Archaeology of the Ganga Plain
— Cultural-Historical Dimensions —

Archaeology of the Ganga Plain

— Cultural-Historical Dimensions —

Purushottam Singh

Indian Institute of Advanced Study
Shimla

Aryan Books International
New Delhi

'If the Indus gave India a name, it may almost be said that the Ganges gave India a faith, and is at least as worthy as her sister of our solicitude'

—Sir Mortimer Wheeler, 1949:10

ARCHAEOLOGY OF THE GANGA PLAIN
(Cultural-Historical Dimensions)

ISBN: 978-81-7305-392-4

First published in **2010** by
INDIAN INSTITUTE OF ADVANCED STUDY
Rashtrapati Nivas, Shimla-171 005

and

ARYAN BOOKS INTERNATIONAL
Pooja Apartments, 4B, Ansari Road, New Delhi-110 002 (India)
Tel.: 23287589, 23255799; Fax: 91-11-23270385
E-mail: aryanbooks@vsnl.com, aryanbooks@gmail.com

Computer Typeset and Printed in India at
ABI Prints & Publishing Co., New Delhi

Dedicated to the sacred memory of my wife
Shrimati Champa Devi
who was a constant source of inspiration
in all my academic pursuits

Preface

The present monograph is updated version of my research project entitled *Cultural-Historical Dimensions of Recent Archaeological Discoveries in the Middle Ganga Plain.* It was carried out at the Indian Institute of Advanced Study, Shimla during September 2002-July 2005. This study was made possible through award of a fellowship by the Institute. My grateful thanks are due to the Governing Body, its then Chairperson, Professor G.C. Pande, and then Director, Professor V.C. Srivastava. His successor, Professor Bhuvan Chandel always encouraged me in my research work and provided administrative and financial support to hold a Seminar on the Archaeology of the Middle Ganga Plain at Lucknow on 13-14 March 2004. The proceedings of the Seminar have been been published in *Pragdhara,* No. 15. I am deeply beholden to Professor Peter Ronald deSouza, the present Director, for providing administrative support. The officers of the Institute, Sarvashri T.K. Majumdar, A.K. Sharma, Kundan Lal Sharma, Dr. Debarshi Sen, Kulbhushan Sharma and Late Shri S.A. Jabbar were always ready to provide every assistance. I thank them all.

Academic help was provided by a number of scholars. My sincere thanks are due to Professor V.N. Misra for providing me reprints of his papers published in inaccessible journals. Professor V.D. Misra brought to my notice some latest publications of his Department. Professor I.B. Singh provided reprints of papers on his latest researches on the geomorphology of Ganga basin. Dr. Rakesh Tewari and Professor J.N. Pal provided the latest and often unpublished data relating to their researches. Dr. K.S. Saraswat studied the archaeobotanical samples from my sites and other places and promptly communicated the results of his study.

Dr. R.N. Singh shared his findings on the archaeometallurgical analysis of copper axe from Imlidih Khurd. I sincerely acknowledge the contributions of all these scholars to the completion of this book and wish to thank them all.

The illustrations contained in this book were provided by Professor P.N. Singh, Head, Department of AIHC & Archaeology, BHU, Varanasi. Dr. R.N. Singh, Dr. A.K. Singh and Shri Varun Sinha helped in the preparation of the illustrations. The press copy of this manuscript was prepared by Dr. Chandra Bhal Srivastava. The proofs were corrected by Dr. Ranjit Pratap Singh and Km. Vindhya Singh. Dr. Santosh Kumar Singh helped me in various ways. I express my gratefulness and thanks to each one of them.

I am thankful to Shri Vikas Arya of Aryan Books International, New Delhi for the efficient and expeditious publication of this book.

Varanasi **Purushottam Singh**
Deepavali, 17 October 2009

Contents

Illustrations

MAPS AND FIGURES

PLATES

1
Introduction

HISTORY OF RESEARCH

The northern part of Middle Ganga plain, known as the Sarayupar plain, is studded with archaeological sites associated with the life of the Buddha. These sites attracted the attention of early explorers in the sixties and seventies of the nineteenth century. The first archaeological exploration of this region was initiated by A.C.L. Carllyle in 1874-75 and 1875-76 under the guidance of Alexander Cunningham. Subsequently in 1890, A. Fuhrer (1891) explored some more sites in this region. In February 1897, Vincent A. Smith identified Piprahwa as a stupa site in course of his explorations. In the subsequent year, W.C. Peppe excavated this stupa and found the famous Piprahwa vase containing the relics of Buddha along with beads, crystals, gold ornaments and cut stars. In the year 1899, P.C. Mukherji carried out archaeological investigation in the Nepal frontier. He identified Tilaura Kot with Kapilvastu and supported Fuhrer in his identification of the stupa of Gothwa with Krakuchchanda's stupa and of the structures on the bank of the Sagar with the stupas commemorating the massacre of the Sakyas. However, all these explorations were carried out with a view to identifying the Buddhist sites only and the importance of ceramic evidence so commonly used today in the identification of protohistoric sites was not realized in those days.

After the end of the nineteenth century, no significant archaeological investigation was carried out for the subsequent six decades and it was only in 1961-62 that a team of archaeologists of the University of Gorakhpur led by G.C. Pande, S.N. Chaturvedi and S.N. Tripathi conducted excavations at the well-known site of Sohgaura, situated on the confluence

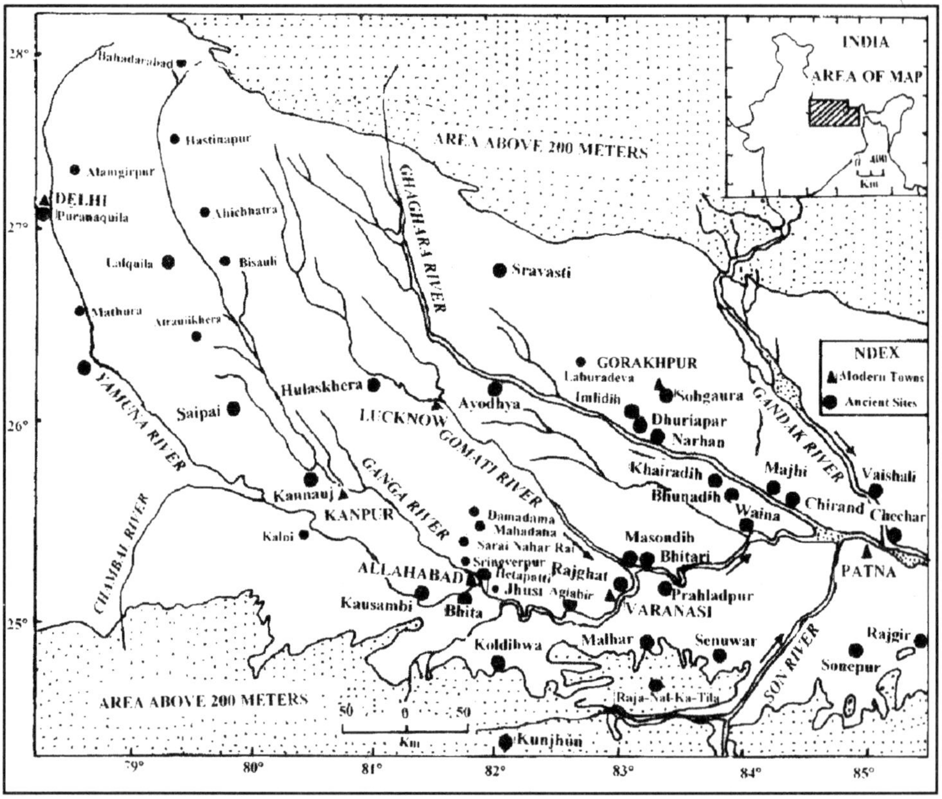

Fig. 1. Archaeological sites of the Ganga plain

of the Ami and Rapti rivers in district Gorakhpur. In the subsequent year, a team of archaeologists of the Banaras Hindu University explored some parts of Basti district under the supervision of A.K. Narain. In 1964, S.K. Bhatt of the same university conducted a village-to-village survey in Basti district and located 67 archaeological sites belonging to the early historical period. This trail was followed by Satish Chandra Singh of the same university who explored the present-day districts of Basti and Sant Ravidas Nagar and identified 147 sites (Singh, S.C., 1991).

EXCAVATION OF EARLY HISTORICAL CITY-SITES

The archaeologist's spade was active at several sites in the Middle Ganga plain during the first three decades of the 20th century, but little attention was paid to close observation and systematic recording of stratification. The main aim was to expose the structures and collection of sculptures, coins, sealings and epigraphs, in the largest number possible (Sharma, 1953: 143). Some of the early historical sites like Sarnath, Kasia, Rajgir,

Lumbini, and Bodh Gaya are connected by literary tradition with the life of the Buddha (ca. 563-483 BC).

Sarnath, the place of First Sermon, was excavated sporadically by far too many hands, including Cunnigham in 1835-36, before its systematic excavation by the Archaeological Survey of India between 1904 and 1928 by F.C. Oertel, John Marshall and others which revealed a town of stupas and monasteries. The earliest structural remains of this place are dated to the Maurya period and some of them are ascribed to Ashoka (Sharma, 1953:143).

Kushinagar (modern Kasia in district Deoria in eastern Uttar Pradesh), the place of death (*Mahaparinirvana*) of the Buddha, was partially excavated by A.C.L. Carlleyle in 1876 and subsequently between 1904 and 1912 by the Archaeological Survey of India. This area is studded with remains of which eight monasteries with the usual plans were excavated but nothing earlier than Kushana coins was found (Ghosh, 1989, Vol. II, 247).

Rajagriha, Sravasti, Vaishali, Sankasya and Kausambi are some of the other important places associated with the life of the Buddha. Of these, Rajagriha (modern Rajgir, about 60 miles south-east of Patna) still awaits a planned and systematic excavation although it was examined by Cunnigham and his assistants, followed later by John Marshall and V.H. Jackson in 1913-14. Section scraping by Shri A. Ghosh in 1950 yielded deposits datable to circa 500-200 BC. D.R. Patil excavated this place and exposed two large elliptical halls with subsidiary rooms within a compound wall.

Buddha passed many years of his life at Jetavana monastery at Sravasti, identified with Saheth-Maheth, on the borders of Gonda and Bahraich districts of Uttar Pradesh. This site has attracted the attention of archaeologists right from the days of A. Cunnigham. Early in the 20th century excavations were conducted here by J. Ph. Vogel, John Marshall and D.R. Sahni between 1907-8 and 1910-11, as a result of which numerous stupas, monasteries and temples were exposed. The earliest of them goes back to Kushana times; the latest datable object is a copper-plate of the Gahadavala ruler Govindachandra (12th century) granting land to Jetavana monastery. This site was re-examined by K.K. Sinha in 1959 (Sinha,1967) and a team of Japanese scholars of Kansai University conducted excavations at Jetavana from 1986 to 1989 (Takahashi *et al.*, 1999-2000). The results of the last-named excavation yielded the following culture-sequence:

Period I: BRW/BSW Phase, 8th to 7th century BC
Period II: Early NBPW Phase, 6th to 4th century BC

Period III: Late NBPW Phase, 3rd to 1st century BC
Period IV: Kushana Phase, 1st to 3rd century AD
Period V: Gupta Phase, 4th to 6th century AD
Period VI: Post-Gupta Phase, 7th to 10th century AD

Vaishali, the reputed birth-place of Mahavira and capital of the oligarchical Lichchhavis from early times, was the scene of the Second Buddhist Council held about a hundred years after Buddha's death. Identified with Basarh in Muzaffarpur district, Bihar, the fortified ruins of the city comprise a prominent fort, over 500 x 240 m, known as Raja-Bishal-ka-Garh, and identified by Cunningham as Vaishali. This fort was excavated by T. Bloch in 1903-4 and D.B. Spooner in 1913-14. While the lower levels were not reached, a vast number of Gupta seals and punch-marked coins were found. The site was re-excavated by Krishna Deva and V. Misra in 1950 and between 1958 and 1962 by A.S. Altekar on behalf of the K.P. Jayaswal Research Institute. The excavation included the areas of Kharauna Pokhar, Raja-Bishal-ka-Garh, Chakramdas, Lalpura, Kolhua and Virpur. The Garh area shows that it was under occupation from at least 500 BC, as in the lowest layers black-and-red ware is found with the NBPW. An important discovery was a stupa, originally of mud but later on encased in brick, which has been taken to be the one built over the corporeal relics of the Buddha by the Lichchhavis.

Kausambi (modern Kosam, 53 km from Allahabad on the northern bank of the Yamuna) had attracted the attention of A. Cunningham. In 1937-38, N.G. Majumdar of the Archaeological Survey of India excavated a small area near the Ashokan pillar. Extensive excavations were undertaken by the University of Allahabad under G.R. Sharma from 1949-50 to 1966-67. The excavations were conducted in four main areas: (1) the pillar area, (2) the defence complex, (3) the Ghositarama area, and (4) the palace complex. The earliest settlement at Kausambi has been dated to a time-bracket of 1165-885 BC and the ceramics from the earliest strata (Red Ware) has been compared with the pottery from the OCW levels at Atranjikhera. The PGW is represented in Periods II and III (Sharma, 1960, 1969).

About 22 km up the Yamuna from Allahabad, 2 km off its right bank, lies a series of mounds at Bhita. The mounds were superficially excavated in 1909-10 and 1911-12 by J. Marshall. This site seems to represent a township inhabited by a mercantile community. The long occupation ranging from pre-Mauryan time to the Gupta period has been divided in five periods.

The ancient remains of Rajghat on the northern outskirts of Varanasi city is situated near the confluence of the Ganga and Baruna. It represents the ancient city of Varanasi, the capital of the kingdom of Kashi. This site was accidentally discovered in 1940 while earth was being removed for construction of Kashi railway station. The relics comprised clay sealings, terracotta figures and distinctive pottery, including the NBPW. The site was re-examined by A.K. Narain of the Banaras Hindu University in 1957 and again from 1960 to 1967, revealing a continuous sequence of six periods, from before the NBPW to medieval times.

Pataliputra (modern Patna) occupies an important place in the history of ancient India. This capital city was established by Udayin (ca. 459-443 BC) and was the scene of the Third Buddhist Coucil during Ashoka's rule. This city of the Mauryas was situated on the confluence of the Ganga and the Son and measures 9 miles in length and 1.5 miles in width. Apart from the early nineteenth century work of Buchanan and Rennel, A. Cunningham and J.D. Beglar made several attempts to locate the sites of Pataliputra as seen by Fa-Hien of the 5th century and Hiuen Tsang of the 7th century without much success. During 1892-1899, L.A. Wadell carried out excavations at several places in Patna and brought to light remains of wooden beams arranged in a double row. In 1897-98, P.C. Mukherji came across a ditch extending east-west to 76 m. In 1912 and the following years, D.B. Spooner re-excavated Kumrahar and found brick walls of the Gupta period and exposed the Mauryan pillared hall.

The Bulandibagh area which was already tapped by Spooner was re-excavated in 1926-27 by J.A. Page and M. Ghosh, resulting in the discovery of a wooden structure. Kumrahar was excavated again by A.S. Altekar and V. Mishra from 1951-1955 (Altekar and Misra, 1959). This excavation revealed that the habitation of Kumrahar continued from the Mauryan times to AD 600. This site was excavated once again on a modest scale by B.P. Sinha and L.A. Narain in 1955-56 who found black-and-red ware in association with the NBPW. However, the high water table and the present city, largely situated on the ancient settlement, have not permitted excavations on a large enough scale.

DISCOVERY OF NEOLITHIC-CHALCOLITHIC LEVELS

The important excavated Chalcolithic sites in the middle Ganga plain are as follows:

SOHGAURA

This site is situated on the confluence of the Rapti and Ami rivers in the Bansgaon sub-division of Gorakhpur district. It was the find-spot of a bronze plaque with a Mauryan Prakrit inscription. This site was excavated in 1961-62 and again in 1974-75 by the University of Gorakhpur.

Lahuradewa

This site is situated on the bank of a lake in district Sant Kabir Nagar. This site, measuring 220 m east-west and 140 m north-south, was explored by the University of Gorakhpur in 1974-75 and has been under excavation since 2001-02 by the U.P. State Department of Archaeology.

Gulrihwaghat

This site is located about 4 km south-east of Haraiya Tahsil headquarter and roughly 24 km south-west of Basti proper. It is situated on the left bank of the Manwar River. This site was first discovered by S.K. Bhatt in 1965 and excavated in 1967 by the Banaras Hindu University on a small scale. This excavation yielded painted black-and-red ware, black slipped ware and other associated ceramic industries along with stone blades, stone beads and terracotta objects. After examining these finds, the present author is convinced that the finds belong to the Narhan culture.

Narhan

This site is situated on the left bank of the Ghaghara in the Gola sub-division of district Gorakhpur. It was excavated by the present author during 1984-89 (Singh, 1994).

Imlidih Khurd

The inconspicuous mound of Imlidih Khurd is located on the left bank of the Kuwana, a tributary of the Ghaghara, in district Gorakhpur. It was excavated by the present author for three field seasons in 1992, 1993 and 1995.

Khairadih

This small village is situated on the right bank of river Ghaghara, about 40 km downstream of Narhan. It was excavated for five seasons by the Banaras Hindu University during 1980-81 to 1983-84 and again in 1985-86.

Senuwar

This site is situated on the bank of a small river Kudra, 7 km south of Sasaram in district Rohtas, Bihar. It was under excavation by the Banaras Hindu University during 1986-87 and 1989-90. A detailed report on these excavations has been published (Singh, B.P., 2004).

Chirand

It is an important settlement of the Neolithic and Chalcolithic cultures. It is situated on the bank of the Ghaghara in district Saran, Bihar, 11 km east of Chhapra. This site was excavated by the Directorate of Archaeology and Museums, Bihar for seven seasons between 1962-63 and 1972-73. It revealed five broad cultural periods, viz., Pd. I (Neolithic), Pd. II (Chalcolithic), Pd. III (NBPW Culture), Pd. IV (first century BC to third century AD) and Pd. V (late historical). Excavation at Chirand brought to light for the first time, remains of a Neolithic culture in an area where it was least expected. Further, this site provided a continuous sequence of more than 2000 years in this part of the country.

Champa

The ancient settlement of Champa lies in the general area of Nathnagar on the outskirts of modern Bhagalpur town. This site was excavated by the Patna University between 1969-70 and 1976-77 and again in 1982-83 on a limited scale.

Oriup

The ancient settlement of Oriup is situated 2 km south-west of Antichak, the site of ancient Vikramshila in district Bhagalpur, Bihar. Small-scale excavation conducted by the Patna University in 1966-67 (*IAR*, 1966-67:6) has revealed four periods of which the earliest two are relevant in the present context. Period I has yielded plain and painted black-and-red ware, NBPW, black slipped ware and red ware. The other finds include copper bangle, microlithic core, fish hooks and points and styli made of bone, beads of agate and carnelian and terracotta female figurines.

Period II is evidenced by the occurrence of NBPW, grey ware and red ware. A few objects of iron such as spearhead and nails, beads of stone, glass and terracotta, and fish hooks constitute the other antiquities. A Neolithic stone celt and sledge-hammer have also been found. This site was deserted after the end of Period II.

Period III has revealed typical Pala pottery and the last period has been ascribed to medieval times.

Raja Nal Ka Tila

This site is located on the banks of river Karamnasa, in the Sonbhadra district. It was excavated for two seasons during 1996 and 1997 by the U.P. State Department of Archaeology.

MALHAR

This site is also situated on the Karamnasa River in district Varanasi. It was excavated in 1999 by the U.P. State Department of Archaeology. A detailed report on this important excavation has recently appeared (Tewari, *et al.*, 2004).

x x x x x

As its name implies, the Chalcolithic stage is represented by cultures where *Chalkos* (copper) was used (though in limited quantities), along with *Lithos* (stones) in the form of microliths which were used as parts of composite tools. However, in the Middle Ganga plain, the artefacts of copper are very limited and the lithic component is completely missing in sites like Imlidih Khurd, Narhan, Khairadih, etc. and wherever it is present (sites of Sant Kabir Nagar district; Waina in Ballia district and Agiabir in Mirzapur), their number is exceedingly small and it is not clear if their presence made any significant contribution in the economy of these people.

The Neolithic phase in the Middle Ganga plain and the Vindhyas was succeeded by the Chalcolithic cultures. There is no time-gap between the two cultures and a gradual evolution from the former to the latter has been witnessed at a number of sites. The excavations at sites like Sohgaura, Imlidih Khurd, Chirand, Chechar and Senuwar have furnished evidence pertaining to the transitional stage from the preceding Neolithic cultures of the region to the Chalcolithic. The only perceptible change during the Chalcolithic is the introduction of copper in this region sometime in the later half of third millennium BC, which resulted in tremendous activity leading to agricultural surplus in a big way and the consequent increase in human population. Whereas the Neolithic settlements were few and far between, in the Chalcolithic phase the number as well as the size of the settlements increased several fold. Exploration carried out in 14,600 sq. km. area of the Middle Ganga plain has brought to light more than 200 sites. Surely, many more sites lie buried and are yet to be documented. Of the explored sites, about two dozen have been excavated so far (Misra, B.B., 2000: 66). Important among them are Kakoria, Magha, Koldihwa, Khajuri, Banimilia-Bahera, Takiaper, Malhar, Raja Nal Ka Tila in the Vindhyas and Jhusi, Kausambi, Sringaverapura, Rajghat, Prahladpur, Masondih, Sohgaura, Narhan, Imlidih Khurd, Khairadih, Chirand, Chechar, Maner, Oriup, Champa, Sonepur, Taradih, Manjhi and Senuwar in the Ganga Valley.

RECENT EXPLORATIONS IN THE SARAYUPAR PLAIN

The excavations at Narhan in 1984-89 and the identification of Narhan culture in the Sarayupar plain gave a fresh impetus to archaeological activities in this area and archaeologists of the Banaras Hindu University and the U.P. State Archaeological Organisation were on the forefront in this endeavour. In order to trace the extent of Narhan culture, the present author and his colleagues undertook village-to-village exploration along the Kuwana River in districts Gorakhpur and Basti (Singh, P. *et al.*, 1990-91). They identified 22 sites in Gorakhpur and 18 sites in Basti district. Of these, about a dozen sites bearing black-and-red ware, similar to that found at Narhan, were located; prominent among them being Imlidih Khurd, Dhuriapar and Sikridih. Of these, the first two were excavated by the present author. The exploration work was resumed in the subsequent year by the present team (Singh, P. *et al.*, 1991-92) and 18 more settlements, mostly belonging to the Narhan culture were located. At about the same time, B.P. Singh (Singh, B.P., 1990-91) visited the sites of Gularihwaghat and Lahuradewa, earlier explored by S.K. Bhatt and S.N. Chaturvedi and picked up potteries and antiquities of Narhan culture from both sites. He further explored parts of Basti and Siddharth Nagar districts and located as many as 58 sites. Of these, 52 settlements have Kushana occupation; 23 start from the late phase of NBPW culture and continue up to Kushana period and 25 are single culture settlements of the Kushana period. This endeavour received fresh impetus by the explorations of Rakesh Tewari and R.K. Srivastava who explored the Ami River, a major tributary of the Rapti, in districts Siddharth Nagar, Basti and Gorakhpur and located 64 sites of various periods. Of these, three sites yielded cord-impressed pottery (Tewari, R. and R.K. Srivastava, 1993-94).

In order to trace the extension of Narhan culture in the lower reaches of the Ghaghara and its tributaries, we excavated at Waina and Bhunadih, both in district Ballia, and explored this district thoroughly (Singh, P. and B. Singh, 1994-95). We were able to locate 20 sites, some of which belonged to the Narhan culture. As a follow-up of these discoveries, Brahmanand Singh undertook extensive exploration of Ballia district and identified 75 sites of various periods. We resumed our work along the bank of Chhoti Sarju, a tributary of the Ganga (Singh, P. *et al.*, 1996-97) and located 27 ancient settlements in district Ghazipur, 26 in Mau and one in district Ballia. Of these, 6 belong to the Narhan culture, 13 to the NBPW culture and 30 sites are dated to the Kushana-Gupta times. We also explored the adjoining Chandauli district in 1999-2000 and identified 24 sites belonging to the various periods (Singh, P. *et al.*, 1999-2000). At the same time, Vibha Tripathi (Tripathi *et al.*, 2000-2001) explored the palaeo-channel of the Varuna River between Babatpur and Varanasi and identified 14 sites, of which 4 sites yielded the characterstic black-and-red ware pottery which is a hallmark of the Narhan culture.

DISCOVERY OF CHALCOLITHIC SITES IN THE LOWER GANGA VALLEY

With the introduction of copper in limited quantity, eastern India, particularly Bengal and Bihar, witnessed gradual transformation from the Neolithic to the Chalcolithic stage. The Chalcolithic remains of Pandu-Rajar-Dhibi on the Ajay River in Burdwan district had been reported way back in the early sixties but recent years have witnessed the discovery of as many as 72 Chalcolithic sites in this region (Hoque, 1993). Of these, 33 Chalcolithic sites are located in Birbhum, 23 in Burdwan, 8 in Bankura, 7 in Midnapore and 1 in Murshidabad district. Geographically speaking, 47 sites are distributed in the *Rarh* plain, mainly concentrated in the Birbhum-Asansol *Rarh* and sporadically distributed in the Bankura *Rarh*. The distribution of these sites clearly shows that the Chalcolithic people of the lower Ganga valley preferred to settle along river banks (the main rivers being the Dwarkeswar, the Ajay, the Rupnarayan, the Kunoor, the Damodar, the Kansabati, the Kopai, the Kumari and the Mayurakshi). These river valleys provided new and fertile alluvium after the end of the rainy season every year, where cultivation was possible even without ploughing. Another attraction was the abundance of aquatic fauna like fish (including carp), tortoise and snail. Of the 72 known sites, 12 have been excavated and a very brief summary of the results of these excavations is given below:

Mahishadal

Mahishadal, situated on the left bank of the Kopai in the Birbhum district, measures 230 × 135 m. The cultural deposit of 2 m is divisible into two periods: (i) Chalcolithic and (ii) Iron Age. The Chalcolithic phase is represented by ceramics, remains of structures, copper and terracotta objects, microliths and charred rice (*IAR*, 1963-64: 59-60). From this site, wild and cultivated strains of rice (*Oryza rufipogon, Oryza sativa*) (*IAR*, 1982-83: 150) were identified in carbonized grains from a barn. The barn, as the calibrated radiocarbon dates suggest (Possehl, 1988: 186), was burnt down around 920-795 BC. Besides the date, useful data have been worked out from the size, volume and number of barns in the settlement (Ghosh and Nag, 1986). Among the domesticated animals, *Bos indicus Linnaeus* (humped cattle) constituted the largest lot in comparison to buffalo, goat, sheep and pig. Domestic fowls were reared and pariah dog was quite common in this Chalcolithic village (Banerjee, 1981). The most notable copper-finds at Mahishadal is a flat celt which has been equated with an axe type of copper hoards (type IV-A) (Chattopadhyay, 2004: 31-32).

Bahiri

Bahiri, another village settlement, located 7 km east of the market town of Bolpur in Birbhum district, is a cluster of three small mounds. Small-scale excavations conducted by Chakrabarti and Hasan brought to light three cultural periods: (i) Chalcolithic, (ii) Iron Age and (iii) Historical (Chakrabarti and Hasan, 1982:111-24). The Chalcolithic period is represented by pottery, structures, hearths, microliths, bone, terracotta and iron objects and animal remains. As regards metal objects, only three very small copper fragments were recovered from Trench BHR-7, which indicates its restricted use.

Banerjee (1979-80) provides a preliminary report of the faunal data from the site. Cattle, pit, buffalo, dog, chital and *Cervus sp.* were present at the site. Banerjee has not made a period-wise discussion of the material making. It is difficult to know if all the species were common to both the periods or there were any changes.

The bone remains from different sites in West Bengal attest to the prevalence of jungles and grassy vegetation in the region. It is suggested that the inhabitants of the Chalcolithic period engaged in hunting, fishing and animal breeding. The identification of the horse and *Bos(?) Namadicus* at Bharatpur is very interesting. The inhabitants were certainly not pure non-vegetarians because there is evidence of cultivated rice (*Oryza sativa*) from Pandu Rajar Dhibi.

Haraipur

In the village Haraipur, district Birbhum, a small-scale excavation conducted by R.C. Kar (*IAR*, 1964-65: 46) revealed a 3.5 m thick deposit containing remains of Chalcolithic to Historical period. The Chalcolithic phase is represented by ceramics only.

Hatikra

The ancient settlement of Hatikra is located about 24 km north-west of Bolpur railway station in Birbhum district, on the right bank of Dwarkeswar River. The ancient site spread over more than four acres was excavated by N.C. Ghosh and S. Nag (1896:116). The excavation revealed a 2.55 m thick habitational deposit of continuous occupation from the Chalcolithic to the Iron Age. The Chalcolithic phase is marked by ceramics (black-and-red ware), mud floors, stone objects, terrocotta objects and animal remains. The existence of copper is attested by two shapeless small nodules which, on examination, were completely turned into oxides having no core (Chattopadhyay, 2004: 29-30).

Nanur

A small-scale excavation conducted at Nanur, located about 20 km north-west of Bolpur in Birbhum district, has also revealed a culture sequence from Chalcolithic to historical times. The Chalcolithic phase is represented by ceramics only.

Bharatpur

Bharatpur, situated on the left bank of the Damodar, about 7 km south-east of Panagarh railways station in Burdwan district, was excavated for four seasons (from 1971-71 to 1975-76). This excavation has revealed a sequence of four periods: (i) Chalcolithic, (ii) Iron Age, (iii) Gupta, and (iv) Pala. The Chalcolithic phase is represented by ceramics, structures, hearths, copper, stone and bone objects and microliths.

The Chalcolithic phase of the site yielded an assemblage consisting of the remains of fish, soft shelled turtle, domestic fowl, pariah dog, horse, cattle, domestic buffalo, sheep, goat, pig, *Bos? Namadicus,* barasinga, chital, barking deer and nilgai (Banerjee, 1979-80: 163-64). The high frequency of cattle remains suggest that the inhabitants maintained large herds of this animal which possibly played an important role in their economic life.

Barabelun

Barabelun, also known as Baneswar Danga, is located 29 km north-east of Burdwan town, on the bank of Khari River. A small-scale excavation conducted in 1974 revealed remains of three periods: (i) Chalcolithic, (ii) Iron Age, and (iii) Historical. The Chalcolithic period is represented by ceramics, microliths, and copper and bone objects.

Pandu-Rajar-Dhibi

The well-known site, Pandu-Rajar-Dhibi, is situated on the right bank of Ajay River in Burdwan district. It is an extensive site. It was intensively excavated for five seasons between 1961 and 1965 and again for one season during 1984-85. These excavations have revealed a sequence of five periods: Periods I and II-Chalcolithic, Period III-Early Iron Age, Period IV-Late Iron Age, and Period V-Historical. The Chalcolithic phase is represented by the typical ceramics, structures, hearths, burials, copper, bone, stone and terracotta objects and faunal remains. After the excavation of 1984-85, vestiges of lower levels at this site were regrouped period-wise and now the earliest cultural phase has been designated as 'pre-Chalcolithic' on the basis of the presence of potsherds, a hand-made dull ware, charcoal specimens, Neolithic celts, etc. A complete absence of metal was noted in this period. The succeeding Period II has now been divided into two phases, viz., II-A and II-B. Both the phases have been designated as Chalcolithic (this sub-division contains the material of Periods I and II of the excavation conducted during the early sixties). The typical pottery is the black-and-red-ware, both plain and painted; associated with plain red ware and a perforated red ware. It is in Phase II-B that the appearance of iron has been noted and, on account of this, this phase has been designated as Ferro-Chalcolithic (De and Chattopadhyay, 1989: 65). This period was succeeded by the actual Iron Age deposit contained in Period III.

MANGALKOT

The ancient settlement of Mangalkot is situated on the confluence of Ajay and Kunoor rivers in Burdwan district, 30 km south of Pandu-Rajar-Dhibi. The ancient remains are spread over an area of about 2 square kilometres. Excavation conducted by Amita Ray (1990: 130-40) revealed a long history of occupation divisible into the following periods: Period I-Chalcolithic, Period II-Iron Age, Period III-Mauryan and Sunga, Period IV-Kushana, Period V-Gupta, and Period VI-Muslim. The Chalcolithic deposit is 2.5 metres and has yielded ceramics, structures, hearths, copper, iron, bone, stone and terracotta objects and plant and faunal remains.

DIHAR

The ancient site of Dihar is located on the bank of Dwarkeswar River, about 6 km away from Bishnupur town in the Bankura district. It rises some 7 metres from the river bed. Two seasons of excavation were carried out by A.C. Pal (*IAR*, 1983-84: 92-3; 1984-85: 92-5). The cultural deposit of 2.5 metres has been divided into two Periods: I. Chalcolithic and II. Early Historical. Period I is characterized by ceramics, structures, copper, bone objects and microliths.

TULASIPUR

The ancient settlement of Tulasipur is situated just below the confluence of Kansabati and Kumari rivers in Bankura district. A small-scale excavation conducted at this site (Chakrabarti *et al.*, 1982: 39-49; *IAR*, 1967-68: 49-50) revealed three cultural periods ranging from Chalcolithic to late Iron Age. The Chalcolithic phase is represented by ceramics and remains of structures including hearths and iron slag.

TAMLUK

The site of Tamluk (ancient Tamralipti) has been known to scholars from quite some time. It is located on the right bank of the Rupnarayan River in Midnapur district of West Bengal. The site was excavated by M.N. Despande (*IAR*, 1954-55: 19-20) and subsequently by S.K. Mukherjee (*IAR*, 1973-74: 33). The cultural sequence is as follows: Period I-Neolithic, Period II-Chalcolithic, Period III-Early Iron Age, Period IV-Late Iron Age and Gupta. The Chalcolithic phase is represented by ceramics, a small polished stone celt and a variety of bone implements.

Cultural components of the above noted early farming settlements of eastern India have been analyzed by Chattopadhya *et al.* (2007). They observe that black-and-red ware remains throughout the early village farming phase the most endemic type all over eastern India. In South Bihar it is associated with black slipped ware and red slipped ware. Bone and antler implements of different wild and domesticated animals and aquatic species have been recovered from the sites of West Bengal, South Bihar and Orissa. The analysis of bone remains shows that while Chalcolithic inhabitants consumed both the wild and domesticated spices. The wild species comprise different types of deer, wild cattle, wild rat, wild dog, etc. while the domesticated species include humped cattle, buffalo, pig, sheep and goat.

THEORETICAL ISSUES

In order to review the archaeological activities in Uttar Pradesh and to plan future course of action, a Seminar was organized by the U.P. State Archaeological Organisation in October 1990 and for the first time archaeologists from the Archaeological Survey of India, U.P. State Archaeological Organisation and various universities, such as B.H.U., Allahabad, Gorakhpur, Lucknow, Aligarh and individual scholars discussed the future course of action. In due course, during 1995 a joint team of ASI under B.R. Mani and U.P. State Archaeology under Rakesh Tewari re-explored the trans-Ghaghara plains of Sarayupar area and published the preliminary report in *Pragdhara*–6. Under this programme, no less than 200 sites were located and a number of them were excavated. Of these, Siswania, Orai, Pipri, Deoraon and Mundiar were excavated by the Archaeological Survey of India and Lahuradewa by the U.P. State Department of Archaeology (Mani, 2004).

Again, with a view to assess the status, and significance of new discoveries in the middle Ganga plain and to discuss their implications in feature research the Indian Institute of Advanced Study (IIAS), Shimla and the Directorate of U.P. State Archaeology, Department of Culture, Government of Uttar Pradesh jointly organized a Workshop on the Archaeology of the Middle Ganga Plain in Lucknow on 13-14 March 2004. Most of the principal investigators engaged in these works from the Universities of Gorakhpur, Banaras, Allahabad and Lucknow, Archaeological Survey of India, Directorate of the U.P. State Archaeology Department, Geological Survey of India and Birbal Sahni Institute of Palaeobotany participated in this workshop. The presentations on specific disciplines conducted by the respective fields workers, interpretations proposed by the learned scholars and discussions generated in the Workshop led to a clear understanding about the related issues, in the region.

The proceedings of the above Workshop have appeared in the fifteenth issue of *Pragdhara*, Annual Journal of the U.P. State Archaeology Department, in the form of fourteen papers.

In this context, mention may be made of an International Seminar on "First Farmers in Global Perspective" held at Lucknow under the auspices of the Directorate of U.P. State Archaeology Department on 18-20 January 2006. This seminar was attended by some eminent scholars working on the origins of agriculture and related fields. They comprised delegates from Australia, Japan, Sri Lanka, France, U.K. and Canada, besides the Indian participants. Among the many topics discussed, the question of early agricultural beginnings in the Ganga valley came under sharp focus. The proceedings of this seminar have been published in *Pragdhara*-18.

The archaeology of the middle Ganga plain has made great strides manly because of healthy competition among scholars from the Universities of Allahabad, Banaras, Lucknow and Gorakhpur, the U.P. State Department of Archaeology and the Archaeological Survey of India. The publication of *Pragdhara,* the journal of the the U.P. State Archaeology Department, provided a conducive platform for quick publication of the archaeological field reports. The key figure behind this endeavour was the bubbling enthusiasm of Rakesh Tewari, the present Director who has managed to publish eighteen volumes of this journal in as many years. The present author has been associated with this journal from its inception.

Further, the last two decades have witnessed greater participation of natural scientists in understanding archaeological problems and their researches have helped us in understanding the rise of human cultures in the Middle Ganga plain. The increased association of geologists, geomorphologists, human biologists and archaeobotanists coupled with intensive field work by archaeologists has brought paradigm shift in understanding past cultures. Among these, the discovery of Mesolithic in the alluvial plain of the Ganga constitutes a distinct contribution to our knowledge. The biological anthropologists from the USA have recognized the anthropological significance of human osteological discoveries of the Vindhyas and the Ganga plain. In 1975, John Lukacs conducted a preliminary examination of the dentition of the Lekhahia skeletal series. In 1980, Kennedy examined the human skeletal remains from Sarai Nahar Rai and Mahadaha and he published a monograph on the skeletal series of these two sites. He completed the study of skeletal remains from Damdama in 1992 and published his findings (Misra, 1996). The study of dentition of Mesolithic population of North India suggested the presence of heavy dietary stress, indicating a pathology pattern consistent with hunting-foraging and gathering subsistence system and primitive food processing technology. The Mesolithic settlement located on the banks of ox-bow lakes and rivulets facilitated in exploiting rich aquatic fauna. Edible fruits, tubers, roots and grains were also possibly collected from surrounding regions. Querns, mullers and hammers of sandstone and quartzite were used for processing the food. Besides microlithic tools, bone tools also were used for hunting and foraging. Pit hearths were used for roasting non-vegetarian and vegetarian food (Pal, 1996: 270).

The animal bones found from the excavations of the above-named Mesolithic sites of the Ganga plain were first studied by Alur and subsequently by Thomas *et al.* These studies showed that the most common bones belonged to Indian humped cattle, gaur, sambar, chital, nilgai, chinkara, antelope and wild boar. A large percentage of animal bones is fragmentary, broken and charred indicating thereby that meat was roasted for consumption. Considerable dependence on aquatic food resources is indicated by fish bones and tortoise shells (Misra, 1996). The faunal assemblege from Damdama shows that the exploitation pattern indicated a cyclical trend in resource management where changes in mammalian resources were mainly compensated by parallel changes in avian and, to some extent, aquatic fauna (Thomas *et al.*, 1996: 255).

REFERENCES

Altekar, A.S. and V.K. Misra. 1959. *Report on Kumrahar Excavations 1951-55*, Patna, K.P. Jayaswal Institute.

Banerjee, S. 1979-80. The archaeological material from West Bengal in the Zoological Survey of India, *Puratattva*, No. 11: 162-64.

_____. 1981. Animal Remains from Bharatpur, District Burdwan, West Bengal, India, *Records of the Zoological Survey of India*, 79: 193-220.

Bhatt, S.K. 1969-70. Archaeological Explorations in Basti District (U.P.), *Puratattva*, No. 3: 77-88.

Chattopadhyay, P.K. 2004. *Archaeometallurgy in India*, Patna, K.P. Jayaswal Research Institute.

Chattopadhyay, R.K., Rajat Sanyal and Kumkum Bandhopadhyay. 2007. Early Village Farming Settlement in Eastern India: An Appraisal, *Puratattva*, No. 37: 68-93.

Chakrabarti, Dilip K. and S. Jamal Hasan. 1982. The Sequence of Bahiri (Chandra Hazrar Danga), District Birbhum, West Bengal, *Man and Environment*, 6: 111-149.

Chakrabarti, Dilip K. *et al.* 1982. Lithic Industries of Bankura, *Puratattva*, No. 11: 39-48.

De, S. and P.K. Chattopadhyay. 1989. Iron Objects from Pandu Rajar Dhibi, Archaeo-Metallurgical Studies, *Steel India*, 3 (1): 33.

Fuhrer, A. 1891. *Monumental Antiquities and Inscriptions in the North-Western Provinces and Oudh*, ASIR, Vol. II, Allahabad.

Ghosh, A. (ed.). 1989. *An Encyclopaedia of Indian Archaeology*, 2 vols., Delhi, Munshiram Manoharlal.

Ghosh, N.C. and A.K. Nag. 1986. Excavations at Hatikra: A Chalcolithic Site in West Bengal, *Puratattva*, No. 15: 116.

Hoque, M. 1993. *Pre- and Protohistoric Settlement Patterns of the Middle and Lower Ganga Valley*, Ph.D. thesis (unpublished), Pune, Deccan College.

Mani, B.R. 2004. On Sensitizing Recent Achievements and Future Prospects for Archaeological Investigations in Middle Ganga Plain, Paper read in the *Workshop on the Archaeology of the Middle Ganga Plain*, held at Lucknow on 13-14 March 2004.

Misra, B.B. 2000. Chalcolithic Culture of the Northern Vindhyays and the Mid Ganga Valley, in S.C. Bhattacharya *et al.* (eds.), *Peeping through the Past* (Prof. G.R. Sharma Memorial Volume), Allahabad, University of Allahabad: 66-85.

Misra, V.D. 1996. History and Context of Mesolithic Research at Allahabad University, Allahabad, India, in G.D. Afanas'ev, S. Cleuziou, J.R. Lukacs and M. Tosi (eds.), *Bioarchaeology of Mesolithic India: An Integrated Approach*, Colloquium XXXIII of the International Union of Prehistoric and Protohistoric Sciences, Forli, ABACO Edizioni: 245-250.

Pal, J.N. 1996. Lithic Use Wear Analysis and Subsistence Activities Among the Mesolithic People of North India, in G.D. Afanas'ev, S. Cleuziou, J.R. Lukacs and M. Tosi (eds.), *Bioarchaeology of Mesolithic India: An Integrated Approach*, Colloquium XXXIII of the International Union of Prehistoric and Protohistoric Sciences, Forli, ABACO Edizioni: 267-277.

Possehl, Gregory L. 1988. Radiocarbon dates from South Asia, *Man and Environment*, XII: 159-196.

Ray, Amita. 1990. Archaeology of Mangalkot, in A. Ray and S. Mukherjee (eds.), *Historical Archaeology of India: A Dialogue between Archaeologists and Historians*, New Delhi, Books and Books: 131-140.

Sharma, G.R. 1960. *Excavations at Kausambi (1957-59)*, Allahabad, University of Allahabad.

_____. 1969. *Excavations at Kausambi*, Memoirs of the Archaeological Survey of India, No. 74, New Delhi, Archaeological Survey of India.

Sharma, Y. D. 1953. Exploration of Historical Sites, *Ancient India*, No. 9: 116-169.

Singh, Brahmanand. 1995-96. Ballia Janapada Ka Puratattvika Utkhanana (Hindi), *Pragdhara*, No. 6: 135-148.

Singh, B.P. 1990-91. Gulrihwaghat and Lohra Dewa: Chalcolithic Settlements in District Basti, Uttar Pradesh, *Pragdhara*, No. 1: 89-91.

_____. 2004. *Early Farming Communities of the Kaimur (Excavations at Senuwar)*, Jaipur, Publication Scheme.

Singh, B.P. and R. Kumar. 1993-94. Explorations in Districts Basti and Siddhartha Nagar in the Saryupar Plain of Eastern Uttar Pradeh, *Pragdhara*, No. 4: 1-12.

Singh, P. 1994. *Excavations at Narhan (1984-89)*, Varanasi & New Delhi, Banaras Hindu University & B.R. Publishing Corporation.

Singh, P., A.K. Singh and I.J. Singh. 1990-91. Explorations along the Kuwana River in Districts Gorakhpur and Basti, *Pragdhara*, No. 1: 69-82.

_____. 1991-92. On the Trails of Narhan Culture, *Pragdhara*, No. 2: 33-44.

Singh, P., A.K. Singh and Brahmanand Singh. 1994-95. Protohistoric Investigations in Ballia District, U.P., *Pragdhara*, No. 5: 21-36.

Singh, P., A.K. Singh and R.N. Singh. 1996-97. Explorations Along the Chhoti Sarju (Tons) River, *Pragdhara*, No. 7: 33-50.

Singh, P., R. Tewari and R.N. Singh. 1999-2000. Explorations in Chandauli District, (U.P.), *Pragdhara*, No. 10: 135-148.

Singh, S.C. 1991. *Archaeology of North Eastern Uttar Pradesh: With Special Reference to Basti District*, unpublished Ph.D. Thesis, Banaras Hindu University.

Sinha, K.K. 1967. *Excavations at Sravasti-1959*, Varanasi, Banaras Hindu University.

Takahashi, T., T. Yamaoka, F. Yoneda and A. Uesugi. 1999-2000. The Ancient City of Sravasti: Its Significance on the Urbanisation of North India, *Puratattva*, No. 30: 74-90.

Tewari, Rakesh and R.K. Srivastava. 1993-94. Explorations Along the Ami River and Its Nearby Areas in Districts Siddhartha Nagar, Basti and Gorakhpur, *Pragdhara*, No. 4: 13-39.

Tewari, Rakesh, R.K. Srivatava and K.K. Singh. 2004. Report of the Excavations at Malhar, District Chandauli (Uttar Pradesh) India: 1998-99, *Pragdhara*, No. 14: 1-112.

Thomas, P.K., P.P. Joglekar, V.D. Misra, J.N. Pandey and J.N. Pal. 1996. Faunal Evidence for the Mesolithic Food Economy of the Gangetic Plain with Special Reference to Damdama, in G.D. Afanas'ev, S. Cleuziou, J.R. Lukacs and M. Tosi (eds.), *Bioarchaeology of Mesolithic India: An Integrated Approach*, Colloquium XXXIII of the International Union of Prehistoric and Protohistoric Sciences, Forli, ABACO Edizioni: 255-266.

Tripathi, Vibha, A.K. Singh and Santosh Kumar. 2000-2001. Explorations Along the Palaeo-channel of River Varuna, *Pragdhara*, No. 11: 125-130.

2

Geographical Background

The Plain of Northern India – stretching for more than 3200 km from the Arabian Sea to the Bay of Bengal – is largely the creation of the mighty Ganga and its tributaries. Sir Dudley Stamp was greatly impressed by the flatness of the plain and its gentle seaward slope. He writes:

> There are several outstanding features of this amazing area. One is the dead flatness of the plain – not a hill, scarcely a mound to break the monotony of the level surface. So gentle is the seaward slope that it is imperceptible to the eye. Nearly a thousand miles from its mouth, the Ganga is only 900 feet above sea level. Another feature is the sudden rise of the Himalayas from the level plain. True, there are foothills, such as the Siwalik, in places, but they occupy, if present at all, a zone which is inconspicuous in its width....The third feature of note is the immense thickness, enormous width and uniform character of the alluvium which forms the subsoil of the plain. A distinction is made between the 'older alluvium' in which certain salts have been segregated by circulating waters and form hard calcareous nodules (kankar) and the 'newer alluvium' in which such concretions are absent. But otherwise the uniformity is amazing. No a rock, not even a pebble is present, to alter the uniform character of the alluvium' (Stamp, 1967: 198-99).

The Ganga plain is a peripheral foreland basin. A foreland basin is formed as a results of compressional stresses developed in the under thrusting plate due to collision and by the vertical load of the thrust-fold belt in the orogen. The main reason for the development of a foreland basin in front of an orogen is flexing of the lithosphere (Singh, I.B., 1996:103).

As stated above, the Ganga plain is a peripheral foreland basin which came into existence in Early Miocene, expanded in the Middle Miocene, and attained its present form in Late Quaternary. The stage-wise evolution of Ganga plain took place in response to the thrust-fold belt loading events in the Himalaya and consequent south-ward expansion of the basin (Singh, I.B., 1996: 133). The basin expanded in the middle Miocene and attained its present configuration in the late Quaternary. Presently, the Ganga plain foreland basin is in a mature stage of evolution, with oversupply of sediment and undefiled condition, building to 300-5 m above sea level, exclusively by fluvial processes (Singh, I.B., 1996: 99). The main rivers of the Ganga plain, mainly the Ganga, Yamuna, Gomati, Ghaghara, etc. show very wide river valleys in which the present-day active channel and its flood plain is entrenched. They are the areas of sand deposition in the Ganga plain. The residence time of these main rivers in the valleys is on the order of 10-10 years during which several climatic and base-level changes have also transformed the character of the river channels and the nature of sediment (Singh, I.B., 1996: 129).

The Ganga plain extends from the Yamuna River in the west to the western borders of Bangladesh covering a distance of about 1,400 km and an average width of 300 km (between the Siwaliks in the north and the Peninsular lands in the south). It occupies a total area of about 3,57,000 sq. km and is drained by the Ganga and its tributaries like the Yamuna, and Son in the south and Ramganga, Ghaghara, Gandak and Kosi in the north. All through its course in the plains, the river is a braided stream bordered by low-lying depressions which get flooded during rains. The plain has a general gradient of about 15 cm per km from north-west to south-east although there are many micro-slopes. The maximum height is found near Saharanpur (276 m) from where it goes on decreasing towards the Sagar Islands.

Following L.D. Stamp, O.H.K. Spate and R.L. Singh, the Ganga plain may be divided into three smaller physiographic units:

1. The Upper Ganga Plain
2. The Middle Ganga Plain
3. The Lower Ganga Plain.

THE UPPER GANGA PLAIN

This region is bordered by the Yamuna River in the west and the south, the Siwalik hills in the north and 100 m contour line (Allahabad-Faizabad railway line) in the east. It occupies a total area of 1,49,029 sq. km, which is about 63% of the total area of Uttar Pradesh. The region has an average elevation between 100 and 300 m with average slope of 24 cm per km towards the south-east. Besides the Ganga and Yamuna, other important rivers of the region include Ramganga, Gomati, Ghaghara and Rapti, etc. As the gradient decreases, drainage becomes more sluggish towards south-east with numerous abandoned courses, ox-bow lakes and sandy stretches. Although featureless plain, the topographic prominences include a 32 km wide zone of unassorted sediments along the foothills of the Siwaliks called Bhabar, followed by a zone of seepage with fine sand, silt and clay (called Terai), the ravine landscape or a bad land topography in the Yamuna-lower Chambal tract, the areas of older alluvium beyond the flood level (the Bangar or Uparhar), the areas of lower alluvium susceptible to frequent flooding (the Khadar or Tarhar), the undulating sandy uplands (called Bhur) along the eastern bank of the Ganga in Moradabad and Bijnor districts, the river bluffs (levees), and the abandoned channels forming ox-bow lakes and meandering courses of the rivers.

THE MIDDLE GANGA PLAIN

The Middle Ganga plain stretches for about 300 km from the Himalayan foothills in the north and Vindhyan ranges in the south. It attained its present form during the post-Tertiary period when this deep trough was filled up by fine alluvium brought down by the Himalayas in the north with an average thickness of 1300-1400 metres. In pre-historic times when this deep trough was filled up by fine alluvium brought down by the Himalayas in the historic times, the main river Ganga watered by several tributaries flowed sluggishly in meandering fashion forming ox-bow lakes, some of which are perennial. These lakes were rich in aquatic fauna and the lands around them were covered with wild grasses, many of which have edible grains. With the onset of milder climate of the Holocene, the marshy land gradually turned into good grassland which attracted small animals.

R.L. Singh (1971: 183) defines the Middle Ganga plain as follows:

Though not a clear-cut physical unit, the Middle Ganga plain (24°30′ N-27°50′ N and 81°47′ E-87°50′ E) is a large physical area (1,44,409 km), and it is the immense human, cultural and economic significance that makes it the heart region of India. It covers the Bihar plains and Eastern Uttar Pradesh in its entirety lying on either side of the Ganga and Saryu (Ghaghara) within the Himalayan and the Peninsular ramparts on the north and south respectively. The western and eastern sides of the region are wide open forming as it does, the central part of the east-west continuum of the vast isotropic Ganga plain – there is no physical boundary as the plain imperceptibly opens up in the west from out of the Upper Ganga plain and so invisibly dies out in the Lower Ganga plain in the east.

The Middle Ganga plain is bounded by the Ganga-Yamuna confluence in the west and the West Bengal and Bihar border in the east, Himalayas in the north and the Vindhyas in the south. The area includes modern eastern Uttar Pradesh and parts of Bihar. The northern boundary of the region runs along the Indo-Nepal international boundary, while the 150 m contour marks the southern boundary along the Vindhyan-Rohtasgarh-Chotanagpur plateaux. The western boundary runs along the 100 m contour while the eastern limit corresponds to the Bihar-Bengal state boundary. The maximum length from east to west is about 600 km while its width from north to south approximates 330 km. The surface is extremely low and level with heights varying from 100 m in the north-west to 75 m in the north-east and 30 m in the south-east. The general slope north of the Ganga (20 cm/km) is from north-west to south-east while in the south of the Ganga, it is from south-west to north-east (9 cm/km).

The average thickness of the alluvium lies between 1300 and 1400 m but the depth increases up to 8,00-10,000 m along the Himalayas. In fact, there are two large troughs, which may be called Gorakhpur trough and Raxaul-Motihari trough of over 8,000 m deep. South of the Ghaghara in the Eastern U.P. plain and the Bihar plain, the depth of alluvium falls below 1500-3000 m, except a few patches in the Ganga-Ghaghara interfluve being deeper. The entire region has suffered great down-warping due to the Himalayan upheaval. The basal rocks seem to have faulted transversely at places and dislocations in the earth's crust along such pre-existing faults or cracks cause earthquakes. Fault lines can be seen running N-S or NE-WE, one trough west of Muzaffarpur and Patna and the other east of Purnea.

The alluvial deposits have less *Kankar* formention owing to more riverine character of the plain and higher incidence of *Khadar* lands. The region is a homogeneous and featureless plain where monotony is broken by local eminences like river levees and bluffs, sandy features like the *Dhus* of the Saryupar, the ox-bow lakes, *tals* and marshy lands (*Chaurs)* of north Bihar, the badlands and ravines of the Sai and the Gomati rivers and low-lands (*Jala* or *Tal*) of south Bihar. Besides Ganga, Gomati, Ghaghara, Rapti, Gandak, Kosi (in the north), and Son (in the south) are other important rivers of the region. These rivers very often change their courses and cause severe floods. The Kosi, called 'sorrow of Bihar', has shifted its course over 120 km in recent times.

The relief features of the entire Saryupar and North Bihar plain are a series of alluvial cones formed by the main rivers along with the inter-cones (with less gradient). There are numerous ox-bow lakes, *tals* and dead or deserted channels of the rivers. In Ganga-Ghaghara Doab region the Bhangar is more extensive. The alluvium deposited in the Ganga plain South has been brought from the southern uplands and is relatively coarser. It also lacks lakes and *tals* except in Patna district. East of the Son in the Magadh-Anga. Plain, there are a number of hills running in SW-NE direction (Tiwari, 2003).

THE LOWER GANGA PLAIN

The Lower Ganga plain incorporating an area of 80,968 sq. km, extended from the foot of the Darjeeling Himalaya in the north to the Bay of Bengal in the south (maximum length about 580 km) and from the eastern margin of the Chotanagpur Plateau in the west to the borders of Bangladesh and Assam in the east (maximum width about 200 km). Its western boundary roughly corresponds with 150 m contour, while Indo-Bangladesh international border forms the eastern limit. It includes the Kishanganj tahsil of Purnia district (Bihar) and the whole of West Bengal (excluding the Purulia and Darjeeling districts). Though the whole of this plain is now perceived as deltaic, the real delta constitutes about two-thirds of this Plain lying to the south of the Rajmahal-Garo alignment and even continuing into Bangladesh. Ganga delta is probably the largest delta in the world. The eastern part of the Plain is drained by the rivers Kartoya, Tista, Jaldhakia, Torsa and Sankosh joining the Brahmaputra, and the western part by the tributaries Mahananda, Purnabhaba, Ajay, Damodar, Dwarkeswar and Rupnarayan of Ganga (Padma-Bhagirathi). In the extreme south-west, Kasai and Subarnarekha are the other rivers. The general slope of the region is towards the south-east and in the delta proper the gradient is less than 2 cm per km (Tiwari, 2003: 76).

The Lower Ganga plain has been formed by the down-warping of a part of the Peninsular landmass (between Rajmahal hills and Meghalaya Plateau) and its subsequent sedimentation by the Ganga and the Brahmaputra river systems (which came into being by the disintegration of the Indobrahma system). The average height of the region above sea level is 50 m, which reaches to a maximum of above 150 m in the extreme north (Darjeeling hills) and south-west (Rajmahal hills) and descends to merely 6 m near Kolkata and 3 m near Sagar Island. The plain has a monotonous surface dissected frequently by the channels of the main streams and their tributaries. On detailed study, there are four areas where the relative relief is somewhat significant (about 12 m to 30 m). These include: (i) the Malda West Dinajpur tract showing inliers of the lateritic alluvium, (ii) the tract bordering the Chotanagpur Highlands where the Gondawanas and the lateritic alluvium are found, (iii) the Midnapur Coast consisting of sand dune terraces, and (iv) the *Duars* (Tarai) of Jalpaiguri and Darjeeling, comprising the submontane tract. Elsewhere the lakes, swamps, marshes and the levees are the only components of the physical landscape (Tiwari, 2003: 76).

On the basis of river system, the Middle Ganga plain is further sub-divided into:

1. The Ganga Plain North and
2. The Ganga Plain South

The former is further sub-divisible into (i) the Ganga-Ghaghara doab, (ii) the Ghaghara-Gandak interfluve, (iii) the Gandak-Kosi interfluve, and (iv) the Kosi-Mahananda interfluve.

The Ganga plain South is also further sub-divisible into (a) the region to the west of Karmnasa, (b) Karmnasa east interfluve, (c) Lower Son valley, and (d) Magadha-Anga Plain. Needless to say, the Ganga remains the lifeline of the Middle Ganga plain (Singh, R.L. 1971: 190).

The Ganga-Ghaghara doab has a different physiography. Although there are a number of *tals*, ox-bow lakes and deserted channels of river, particularly along the Ghaghara and in the eastern parts (i.e., Suraha *tal* in Ballia), most of the land is Bhangar, which is not subjected to annual floods. The Gomati divides it diagonally into two halves.

The Ghaghara-Gandak interfluve is diagonally divided by the Rapti while other streams like the Burhi Rapti, the Kuwana, the Chhoti Gandak and other rivers also drain this area. There are numerous ox-bow lakes, *tals* and dead or deserted channels of the rivers. The *tals* like Ramgarh, Chando, Bukhira, Chillua, Likhia, etc. have resulted due to the changes in the courses of the various rivers.

The same zones follow in the North Bihar Plain where the land is also dotted with lakes and elongated chaurs and dead channels. The Kosi-Mahananda interfluve has more of these features as the river is notorious for its shifting channels (Singh, R.L. 1971: 192).

THE DRAINAGE SYSTEM

The drainage system of the Middle Ganga plain is governed by the general life of the land which slopes from the north-west to the south-east. The entire region is drained by the Ganga system. The Ganga is the trunk river of the Ganga plain covering a distance of about 2000 km within the alluvial plain. It is a Himalayan source river having a large catchment in the mountains. It runs through Piedmont plain and its Megafan deposits in almost N-S direction; and acquiring; swinging to the NW-SE trend in the Central Alluvial Plain, and acquiring W-E trend when it becomes the axial river (Singh, I.B., 1996: 130).

As stated above, the Ganga is the most important river system of India which drains over a quarter of the country's surface area. Its flood plain is the granary house of the country supporting the largest concentration of human population. Its banks are dotted with important cities and its water is utilised for irrigation, hydel generation, industrial uses and drinking purposes.

The Ganga proper is formed by the confluence of the Alaknanda and the Bhagirathi at Deva Prayag. The former consists of the Dhauli (rising in the Zanskar Range near Niti Pass) and the Vishnu Ganga (originating from Mount Kamet 7756 m near Mana Pass) meeting at Joshimath or Vishnu Prayag. The Pindar River rising from Nanda Devi and East Trisul (6803 m) joins the Alaknanda at Karna Prayag while the Mandakini or Kali Ganga meets it at Rudra Prayag. The source of Bhagirathi lies in the Gangotri glacier (25 km long) at a point called Gaumukh (3900 m). It is joined by the Jahnavi and forms a deep gorge near Bandarpunch (Tiwari, 2003: 101).

Emerging out of the Himalayas as near Hardwar, the Ganga flows majestically for 1200 km east-wards, turns south and then flanks the eastern face of the Rajmahal hills. Near Dulian the waters divide. One branch passes into Bangladesh, the other flows through the Indian territory under the name of Bhagirathi or Hooghly and enters the Bay of Bengal at the southern tip of Sagar island. The lower reach about 300 km long, does not carry enough water because of the eastward shifting of the river. All through its course in the plains, the Ganga flows along a braided channel with sandbanks and is bordered on either side by low-lying depressions which get flooded during the rains. The river receives two important tributaries on its right bank, the Yamuna and the Son, and three on its left bank, the Ghaghara (Sarju), the Gandak and the Kosi.

The Yamuna

The Yamuna (length 1,384 km, drainage area 3,59,000 km) is the most important tributary of the Ganga. It rises on the western slopes of Bandarpunch in the Jamnotri glacier and runs almost parallel to Ganga and joins the latter at Prayag (Allahabad). In its upper reaches it is joined by the Tons, the Giri and the Asan. Its tributaries include the Chambal,

Betwa and Ken and Sind from the south and the Hindan, the Rind, the Sengar, the Non, the Baruna and the Sasur Khaderi from the north. Geologists believe that the Yamuna earlier flowed to the south and south-west into Rajasthan sharing its waters with the Saraswati. Much of the water of the river is taken out in the western and eastern Yamuna and Agra canal for irrigation purposes. During the medieval period it was also an important means of transport, which declined in recent times due to the development of railways and roads (Tiwari, 2003: 101).

For the greater part of its course the Yamuna flows between high banks, considerably dissected at places by gulley erosion. It runs for 800 km parallel to the Ganga and joins it at Allahabad, having received a number of tributaries from the Central Highlands, on its right bank – the Chambal, Sind, Betwa and Ken (*Gazetteer of India*: 36).

The Ghaghara

The Ghaghara (Karnali or Kauriala) rises in the glaciers of Mapchachungo, north-west of Taklakot and collecting the waters of the Tila, the Seti and the Beri rivers carves out a deep 600 m gorge at Shgishapani. In the plains it is joined by the Sarda (Kali or Kaliganga) and flows south-eastward so as to meet the Ganga at Chapra. It has a total length of 1,080 km with a catchment area of 1,27,500 km (55% lying in Nepal) and average annual water yield of 94,400 million m (Tiwari, 2003: 101).

In the Eastern U.P. Plain, while the Ganga receives the Sarayupar waters through the Ghaghara joining it west of Patna (near Chhapra), most of the waters of the Ganga-Ghaghara Doab East are received directly through independent large and small tributaries, the Gomati, the Chhoti Saryu, the Mangai, the Besu, and the Gangi in the Gomati-Ghaghara interfluve, while the Varuna is the only important stream in the Gomati-Ganga interfluve (Singh, R.L., 1971: 194).

The Ghaghara is the recepient of all drainage of the Sarayupar west of the Gandak through its tributaries like the Kuwana, the Rapti, the Chhoti Gandak and other smaller ones. The Ghaghara is highly notorious for its floods and changing courses and capacity of rendering vast agricultural tracts into sand flats (Singh, R.L., 1971: 195). Other streams like the Rapti, although equally notorious, deposit fertile silt and provide highly fertile agricultural tracts.

The Gandak

The Gandak (Sadanira, Saligrami in Nepal, or Narayani in the plains) comprises two streams – the Kaligandak rising close to Photu Pass near

Muktinath and the Trisulganga, north of Gosainthan (8,013 m). It cuts through the Mahabharat Range and covering a distance of 425 km joins the Ganga near Patna. Its total catchment area is 48,500 km, of which 9,540 km lies in India (average annual flow 52,200 million m) (Tiwari, 2003: 101-02).

In between the Gandak on the west and the Kosi system on the east, the Burhi Gandak is the chief tributary of the Ganga and receives the waters of the Baghmati.

The Kosi

The Kosi (Kausika) is the largest of the tributaries of the Ganga. It consists of seven streams of which the main stream, Arun (Phungchu in Tibet), rises to the north of Gosainthan. It has a total length of 730 km with a drainage area of 86,900 km (in India 21,500 km) and average annual flow of 61,560 million m. The Kosi is notorious for its frequent and disastrous floods and shifting of courses. It is also called 'the sorrow of Bihar'. The river flowed by Purnea 200 years ago but its present course is about 160 km to the west of that place ravaging an area of about 10,500 km. It now meets the Ganga 32 km west of Manihari (formerly near Manihari) (Tiwari, 2003: 102). A striking feature of the river is that after the impetusity of youth, there is a sudden constriction of the advanced age, a sudden leap from the degraded to the aggraded stage with no graded interval (Singh, R.L., 1971: 196).

The Kosi, formed by seven important streams (*Sapt-Kosi*) in eastern Nepal, receives no tributary in the plains because of its raised bed; it meets the Ganga at present near Kargola. It is the sorrow of Bihar and the wildest and the most devastative of the Indian rivers, and flows through several capricious channels. It deposits infertile sediments consisting of micaceous sands and renders vast fertile lands into sandy and marshy flats. The river has several distributaries like the Saura, the Kamla, the Barhnadi, the Dhusan, the Tilabeh and its tributaries like the Sugarwa, the Balan, the Kamla, etc.; most of these are seasonal (Singh, R.L., 1971: 196).

The Son

The Son (Swarna Nadi) is a large river (length 780 km: drainage area 71,900 km) rising from the Amarkantak plateau not far off from the source of the Narmada. It first flows in north-westerly direction and then takes a north-easterly course to meet the Ganga near Arrah (west of the Patna). In the plains of Bihar, it has wide bed (4.8 km) and assumes huge size during rains. The confluence of the river with Ganga is gradually shifting towards west (in AD 1750 at Maner) (Tiwari, 2003: 102).

The Ganga receives numerous tributaries from the Southern Uplands among which the Son is the largest. The channel of this river is very wide (about 5 km at Dehri), but the flood-plain is narrow, only 3 to 5 km wide. The river has been notorious for its changing courses in the past, as is traceable from several old beds on its east, but has been tamed squarely with the anicut at Dehri and now more so with the Indrapuri Barrage, a few km upstream (Singh, R.L., 1971: 196).

The tributaries of the Ganga west of the Son are smaller – the Karnauti, the Ojnala, the Khejuri, the Chatar, the Jargo, the Tons and the Karmanasa. Those on the east of the Son are the Punpun, the Mohini and the Chandan (Singh, R.L., 1971: 196).

RAINFALL

Moving eastwards from Allahabad into the middle Ganga plain, the rainfall increases. It ranges from about 40 inches in the west to about 70 inches in the east. The rainfall, though torrential and ample, is apt to be variable and, while true droughts are rare, the vicissitudes of the rainfall introduce an element of insecurity into farming (Robinson, 1966: 169).

CROPS

The characteristic crops of *rabi* and *kharif* of the Upper Ganga plain are now replaced by a threefold harvest system; crops are planted to enable three distinct harvests to be secured.

1. The autumn or *bhadai* harvest – maize, millets, quick growing rice and some Jute in the eastern parts.
2. The winter or *aghani* harvest – the main rice crop is planted in and grows during the wet season and is harvested in December or Jaunary; and
3. The spring or *rabi* harvest – catch crop of little value such as gram and chickling vetch, usually follow on after the *aghani* harvest. In noting this division of the agricultural calendar, it should be emphasised that not all three harvests are obtained from a single piece of land in a twelve-month period (Robinson, 1966: 169).

Rice is the chief crop of the Middle Ganga plain with about three times the acreage devoted to barley and wheat, the two next most important food crops. Millet is of little importance as are jowar and bajra. A considerable area is sown to oilseeds and to sugarcane. Cotton as a crop fades out in this region and is of little consequence except in the

Tirhut area between the Gandak and Kosi rivers. On the other hand, jute makes its appearance in the extreme east in the Bhagalpur area and is of increasing importance. Small quantities of tobacco are grown mainly in the east. It is interesting to note that indigo and opium, both formerly cash crops, have now practically disappeared from the scene (Robinson, 1966: 169-70).

FLOODS

Floods are a recurring feature of the region, more particularly in the Northern Ganga plain. Not infrequently, when the Ganga itself remains in spate, and thwarts the incoming water from its numerous tributaries in the region, large areas get flooded leading to breaks of transport system and devastation of life and property.

CHANGES IN THE COURSES OF RIVERS

The rivers have played effective role in the origin and growth of human settlements up to the introduction of modern means of transportation, and most of the towns of the region have thus grown along the rivers and at confluence points, taking therein advantage in several ways. The towns like Ballia have shifted their sites along with a shift in course of the Ganga. The rivers of the Middle Ganga plain have shifted their courses frequently covering wide areas throughout the historic times, as is reflected by the remnants of their former beds in the form of ox-bow lakes, meander loops, dead arms, *chaurs, tals* and ruins of settlements, etc. For instance, the Ganga has shifted over 55 km to the south of Allahabad (Kennedy, 2000: 202) and over 35 km between Bhojpur *tal* and Surha *tal* causing changes in the site of Ballia (Singh, R.L., 1971: 197). Town and river ports like Gola, Barhaj, etc. have been affected by similar shift of the Ghaghara. The Kosi, the most dynamic among the rivers, has marched about 120 km during the last two hundred years from near the town of Purnea up to the Tiljuga within Darbhanga district (Singh, R.L., 1971: 197).

The river morphology and the changes in the course of the Ganga and its major tributaries – the Ghaghara, the Son, the Kosi and the Gandak – have been studied by Satis Chandra Singh (1973). His study shows that the master stream, the Ganga, exhibits gradual and slow changes, swinging north-south through meandering process over a large section from Allahabad to Chapra. The Ghaghara shows a few braidings and slight meanderings. Its swifter currents have caused shifts southwards and northwards and at places have occupied the beds of its tributaries ¾ the Kuwana and the Rapti. The most conspicuous changes in its course have taken place near its confluence with the Ganga. The Son has also considerably oscillated its course near the confluence with the Ganga, the upper course being, more or less, stabilized. The Kosi is known as the 'sorrow of Bihar' for striking changes in its course from east to west or vice-versa below Chatra in the process of its fan extension which has led to the formation of an extensive alluvial cone.

THE OX-BOW LAKES

A striking feature of the Middle Ganga plain, particularly its western section, is the existence of a large number of horse-shoe or ox-bow lakes. A large number of them have been filled up partly by nature and partly by man but many of them still survive. These lakes were formed by the meander of the Ganga and represent the various stages in the withdrawal of the river to its present channel. In fact, it has been claimed that the Ganga shifted its course some 55 km south-ward during terminal Pleistocene time (Kennedy, 2000: 202). At some places these horse-shoe lake formations have been studied. The available evidence suggests that in the beginning there was very arid climatic condition followed by arid, semi-arid and semi-humid conditions (Misra and Gupta, 1995: 22).

The formation of these lakes, the change in the life of the Ganga, and the deepening of its channel are evidently part of the same process and may be due to a sharp change in climate and also to the lowering of the sea-level (Sharma, 1975: 9).

PRE-HOLOCENE ARIDITY AND CHANGE IN THE LIFE-CYCLE OF THE GANGA

On the basis of their study of the continental shelf off Maharashtra, Agrawal and Kusumgar (1974: 50) have come to the conclusion that in circa 11000 BP the sea level was several fathoms lower than at present. Further, on the basis of stratigraphical and palaeo-ecological studies Gurdip Singh (1974) concluded that there was severe pre-Holocene aridity in the area of Rajasthan lakes and that the present basins of the lakes were probably covered during the pre-Holocene time by the damming of ancient valleys by wind-borne sand at a time when the sand-dunes were still active. Allchin and Goudie (1971) have noticed a similar phenomenon in Gujarat and the dunes, according to them, were formed in this very period of aridity under similar conditions.

Sharma (1975: 13) believes that the intense aridity that marked the closing period of Pleistocene and the fall of the ocean level were responsible for a cataclysmic change in the life-cycle of the Ganga. He observes:

> The river, which had been building its valley since its arrival in the plains down the Himalayas, suddenly started cutting its bed and receding further south to its present course. As it has been observed earlier, the present water level is about 25 metres lower than the level of the last deposit of the river. In the course of its movement to its present channel many of the meanders of the old courses were converted into horse-shoe or ox-bow lakes of varying sizes enclosing recently formed sandy silty alluvium. In this land surface must have appeared, on account of the freshness and fertility of the soil, a rich vegetation. The Vindhyas on account of aridity must have been comparatively denuded of vegetation, and scarcity of fodder and water must have driven the animals to more hospitable region of the Ganga alluvium. The deep lakes were another source of food supply and a perennial source of water (Sharma, 1975: 13).

PALAEO-ENVIRONMENT AND ANTHROPOGENIC ACTIVITY IN THE MIDDLE GANGA PLAIN

As compared to the lakes and sand-dunes of Rajasthan and Kashmir valley, the palaeoclimatic data regarding the Ganga Valley is meagre indeed. The first attempt in this direction was made by H.P. Gupta (1976) who collected a pollen sequence from an ox-bow lake in Pratapgarh district of Uttar Pradesh. He concluded:

> The climatic sequence as determined from the bio-stratigraphy of the lake-basin has been grouped into four phases (I-IV). The general vegetation pattern is rather uniform and is tipped more towards open savannah forest with vast stretches of grasslands and a few scattered stands of arboreal vegetation. However, it has been observed that Gupta's chronology has poor control and is not of much use in the present context (Agrawal and Kharakwal, 2003: 20).

According to a more recent study by Kumar *et al.* (1996), development of morphology and soils of the study area in the Ganga plain can be considered to have taken place in the following three stages (Agrawal and Kharakwal, 2003: 20).

Stage I (10000-8000 BP): Large areas of the Indo-Ganga plains experienced a long spell of dry and cold climate during the last glaciation, effects of which were felt till about 6000 years. The study area, however, has surficial soil deposits that are no older than circa 10000 years. During the period starting from the Early Holocene, vegetation was scant; rivers had braided nature over vast stretches due to low and variable discharge and high sediment load. Soils developed with concentration of salts near the surface and precipitation of pedogenic calcite in the subsurface over only small upland areas in the east and north-east.

***Stage II (8000-5000 BP)*:** This stage started with uplift of the Lower Ganga-Yamuna Block and corresponding activity along Ganga, Yamuna and Meerut Faults. Till about 6000 BP, climate continued to be cold and dry and later it was warmer and wetter. This led to higher vegetation in the area and higher discharge and low sediment load of the streams.

***Stage III (5000-2500 BP)*:** At the start of this stage, the Upper Ganga-Yamuna Block subsided and became a site of deposition. Also, the Yamuna River, which was flowing in Haryana (west of the present area) and was a part of the Indus system, shifted to south and became a tributary of the Ganga River. Both the Yamuna and Ganga rivers deposited sediments in the Gn-YP. Lateral erosion by the two rivers modified the northern boundary of the Lower Ganga-Yamuna Block and changed it to V-shaped with end pointing to the north. These plains were also the hub of activity of the Ochre Coloured Pottery (3900-3000 BP) and Painted Grey Ware (3000-2600 BP) cultures.

An increase in rainfall and improved drainage led to some regressive pedogenesis in Gn-Y1 (NSA) adjoining the Ganga and Yamuna rivers and the Gn-Rgl. Salts and pedogenic calcrete were washed down partially to completely to the deeper levels (Kumar *et al.*, 1996: 307).

This study by Kumar *et al.* also is in conformity with the general pattern of climatic amelioration during mid-Holocene in all the three regions of Kashmir, Rajasthan and the Ganga valley.

A most recent attempt in tracing the late glacial and Holocene environment changes in the Ganga plain comes from Sanai lake, which is part of a linear belt of lakes in the Central Ganga plain. Most of these lakes are considered to be formed in early Holocene and were gradually filled in response to changing climate during the late Holocene to present day. Stable isotope, elemental geochemistry and pollen analysis of sediment profile from Sanai lake were used to document climatic oscillations during the last ~ 15,000 yr in Indian subcontinent (Sharma *et al.*, 2004). This study provided the following climatic scenario (Sharma *et al.*, 2004: 157):

1. Humid conditions before ~ 15,000 14C yr BP.
2. Comparatively arid conditions from 15,000-13,000 14C yr BP.
3. Enhanced humidity around 13,000 14C yr BP.
4. Dry phase around an estimated age of 11,500-10,500 14C yr BP.
5. Early to Mid Holocene climatic optimum from ~ 10,000 to 5800 14C yr BP.
6. Arid conditions during 5000 to 2000 14C yr BP.
7. Evidence of climatic amelioration from ~ 1700 14C yr BP onwards.

The climatic oscillations recorded from the Sanai lake match broadly with the climatic records from other parts of the Indian subcontinent, suggesting that these oscillations are an expression of broad scale probably global climatic changes rather than local climatic variations.

PALYNOLOGICAL INVESTIGATIONS IN THE LAHURADEWA LAKE

Mention may be made in this context of the palynological investigations currently under progress in the Lahuradewa lake in Sant Kabir Nagar district of eastern Uttar Pradesh. The Neolithic settlement of Lahuradewa is surrounded by a large lake and a 2, 80 m deep trench was dug on the dried margin of this ancient lake located in the vicinity of the archaeological site for the collection of sediment profile (Chauhan *et al.*, 2004). Two sets of samples each comprising 28 were collected from this profile at an interval of 10 cm for pollen and chemical analyses along with 10 radiocarbon dating samples at larger intervals. The profile has been dated to 9210+170 years BP at 2.70-2.80 m depth, 8710+90 years BP at 2.50-2.60 m depth and 7010+170 years BP at 2.30-2.40 m depth from the lower horizon. Radiocarbon dates from the upper part of the profile are awaited.

The preliminary pollen analysis based on 23 samples between 0-2.30 m depth of the profile, in general, has demonstrated the presence of open vegetation, mainly comprising grasses, sedges, Asteraceae, *Polygonum* sp., Chenopodiaceae/Amaranthaceae, Malvaceae, etc., together with sparsely distributed trees of *Madhuca indica* (Mahua), *Syzygium* sp. (Jamun), *Embica officinalis* (Anwala), *Aegle mamelos* (Bel), *Acacia* (Babul), *Bombax malabaricum* (Semal), *Holoptelea* (Chilbil), *Terminalia, Shorea robusta* (Sal), *Barringto*, etc. since 7000 yrs BP. The overall presence of a good number of deciduous trees denotes the tropical monsoonal climate in the region. The recovery of Cerelia together with othe culture pollen taxa, viz., Cannabis sativa, Chenopodiaceae/Amaranthacea, Artemisia, Brassicaceae and Caryophyllacea since 7000 yrs BP onwards suggests that this region was under some sort of agricultural practices. The existence of the lake has been witnessed as clearly manifested by the record of pollen of aquatic plants such as *Potamogeton, Nymphoides, Jussieua, Typha* and algal remains of *Botryococcus*. Interestingly, the consistent occurrence of *Trapa* (Singhara) between the depths of 2.00-1.50 m, tentatively dated to 6000-3250 yrs BP, reveals that the lake was quite deep and perpetually extending even in the close vicinity of human settlement at the excavation site owing to prevailing favourable climatic conditions. The Singhara fruits (*Trapa*), in all likelihood, would have been exploited by the ancient settlers for subsistence during this period. The pollen of temperate and high altitude plants, like *Pinus* (Chirpine), *Cedrus* (Deodar), *Alnus* (Alder), *Betula* (Birch) and *Ephedra* denote their transportation by wind or water from the Himalayan region.

The pollen analytical investigation from the lowest horizon at the depth of 2.40-2.80 m, dating back from 8710+90 yrs BP to 9210+170 yrs BP, is in progress.

Commenting upon the palaeo-environments and anthropogenic activity in the Ganga plain during the Quaternary, Indra Bir Singh (2004a) writes:

Systematic geomorphic studies, geochemical-mineralogical investigations, chronometry using luminescence method, radiocarbon dating and palynological studies have helped us to reconstruct the events of base-level tectonic activity and climate change during Late Quaternary which are often intermixed and difficult to separate.

An important inference of these studies is that the Ganga plain, at least for the last 45 kyrs, was a grassland with few thickets and patches of forest. The landscape had some high grounds, represented by alluvial ridges and natural levees. Large number of small and large water bodies (ponds and lakes) and minor channels were prominent features of the landscape. There is a continuous record of palynological evidence of grassland for about last 15 kyrs. During the last glacial maxima (LGM), the landform supported a dense network of minor tributaries, many of the ephemeral character. These channels became very prominent around 13 kyrs with increased monsoon rainfall. A tectonic event between 8-5 kyrs transformed this landscape of dense river channels into a landscape of ponds and lakes. High monsoon rainfall during 13-6 kyrs supported large lakes. 5-4 kyrs is a dry climate phase causing shrinkage and siltation of the lakes. Study of bovid teeth enamel suggest century-scale monsoon rainfall changes in the last 4 kyrs.

The Ganga Plain with high grounds for settlement, plenty of water and rich fauna and flora in the grassland attracted humans since Palaeolithic time. The find of Middle Palaeolithic archaeological site at Kalpi, in Yamuna valley dated around 45 kyrs with rich faunal remains and large variety of bone tool implements suggest early occupation of the Ganga Plain by humans. The upwarps and ponds, developed during Early Holocene, provided ideal sites for the Mesolithic people (8-4 kyrs) in Pratapgarh region. There is also evidence of Mesolithic occupation of Kalpi region. Large-scale human settlement in Ganga Plain took place around 3.5-3.0 kyrs on the high grounds close to the lakes and small rivers . Later during 3.2 kyrs, sites close to large rivers were occupied.

Thus, it seems reasonable to assume that Ganga Plain was well occupied by the humans since Middle Palaeolithic time. There is evidence of agricultural activity in the form of cultural pollens since last 15 kyrs. The Ganga plain is an area of active sedimentation and the age of the surface sediments is mostly Late Holocene. Evidence of early human settlements are probably buried in the sub-surface and can be studied in cliff-sections, deeper excavations in appropriate sites and areas of upliftment undergoing erosion (Pratapgarh region). Proper understanding of the microgeomorphic features, landscape evolution and past climate can help in understanding the human settlement in the Ganga Plain. These studies are also important to investigate the changes in the landscape due to the anthropogenic activity of early settlers. It would help us to differentiate between changes in the landscape due to natural causes from those of the anthropogenic activity.

ANTHROPOGENIC ACTIVITY

The oldest record of human activity in the Ganga plain is from Mau in Banda (presently Chitrakoot) district from a cliff section of Yamuna, where early Palaeolithic artefacts were recorded from the lowest horizon (*IAR*, 1968-69: 34; Singh, I.B., 2001-2002: 16).

The nearest site in the Vindhyan hills, which has yielded both Lower and Middle Palaeolithic industries from the surface, is a site named Lahchura, located near the tri-junction of Hamirpur and Jhansi districts of Uttar Pradesh and Chhatarpur district of Madhya Pradesh. This site is situated on the river Dhasan, a tributary of the Betwa. On typological considerations, the label 'Palaeolithic' has been assigned to this industry (Pant, 1982: 39-49, 72-76).

But the most significant discovery of human activity in the Ganga plain comes from Kalpi in district Jalaun in U.P. The Kalpi section is located on the southern bank of the Yamuna River, trending NW-SE, about 20 m thick extending over one km and divisible into three stratigraphic units, designated formally as Events (Singh *et al.*, 1999; Singh, 2004b). Event I makes the 5 m thick lower part of the succession composed of essentially reddish to know – coloured silty sediments, highly mottled with distinct different types of calcretized urrows and scattered calcrete nodules.

Event II is about 4 m thick succession of light grey micaceous fine sand. This Event has yielded a 3.54 m long elephant tusk, a 1 m long shoulder blade of elephant and molars of bovides. The meticulous field investigations carried out by a team of the Department of Geology, Lucknow University into the sediments of the Yamuna River section between the railway and road bridges at this site, during the last five years have proved beyond doubt that human groups occupied the region around 45000 years BP (Tewari *et al.*, 2002: 12). Here the stone and bone implements occur in a definite stratigraphic horizon, which has been dated by various dating methods. This artefact yielding horizon is present in Event II which also provided a variety of vertebrate faunal remains listed above. The presence of elephant and other animals seems to suggest a humid climate during the deposition of this horizon (Singh, I.B. *et al.*, 1999).

THE TOOL ASSEMBLAGE

As stated above, lithic and bone artefacts, chronologically assignable to Middle Palaeolithic, were recorded from Event II of the Kalpi section. The lithic artefacts comprise flakes and chips detached from quartzite pebbles. However, a few flakes of chert also occur. A total collection of 65 lithic artefacts was made between March 1997 and June 2002. The pebble tools comprise unifacial and bifacial tools and the flake tools include typical and atypical varieties.

Besides, a sizeable number of fossilised bones including those showing definite evidence of human activity, were collected from Event II. A considerable proposition of them apparently appears charred in varying degrees. Several bones bearing cut-marks and worked edges were also found. The bone artefacts are generally made on elongated pieces of bones of various sizes, split vertically from long bones. Amongst them, points are maximum in number. The other types comprise burins, end scrapers, notched tools and atypical end scrapers. In view of the typological and also chronological considerations, the stone and bone industry of Kalpi has been placed in the Middle Palaeolithic period.

Thus, the above investigations record for the first time the occurrence of a variety of vertebrate fauna along with evidence for human occupation in Event II, assignable to Late Pleistocene.

CHRONOLOGY

The Kalpi succession has been dated by luminescence method using Infrared Stimulated Luminescence (IRSL) technique. A total of seven samples were collected in steel tubes along the exposed cliff section in 1998 and dated at Physical Research Laboratory. In view of the fine-grained nature of samples, the dating analysis was done using IRSL from polyminerallic fine grains in the size range of 4-11 um. The estimated IRSL ages of different samples of the Kalpi section show that the basal part of Event I gives an age of 76+11 ka while the top of Event is 54+12 ka. The basal part of Event II is 45+9 ka. The basal part of Event III is 43-7 ka. Thus, it is logical to infer that artefact yielding basal Event II is about 45 ka in age.

Luminescence dates of Kalpi section have been preferred over the earlier 14C dates because first, the time-frame of the deposit fall near the lower limit of 14C dating technique, second, the 14C dating was done on calcrete nodules which have some inherent problems, and third, seven TL dates are available in the section giving stratigraphically consistent ages.

It may be noted that the stone tool assemblage and the bone implements are so far recovered from the basal and middle parts of the Event II deposits. The stone tools have been recovered from a limited area of about 50 m lateral extent. On the contrary, the bone implements are recorded from a fairly large area of a few hundred metres. The stratigraphic horizon containing this tool assemblage is dated about 45,000 yrs BP, which makes it a Middle Palaeolithic industry.

In the Ganga-Gomati interfluve, there are nearly two hundred Mesolithic settlements in and around Pratapgarh district dated around 10-8 thousand years BP. Most of these sites are located on the mounds (natural levees raised flood plain) close to the lakes, the most famous being Sarai Nahar Rai, Mahadaha and Damdama. It suggests occupation of higher mounds close to the lakes during 10-8 ka.

Besides, palynological study of Sanai *Tal* in Rae Bareli district indicates the presence of anthropogenic pollen during early to middle Holocene. In the Ganga-Gomati interfluve region of Lucknow area, few exceptional archaeological sites are dated around 2.5 ka. Thus, large-scale habitation of Ganga-Gomati interfluve took place between 3-2.5 ka. (Singh, I.B., 2001-2002: 16). Most of the habitation sites are located on the mounds adjacent to the lakes. These mounds represent natural levees or raised flood plain, which were beyond flooding. Some sites are also present on the cliffs and banks of minor rivers, and a few on the cliffs along large rivers. This process of large-scale human settlement continued throughout the last 3500 years with distinct cultural changes.

As stated earlier, the area around Lahuradewa site and the adjoining lake in district Sant Kabir Nagar of eastern Uttar Pradesh has been subjected to a multi-disciplinary research by a team of scientists from the Lucknow University, Birbal Sahni Institute of Palaeobotany and the Directorate of Archaeology, Uttar Pradesh. This study has brought to light significant results which can be summarised as follows (Tewari *et al.*, 2004b):

1. This study has provided significant information regarding human activity, domestication of rice, palaeovegetation and palaeoclimate in the Lahuradewa area from about 10,000 yr. BP. The respective lacustrine and archaeological sediments are dated on the basis of over a dozen conventional radiocarbon and two AMS dates.
2. The consistent presence of micro-charcoal recorded in the successive lake sediments indicates fires caused by human activity for slash and burn cultivation in the area since about 10,000 yr. The evidence of micro-charcoal and Cerealia pollen since about 15,000 yr. BP found in the studies in Sanai *Tal* (Rae Bareli district) taken together with a good number of radiocarbon dates, generally termed as erratic, for the charcoal samples from different archaeological sites, such as Dadupur (Lucknow district) and Bateswar (Agra district), also attest human activity prevailing in a larger area of the Ganga plain during the late Pleistocene and early Holocene.
3. The presence of wild rice is marked in the Lahuradewa Lake-sediments from about 10,000 yr. BP. An AMS radiocarbon date of about mid-eighth millennia BP (cal. mid-ninth millennia BP) for a husk-clot of a domesticated rice grain found in the lowest archaeological deposit and the presence of phytoliths and Cerealia pollen in lake sediments during 7th-8th millennium BP is indicative of well-developed agriculture during that period. Since the identifiable morphological features of a domesticated variety of grain develop in a considerably long span of time, these evidences suggest commencement of cultivation and domestication of rice much earlier may be during the terminal Pleistocene or beginning of Holocene. Considering the earlier evidence regarding the cultivation of rice known from Koldihwa, Kunjhun, Malhar, Senuwar, Chirand and Imlidih Khurd, etc. along with that of Lahuradewa, Damdama and Khairadih located in the Vindhyan hills and Ganga plain, it appears that the rice was being grown in the whole of this area during the earlier half of the Holocene. Further sustained and focussed researches at other suitable archaeological sites and lake sediments may prove this region as an independent zone for the evolution of rice cultivation and domestication.
4. The studies pertaining to carbon isotope, pollens and phytoliths, etc. suggest that the area around Lahuradewa was a swamp with grass vegetation since 10,000 yr. BP. The lake expanded around 7000 BP and reached its maximum around 5000 yr. BP with the increase of rainfall. During circa 9500 to 8700 yr. BP, open vegetation chiefly

constituting of grass together with meagre trees and thickets occurred in the region under cool and dry climate condition, between about 8700 to 5700 yr. BP rainfall increases, and grassland incorporated more trees.

REFERENCES

Agrawal, D. P. and S. Kusumgar. 1974. *Prehistoric Chronology and Radiocarbon Dating in India*, Delhi, Munshiram Manoharlal.

Agrawal, D.P. and J.S. Kharakwal. 2002. *South Asian Prehistory: A Multidisciplinary Study*, New Delhi, Aryan Books International.

_____. 2003. *Bronze and Iron Ages in South Asia*, New Delhi, Aryan Books International.

Allchin, F. R. and A. Goudie. 1971. Dunes, Aridity and Early Man in Gujarat, *Western Asia Man*, Vol. 6 (June 1971), No. 2: 251.

Chauhan, M.S., A.K. Pokharia, R. Tewari and I.B. Singh. 2004. Preliminary pollen analytical investigation on early Holocene sediments from Lahuradewa Lake, District Sant Kabir Nagar, U. P. Paper read in the *Workshop on the Archaeology of the Middle Ganga Plain*, Lucknow, on 13-14 March 2004.

Diwakar, R.R. 1959. *Bihar Through the Ages*, Bombay, Orient Longman.

Government of India. 1965. *The Gazetteer of India*, Vol. I, Country and People, New Delhi, Publication Division.

Gupta, H.P. 1976. Holocene Palynology from Meander Lake in the Ganga Valley, District Pratapgarh, Uttar Pradesh, *The Palaeobotanist*, 25: 109-119.

Kennedy, K.A.R. 2000. *God-Apes and Fossil Men: Palaeoanthropology of South Asia*, Ann Arbor, The University of Michigan Press.

Kumar, Sudhir, B. Prakash, M.L. Manchanda, A.K. Singhvi and Pankaj Srivastava. 1996. Holocene land form and soil evolution of the Western Gangetic plains: implications of neotectonics and climate, *Geomorph. N.F. Suppl-Bd.*103: 283-312.

Misra, V.D. and M.C. Gupta. 1995. Pre-NBP cultures in the Mid-Ganga Valley, *Prof. Agam Prasad Mathur Felicitation Volume*, Vol. III, Agra, Huzuri Bhavan, Peepal Mandi, 21-34.

Pandey, M.S. 1963. *The Historical Geography and Topography of Bihar*, Varanasi, Motilal Banarsidass.

Pant, P. C. 1982. *Prehistoric Uttar Pradesh*, Delhi, Agam Kala Prakashan.

Robinson, H. 1966. *Monsoon Asia*, London, Macdonald and Evans Ltd.

Sharma, G.R. 1975. Seasonal Migrations and Mesolithic Lake cultures of the Ganga Valley, *K.C. Chattopadhyay Memorial Volume*, Allahabad, Allahabad University, 1-21.

Sharma, C., M.S. Chauhan *et al.* 2001. Proxy records of Holocene Vegetation and climate changes from Sanai Tal, Central Ganga plain, *Geol-Surv India spl. Publication*, 65 (iii): 199-202.

Sharma, S., M. Joachimski, M. Sharma, H.J. Tobschall, I.B. Singh, C. Sharma, M.S. Chauhan and G. Morgenroth. 2004. Late Glacial and Holocene Environmental

Changes in Ganga Plain, Northern India, *Quaternary Science Reviews*, 23: 145-159.

Singh, Gurdip. 1974. Late Quaternary history of vegetation and climate of Rajasthan desert, India, *Philosophical Themes of Royal Society*, London Ser. 267, 467-501.

Singh, I.B. 1996. Geological Evolution of Ganga Plain: An Overview, *Journal of the Palaeontological Society of India*, No. 41: 99-137.

——. 2001-2002. Late Quaternary evolution of Ganga Plain and proxy records of climate change, neotectonics and anthropogenic activity, *Pragdhara*, No. 12: 1-25.

——. 2004a. Palaeoenvironments and Anthropogenic activity in the Quaternary of Ganga Plain, Paper read in the *Workshop on the Archaeology of the Middle Ganga Plain*, Lucknow, on 13-14 March 2004.

——. 2004b. Quaternary Palaeoenvironments of the Ganga Plain and Anthropogenic Activity, *Presidential address: Indian Society for Prehistoric and Quaternary Studies, XXXIIth Session*, Lucknow, 28-31 December 2004.

Singh, I.B., Shikha Sharma, Maneesh Sharma, Pradeep Srivastava and Govindaraja Rajagopalan. 1999. Evidence of human occupation and humid climate of 30 ka in the alluvium of southern climate plain. *Current Science*, 76 (No. 7) 10 April 1999: 1022-1026.

Singh, R.L. (ed.). 1971. *India: A Regional Geography*, Varanasi, National Geographical Society of India.

Singh, S.C. 1973. *Changes in the courses of rivers and their effects on the urban settlements in the Middle Ganga Plain*, Varanasi, National Geographical Society of India.

Stamp, Sir Dudley. 1967. *Asia: A Regional and Economic Geography*, London, Methuen & Co.

Tewari, Rakesh, P.C. Pant, I.B. Singh, S. Sharma, M. Sharma, P. Srivastava, A.K. Singhvi, P.K. Mishra and H.J. Tobschall. 2002. Middle Palaeolithic Human Activity and Palaeoclimate at Kalpi in Yamuna Valley, Ganga Plain, *Man and Environment*, XXVII (2): 1-14.

Tewari, Rakesh, R.K. Srivastava, K.K. Singh, Ram Vinay, G.C. Singh and Rajiv Trivedi. 2004a. Recent archaeological excavations in the Middle Ganga Plain and North Vindhyas, Paper read in the *Workshop on the Archaeology of the Middle Ganga Plain*, Lucknow, on 13-14 March 2004.

Tewari, Rakesh, R.K. Srivastava, K.K. Singh, K.S. Saraswat, I.B. Singh, M.S. Chauhan, B. Shekar, A.K. Pokharia, A. Saxena, V. Prasad, M. Sharma and P.P. Joglekar. 2004b. Archaeological Studies in the Lahuradewa Area, Ganga Plain: Epilogue: Implications for the Archaeogical Studies in Ganga Plain, Paper read in *The Annual Conference of the IAS, ISPQS, and IHC and the National Seminar on the Archaeology of the Ganga Plain*, Lucknow, 28-31 December 2004.

Tiwari, R.C. 2003. *Geography of India*, Allahabad, Prayag Pustak Bhandar.

3

Epi-Palaeolithic and Mesolithic Cultures

INTRODUCTION

The Mesolithic phase constitutes a transitional stage from the Pālaeolithic to Neolithic. The Mesolithic sites, characterized by microliths, have been reported from different ecological zones, across the length and width of the country, excepting from the major portion of the Indo-Gangetic plain and the north-eastern part of India. The technology of Mesolithic is primarily based on microliths. These are tiny tools made from micro-blades of one to five centimetres length, by blunting one or more sides with steep re-touch. The main tool-types are backed blades, obliquely truncated blades, points, crescents, triangles and trapezes. These microliths were used as components of spear-heads, arrow-heads, knives, sickles, harpoons and daggers (Misra, 2001: 498). They were fitted into grooves in bone, wood and reed shafts and joined together by natural adhesives like gum and resin. Evidence for such hafting comes from later sites in India and from Mesolithic and Neolithic sites in Western Asia, Africa and Europe. The use of bow and arrow for hunting became common during this period.

Archaeological investigations have revealed that the first forays of prehistoric man in the Middle Ganga plain were made at the fag end of the terminal Pleistocene and at the beginning of early Holocene period. This stage is known as the Epipalaeolithic (a transitional phase from the Late Upper Palaeolithic to the early Mesolithic). During this stage the Stone Age man from the Vindhyas used to cross the Ganga and Yamuna rivers in the north and colonise the Ganga plain. It is believed that change in climate – resulting in paucity of food resource in the Vindhyas – might be the reason for this migration. In the Holocene period return of moderate climate resulting in rich food resource in the Ganga plain and population pressure in the Vindhyas forced the Stone Age man to colonise the Ganga plain on a larger scale. Six sites of the Epipalaeolithic phase – Mandah, Shalhipur, Suleman Parbatpur in Pratapgarh district, Kurha and Ahiri in Allahabad district and Garhwa in Varanasi district – have been located. Scatter of artefacts on hard concretionary plastic clay horizon has been found. The tools are made on chert of varying shades and occasionally on chalcedony. The finished tools comprise retouched blades, backed blades, notches, points/drills, burins, scrapers and lunates. The unmodified waste is divisible into blades, flakes, cores and chips. The artefacts are highly patinated. The artefact-bearing horizon is thin and indicates that these were seasonal camp sites. The artefacts generally exposed on present surface are mostly fragmentary. No biological remains have been found from these surface sites (Pal, 2002: 67).

HISTORY OF RESEARCH

In India the microlithic tools were first discovered as early as 1867-68 by A.C.L. Carlleyle, an Assistant of Sir Alexander Cunningham, the first Director General of the Archaeological Survey of India, in the caves and rock-shelters of the Kaimur ranges of the Vindhyan hills. Subsequently, in 1880-81 he excavated some of the rock-shelters and came across microliths and other stone tools, living floors with hearths containing animal bones, ash and charcoal and human burials. At about the same time, Carlleyle's contemporary, Robert Bruce Foote discovered many microlithic sites in different parts of South India and in Gujarat, including the now famous site of Langhnaj. Small scale diggings of microlith-bearing deposits were carried out by G.R. Hunter and D.H. Gordon in the rock-shelters at Pachmarhi in Madhya Pradesh in the thirties of the last century. However, significant advance in our knowledge of this period was made only when H.D. Sankalia undertook excavation at Langhnaj and other sites in Gujarat in the early forties of the last century. Among Sankalia's contemporaries who contributed to the study of the Mesolithic period, mention may be made of A. Aiyappan, K.R.U. Todd and G.R. Sharma. While Aiyappan explored the *teri* sites of Sawyerpuram and published analysis of its microlithic industry, Todd explored the microlithic sites on the Islands of Bombay. G.R. Sharma with his colleagues R.K. Varma, V.D. Misra, B.B. Misra, J.N. Pandey and J.N. Pal discovered and excavated many Mesolithic sites in Mirzapur district; the Balen valley in Allahabad district; and in the Ganga valley in Pratapgarh district. One of the pioneers in the

Mesolithic studies in India is V.N. Misra who explored the Berach basin in south Rajasthan and discovered more than thirty Mesolithic sites. He excavated two sites – Tilwara and Bagor – in districts Barmer and Bhilwara respectively, both in Rajasthan, which unfolded many hitherto unknown facets of this culture. In the last four decades several thousand Mesolithic sites have been discovered in widely separated areas of India and as many as thirty-five of them have been excavated on varying scale. The important excavated sites are Langhnaj in Gujarat, Birbhanpur in West Bengal, Tilwara and Bagor in Rajasthan, Chopani Mando and Lekhahia in the Vindhyan hills and Sarai Nahar Rai, Mahadaha and Damdama in the middle Ganga plain. In order to comprehend the full significance of the Mesolithic phase in the Ganga valley, it is imperative to study them in relation to the Mesolithic culture of the Vindhyas.

MESOLITHIC SITES OF THE VINDHYAS AND THE GANGA VALLEY

More than 500 Mesolithic sites have been located in surface explorations in the eastern Vindhyas and the middle Ganga valley, of which 204 sites are located in the middle Ganga valley and the rest are in the Vindhyan area. In the Vindhyas microliths have been obtained littered either in the open-air settlements or in rock-shelters. In the middle Ganga Valley, Mesolithic sites have been found in parts of Allahabad (6 sites), Pratapgarh (177 sites), Jaunpur (14 sites), Sultanpur (5 sites) and Varanasi (only 2 sites) districts of Uttar Pradesh (Pandey, 1990: 311). Their occurrence have been noticed on the old banks of the Ganga, the *Bhagar* formation and on or near horse-shoe lakes (Misra, 1997: 32).

Among the excavated Mesolithic sites in the Vindhyan hills and the Ganga valley, mention may be made of Baghaikhor, Lekhahia, Morhana Pahar, Bhadahwan, Laharia Dih, Chopani Mando, Baghor II, Medhauli, Banki, Ghagharia, Dhanuhi, Sarai Nahar Rai, Mahadaha and Damdama. Of these, the first ten sites are located in the Vindhyan hills while the last three are situated in the Ganga plain.

The Mesolithic sites of the Vindhyan region are found scattered all over where water and raw material was available. Analysis of the tool assemblages indicates that sometimes the assemblage of one site differs from the others. This is because of the fact that the sites represent different stages of development within the Mesolithic.

The Department of Ancient History, Culture and Archaeology, Allahabad University, has conducted excavations at 13 Mesolithic sites so

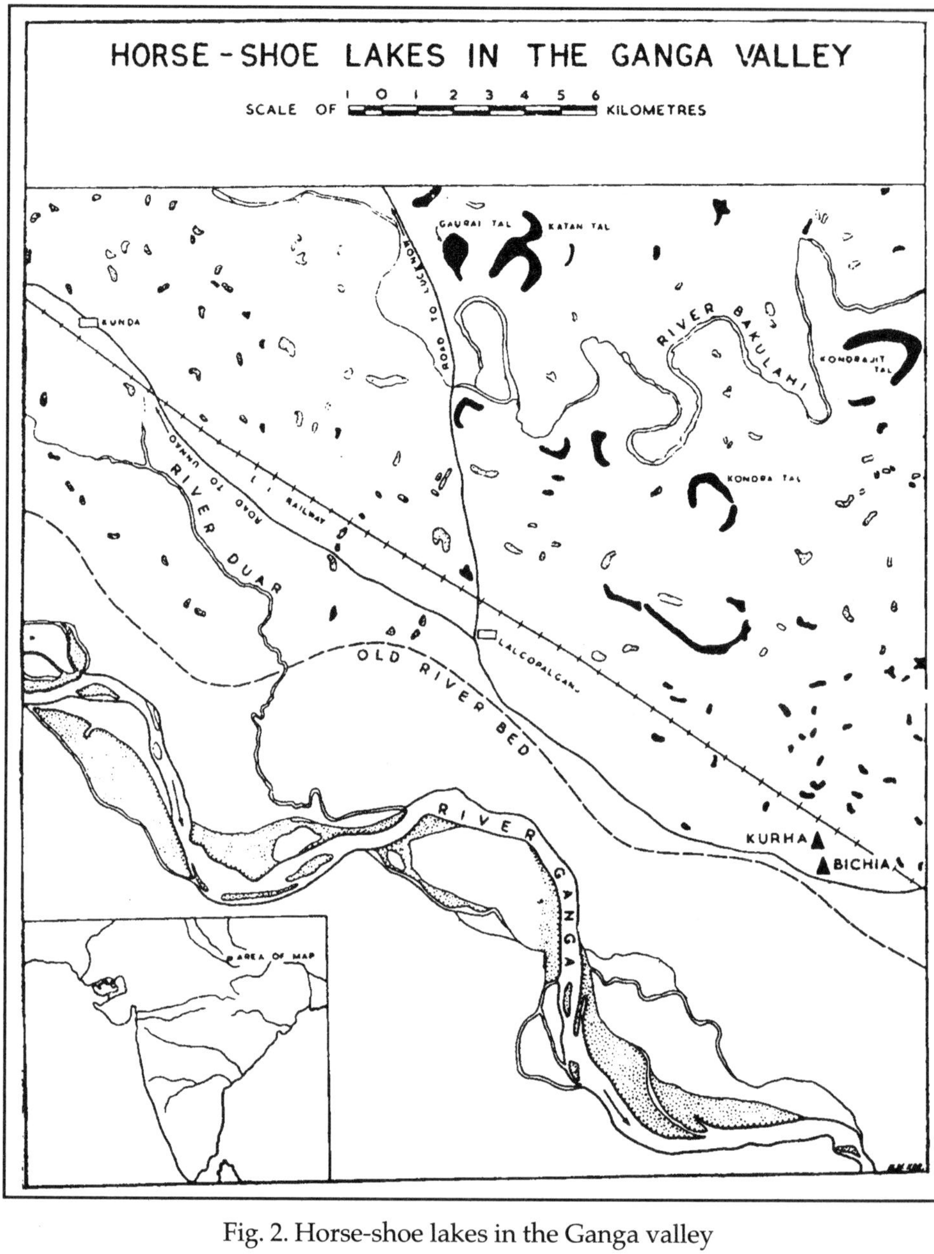

Fig. 2. Horse-shoe lakes in the Ganga valley

far. Of these, as many as 9 sites, viz., Morhana Pahar (Varma, 1986), Baghaikhor (Varma, 1986), Lekhahia (Sharma, 1975; Misra, 1977), Bhadahawan Pahar (Misra, 1977), Chopani Mando (Sharma *et al.*, 1980), Baghor II (Sharma and Clark, 1983), Medhauli (*IAR*, 1982-83), Banki,

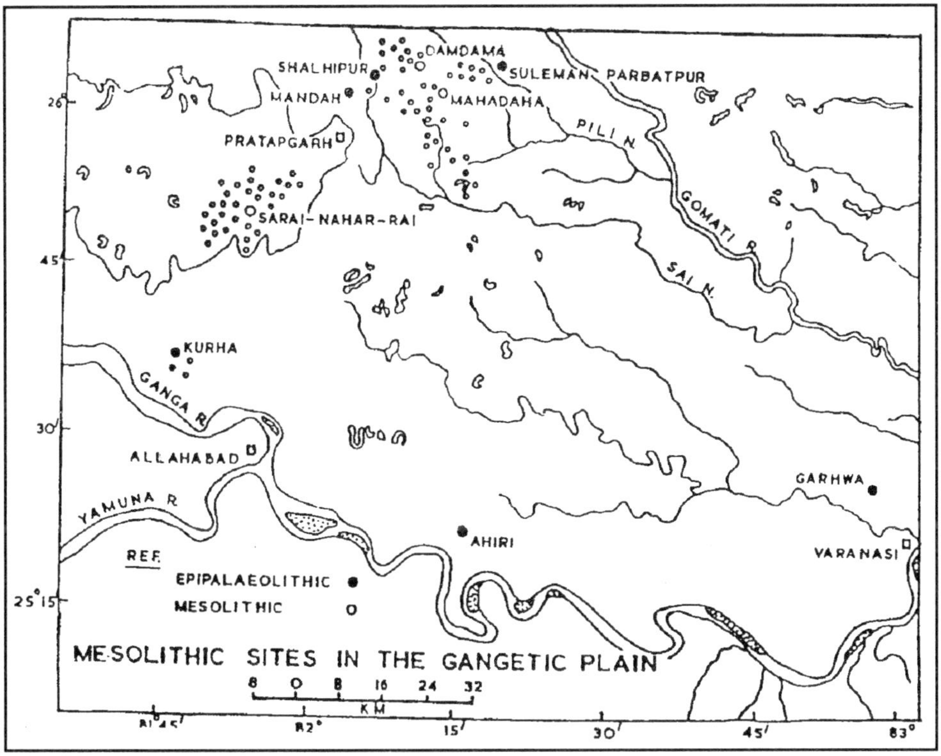

Fig. 3. Distribution of Mesolithic sites in the Ganga plain

Ghagharia (Sharma and Clark, 1983), and Dhanuhi are in the Vindhyan area and the remaining three, viz., Sarai Nahar Rai (Sharma, 1973), Mahadaha and Warikalan-Damdama, are in the middle Ganga valley. Besides, excavation has also been carried out in Lahariadih by the Department of Ancient Indian History, Banaras Hindu University. The excavated sites in the Vindhyas include six rock-shelters – Lekhahia I, Lekhahia II, Baghai-khor, Morahana Pahar, Ghagharia I and Lahariadih (Misra, 1977: 32).

The history of Stone Age archaeology in the Ganga plain goes back to 1969-70 when the Mesolithic site of Sarai Nahar Rai was discovered by the archaeologists of Allahabad University. Though the first human skeleton of the Mesolithic man at Sarai Nahar Rai was excavated by the Anthropological Survey of India in 1970, it was the excavations of 1972 and 1973-74 of Allahabad University which yielded significant results including human skeletons, hearths, animal bones, microliths and other valuable evidences pertaining to habitation and settlement pattern. The results were promptly published by Sharma in 1973 and 1975.

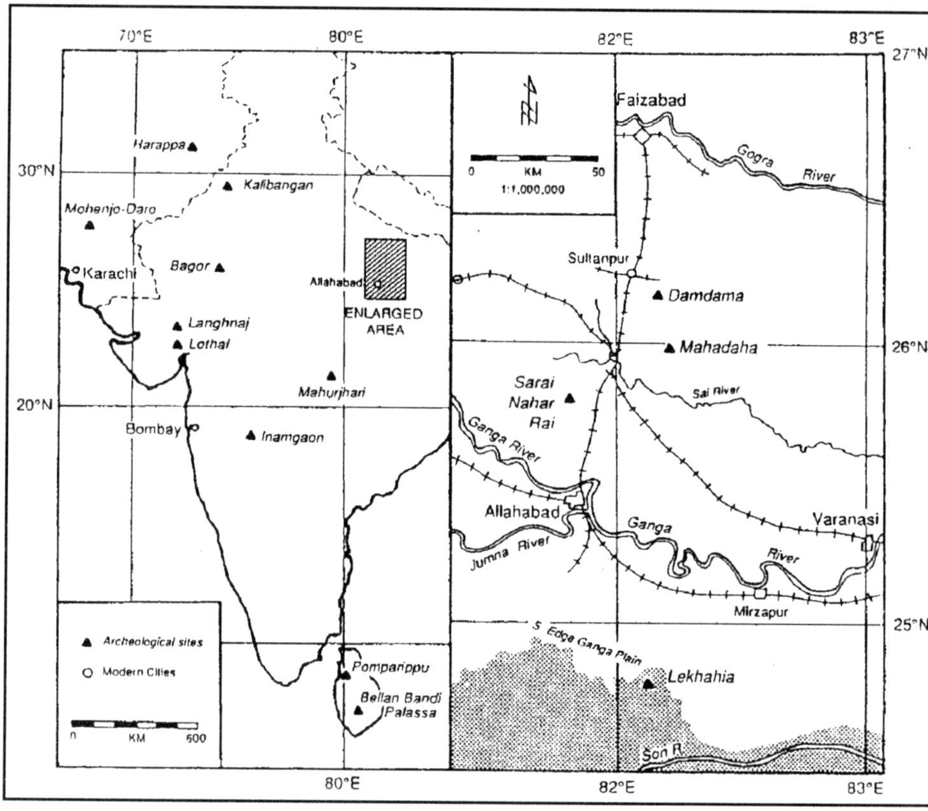

Fig. 4. Location map of Sarai Nahar Rai, Mahadaha and Damadama

The next excavated site was Mahadaha, situated on the western bank of another horse-shoe lake at a distance of 31 km to the north-east of Pratapgarh. This site was brought to light in 1978 and a 60 cm thick occupation, divisible into 4 layers, was excavated in 1977-78 and 1978-79. The excavations yielded 35 oval or circular pit-hearths, 28 human graves and several patches of burnt floors/plasters along with microliths, bone tools, querns, mullers and hammerstone fragments.

The third excavated site is Damdama, situated on a slightly raised ground at the confluence of two branches of Tambura Nala, a tributary of the Pili Nadi, which discharges itself into the Sai River. This site was discovered in 1978 and was excavated continuously for seven seasons since 1982-83, which brought to light 41 human graves, several pit-hearths, microliths, bone objects and grinding stones.

The principal excavated sites are described as follows:

CHOPANI MANDO

Chopani Mando is situated on the middle terrace of the Balen River, about 77 km south-east of Allahabad. This site is spread on an area of roughly 15,000 square metres, of which nearly 680 square metre area was excavated to varying depths from 30 cm to 80 cm. This excavation, conducted in 1967 and again in 1977-78, brought to light ten layers divisible into three uninterrupted cultural phases: Epi-Palaeolithic, Mesolithic, and Advanced Mesolithic or Proto-Neolithic.

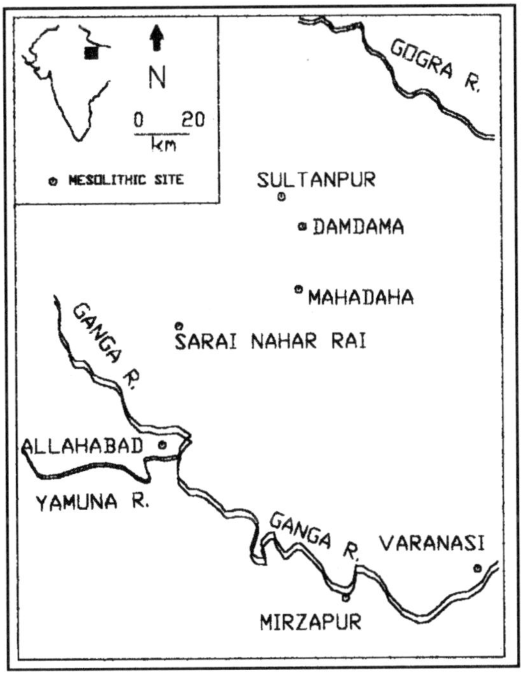

Fig. 5. Location map of principal excavated sites

EPI-PALAEOLITHIC

Layer 10 belonging to this phase has yielded both Upper Palaeolithic (20%) and Early Mesolithic (80%) artefacts. The assemblage comprises large and broad blades, burins, parallel-sided blades, blunted back borers, scrapers and points along with numerous cores, flakes and blanks, mostly fashioned on cherty material.

EARLY MESOLITHIC

This phase is divided into sub-phases A and B on the basis of the absence and presence of geometric tool shapes. Early Mesolithic sub-phase A is marked by non-geometric microliths unassociated with pottery and is represented in layers 9 and 8. Early Mesolithic sub-phase B, represented by layers 7 to 4, yielded geometric microliths, also unassociated with pottery.

ADVANCED MESOLITHIC OR PROTO-NEOLITHIC

This phase is represented in layers 3 to 1. Besides microlithic tools, cores, flakes and debitage, plans of as many as 13 circular or oval huts and four hearths have been exposed. The huts lie very close to each other, varying in diameter from 4.5 m. to 2.5 m. On the floor of the huts is a concentration of microliths and stone pieces, potsherds, fragmentary animal bones, charcoal pieces, burnt clay lumps with reed and bamboo impressions, hammerstones and anvils of different sizes and shapes. This phase is also characterized by the emergence of handmade pottery comprising ill-fired *khaki*-coloured ware, ochrous red ware and moulded or stamped ware. Bowls or vases of medium to small size with featureless rims are the only shapes met with in all the above wares. A few burnt clay lumps from the Proto-Neolithic levels of the sites contain rice or husk impressions of a wild variety of rice. This is an important discovery, particularly in view of the occurrence of domesticated rice and handmade pottery from the Neolithic levels at Koldihwa and Mahagara in the same region.

The excavation have yielded as many as 4624 bone fragments. The majority of them (4455) come from the Advanced Mesolithic Phase (Phase III) of the settlement (Sharma *et al.*, 1980: 69). The bone remains were selected for identification. They belonged to the advanced Mesolithic phase. Alur (1980: 206) who studied the material opines that only two could yield to identification for the rest were too fragmentary. The animals identified are cattle and sheep/goat of wild variety. The cattle specimen identified that it belongs to a large-sized animal. The size of the horn-core of sheep or goat indicates that it belongs to a mature animal, "the height of which would be little above the average goat of today" (Alur, 1980: 207).

Commenting on the importance and contributions of the proto-neolithc phase at Chopani, Mando R.K. Varma (2003: 6-7) remarks that this phase is important from a number of viewpoints:

1. It brings out a change in the living pattern within the Mesolithic. The appearance of quern and mullers indicate that these people substituted their subsistence economy with vegetal food. It further finds support from the discovery of wild rice in the lumps of burnt clay and the use of rice husk and straw as degraissants. In Vindhya-region wild rice has been discovered for the first time on a Mesolithic settlement.
2. It is presumed that the return of the people from the Ganga Valley gave a new impetus to the Mesolithic folk of the Vindhyan region. These people probably introduced the exploitation of vegetal food and its processing. Out of all the wild cereals and seeds, rice was chosen as their favourite item. It seems to have been available in plenty in wild form in river valleys of the Belan and its tributaries. We find that in Phase III at Chopani Mando, wild rice is available in burnt lump of clay. Querns and mullers also are introduced at this stage. We have seen that pottery purely hand-made is also

introduced at this juncture of time. Each piece of pottery differs from the other. "It is evident that each pottery piece was an individual creation" (Sharma *et al.*, 1980: 15). It is clear from this that it was a completely recent innovation at the site. Here it would not be out of place to mention that excavations carried out in the Bhainsore group of rock-shelters consisting of Mohahana Pahar, Baghaikhor and Lekhahia, pottery appears in the third stage, that is, after the introduction of geometric shapes. The pottery collected from these places is extremely fragile and some pieces are impressed and some resemblance may be observed with the cord impressed ware of Koldihwa and Mahagara. But no quern and muller was found associated with them. It seems pottery appears before the introduction of querns and mullers.

3. It seems that the site of Chopani Mando was deserted before the introduction of cultivation. Though cultivation did not start here but the stage was set for a take-off. It is a well-known phenomenon that cultural development is a cumulative process in which inventions and innovations take place only when the necessary antecedents already exist. Here everything was at a breaking point but unfortunately before the introduction of agriculture or cultivation, the site was deserted and the focus now shifts to Koldihwa and Mahagara, which are at a distance of not more than three kilometres south-west as the crow flies from the site of Chopani Mando in the Belan valley.

Sarai Nahar Rai

Mesolithic settlements in the Ganga valley in districts Allahabad and Pratapgarh are centred on the shores of the lakes formed by abandoned meanders of changing river courses. Among the first site to be excavated is Sarai Nahar Rai, situated at a distance of 15 km south-west of Pratapgarh on one such lake. The implementiferous locality of this site has an area of 1,800 square metres which was excavated for two seasons during 1971-73. This excavation revealed eleven graves (one with four burials), eight pit-hearths and a hut floor.

It is believed that the lake near Sarai Nahar Rai was much larger in extent about 8,000 years ago. It provided hospitable conditions to large animals such as the bison, rhinoceros, stag, etc., bones of which have been found at this site. Besides, bones of smaller games like the fish, tortoise and shells have also been found. The habitational remains constitute hearths, a limited number of post-holes and paved flooring. The area having a paved floor and post-holed enclosure has been identified as a community hearth (Sharma, 1973, 1975).

Sarai Nahar Rai provided for the first time, evidence regarding disposal of the dead in the mid-Ganga valley. Out of the total number of 15 burials, eleven were exposed. From 10 graves skeletal remains of single individuals were found while in one grave four individuals were buried at one and the same time. The dead were buried in oblong pits in extended position in west-east orientation. The right hand in the case of the male and the left in the case of female was place across the abdomen. The grave goods comprise microliths and a particular type of shells. The skeletal remains belong to 16 to 30 years old males and females with well-built structures, the average height being 1.80 m.

Excavations have yielded a large number of animal bones in charred, semi-charred and uncharred conditions (*IAR*, 1971-72: 48-49; Misra, 1977: 61). K.R. Alur (1980) has studied the bones from the site. They come from two locations: hearths and floor area. Those recovered from the former were in different stages of roasting with extensive soot deposition on them (Alur, 1980: 207). The species represented in the assemblage are cattle, bison, hippopotamus, sheep, goat, deer, stag, elephant and tortoise. The presence of the medullary cavity in the bones remains of cattle and sheep/goat hint that most of the animals on the site were in wild state (Alur, 1980: 208). Cattle are estimated to be taller. Various breeds of sheep/goat are encountered, which is reflected in the disparity of size. They were tall and hefty. Alur (1980: 210) opines that "In cattle sheep/goat majority of the animals indicated their wild affinity, while in all other animals the entire flock was of wild origin." There is a suggestion in the statement that some cattle and sheep/goat may not have been wild. This issue deserves careful consideration.

Roasting and chopping marks are identified on some cattle, barasinga, hippo and tortoise remains. About eight samples bear chopping marks. Alur (1980: 209) notes that this is an associate symptom of roasting for chopping is resorted to after roasting the flesh to detach it from its point of adherence. These marks indicate that the process was entirely food-oriented. The find of bones of animals of wild variety suggests the practice of hunting. Tortoise collected from lakes was an article of diet (Sahu, 1988: 97-98).

Mahadaha

This site is situated at a distance of five km north of Patti, in the Patti sub-division of Pratapgarh district. This site is situated on the western bank of an ancient horse-shoe lake. A number of human burials were exposed at this site in 1953 during the digging operation of the Jaunpur Minor, a branch of the Sharda Sahayak Canal, but the full archaeological potential of the site was realized in the excavation of 1977-78 and 1978-79, conducted by the University of Allahabad. This excavation revealed three distinct complexes:

1. Cemetery-cum-habitation complex
2. The butchering complex and
3. The lake complex

The cemetery-cum-habitation complex comprises mainly the burials and hearths. The butchering area is situated to the east of this complex. The excavation revealed a 60 cm thick habitational deposit, divisible into four layers (Joglekar, Misra *et al.*, 2003). During the two seasons of excavations at the site, as many as twenty-eight human graves and thirty-five hearths were excavated. All the burials with one exception were extended burials in which skeletons were placed in the supine position. The general orientation of skeletons was west-east, with the head to the west. Barring two, all the graves contained the skeletal remains of single individuals, male or female. In two graves, two individuals were found buried. While both these skeletons interred in Grave X were male, the skeletons buried in Grave IX were male and female. Burial goods found in some graves comprised bone ornaments, charred and semi-charred animal bones, microliths, bone arrowheads, etc. A noteworthy feature of these burials is that most of the individuals buried at Mahadaha died young. There was one individual, a female, whose age was estimated between 40-50 years.

The hearths excavated at this site belong to the category of pit-hearths. These were oval or circular in shape. These hearths yielded burnt clay lumps and bone fragments.

Excavation conducted in the butchering complex yielded animal bones. This indicates that the Mesolithic hunters used to bring the carcass of small game and the dismembered parts of big animals and cut them into small pieces in the area. This area was also used for fabricating bone tools and ornaments. Majority of available bones belong to stag and deer.

The microlithic assemblage of Mahadaha include chips, cores, core-fragments and finished tools which comprise scrapers, points, blades, blunted backed blades, borers, lunates, triangles and trapezes. These tools are fashioned on chert, chalcedony, carnelian, agate, quartz and crystal. However, their number is comparatively small because of the non-availability of required semi-precious stones in the Ganga valley. Besides, querns, mullers, anvils, hammers, sharpeners and sling-balls, made of sandstone and quartzite, were obtained from excavations. This suggests that the Mesolithic man at Mahadaha started gathering wild grains and other edibles for food.

The paucity of stone tools at this site was compensated by manufacturing tools of bone. These implements consist of arrowheads, points, blades, knives, chisels, scrapers and saw, etc. Small-sized horn cores, mostly of stag, were also used as tools.

During excavations, thousands of animal bones were unearthed from the lake area, the butchering area and the cementry-cum-habitation area. The character of the bones recovered in the three different areas and the species represented by them are identical. The occurrence of thousands of animal bones in the lake area indicates that the Mesolithic people at the site had dumped the refuge of the hearths and habitation area in the lake after consuming the adhered flesh (Sharma *et al.*, 1980: 101). The sheer volume of the refuge suggests deliberate human action and precludes the role of any natural agency.

Alur (1980) has examined 768 specimens from the site, of which 319 belong to the lake area, 165 to the butchering area and 284 to the cemetery-cum-habitation area. More than 95% of the total collection of bones were in various stages of fossilization (Alur, 1980: 211). Alur had identified the remains of cattle, sheep/goat, antelope, deer, bison, hippopotamus, swine, horse, carnivores rat (*Rattus rattus*) tortoise, fish and birds (*Gallus galliformes*).

Cattle bones, which dominated the collection, belong to two sizes of animals – one massive and other medium-sized. Their morphological characters suggest that they belong to wild species (Alur, 1980: 211). Four grades of sheep/goat are identified, which suggest their wild affinity. The bones of smaller size compare favourably with modern small-sized cattle. The bones of large sheep/goat constitute about 10% to 12% of the total sample of these species (Alur, 1980: 211). The swine is represented by both immature animals and the wild boar. The latter is indicated by the evidence of the find of tust. Of interest is the find of a molar of a pig. Alur (1980: 215, specimen no. 15) observes that "its size and nature of wearing indicates its domesticated origin." In Alur's observation there seems to be some suggestion for the appearance of the herding of pig in some stage of the Mesolithic. There is a solitary incisor of the horse which belongs to a small-sized pony (Alur, 1980: 212). The carnivore remains have not been identified to the level of species. Bird remains have been identified which belong to the species *Gallus* of the order *Galliformes*. The antelope and deer remains are prolific at the site, especially in the lake area. The hippo too is represented by a large number of skeletal remains in the collection (Sahu, 1988: 99-100).

The faunal assemblage of Mahadaha was also studied by P.P. Joglekar *et al.* (2003). They remark that a wide spectrum of animals was utilized during Mesolithic phase. Animals were not only consumed but also their bones, teeth and antlers were utilized for making a variety of tools. Since there was no evidence of any domestic species, it can be securely concluded that the economy of the Mesolithic Mahadaha inhabitants was completely based on hunting-gathering/foraging-collecting. Carcasses of some of the large animals such as wide buffalo, gaur, rhinoceros and elephants were scavenged to obtain meat and/or the bones for making tools (Joglekar *et al.*, 2003: 116). The reptiles, fish and birds played a supplementary role in the food economy during the Mesolithic phase at Mahadaha.

As regards the chronology of the Mesolithic culture at Mahadaha, V.D. Misra (In Joglekar *et al.*, 2003: 23-25) writes: For computing the chronology of the Mesolithic culture at Mahadaha, the following points deserve attention:

1. That no potsherds were obtained from the site indicating thereby that these people were not familiar with pottery, even the hand-made one.
2. That all the animal bones obtained from the site belong to the wild category indicating thereby that during the Mesolithic settlement at the site, the process of domestication had not set in.
3. That the occurrence of the bones of animals like those of elephant, bison, rhinoceros and possibly hippopotamus in the Mesolithic settlement suggests a comparatively humid climatic condition at that time.
4. That the occurrence of the fragments of querns and mullers at the site in appreciable number would suggest that in the life of the Mesolithic people at Mahadaha gathering of wild grains and other edibles has started playing some role otherwise the presence of these food-processing equipments could not be easily explained. In this connection we have to keep in mind that for manufacturing these equipments, sandstone and quartzite had to be obtained only from the Vindhyan area as stone as such was not available in the Ganga valley. On this point the Mesolithic culture of Mahadaha tallies as well with its counterparts not only of the middle Ganga valley but those of the Vindhyan area as well. Fragments of querns, mullers, etc. were obtained in appreciable number from Damdama and Sarai Nahar Rai in the

middle Ganga Valley and Chopani Mando in the Belan Valley, and Baghor II, Medhauli and Banki in the Son Valley. The available evidence, thus, indicates that in the life of the Mesolithic people whether in the Vindhyan area or in the Ganga Valley gathering of wild edible grains had started playing some role. Thus along with hunting wild animals, collecting aquatic creatures like turtle and fish and killing birds, these people had started augmenting their dietary items with the wild edible grains as well.

The combined testimony of the above factors would strongly suggest that the Mesolithic people at Mahadaha were still leading a Mesolithic way of life. The indication of a comparative mild climatic condition during the time would make a strong case for placing them in the early phase of the Holocene, if not at the end of the Pleistocene. However, the calibrated range of three radiocarbon dates obtained from Mahadaha range from 1385-885 BC to 2675-2215 BC (Possehl and Rissman, 1992: 472-73). On the basis of these dates, a comparatively late date for the site has been suggested. But in this connection mention may be made of the significance of the radiocarbon/thermoluminescent dates obtained from Sarai Nahar Rai and Damdama both in the Pratapgarh district like that of Mahadaha. Date obtained from Sarai Nahar Rai reads 8395±110 BC. A thermoluminescent date from Damdama indicates an antiquity between 5000 BC to 7000 BC. Two AMS C^{14} dates from Damdama read 6690±65 BC (Lukacs *et al.*, 1996). All the three excavated Mesolithic sites – Sarai Nahar Rai, Damdama and Mahadaha – have yielded almost identical archaeological material whether it be burial practices, human skeletal remains, the animal bones, the bone objects and lithic components – microliths on the one hand and fragments of quern, muller, etc. on the other. The corpus of these evidences would suggest a high antiquity for the Mesolithic culture of Mahadaha also. From the Vindhyan area also matching evidence arguing for a high antiquity of the Mesolithic culture has been obtained. From Baghor II a date reading 6380 BC (Possehl and Rissman, 1992) has obtained. Barkhera and Adamgarh have yielded dates reading 5520 BC and 5505 BC respectively (Misra, 2002). Two AMS C^{14} dates from Lekhahia Rockshelter I read 6420±75 BC and 6050±75 BC (Lukacs *et al.*, 1996). For the Mesolithic Paisra a radiocarbon date reading 7420±110 BC has been obtained (Pant and Jayaswal, 1991: 139).

DAMDAMA

This site is situated in Warikalan, a revenue village in Patti sub-division of Pratapgarh district, five km towards the north-west of Mahadaha. The

Mesolithic settlement is spread over a slightly raised ground on the confluence of the two branches of the Tambura Nala, a tributary of the Pili Nadi which discharges itself in the river Sai. This site was discovered in 1978 and was extensively explored between 1979-1982.

The lithic industry of Damdama comprises microliths including finished tools, used flakes and debitage. They may be described as pre-pottery and geometric in nature. Blade tools form the largest single category, followed by triangles, lunates, flake tools, scrapers and trapeze. The artefacts are made on chalcedony, chert, quartz, agate and carnelian. Bone tools form an important part of the artefactual repertoire at this site. Arrowheads made of split bones are important tool type. Bone horn cores were used as tools for digging and engraving. A large number of stone objects comprising querns, mullers and anvils were found. These tool were presumably used for processing vegetal food. Seeds of millets collected by flotation technique from the excavation shows that this cereal formed an important component of their diet. Ornaments (pendants, beads and bangles) made of bone and ivory provide an indication of the aesthetic sense of the Mesolithic man of the Ganga valley.

At Warikalan-Damdama, forty-one graves were exposed. Of these, thirty-five graves yielded skeletal remains of single individuals. In five graves double burials were encountered. One grave yielded skeletal remains of three individuals. Of the double burials, in four cases, the skeletal remains were those of male and female. In one grave both skeletons appeared to be those of males. The triple burial at this site yielded skeletal remains of two males and one female.

The presence of gaur on the Indian bison is interesting. This animal lives in high altitudes and hilly areas and is not native to the Ganga valley. Indian gaur is also available in the Terai region. Hence, it is possible that during the winter season some of these animals may have migrated to the plains where they were killed by predators or trapped by man.

The faunal material from Damdama was very systematically collected by sieving the entire deposit. As a result, 21,000 bone fragments were collected. This entire collection studied by Thomas *et al.* (1996). More than 30 species of animals have been identified, comprising mammals (NSIP-77.39%), reptiles (12.1%), fish (1.25%) and molluscs (0.30%). Mammals constituted a major source of food at Damdama. The majority of species among the mammals are six species of deer, which together constituted 2874 bones (79.89%). Of this, the mouse deer and the musk deer are negligible (only 2 and 1 bone, respectively). The antelopes in general (nilgai, blackbuck, chowsingha and chinkara) had a very small share, i.e., 2.26 %

(92/4054 bones), though the bones of the blackbuck were in sizable number. Except for isolated representation of bones of blackbucks in the bottom layers, a majority of the antelope bones have been found in the upper part of the cultural deposit, especially between layers I to 3. Therefore, scarcity of antelopes at Damdama also suggests the differential habitats of deer and antelopes. The wild pig (*Sus scrofa*) were 2.52% in the collection. Thus, it is clear that the Mesolithic people at Damdama were mainly dependent of venison.

Among the animals identified at Damdama, a few bones of large mammals like elephant, rhinoceros, gaur, wild buffalo and possible wild cattle were also found, which constituted about 9.52% in the total collection of identifiable bones at the site. However, the hinting of such large mammals and their use in the daily diet of the people is difficult to postulate looking at the technological level of the Mesolithic population. Probably the carcasses or the isolated bones were collected and were utilized for making bone tools. However, it is to be noted that a majority of these bones at Damdama have cut marks. Thus, possibly the bones were cut off from the original carcass and were dumped at one place near the settlement for further use.

The size range of animals present at Damdama is as follows (Thomas *et al.*, 1996: 260):

Size range	Animals
<5 kg	Mongoose, Red Fox
5-10 kg	Jackal
10-20 kg	Mouse deer, Pigmy Hog, Wolf
20-50 kg	Chowsingha, Muntjak, Hog deer, Chinkara, Blackbuck
50-100 kg	Wild goat, chital, Musk deer
100-200 kg	Wild Boar
200-500 kg	Sambar, Nilgai

EMERGING PICTURE

A survey of the data presented above gives some idea about the topography, distribution and settlement pattern, technology and material culture of the Mesolithic people as also the subsistence pattern of these folk. This can be summarized as follows:

Topography

The region of Middle Ganga valley under study is located between the Ganga in the south and the Gomati in the north, covering the northern part of the Allahabad district and Pratapgarh, Sultanpur, Jaunpur and Varanasi districts of eastern Uttar Pradesh. Geographically speaking, the middle Ganga plain is of a very recent age and its surface has been built up by the silting action of its streams during the Pleistocene. In the Middle Ganga valley, the Ganga is the master stream and is the recipient of all water lines like the Gomati, the Sai, the Varuna, and their numerous seasonal tributary streams. Except the Ganga, all other rivers rise in the marshy plains. Gomati and Sai have occasional badlands and revines. There is a great development of dead arms, deferred junctions, *Jhils* and natural *Tals* in their plains (Spate, 1967: 547). The general slope of the region is towards south-east.

The Lakes of the Ganga Valley

As a large number of Mesolithic settlements of the mid Ganga valley are located along the horse-shoe on ax-bow lakes, it would be interesting to understand their nature and process of formation. Of the 198 sites of the Mesolithic culture reported from the mid Ganga valley, as many as 100 sites are situated on the banks of these lakes, out of which 95 are located in an area of 600 square kilometres around Sarai Nahar Rai (Sharma, 1975: 9).

The horse-shoe lakes form an important feature of the morphology of the plains. A large number of them have now been filled up partly by nature and partly by man, but many of them still survive and they cover an area ranging from 20-46 to 1.92 square kilometres. These lakes were formed out of the meander of the Ganga and represent the various stages in the withdrawal of the river to its present channel. The formation of these lakes, the change in the life of the Ganga, and the deepening of its channel are evidently part of the same process and may be lowering of the sea level (Sharma, 1975: 9).

Geological and palaeo-ecological studies carried out by Gurdip Singh in Rajasthan and by Allchin and Goudie in Gujarat have shown that extreme dryness marked the last stage of Pleistocene in the area of Rajasthan lakes and in the sand dunes of Gujarat respectively. It is believed that intense aridity that marked the closing period of Pleistocene and the fall of the ocean level were responsible for a cataclysmic change in the life cycle of the Ganga. The river, which had been building its valley since its arrival in the plains down the Himalayas, suddently started cutting its bed and receding further south to its present course. As stated earlier, the present water level is about 25 metres lower than the level of the last deposit of the river. In the course of movement to its present channel, many of the meanders of the old courses were converted into horse-shoe or ox-bow lakes of varying sizes. In this land surface must have appeared, on account of the freshness and fertility of the soil, a rich vegetation. The Vindhyas on account of aridity must have been comparatively denuded of vegetation, and scarcity of fodder and water must have driven the animals to more hospitable regions of the Ganga alluvium. The deep lakes were another source of food supply and a perennial source of water.

Distribution and Settlement Pattern

The Mesolithic sites have a fairly dense but discontinuous distribution in Pratapgarh district and sporadic occurrences in Allahabad, Sultanpur, Jaunpur and Varanasi districts. The distribution disparity is probably the result of uneven explorations but could also be due to micro-level environmental differences among the districts concerned. This latter possibility is yet to be investigated (Pandey, 1990: 311). Mesolithic settlement pattern in the middle Ganga valley is represented by sites in three characteristic locations:

1. along rivulets and their seasonal tributaries,
2. in close association to horse-shoe lakes, and
3. away from rivers and lakes.

Location of settlements along rivulets and lakes is obviously related to the availability of water and aquatic resources. Another reason for this bias may be the presence of dense forests in inland areas. The settlements are located generally on elevated barren land (*Usar*) and are away from the reach of annual floods.

The settlements are generally small in size. Most of these measure between 5 m square to 4.5 m square in area (Pandey, 1990: 312). There are a few larger settlements like Sarai Nahar Rai (1,800 square metres), Mahadaha (8,000 square metres) and Damdama (8,750 square metres). Average spacing between two sites is between 5 and 10 km in Pratapgarh district but this spacing is slightly more in other districts.

Technology and Material Culture

Microlithic industries of India present considerable variation in typology, technology and raw materials used in the manufacture of tools. As attested in rock paintings, microliths were used as components of arrowheads, sprearheads, daggers, sickles and harpoons. Besides, other types of tools, like scrapers, points and burins were also used. In addition to flaked stone tools, some implements include hammerstones, sling balls, perforated discs or ring-stones and querns and rubbers. There is also evidence for the use of bone and antler tools. Bone points, pendants and antlers with sharp cut marks have been found in the Mesolithic deposits of Bhimbetka caves. But the best evidence for bone and antler work comes from Mahadaha in the Ganga valley. Bone and antler tools include arrowheads, points, blades, knives, chisels, scrapers and saw. Besides, a number of rings cut from antlers and worn as earrings and necklaces have been found from this site.

The noteworthy traits of Mesolithic technology of the Middle Ganga valley is (i) the use of microliths, (ii) use of bone tools and ornaments, and (iii) use of heavy-duty tools such as querns, rubbers, anvils, hammerstones, sling balls and sharpeners of grey sandstone. It may be noted that the latter two traits occur only at the excavated sites. Their disribution furnishes a striking example of what can be learnt from the occurrence and non-occurrence of raw material in a particular region. In the present case, raw material had to be brought in from outside. The presence of waste flakes and tiny chips suggests that raw material was taken to these sites and worked there. The nearest source of raw material is the Vindhyan hills, about 100 km to the south as the crow flies.

Our knowledge of the material culture of the Mesolithic people is very limited, mainly because of the poor survival of the items made of organic materials. In Central India, Mesolithic people often inhabited readily available rock shelters. But from one shelter at Bhimbetka, there is evidence that they raised a stone wall inside a shelter to partition off some area. Rock paintings show circular huts made of tree branches and leaves. There is also evidence of circular stone-lined huts from Bagor and Tilwara. At Sarai Nahar Rai, a rectangular floor made by ramming clay has been found. Post-holes found at the corners of this floor suggest some kind of a superstructure over the floor. Material possessions ot the social units included bows and arrows, spears, traps and nets, lower and upper grinding stones for processing food, stone hammers, sling balls, ring-stones, bone and antler tools and ornaments. Rock paintings also show that both men and women wore some kind of dress around the waist, probably made of leaves. Hunters are often shown wearing masks. Human skeletons in the burials from Mahadaha in the Ganga valley are shown wearing earring and necklaces made of rings cut from antlers.

SUBSISTENCE

Commenting upon the susbsistence pattern of the Mesolithic people, V.N. Misra (1996: 323) writes:

Knowledge of the subsistence pattern of the Mesolithic people is mainly based on the animal bones which have been found in large quantities and often in well-preserved condition at several sites. This is supplemented by depictions of scenes of hunting, trapping, fishing and plant food collecting in the rock paintings. The animals most commonly represented in the bone record are Indian humped cattle, gaur, buffalo, sambar, chital, gazelle, hog deer, *nilgai*, fox and jackal. Besides, *barasingha* and rhinoceros were hunted at Langhnaj, elephant at Sarai Nahar Rai and porcupine at Adamgarh. At Bagor there are bones of tortoise and fish and at Sarai-Nahar-Rai of tortoise. Paintings at Bhimbetka and other sites show hunting of a variety of animals by spear and bow and arrow and by trapping and snaring. There are also scenes of trapping of rats and of fishing. Besides, at Bagor and Adamgarh there is evidence of domestication of cattle and sheep and goat. The bones occur in broken, spilt open and charred condition, showing that meat was cooked on open fires and marrow was extracted from bones. Paintings in rock shelters at Bhimbetka and other places show scenes of plant food and honey collection. Besides, the deciduous forest country in central and eastern India where a larger number of Mesolithic sites are located, is very rich in a variety of plant foods which are even today extensively exploited by the local aboriginal populations and there is no reason to believe that ancient hunter-gatherers did not do the same.

A preliminary study of the plant remains from Damdama by Kajale (1990) and Saraswat revealed several wild plant remains (wild grasses, millet-like grains, jujube and some charcoal fragments).

The first attempt of pollen analysis by H.P. Gupta (1976) of a horse-shoe lake in the vicinity of Sarai Nahar Rai was supplemented by that of M.D. Kajale and V.C. Deotare (1988-89: 27-30) who carried out pollen analysis from an ox-bow lake adjacent to the Mesolithic site of Damdama. The samples were collected from a freshly dug trench of 3 × 3 × 2 m in the dried lake bed. Of the eighteen samples processed, the 15 from the lower levels were found to be extremely poor. The upper 3 samples yielded a few pollen representing superficial incorporation. A few fungal spores were present in the lower level samples (Kajale and Deotare, 1988-89: 29). Thus, despite lacustral nature of the deposits analysed, there is hardly any preservation of the pollen. However, a large number of grinding stones, querns and muller-cum-envils with heavy use-marks and lustrous polished surface suggests inclusion of vegetal food in the diet (Pal, 2002: 75).

The Gangetic Mesolithic is extremely rich in faunal remains. Thomas and Joglekar have identified more than 30 species of animals comprising mammals, reptiles, birds, fishes and molluscs. Among the most frequent animals are six species of deer (Thomas *et al.*, 1996), buffalo, cattle, bison, *nilgai*, elephant, rhinoceros, wild pig and hog. The majority of animal bones are in charred and semi-charred condition suggesting thereby that roasted meat was consumed. Thus, we may infer that the Mesolithic people hunted wild animals and gathered edible fruits, grains and tubers from surrounding forests.

HUMAN BURIALS

Human skeletal remains have been found buried at a number of Mesolithic settlements in the Vindhyas. The rock shelters of Bangai Khor and Lekhahia in Sonbhadra district have yielded 1 and 27 skeletons respectively. With a single exception of Lakhahia, skeleton No. 4 placed in flexed position, all the skeletons are found placed in extended position. Mesolithic burials have also been reported from Dorothy Deep and Jambu Deep rock shelters (Hunter, 1935-36), Bagor (Misra, 1972) and Langhnaj (Ehrhardt and Kennedy, 1965). In the Ganga valley as well as the Vindhyas, with a few exception, the skeletons were found oriented west-east, with the skull lying in the west. In a few cases east-west orientation was also noted.

A few skeletons, both in the Vindhyas and Ganga valley were found with burial goods, whether in the form of animal bones as in the case of Lekhahia or bone ornaments and arrowheads, as in the case of Mahadaha and Damdama. It is not unlikely that microliths might have also been offered as burial goods (Misra, 1997: 35).

The excavations at the three Mesolithic sites in the mid Ganga valley have revealed a good number of human burials within the habitation area which throw valuable light on the mortuary practices, rituals, eschatological beliefs, dietary behaviour, palaeopathology and social structure of the Mesolithic people. The dead were generally buried in the vicinity of hearths. There are extended human burials in shallow, oblong grave pits in supine position. There are only exceptions, one at Mahadaha and two at Damdama of crouched/flexed burials.

Burials at Sarai Nahar Rai

The excavations at Sarai Nahar Rai revealed 14 human burials in eleven graves as the overlying deposits at the site was washed away, these burials represent the earliest phase of this culture at the site. All the graves were shallow and oblong and the dead were placed in an extended and supine position. In every case, one hand was lying by the side of the body and the other was placed across the abdomen. The orientation of the skeleton was from west to east, with the skull pointing to the west. The graves were carefully prepared and were provided with a 3-4 cm thick, soft cushion of soil. The graves were filled up with earth. Among the grave goods, mention may be made of microlithic tools and animal bones.

Barring Grave No. VII, each of the other graves contained a single skeleton. Grave No. VII was intentionally widened to receive four individuals who were buried at the same time. Two of these skeletons belong to males, while the other two have been identified as female. It is interesting to note that the males were placed to the right of the females. Even today, Hindu rituals related to disposal off the dead require husbands and wives to be positioned in a similar manner.

Except for the skeleton in Grave No. II, which seems to be that of a child, most of the skeletons fall within the age group of 16 to 28 years. The skeletons of Grave Nos. V and IX may be assigned in age group of 30 to 35 years, and 28 to 34 years, respectively. On an average, the skeletons measure about 1.80 m in height. Out of 14 skeletons exposed at the site, 9 are of males and 4 are of females. The sex of the child in Grave No. II could not be determined.

Burials at Mahadaha

Twenty-eight graves containing 32 skeletons were excavated at Mahadaha. The graves located between the embankment and the canal were disturbed during the digging of the canal. Stratigraphically, and on the basis of superimposition, the graves are ascribed to four different phases of the Mesolithic culture. Three graves belong to Phase I, two to Phase II, ten to Phase III, and thirteen to Phase IV.

The graves, like those of Sarai Nahar Rai, were shallow and oblong, and except for two graves (Nos. I and IV), were meant for single burials. The skeletons were either oriented west-east or east-west. In a few cases, however, there was no specific orientation.

> All the burials, except for Grave No. XXV were of the extended type and the dead were placed in a supine position, with the head tilted to the left or right. Although in a majority of cases the hands were placed alongside the body, in one instance the left lower arm was placed on the chest and the right arm lay along the body. In another burial, one hand was placed on the abdomen and the other alongside the body. One skeleton had both its hands on the chest. In the grave, the dead were generally placed on a 4 to 6 cm cushion of soil. Some of the graves contained burial goods such as bone rings, bone arrowheads, microliths, rubbed ochre piece and animal bones.

Burials at Damdama

The Mesolithic site of Damdama was under excavation for five seasons (between 1983 and 1987) which brought to light interesting evidence of human burial practices. The excavations in western and central sectors of the settlement revealed as many as 41 graves. The eastern sector did not yield burials, but their existence cannot be ruled out.

Forty-one graves have been located and exposed at Damdama. Among these, Grave Nos. VI and XXVI are double burials, while Grave No. XVIII is a multiple burial containing three individuals (Pal, 1988). The rest of the burials are single burials, their orientation being west-east, with the head facing west. Graves I and XIX, however, belong to the late phase in which the skeletons were laid out in an east-west direction. The skeletons in each of the burials, except for two, have been placed in an extended position. In Graves I and XXVIII, the skeletons have been found in a flexed position. The position of the skeletons in Graves VIII and XI differ from the rest in that the skeleton in Grave XI has been placed in a prone position, while that in Grave VIII is in a lateral position. The other skeletons are in a supine position. The graves are shallow and oblong with tapering sides. It has been noticed that in most cases a hearth is situated next to a burial. Commenting upon these burials, Pal has made some interesting observations. He writes (Pal, 1992: 42-44):

> Most of the bodies are placed in shallow oblong pits in the extended position. There are only three exceptions to this, one at Mahadaha, and two at Damdama where evidence of flexed burials has been found (Pal, 1988). The individuals buried in a flexed position may have either been victims of punishment or they may have been *sanyasis*. Even today the corpses of *sanyasis* are immersed in rivers or buried in a sitting posture. The skeletons are generally found in a supine position, but in a few graves at Damdama, the skeletons were placed in a prone or lateral position. With a few exceptions, then skeletons are oriented west to east, or east to west, possibly signifying the positions of the sun and the moon.

The burials represent all the groups, particularly those of young individuals, thus suggesting that the life span of people during the Mesolithic was quite short. The multiple burials probably signify the development of strong family ties. However, it is difficult to explain the significance of the burial of three individuals, two males and one female, in a single grave (No. XVIII) at Damdama. On the whole, it seems that multiple burials were associated with individuals who occupied an important place in society. This is suggested by the presence of long bone arrowheads in the burials at Damdama, and by the discovery of a bone necklace and earring at Mahadaha.

Couple and Multiple Burials

As stated earlier, Grave VIII at Sarai Nahar Rai yielded multiple skeletons comprising two couples of a male and a female each. The couples were interred in the specially prepared grave in two tiers – one above in other. In both cases, the female was placed in the grave to the left of the male skeleton. Further, in each case the male was placed in the grave first and followed by the female. From the careful placing of the bodies in the grave, it is clear that all the four skeletons were buried at one and the same time simultaneously. The skeletons were buried in west-east direction, the head being towards the west.

At Mahadaha, 28 graves were excavated. Of these, grave Nos. I and V revealed the evidence of couple burials. Grave I was made to receive two individuals side by side. Of the two skeletons, skeleton No. 1 was that of a female and was placed to the left of the skeleton No. 2. Skeleton No. 2 was placed first in the grave and the skeleton No. 1 followed. Unfortunately, the sex of skeleton No. 2 could not be determined. On the analogy of similar burials it is presumed to be that of a male (Varma, 1997: 30). The orientation of the grave is west-east with the head being towards the west.

Grave No. V at Mahadaha also revealed the evidence of couple burial in which a male and a female skeleton were found placed one above the other in two tiers with the female on the top. The available evidence indicates that both the skeletons were buried simultaneously and the male was the first to be placed in the grave. The grave was oriented west-east with the heads lying towards the west.

At Damdama forty-one graves were excavated. Of these, five revealed double burials each and one multiple burial. All the burials were oriented west-east.

Grave No. XVI is the earliest couple-burial at the site. In this grave two individuals were placed side by side in west-east direction, the head being towards the west. Both the skeletons were buried simultaneously. The skeleton which was placed first in the grave was that of a male. The other skeleton which followed the earlier skeleton has also been described as male. But this identification needs to be rechecked (Varma, 1997: 31).

In Grave No. XX a male and a female were buried together in west-east orientation. Both then skeletons were buried one and the same time and in this case also the male was placed first in the grave.

Among all the couple burials, Grave No. VI is unique from a number of points of view. The burial is not only oriented north-south but the skulls of both the male and female were placed in the opposite direction. The head of the male was towards the north while that of the female was towards the south. In this case also the grave was dug to accommodate the couple simultaneously. The archaeological evidence is conclusive on the point that the male was placed first in the grave and the female followed.

Grave No. XXX also yielded a couple-burial – a male and a female. In this case too, both the dead were buried at the same time. The male was placed in the grave first and the female followed. The grave was oriented west-east with the skulls on the west.

Grave No. XXXVI at Damdama also yielded skeletons of a male and a female. They were buried together at one and the same time in west-east direction with head towards the west. In this case also the male was buried first and the female followed. The female skeleton in this grave has been placed in prone position and the male in supine condition.

Grave No. XVIII at Damdama was unique. It revealed three skeletons which were buried at one and the same time in west-east direction with their heads towards the west. The skeletons have been numbered A, B and C. The skeleton A was the first to be placed in the grave and it was followed by skeletons B and C. Both A and B are males while C is that of a female.

The above discussion about the couple or multiple burial of the Mesolithic period in the Ganga valley brings out certain important features (Varma, 1997: 31):

1. All the graves that have yielded double burial contain one male and one female skeleton. There is only one doubtful exception of Grave No. XVI at Damdama, in which probably two males were buried together. But there is, so far, no example of double female burial.
2. In all the graves, the male skeleton was the first to be placed in the grave and the female followed.
3. In all the graves, the dead were interred simultaneously without any time-gap and the grave was originally prepared to accommodate more than one skeleton.
4. The orientation of all the graves is west-east with the head towards west facing each other with the exception of Grave No. VI at Damdama, in which the orientation of the grave is north-south and the male and the female have been placed in opposite directions.
5. In almost all the cases the female has been placed to the left of the male skeleton. The exceptions are graves Nos. XX and XXXVI. In Grave No. XX, the female seems to have been placed to the right of the male. In Grave No. XXXVI the female has been placed in prone position to the right of the male skeleton and in Grave No. VI, the male and the female have been buried in opposite direction.

6. Generally, the couples were buried side by side in supine position but in Grave No. V at Mahadaha they have been placed one above the other in two tiers. In the multiple burial at Sarai Nahar Rai, which revealed skeletons of two couples, the couples were placed side by side though one couple was placed over the other.
7. Among all the burials discussed above, the burial No. XVIII poses different problems. This grave yielded three skeletons – one female and two males. But in this grave, too, the first to be placed in the grave was a male followed by the other male and female respectively. What does it indicate? Does it mean polygamy? If we consider male and female buried together in a grave as couple burial, could this burial be said to be a polygamous burial.

Varma further writes (1997: 33):

1. The Mesolithic couple burials of the Ganga Valley are of special significance. The consistency in which male and female are found together in double burials points to the fact that they are not simple double burials but they are couple burials. The concept of male-female relationship which later ended in the evolution of the institution of marriage or the concept of a family unit consisting of a male and female can be tracked in its most rudimentary form to the Mesolithic society of the Ganga Valley. Further, it may be pointed out that the couples in the burials belong to almost the same age group. The formation of smaller units is also attested to by the discovery of small hearths. Hunting no doubt was a social event in which all participated but the same may not be true regarding gathering economy. When dependence on vegetal food increased and gathering became the main source of livelihood, the formation of smaller family units must have started because community processing of vegetal food is not an easily feasible proposition. Moreover, with the development of gathering economy, the concept of individual ownership must have played an important role in the formation of smaller family units.
2. The above description and discussion of the couple and multiple couple burials raise certain important issues. The first and the foremost question is: are these burials accidental? These could have been taken at accidental burials. Had they been merely double burials, had no stereotyped pattern being followed in the placement of male and female in the grave, etc. Since a set pattern has been followed, these cannot be termed as accidental burials.

3. The next question that follows is still complicated. How was it that the male and the female died simultaneously? Was it a case of accident, quarrel, feud, epidemic, or any such happening? If it was so, why were only a male and a female affected? This also seems to be improbable. There can be yet another possibility. After the death of one – male or female – the other died of shock and grief, committed suicide or was killed are the other possibility. At this stage of our knowledge, it is very difficult to give any specific answer. The only thing that can be said positively is that after the death of a couple a set pattern of burial practice was followed.

THE PEOPLE

Human skeletons obtained from Sarai Nahar Rai and other sites of the Middle Ganga Plain have been studied by K.A.R. Kennedy who believes that the people of Sarai Nahar Rai were anatomically modern homonids, i.e., Homo sapiens bearing some physical resemblances to their sapient collaterals to the west of the Indus. The Sarai Nahar Rai population is characterised by a spectrum of phenotypic characteristics peculiar to itself with respect to cranial architecture. These ancient people of the Ganga Valley have large and musculary robust skulls, which range from low mesocrany to hyperdolichocrany. These people had large and robust skulls and they were relatively tall, with the status of males at Sarai Nahar Rai being approximately 173.93 cm to 192.08 cm. Kennedy feels that their large body size and distinctive features reflect a regional adaptation leading to large body size (Varma, 1992: 55).

Kennedy has made a comparative study of the skeletal remains from Sarai Nahar Rai and Mahadaha. He remarks that whatever phenotypic traits might be interpreted as indicators of genetic affinity in ancient populations, as exemplified in the present study of the morphometric data from Sarai Nahar Rai and Mahadaha, certain of these biological features need to be assessed as parallel skeletal adaptations shared by populations surviving under the particular stresses of a similar socio-economic life way. Genetic continua are not excluded from consideration, as indeed appears to be the case for some of the Mesolithic people of Sri Lanka and the Veddas of the historic period, but in case of the Mesolithic Gangetic populations their configuration of skeletal features is not represented in any living population of the Indian subcontinent. It is tempting to look to isolated tribal people for 'survivors' of these earlier communities, particularly among those ethnic enclaves still practising a hunting-foraging strategy. But these groups are not 'living fossils' of ancient humans, as attested by the varying incidences of gene flow and trade networks between tribal and food-producing communities. Why this socio-economic lifeway continues it is because it is a viable survival strategy offering advantages cultural and biological, over the settled farming-pastoral patterns of subsistence. Food-production demands a biological cost as a consequence of greater population density, dependency upon weather for harvesting, diseases of domesticated animals and plants, and the increase of social challenges emerging from cultural institutions accompanying sedentary life in villages and urban centres. These dynamic differences are recorded in skeletal and dental tissues of ancient and modern people and allow the palaeoanthropologist to reconstruct the life histories of individuals as well as the demographic patterns of their populations (Kennedy, 1996: 295).

In 1991, Lukacs began a study of the 47 human skeletons from 41 graves from Damdama in collaboration with J.N. Pal and Greg C. Nelson. It was determined that 50 per cent of the skeletons were male, 40 per cent female, and nine of undetermined sex.

SEX AND AGE DISTRIBUTION

The Sarai Nahar Rai skeletal series is composed of 15 specimens. Of the 10 specimens studied by Kennedy, 7 are males and 3 are females. Children were not found at the site, although immature skeletons appear in the series from Mahadaha. The present sample is too small to suggest that Sarai Nahar Rai was predominantly a cemetery for males.

The extremes of the age range for males in the series is 16 to 34 years at the time of death, with mean age ranges of 17 to 31 years. This has a cumulative mean of 23.23 years. The last figure is not statistically different from the cumulative mean of 22.33 years for females whose extremes of age range are 15 to 35 years with mean age ranges of 16 to 32.5 years. There is no reason to believe one sex had a significantly greater lifespan than the other sex. It is interesting to note that these sex and age ranges for Sarai Nahar Rai do not coincide with the ranges obtained from the considerably larger skeletal series from Mahadaha. Of the 26 specimens described from Mahadaha, 18 are identified as males, 6 as females, one is of uncertain sex, and there is a single child skeleton. The age range for Mahadaha males is 7 to 40 years, and form young adulthood to 60+ years for Mahadaha females. The average ages at time of death for males and females at Sarai Nahar Rai agree well with death age means for Mesolithic populations elsewhere in India, in Sri Lanka and in Eurasia (Kennedy *et al.*, 1984-85: 23-24).

Taking a broad view of skeletons from all these three sites, Kennedy (2000: 230) remarks that the phenotypic pattern of the Gangetic Mesolithic people is unique, and when comparative studies with other prehistoric South Asian population were conducted, it appeared that degrees of relationship are distant and that the people of Sarai Nahar Rai and Mahadaha contributed little biologically to later inhabitants of their region and beyond.

AESTHETIC SENSE

These people had a developed aesthetic sense and they had devised ways and means to decorate themselves. From Mahadaha burials, ear-rings or necklaces have been recovered from three graves. Two males were buried adorned with necklaces made of antler rings. At Damdama, in Grave No. 7, a pendant along with two bone arrowheads were found. The form of these items is socio-technique and may have been significant of particular status in society (Varma, 1992: 55).

CHRONOLOGY

Commenting upon the chronology of the Mesolithic cultures of India, V.N. Misra (2002: 34-37) writes:

> Although not all the excavated sites have been dated by radiometric methods, the chronology of the Mesolithic period can be determined on the basis of around 50 uncalibrated radiocarbon dates from 20 sites and eight TL dates from three sites. The oldest available date is 10100+100 B.P. and it comes from the site of Inamgaon near Pune. A date of c. 10000 B.P. is known from Sarai Nahar Rai, but, as it is obtained from uncharred bone, its reliability is low. From Bhimbetka the oldest dates is 7790 B.P., and from Adamgarh it is 6430 B.P. The beginning of the microlithic industries can therefore be assigned to c. 12000 B.P. However, it needs to be pointed out that microlithic industries in Sri Lanka are dated by radiocarbon as early as 35000 B.P. Since the microlithic industry of the *teris* of Tamil Nadu is closely similar to that of Sri Lankan caves, it is reasonable to assume that the *teri* microlithic industry should be of equal antiquity. Two dates from Phase II of Bagor, which has an association of copper tools and pottery with microliths, are 4715 B.P. and 4060 B.P. Several dates from the upper levels of Bhimbetka shelters have readings between 3000 and 2000 B.P. It is significant that Mesolithic occupation in central Indian caves as well as on the sand dunes in western India came to an end soon after the beginning of the Christian era. Iron first appeared in the Ganga valley at the beginning of first millennium BC and slowly diffused to other parts of the country. As iron tools began to be available to microlith-using hunter-gatherer communities, they started giving

up the use of stone technology. Both archaeological data and radiocarbon dates suggest that the use of stone tools had completely disappeared by the beginning of the Christian era. The Stone Age finally ended after the introduction and diffusion of iron technology.

As regards the chronology of the Mesolithic phase in the Ganga valley, it may be admitted that it is still not firmly established. Two radiocarbon dates have been obtained from Sarai Nahar Rai on bone samples reading 10050+110 BP and 2660+120 BP. The former date seems to represent the early phase of the culture. The preliminary analysis of the thermoluminescence sample from Damdama by A.K. Singhvi of Physical Research Laboratory, Ahmedabad, indicates an antiquity between 5000 and 7000 BP. Two AMS C-14 dates from Damdama reading 8865+65 BP (from the earliest phase) and 8640+65 BP (from Phase VII) suggests an early Holocene antiquity for the site. A time span of 8000 BC to 2000 BC may be proposed for the Mesolithic phase of the Ganga valley (Pal, 2002: 77).

Table 1. Radiocarbon dates for Mesolithic sites of the Gangetic plain

Site	Dates
Damdama	8865 ± 65[1] 5550 ± 60[2] (st 1)
Mahadaha	6160 ± 60[2] (st 4) 4680 ± 80[2] (st 1) 4110 ± 60[2] (st 2) 4010 ± 120 3840 ± 130 2880 ± 250
Sarai Nahar Rai	10395 ± 110 (burned bone) 10050 ± 110 (burned bone) 5040 ± 50[2] (surface) 2860 ± 120

Taken from Misra, V.D. (1977: 67); Kennedy *et al.* (1992); Allchin and Allchin (1982: 79); Kennedy *et al.* (1986: 52); Lucas *et al.* (1996); Lucas (n.d.)

[1] Dates obtained from Accelerated Mass Spectroscopy (AMS) techniques on bio-apatite from bone.

[2] Dates obtained from AMS dating technique on bio-apatite from bovid teeth.

In this connection, the observations of Lukacs *et al.* (1996) is worth reproducing. They write:

> Bone samples from Damdama and Lekhahia were analysed to help resolve issues regarding the antiquity and dietary pattern of these mesolithic occupants of north India. The data presented here constitute the first report of AMS 14C

dates in south Asian prehistory, and tentatively suggest an early Holocene age for these sites. The AMS dates for Damdama are the first radiometric dates for this site, which can now be placed in the first half of the 7th millennium BC (8865-8640 BP). Previously dated to approximately ± 4000 BP, the antiquity of Lekhahia is now estimated at between 8370 and 8000 BP. These new dates have major implications for understanding hunter-gatherer population dynamics.

Table 2. Radiocarbon dates for Mesolithic skeletons from North India

Site	Unit	Layer	Date	Lab Sample Number	Material Dated	Source
Lekhahia	Phase III	4	3560 ± 110	TF-417	bone	Agarwal & Kusumgar, 1969
	Phase I	8	4240 ± 115	TF-419	bone	
Mahadaha	Loc XII-XIV	2	4010 ± 120	BS-136	charred	Rajagopalan *et al.*, 1982
	Loc XII-XVIII	3	2880 ± 250	BS-137	bone	
	Loc VI-XII	4	3840 ± 130	BS-138	carbonate	
Sarai Nahar Rai	Hearth1/A3	?	2860 ± 120	TF-1356	bone	Agarwal & Kusumgar, 1975
	Hearth 2/B4	1	10050 ± 110	TF-1359	charred bone	Agarwal & Kusumgar, 1973

Table 3. New AMS C[14] dates for Mesolithic skeletons from North India[1]

Site	Phase	Layer	Date[2]	Lab Sample Number	Skeleton Number
Damdama	VIII		8640 ± 65	GX-20829-AMS	DDM-36a
	I		8865 ± 65	GX-20827-AMS	DDM-12
Lekhahia	III	3	8370 ± 75	GX-20983-AMS	LKH-4
	II	6	8000 ± 75	GX-20984-AMS	LKH-13

[1] AMS Accelerator Mass Spectrometry.

[2] These dates are in C^{14} years BP and have been C^{13} corrected.

REFERENCES

Agrawal, D.P. and J.S. Kharakwal. 2002. *South Asian Prehistory*, New Delhi, Aryan Books International.

Allchin, B., A. Goudie and K.T.M. Hegde. 1978. *Prehistory and Palaeogeography of the Great Indian Desert*, London, Academic Press.

Alur, K.R. 1980. Faunal remains from the Vindhyas and the Ganga Valley, in G.R. Sharma, V.D. Misra, D. Mandal, B.B. Misra and J.N. Pal (eds.), *Beginning of Agriculture*, Allahabad, Abinash Prakashan: 201-227.

Chattopadhyay, U.C. 1988. Subsistence Variability and Complex Social formations in Prehistoric Ganga Valley: Problems and Prospects, *Man and Environment*, XII: 135-52.

Chattopadhyay, I. and U.C. Chattopadhyay. 1990. The Spatial Organization of Mortuary Practices in the Mesolithic Ganga Valley, in N.C. Ghosh and S. Chakrabarti (eds.), *Adaptation and other essays*, Santiniketan, Vishwa Bharati: 103-21.

Dutta, P.C. 1984. Sarai Nahar Rai Man: The First and Oldest Human Fossil Record in South Asia, *Anthropologie*, 23 (1): 35-50.

Ehrhardt, S. and K.A.R. Kennedy. 1965. *Excavations at Langhnaj*, Part III (Human Remains), Poona, Deccan College.

Gupta, H.P. 1976. Holocene Palynology from Meander Lake in the Ganga Valley, District Pratapgarh, Uttar Pradesh, *The Palaeobotanist*, 25: 109-119.

Hunter, G.R. 1945-46. Interim Report on the Excavations in the Mahadeo Hills, *Nagpur University Journal*, No. 1: 28-57.

Joglekar, P.P., V.D. Misra, J.N. Pal and M.C. Gupta. 2003. *Mesolithic Mahadaha: The Faunal Remains*, Allahabad, Department of A.H.C. & Archaeology, University of Allahabad.

Kajale, M.D. and B.C. Deotare. 1988-89. Pollen Analysis and Chemical Examination of a Prehistoric Lake Site at Damdama, *Puratattva*, No. 19: 27-30.

Kennedy, K.A.R., Christopher B. Burrow and Nancy C. Lovell. 1984-85. Mesolithic Human Remains from the Gangetic Plain: Sarai Nahar Rai, *Puratattva*, No. 15: 1-55.

Kennedy, Kenneth A.R. 1996. Skeletal Adaptations of Mesolithc Hunter-Foragers of North India: Mahadaha and Sarai Nahar Rai Compared, in G.D. Afanas'ev, S. Cleuziou, J.R. Lukacs and M. Tosi (eds.), *Bioarchaeology of Mesolithic India: An Integrated Approach*, Colloquium XXXIII of the International Union of Prehistoric and Protohistoric Sciences, Forli, ABACO Edizioni: 291-300.

——. *God-Apes and Fossil Men: Palaeoanthropology in South Asia*, Ann Arbor, The University of Michigan Press.

Lukacs, J.R. and J.N. Pal. 1992. Dental Anthropology of the Mesolithic Hunter-Gathers: A Preliminary Reports on the Mahadaha and Sarai Nahar Rai Dentition, *Man and Environment*, XVII (2): 45-55.

Lukacs, J.R., J.N. Pal and V.D. Misra. 1996. Chronology and Diet in Mesolithic North India: A Preliminary Report on New AMS C14 dates, 13C Isotope Values, and their Significance, in G.D. Afanas'ev, S. Cleuziou, J.R. Lukacs and M. Tosi (eds.), *Bioarchaeology of Mesolithic India: An Integrated Approach*, Colloquium XXXIII of the International Union of Prehistoric and Protohistoric Sciences, Forli, ABACO Edizioni: 301-311.

Misra, V.D. 1997. The Mesolithic Cultures of the Vindhyas and the Ganga Valley with Special Reference to Environment and Archaeology, in B.M. Khanduri and Vinod Nautiyal (eds.), *Him-Kanti* (Prof. K.P. Nautiyal Felicitation Volume), Delhi, Book India Publishing Co. 32-38.

——. 1977. *Some Aspects of Indian Archaeology*, Allahabad, Prabhat Prakashan.

_____. 1999. A Brief Note on Indian Stone Age Archaeology, in G.C. Pande (ed.), *The Dawn of Indian Civilisation (upto c. 600 BC)*, Vol. I, Part I: 129-138.

_____. 1999. Agriculture, Domestication of Animals and Ceramic and Other Industries in Prehistoric India: Mesolithic and Neolithic, in G.C. Pande (ed.), *The Dawn of Indian Civilisation (upto c. 600 BC)*, Vol. I, Part I: 233-266.

Misra, V.D. and J.N. Pal (eds.). 2002. *Mesolithic India*, Allahabad, Department of A.H.C. & Archaeology, University of Allahabad.

Misra, V.N. 1972. Burials from Prehistoric Bagor, Rajasthan, in S.B. Deo (ed.), *Archaeological Congress and Seminar Papers*, Nagpur, Nagpur University: 58-65.

_____. 1996. Mesolithic India: History and Current Status of Research, in G.D. Afanas'ev, S. Cleuziou, J.R. Lukacs and M. Tosi (eds.), *Bioarchaeology of Mesolithic India: An Integrated Approach*, Colloquium XXXIII of the International Union of Prehistoric and Protohistoric Sciences, Forli, ABACO Edizioni, 321-328.

_____. 2001. Prehistoric Human Colonisation of India, *Journal of Biosciences*, 26 (4), Supplement: 491-531.

_____. 2002. Keynote Address, in V.D. Misra and J.N. Pal (eds.), *Mesolithic India*, Allahabad, University of Allahabad: 1-66.

Pal, J.N. 1985. Some New Light on the Mesolithic Burial Practices of the Ganga Valley: Evidence from Mahadaha, Pratapgarh, Uttar Pradesh, *Man and Environment*, IX: 28-37.

_____. 1986. *Archaeology of Southern Uttar Pradesh*, Allahabad, Swabha Prakashan.

_____. 1988. Mesolithic Double Burials from Recent Excavations at Damdama, *Man and Environment*, XII: 115-22.

_____. 1992. Mesolithic Human Burials in the Ganga Plain, North India, *Man and Environment*, XVII (2): 35-55.

_____. 1994. Mesolithic Settlements in the Ganga Plain, *Man and Environment*, XIX (1-2): 91-101.

_____. 2002. The Mesolithic Phase in the Ganga Valley, in K. Paddayya (ed.), *Recent Studies in Indian Archaeology*, ICHR Monograph Series No. 6, New Delhi, Munshiram Manoharlal: 61-80.

Pandey, Neelima. 2006. Subsistence Pattern in Mesolithic Communities of India, *Puratattva*, No. 36: 217-221.

Pandey, J.N. 1985. *Settlement Patterns and Life in the Mesolithic Period in Uttar Pradesh*, D. Phil. Thesis, University of Allahabad (Unpublished).

_____. 1990. Mesolithic in the Middle Ganga Valley, *Bulletin of the Deccan College Post-Graduate & Research Institute*, Pune, 49: 311-316.

Possehl, G. L. and Paul C. Rissman. 1992. The Chronology of Prehistoric India: From Earliest Times to the Iron Age, in Robert W. Ehrich (ed.), *Chronologies in Old World Archaeology*, Vol. I, India. The University of Chicago Press, Chicago and London: 461.

Robbins, Gwen, V.D. Misra, J.N. Pal and M.C. Gupta. 2003. *Mesolithic Damdama: Dental Histology and Age Estimation*, Allahabad, University of Allahabad.

Sahu, B.P. 1988. *From Hunters to Breeders*, Delhi, Anamika Prakashan.

Sharma, G.R. 1973. Mesolithic Lake Cultures in the Ganga Valley, India, *Proceedings of the Prehistoric Society*, 39: 129-146.

——. 1975. Seasonal Migrations and Mesolithic Lake Cultures of the Ganga Valley, in G.R. Sharma (ed.), *K. C. Chattopadhyaya Memorial Volume*, Allahabad, 1-20.

Sharma, G.R., V.D. Misra, D. Mandal, B.B. Misa and J.N. Pal. 1980. From Hunting and Food-Gathering to Domestication of Plants and Animals – Epi–Palaeolithic to Neolithic – Excavation at Chopani Mando, Mahadaha and Mahagara, *History and Archaeology*, I, Allahabad University.

Sharma, G.R., V.D. Misra, D. Mandal and J.N. Pal. 1980. *Beginnings of Agriculture*, Allahabad, Abinash Prakashan.

Sankalia, H.D. 1974. *The Pre and Protohistory of India and Pakistan*, Poona, Deccan College.

——. 1977. *Prehistory of India*, New Delhi, Munshiram Manoharlal.

Sharma, G.R. and J.D. Clarke (eds.). 1983. *Palaeoenvironment and Prehistory in the Middle Son Valley (Madhya Pradesh)*, Allahabad, Abinash Prakashan.

Spate, O.H.K. and A.T.A. Learmonth. 1967. *India and Pakistan: A General Regional Geography*, London, Methuen.

Thomas, P.K., P.P. Joglekar, V.D. Misra, J.N. Pande and J.N. Pal. 1996. Faunal Evidence for the Mesolithic Food Economy of the Gangetic Plain with Special Reference to Damdama, in G.D. Afanas'ev, S. Cleuziou, J.R. Lukacs and M. Tosi (eds.), *Bioarchaeology of Mesolithic India: An Integrated Approach*, Colloquium XXXIII of the International Union of Prehistoric and Protohistoric Sciences, Forli, ABACO Edizioni: 255-66.

Varma, R.K. 1986. *The Mesolithic Age in Mirzapur*, Allahabad, Paramjyoti Prakashan.

——. 1992. Some aspects of the Mesolithic of the Ganga Valley, in Rakesh Tewari (ed.), *Archaeological Perspectives of Uttar Pradesh and Future Prospects*, Part I, Lucknow, U.P. State Archaeological Organisation: 47-57.

——. 1997. Couple and Multiple Couple Burials of the Mesolithic in the Ganga Valley, in J. P. Joshi (ed.), *Facets of Indian Civilization : Recent Perspectives*, (Essays in Honour of Prof. B. B. Lal), New Delhi, Aryan Books International: 29-34.

——. 1999. The Emergence of Culture in the Vindhya-Ganga Region with Special Reference to Old Stone Age, in G.C. Pande (ed.), *The Dawn of Indian Civilisation (upto c. 600 BC)*, Vol. I, Part I: 175-204.

——. 2000. A Note on Some Aspects of Society during the Mesolithic Period, in V.D. Misra and J.N. Pal (eds.), *Social History and Social Theory*, Allahabad, University of Allahabad: 1-6.

——. 2003. *Early Farming Culture of India: Key Note Address*, UGC National Seminar, April 2003, Department of Ancient History, Culture and Archaeology, University of Allahabad, Allahabad.

4

The Neolithic Interlude

The term Neolithic implies a certain stage of culture, not an absolute period of time. This food-producing stage is marked by domestication and exploitation of plant food and animals. In the archaeological record, particularly in India, it is manifested in the shape of polished stone axes, tools, hammer stones, anvils, querns and mullers; microlithic tools and cultivation of earliest cereals like wheat, barley and rice; domestication of sheep/goat, pigs, and cattle; and traces of semi-permanent settlements (in the form of circular huts) and hand-made pottery. In the Vindhyas more than 40 neolithic sites have been identified in the valleys of the Belan, Adwa, Son, Rihand and the Ganga (Singh, 1991: 34; Pal, 1986: 36-38). Of these two sites, Koldihwa and Mahagara were excavated in the 1970s by the University of Allahabad (Sharma *et al.*, 1980) and two others. Tokwa (district Mirzapur), Jhusi and Hetapatti (both in district Allahabad) are presently under excavation by the same university.

In the mid Ganga valley, traces of Neolithic culture were found at Sohgaura in the early sixties of the last century. This site is situated on the confluence of the Ami at the Rapti rivers in district Gorakhpur. In recent years, Neolithic artefacts comprising a limited number of microliths and the characteristic cord impressed, hand-made pottery have been found from more than a dozen sites and of these, Imlidih Khurd and Lahuradeva have been excavated. Microlithic tools have been picked up from Susipar and Gerar in Sant Kabir Nagar district as also from the excavated site of Waina in district Ballia. Details regarding the excavated sites of the Neolithic culture in the Vindhyas and the mid Ganga valley are presented as follow:

KOLDIHWA

Koldihwa is a small village situated at a distance of about 80 km to the south-east of Allahabad, on the left bank of the river Belan in Koraon sub-division of Allahabad district. To the north-east of the village, there is an extensive mound (500 × 200 m). This mound is roughly rectangular in form and has been now divided in small mounds by *Nalas*. This site was excavated by the University of Allahabad under the direction of G.R. Sharma. The Neolithic deposit at this site has a thickness of 45 cm represented by layers 4 and 3. The tools comprised rounded celts with flat sides and rectangular cross-sections made on basalt and granite, ring-stones and microliths. The microlithic assemblage is fashioned on chert, chalcedony, agate, carnalian, jasper and quartz and includes tools, plates, retouched blades, backed blades and scrapers. The bone tools are conspicuous by their absence in the Neolithic strata. The pottery of the Neolithic phase is corded and incised ware of thick fabric, plain red ware and ill-fired, crude black-and-red ware – all hand-made, the first being predominant. It is believed that the cord impression could have been produced by tortoise shell. The incised designs are criss-cross and zig-zag, horizontal or vertical parallel lines. The types are: the shallow, deep, straight sided and lipped bowl; vase with broad mouth and carinated neck; deep trough; storage jar and vessel with tubular spout. The occurrence of stray pieces of corded ware and smaller Neolithic celts of basalt in the succeeding chalcolithic phase may indicate a link with the Neolithic, but the black-and-red ware, black slipped ware and red ware were new features. In Period II the pottery was wheel-turned and made of well-levigated clay, besides being of finer fabric.

The Neolithic people at Koldihwa appear to have practised domestication of animals and cultivation of plants. Remains of rice from the Neolithic deposit is one of the most significant discoveries of this excavation. A preliminary palaeo-botanical analysis of the rice husks by Vishnu Mittre and T.T. Chang reveals that these belong to the domesticated variety. However, a wild grain also was a part of their diet as it is suggested by finding of millet (Pal, 2003: 3). Querns and mullers also inferentially indicate that the people had started cultivation. The evidence of structures at Neolithic Koldihwa is very poor due to limited area of excavation and disturbance of Neolithic strata by later pit activity. However, burnt clay lumps with wattle-and-daub impression obtained in profusion, indicate that they used to live in thatched huts, made of bamboo and wooden posts with mud-plastered screen walls.

The chronology of the three cultures represented at Koldihwa is not free from difficulties. While no 14C date for the Neolithic occupation seems to be known, for the early Chalcolithic phase the two available dates, 4530+185 and 5440+240 BC, are far too early for any Chalcolithic culture of India, and it has been wondered if the samples measured really belonged to the Chalcolithic levels or to the earlier Neolithic ones; even if that is true, the Koldihwa Neolithic itself would much antedate any other Neolithic culture of India, and this would involve *inter alia* the assumption that the site has the oldest record of the cultivation of rice in the world. On the other hand, a 14C date for a sample, also from the lowest Chalcolithic level, reads 1440+120 BC. It has, therefore, been reasonably assumed that the beginning of the Chalcolithic culture of Koldihwa may be pushed back to the 2nd half of the 2nd millennium BC, which is archaeologically quite acceptable (Ghosh, 1989, II: 233).

MAHAGARA

The Neolithic site of Mahagara is situated to the west of revenue village of Kotia on the confluence of old and new Belans just opposite Koldihwa, 80 km south-east of Allahabad. This site was explored in 1976 and excavated during 1976-79 by the University of Allahabad. The site is comparatively well-preserved and is a single culture site containing only Neolithic material. The excavation brought to light 18 hutments. The floors of the huts, circular or oval on plan, vary from 6.70 × 6.25 metres to 5.0 × 3.50 metres. At the periphery of these floors post-holes varying from 6-9 in number were also exposed. The floors of the huts were not rammed or paved. The occurrence of burnt clay lumps with wattle-and-daub impression indicates the use of mud plaster on the screen walls of these huts. The floors are well represented by occupational debris containing potsherds, household implements, bones of animals, etc.

Of the tools and weapons found in excavation, mention may be made of microliths, consisting retouched blades, backed blades, lunates, scrapers, borers, triangles, trapeze and tranchets; rounded celts and bone arrowheads. The other excavated objects comprise querns, mullers, hammers, sling-balls, sharpeners, ring-stones, perforated shell objects (ornaments), clay, dabber, terracotta beads and perforated pottery discs.

The pottery recovered from excavations is grouped into (a) cord-impressed, (b) rusticated, (c) burnished red, and (d) burnished black ware.

Rice husk and rice grain have been found either embedded in pottery as degraissant or separately in charred condition. Similar evidence of rice from Koldihwa has been ascribed to the domesticated variety by Vishnu

Mittre and Chang. Some of the Mahagara specimens may also belong to the same category. The occurrence of the wild variety side by side the domesticated one may not be ruled out (Pal, 2003).

A large number of animal bones have been recoved from the Neolithic levels of Mahagara and Koldihwa. As many as 246 specimens were examined by Alur (1980), of which 95 belonged to Koldihwa and 151 of Mahagara. Eighty-five per cent of the specimens were fossilized. The species identified are: cattle (*Bos indicus*), sheep/goat (*Ovis/capra*), deer (*Cervidae*), horse (*Eguidae*), tortoise (*Chelonia*), wild boar (*Sus scrofa*) and fish.

Cattle bones from Koldihwa and Mahagara are mostly of domesticated variety, though some specimens of wild cattle were also present. In contrast to the high percentage of wild cattle in the Mesolithic, their share receded to a meagre 6.5% in the Neolithic period. Together with this the considerable reduction in size of cattle indicate its domestication. The bones of sheep/goat betray similar consequences. From their gradation into four orders in the Mesolithic, they were reduced to two stable and static breeds. The remains of horse have been traced at Mahagara. The third phalanx, which is a diagnostic bone of horse, has been traced. Amongst the remains, traces of wild affinity could be discerned. Alur (1980: 221) infers that the concerned animal was of the size of a modern pony. Among the wild animals the deer and wild boar are present in the collection. The antelope remnants are dominated by antlers. Alur (1980: 221) opines that "their size variation is so marked that their breed characters are hard to be assessed. However, barasinga is a notable variation". The available aquatic resources were also exploited by Neolithic folk of the Vindhyas (Sahu, 1988: 178).

Pachoh

This Neolithic site also is situated in the Koraon sub-division of Allahabad district, only 2.5 km north-west of Koldihwa near the right bank of the Belan. Microlithic celts, pottery, etc. were collected from the surface. This site was excavated in 1975-76 by the University of Allahabad. The total thickness of cultural deposit, though major portion was washed away and disturbed by cultivation, is 60 cm. Besides the pottery, the excavation brought to light burnt clay lumps, ring-stones, rounded celts and microliths consisting of fluted cores, retouched blades, backed blades, scrapers and points (Sharma *et al.*, 1980: 136).

TOKWA

This important archaeological site is situated on the confluence of the Belan and Adwa rivers in Lalganj sub-division of Mirzapur district of eastern Uttar Pradesh, at a distance of 68 km from Mirzapur city in south-eastern direction and at a distance of 8 km east of Baraundha. It is one of the well-preserved settlements among the Neolithic sites of the Vindhyas (Misra *et al.*, 2000).

The northern margin of the site is flanked by the Belan River while the southern is facing the Adwa. The western margin of the site looks like the peak of a triangle. This site is quite extensive. Even at present it covers an area of about 27579 square m or 6 hectares, extending 400 m along the Belan and Adwa with a width of 150 m in the eastern side. As one moves eastward, the width of the site gets widened. The eastern limit of the site is up to the present-day Tokwa village. For the sake of convenience, the entire site was divided into three sub-parts: Tokwa-1, Tokwa-2 and Tokwa-3 from west to east.

Though the site was discovered long back in the seventies of the last century, it was revisited in 1999 and extensive explorations were done (Misra *et al.*, 2000). Excavation conducted at the site during 2000 and 2002 has revealed cultural relics of Neolithic, Chalcolithic and early Iron Age periods. The explorations at Tokwa resulted in the discovery of hand-made pottery comprising cord-impressed, rusticated, burnished red, burnished black, black-and-red and ordinary red ware on the one hand and black slipped ware and black-and-red ware on the other. The second assemblage of the pottery is wheel-thrown. At Tokwa I two trenches – H-8 and H-9 – in 2000 and two – I-8 and I-9 – in 2003, each measuring 5 square metre were laid out. The combined testimony of the excavations brought to light the archaeological evidence of three cultures: Neolithic, Chalcolithic and Iron Age. The occupational strata, divisible into as many as 16 layers, measured 4.00 m.

Layers 8 to 16 measuring 2.47 m represent the Neolithic horizon at the site. These layers have yielded hand-made cord impressed pottery, rusticated ware and burnished red and burnished black sherds as well. Other antiquities of the period include bone arrowheads, beads fashioned on semi-precious stones and terracotta, fragments of querns, mullers, hammer stones, etc. Microliths fashioned on semi-precious stones include flakes, flake fragments, blades, blade fragments, scrapers, triangles, etc. Preliminary observation to identify the grains obtained by floatation include rice, barley, *til* and *moong*. Some fruits and beans were also found. The analysis and identification of animal species shows that the bones include both wild and domesticated animals. A total of 235 fragments of animal bones were collected from the Neolithic phase. An examination of these remains showed the presence of any two domestic mammalian species (cattle and goat), wild mammal, birds, fish and a single molluscan species. Domestic mammals formed a major component of the Neolithic faunal assemblage (Joglekar *et al.*, 2008: 54). The wild animals from the Neolithic level comprise gaur (*Bos gaures*), nilgai and black-buck (*Antilopes cervicapra*).

From excavation at Tokwa, it appears that there was a gap between the disappearance of the Neolithic culture and arrival of the Chalcolithic culture as these two cultures exhibit different trends in ceramic tradition. While Neolithic pottery is hand-made, the Chalcolithic is wheel-thrown. Among the dates from the Neolithic levels, sample BS 2369 reads 6850 ± 200 BP which on calibration reads 5976-5561 BC.

These investigations have clearly established that:

1. The hilly region of the Kaimurs, rich in both plant and animal food resources, has been a scene of uninterrupted human habitation from Lower Palaeolithic times;
2. From here human groups moved north across the Yamuna and Ganga in the terminal Pleistocene to colonise the alluvial plains of the Ganga; and
3. It was at the interface of the plateau and plain that some enterprising groups crossed the rubicon from hunting-gathering to food production, which slowly led to the large-scale colonisation of the fertile Gangetic plains by farming communities (Misra in Pal, 1986).

Jhusi

The sprawling settlement of Jhusi (identified with ancient Pratisthanpura) is located on the left bank of the Ganga at a distance of about 7 kilometre to the east of Allahabad city and is very close to the confluence of the Ganga and Yamuna. Excavations conducted intermittently by the University of Allahabad at the Samudrakup mound has brought to light a sequence of cultures from the Neolithic to the early medieval times. The earliest settlement belonging to the Neolithic period has a deposit of 1.5 m. This culture was brought to light in the excavation of 2002 and 2003.

The Neolithic inhabitants lived in circular huts having walls of bamboo and reeds. The Neolithic pottery is essentially hand-made. It comprised cord-impressed ware, rusticated bone, burnished red ware, burnished black ware and crude black-and-red ware. Microlithics include various

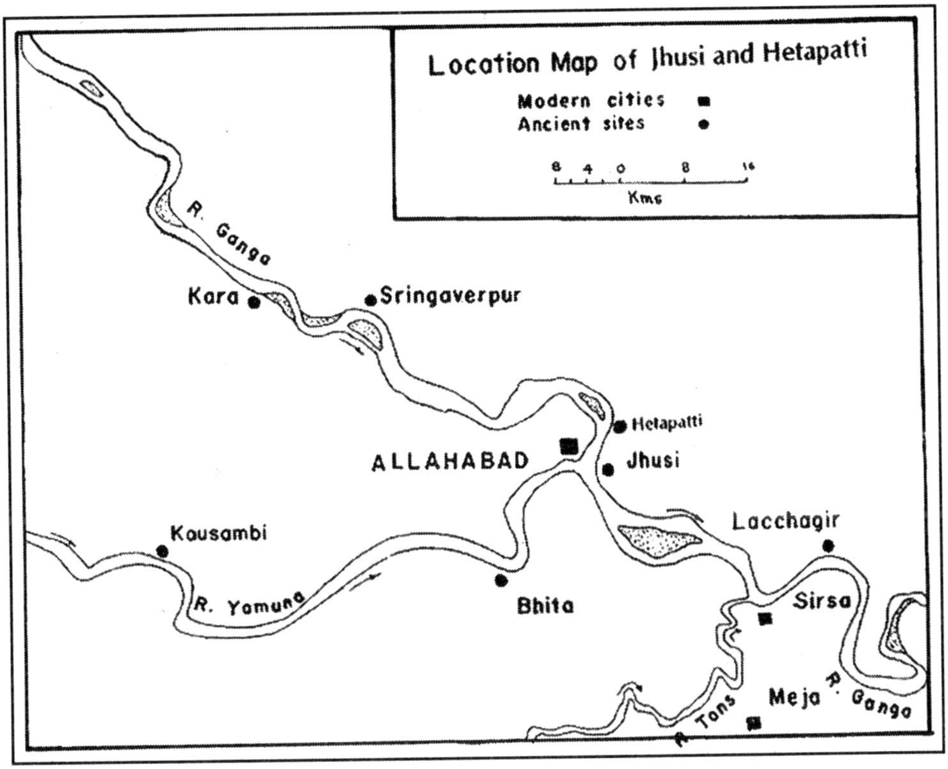

Fig. 6. Location map of Jhusi and Hetapatti

types of blades, escapers, triangles, trapeze, points, drills and lunates made of chart, chalcedony, carnelian and quartz. Micro disc beads and cylindrical beads made of paste material like steatite have been found. The bone tools comprised simple arrowheads. The archaeobotanical remains from the Neolithic strata were examined by Saraswat and Pokharia who have identified grains of barley, *jowar*, bread wheat, rice, lentil, pea, grass pea, horse gram and black gram together with fruit remains of *awala*, grapes and *ber* and oil-seeds comprising *til* or seasame (Pal, 2008: 272). The companions of Neolithic mean were cattle, sheep, goat, boar, barasinga, etc. Fish, turtle and birds definitely constituted important item of their diet (Pal, 2008: 273).

A time gap between the Neolithic and the succeeding Chalcolithic culture at this site has been suspected (Pal, 2008: 266).

Hetapatti

Yet another settlement of Neolithic culture was identified at Hetapatti, located on the left bank of the Ganga, at a distance of about 20 km from

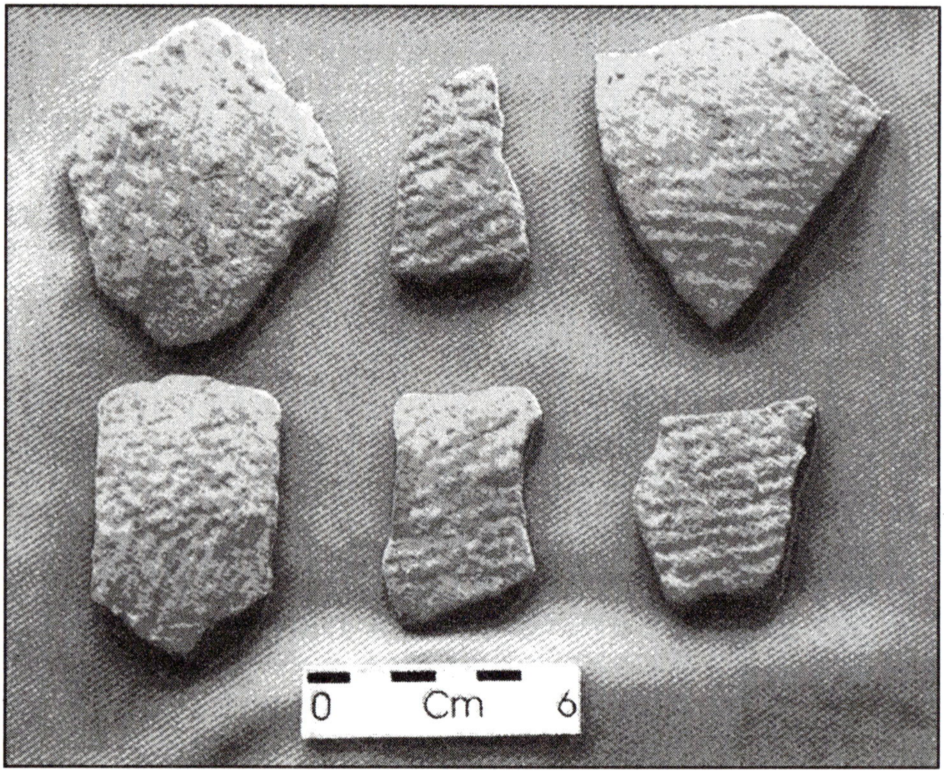

Fig. 7. Hetapatti: Cord-impressed potsherd

Allahabad in north-east direction. The site is under excavation since 2006 by the University of Allahabad (Pal, 2008: 273). The Neolithic deposit at Hetapatti is 60 cm divisible into four layers. This site has yielded hand-made Neolithic pottery characterised by cord-impressed ware, rusticated ware, ordinary red ware with jar, shallow and deep bowls and basins. Hut floors with burnt clay lumps with reed marks suggest wattle-and-daub structures.

Osteological remains from the Hetapatti are under study by Joglekar. This data will help in reconstructing man-animal relationship in the Ganga valley.

NEOLITHIC SITES IN THE MIDDLE GANGA VALLEY

Sohgaura

Perhaps the first Neolithic site excavated in the middle Ganga plain is Sohgaura, situated on the confluence of the rivers Rapti and Ami in the

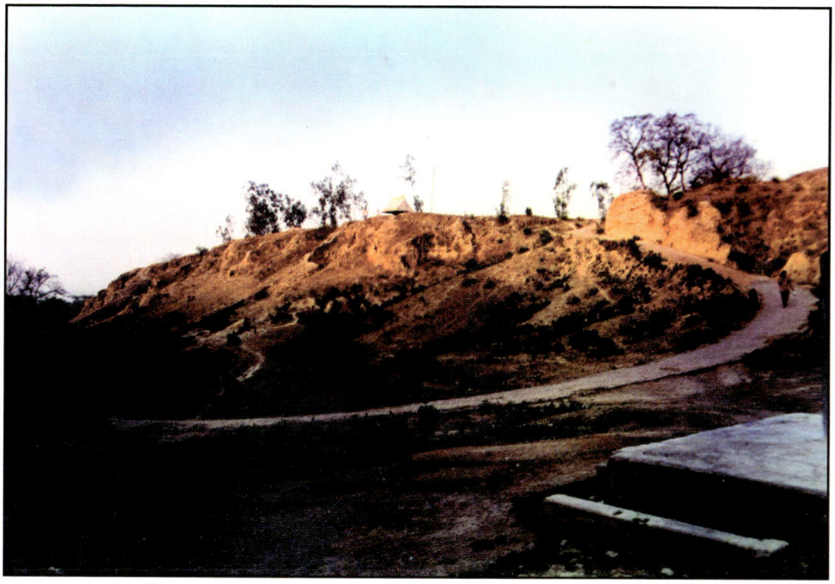

Pl. IA. Jhusi: General view of the Samudrakup mound

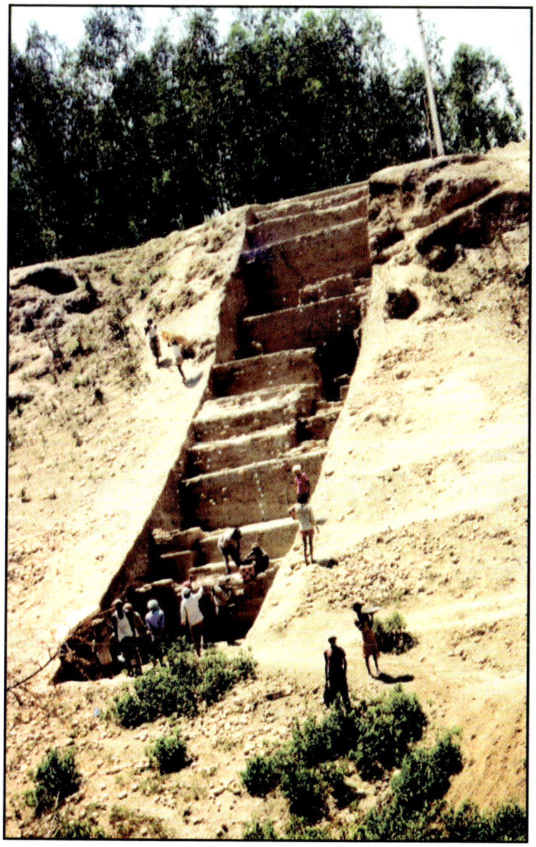

Pl. IB. Jhusi: General view of the excavation-
1995

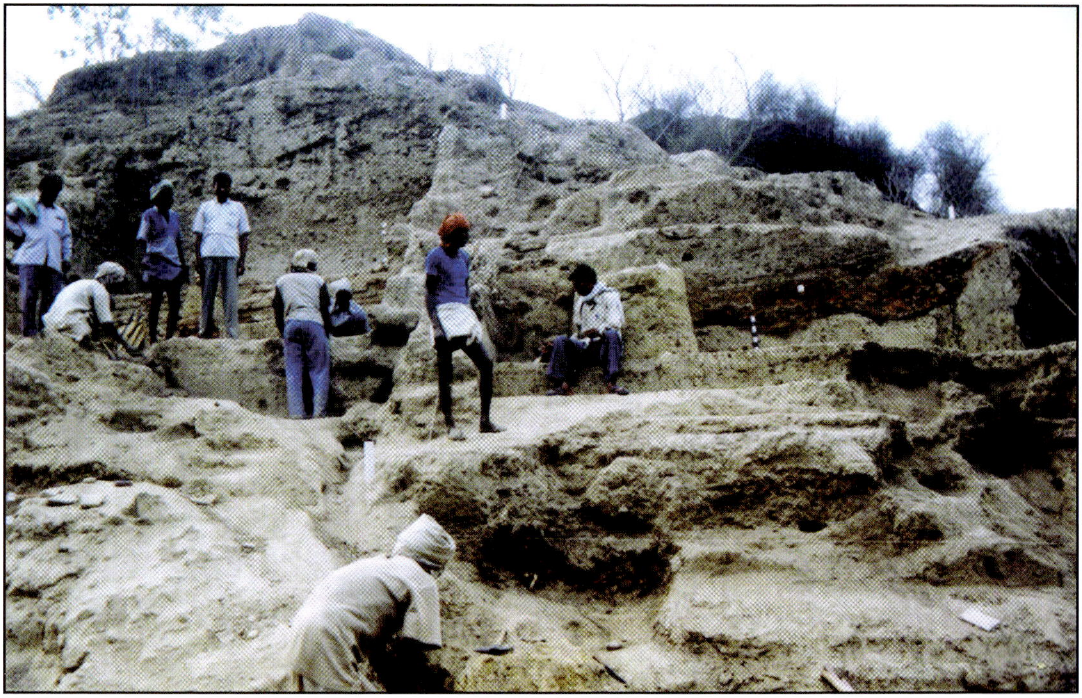

Pl. IIA. Jhusi: General view of the excavation-2003

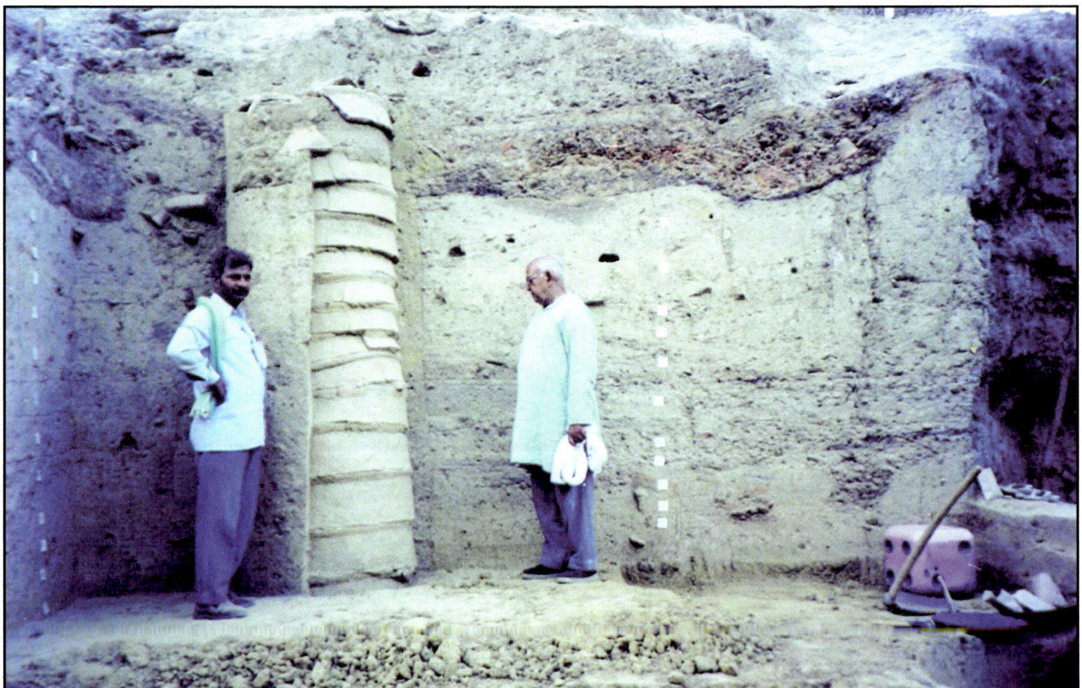

Pl. IIB. Jhusi: General view of the excavated trench-2003

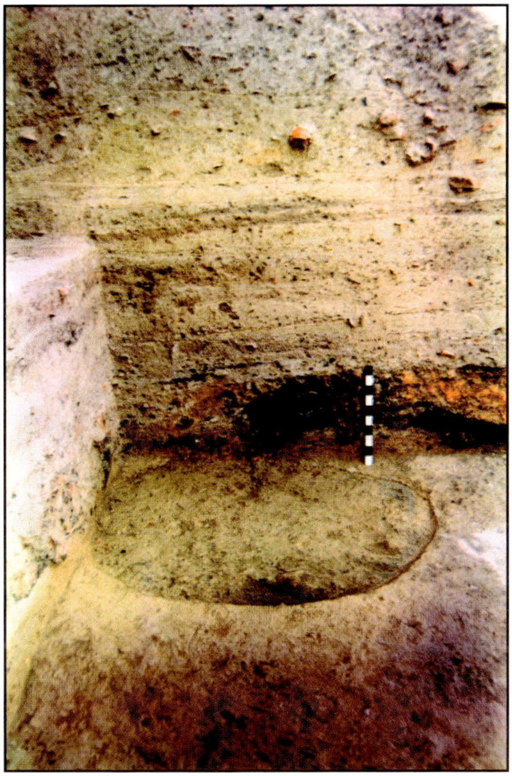

Pl. IIIA. Jhusi: Burnt layer in the section (mid-NBPW phase)

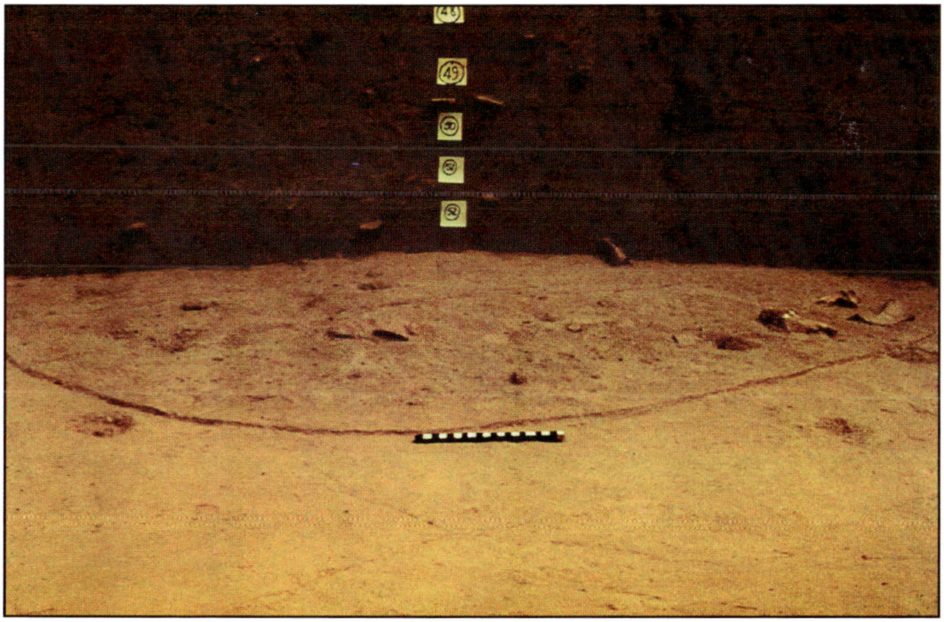

Pl. IIIB. Jhusi: Hut floor

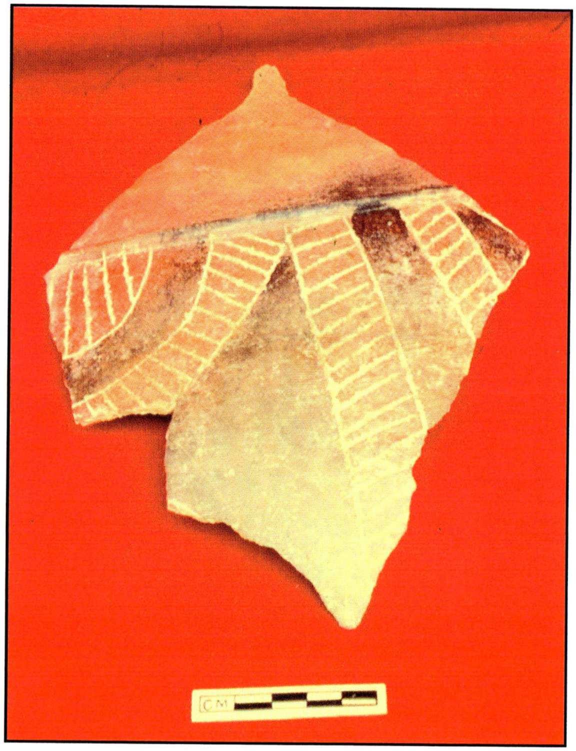

Pl. IVA. Jhusi: Incised and painted potsherd (Chalcolithic)

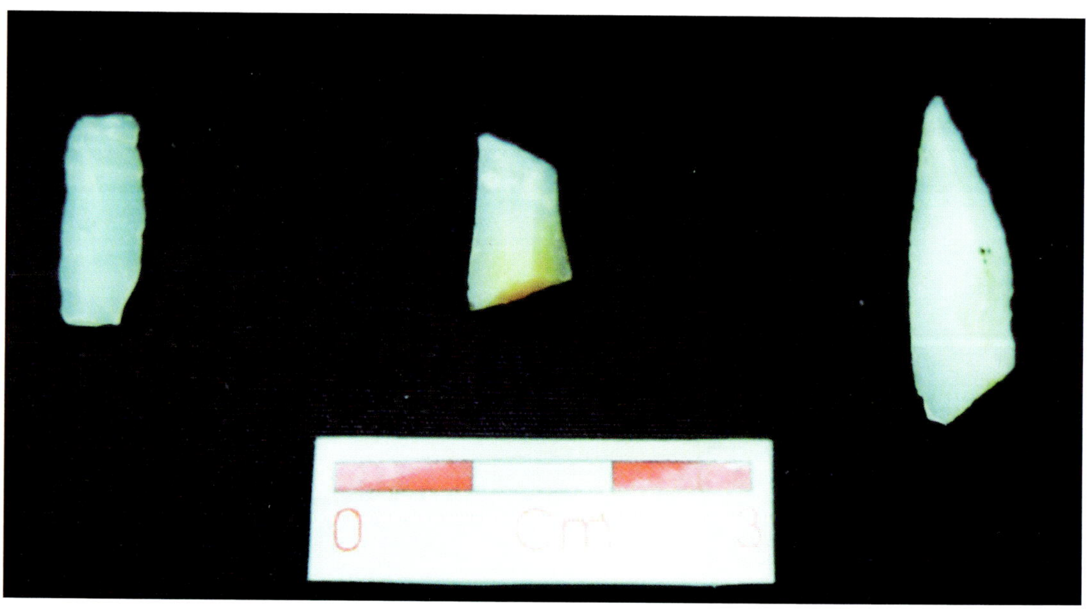

Pl. IVB. Jhusi: Microliths from Period I (Neolithic)

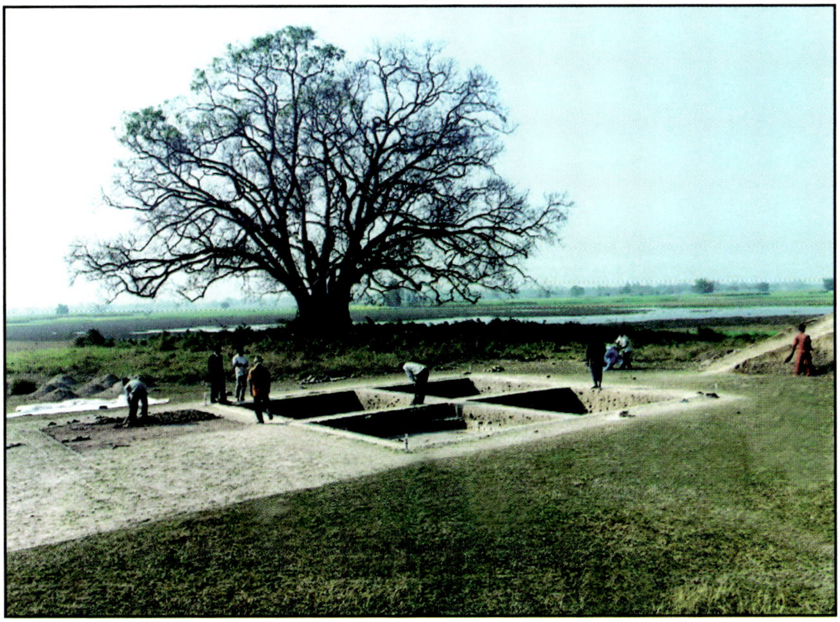

Pl. VA. Lahuradewa: General view of the site

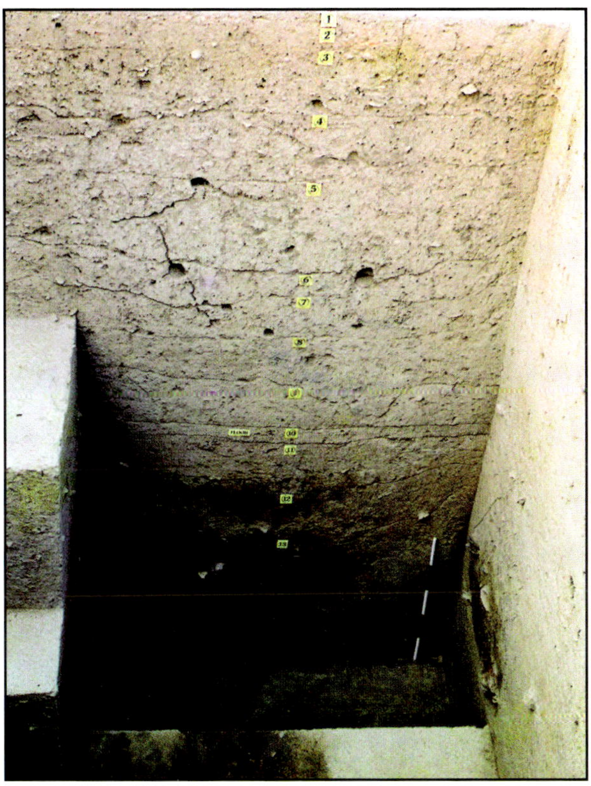

Pl. VB. Lahuradewa: Section facing south (trench No.YAI Qdt-1)

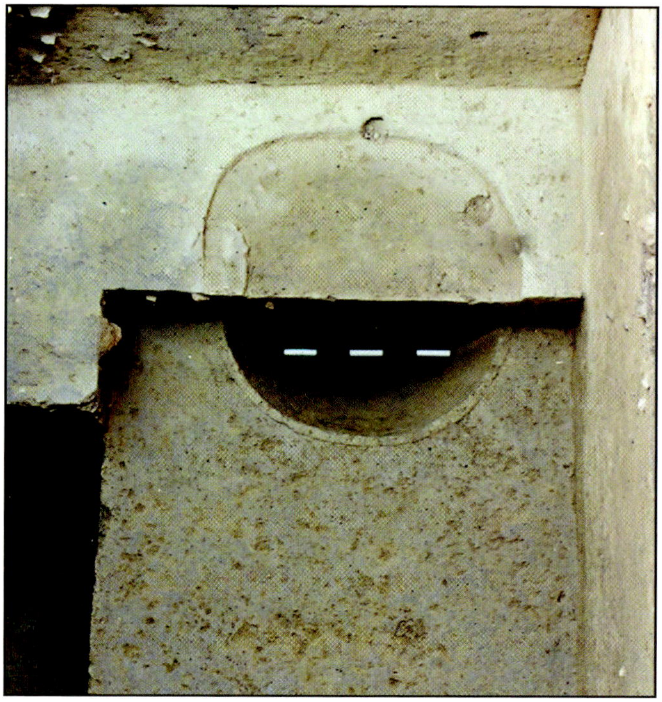

Pl. VIA. Lahuradewa: Earthen bin, dug in natural soil, Period II

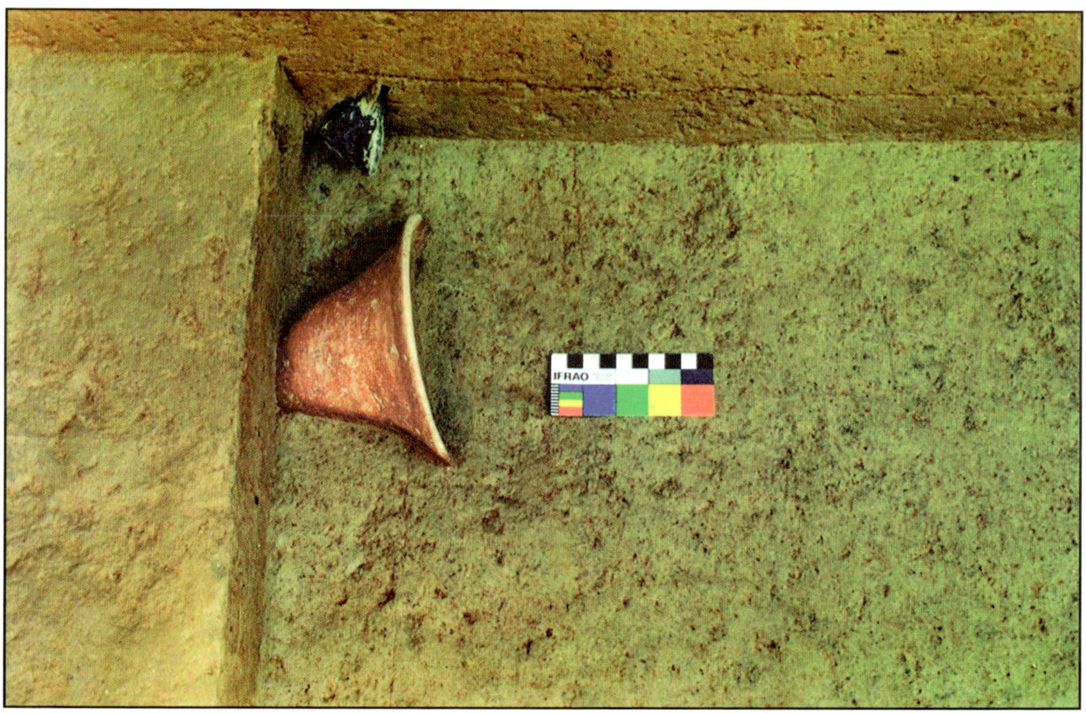

Pl. VIB. Lahuradewa: Dish-on-stand *in situ*, Period IB

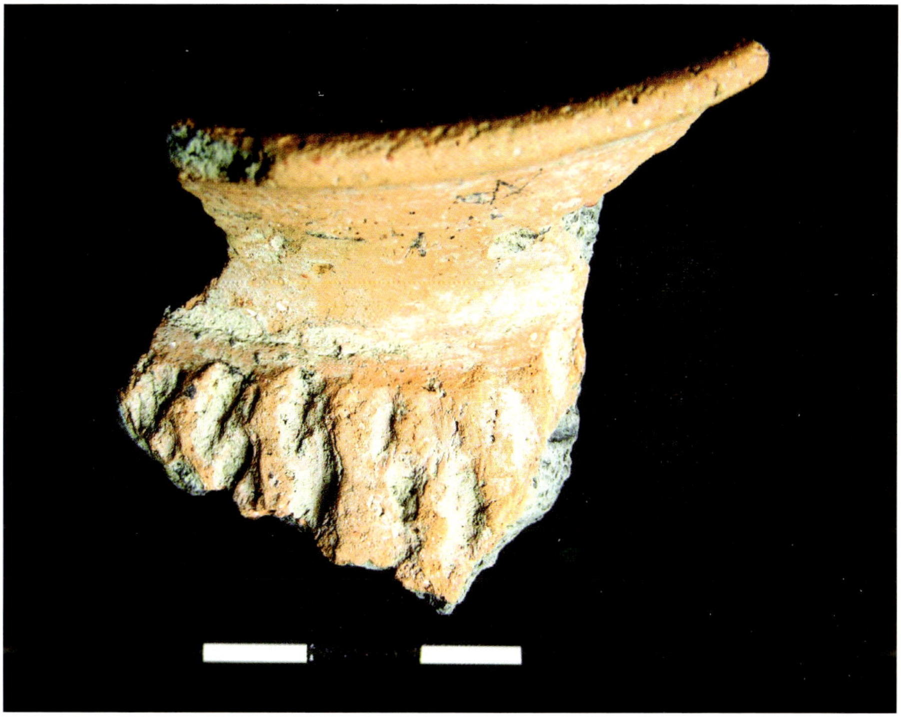

Pl. VIIA. Lahuradewa: Corded ware from Period IA

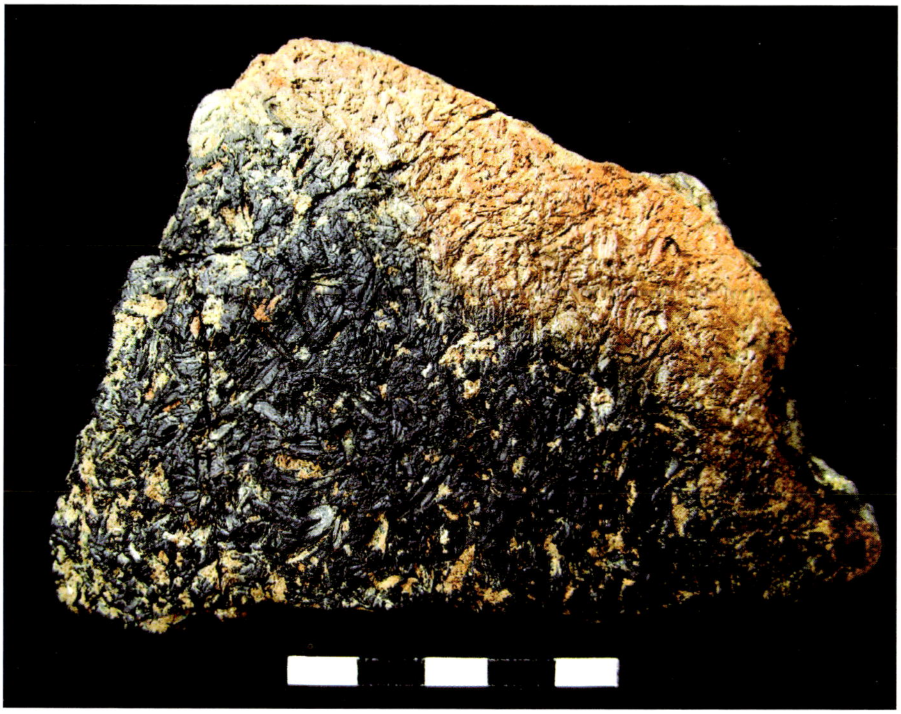

Pl. VIIB. Lahuradewa: Rice husk inclusions in a potsherd, Period IA

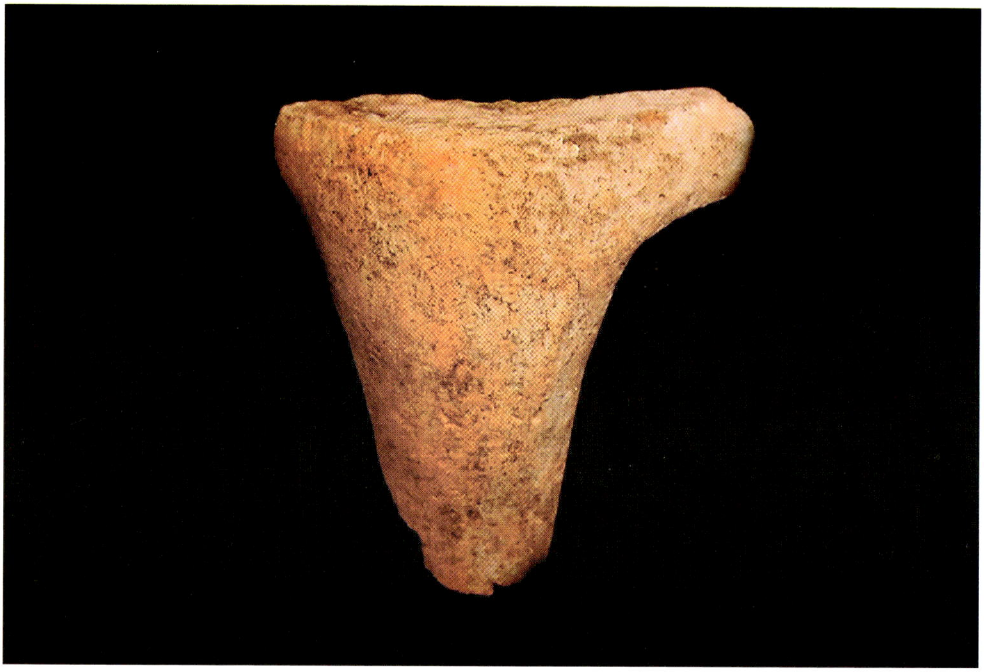

Pl. VIIIA. Lahuradewa: Terracotta leg of a *chauki*, Period II

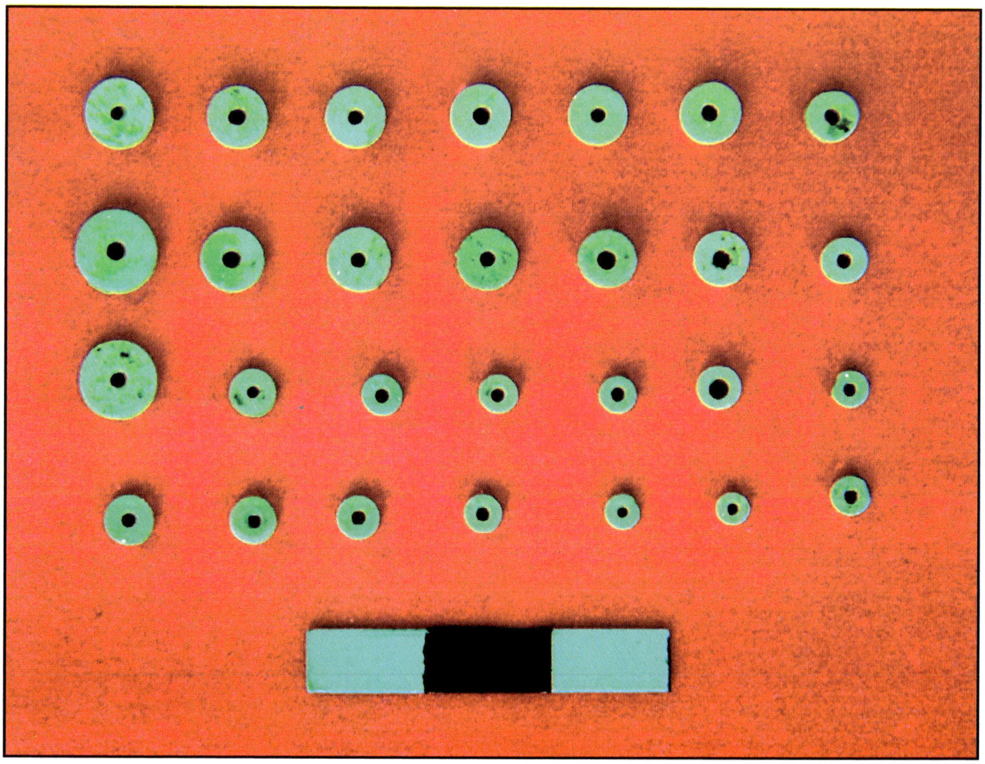

Pl. VIIIB. Lahuradewa: Steatite disc beads, Period II

Basgaon sub-division of Gorakhpur district. The site spreads over an area of 150 acres. It was the find-spot of a bronze plaque with a Mauryan Prakrit inscription recording the setting up a granary for storing grains for famines but the culture sequence of this site was worked out in the first excavation in 1961-62 by the Gorakhpur University, which brought to light a Chalcolithic culture characterized by white painted black-and red-ware along with several other varieties of pottery including black slipped and grey ware with painted design. However, yet another cultural phase at this site was brought to light in 1974-75 when it was again subjected to excavation by the same university. A complete set of cultures at the site was obtained mainly from a 5 metres square trench dug on the north-western corner of the mound. Since the lower levels were exposed only in a small part of the trench, little information could be obtained about the material culture of the early phases. The total cultural deposit of 4.40 metres has been divided into six periods: Period I – Neolithic; Period II – Chalcolithic I; Period III – Chalcolithic II; Period IV – NBPW; Period V – Kushana-Gupta and Period VI – Medieval. It is the earliest period at this site which is relevant in the present context.

The earliest period (Neolithic) is represented by a deposit of 17 cm exposed in a very small area (less than quarter of a 5 metres square trench) and has yielded few antiquities, mainly hand-made pottery. The sherds are very small; only a few provide clues to the shape of the original pots. Most of them are either cord-impressed or rusticated, the former predominating the assembly. The number of the plain red ware is meagre. The pottery is of coarse or medium fabric and is usually ill-fired. As a result, especially in the case of cord-impressed ware, the section does not show uniformity of colour. The only other find is a large-sized burnt clay cake like object (Chaturvedi, 1985: 103).

The cord-impressed ware is the most notable feature of this period. It is made of gritty clay mixed with rice husk, straw, etc., and is usually ill-fired. Cord impression occurs on the exterior of the pots only. It consists mainly of beaded lines usually vertical but at times reveals various patterns. It is believed that the cord-impressed designs could be obtained through tortoise shell impressions (Misra, 1977: 108).

The rusticated ware also is of medium fabric and ill-fired. The term 'rusticated' refers to the application of clay solutions mixed with straw husk, etc. on the exterior of the pots and the device is supposed to have been adopted to strengthen the pots (Sharma *et al.*, 1980: 153). Some of the cord-impressed sherds are also rusticated and a fragment of coarse fabric, dull red in colour, bears the impression of a leaf suggesting that, after the application of clay solution, the leather-hard pot was placed on dried grass and leaves. Plain red ware is represented by a few fragments of globular vessels of coarse and medium fabric.

A fragmentary baked terracotta discoid object with a lenticular section and a diameter of 13.5 cm is the only antiquity other than pottery which has been found in the deposit of this period.

The results of excavations at Sohgaura provided for the first time a glimpse of pre-historic culture in Sarayupar plains but the limited excavations did not provide ample data for understanding the full implications of this discovery. Similarly, the chronology of this Neolithic culture could not be made out as there were no radio-carbon dates from the Neolithic strata. However, it was believed that Period I at Sohagaura came to an end about 1900 BC. As regards the beginning of this culture, it was suggested that the Neolithic phase had a beginning some time in the first half of the third millennium BC (Chaturvedi, 1985: 107).

LAHURADEWA

While conducting archaeological excavations at Sohgaura in 1974-75, the archaeologists of the University of Gorakhpur explored and located a number of sites in district Basti; notable amongst them are Susipar, Ramnagar Ghat, Baragaon, Gerar and Lahuradewa. These sites are located on the high lines of river Kuano and its tributary and yielded the early

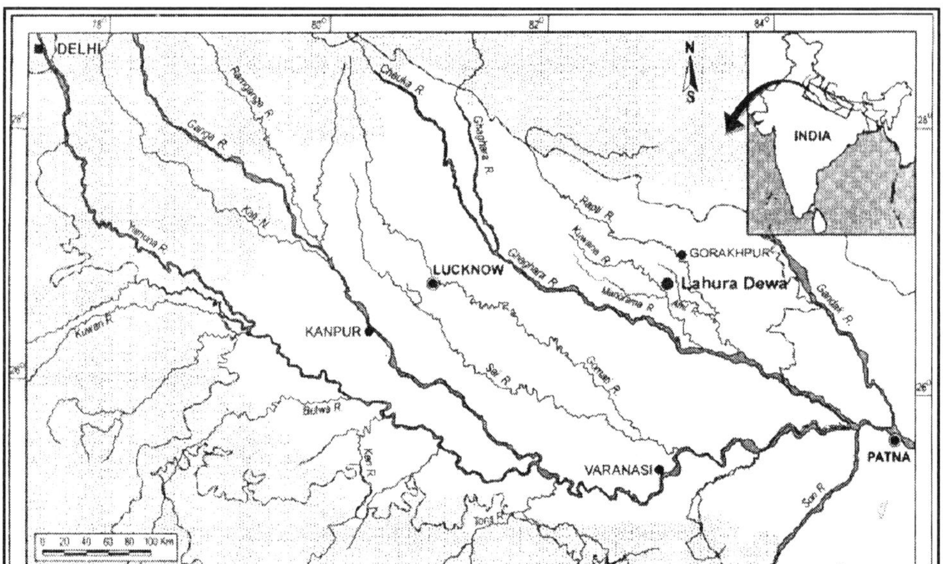

Fig. 8. Map showing location of Lahuradewa in the middle Ganga plain

pottery of Sohgaura (cord-impressed pottery along with lithic assortment comprising chunks, flakes, cores and debitage of fine-grained stones such as chalcedony, quartz, crystal and chert. Subsequently, these sites were visited by a number of scholars from time to time and the most promising of these – Lahuradewa – was selected for excavations by Rakesh Tewari and his team of the Department of Archaeology, Government of Uttar Pradesh.

Lahuradewa is situated on the bank of a lake which surrounds it from three sides. It is located at a distance of about 5 km south of the Basti-Gorakhpur main road from Bhujaini crossing, in district Sant Kabir Nagar. It extends over an area of about 220 m east-west and about 140 m north-south, with an elevation of about 4 metres from the surrounding levels. Excavations conducted for four seasons between 2001 and 2006 have brought to light a five-fold culture sequence as given below:

Period I: Early Farming phase
Period II: Developed Farming phase
Period III: Advanced Farming/Early Iron Age
Period IV: NBPW phase
Period V: Early Historic (Early centuries BC/AD)

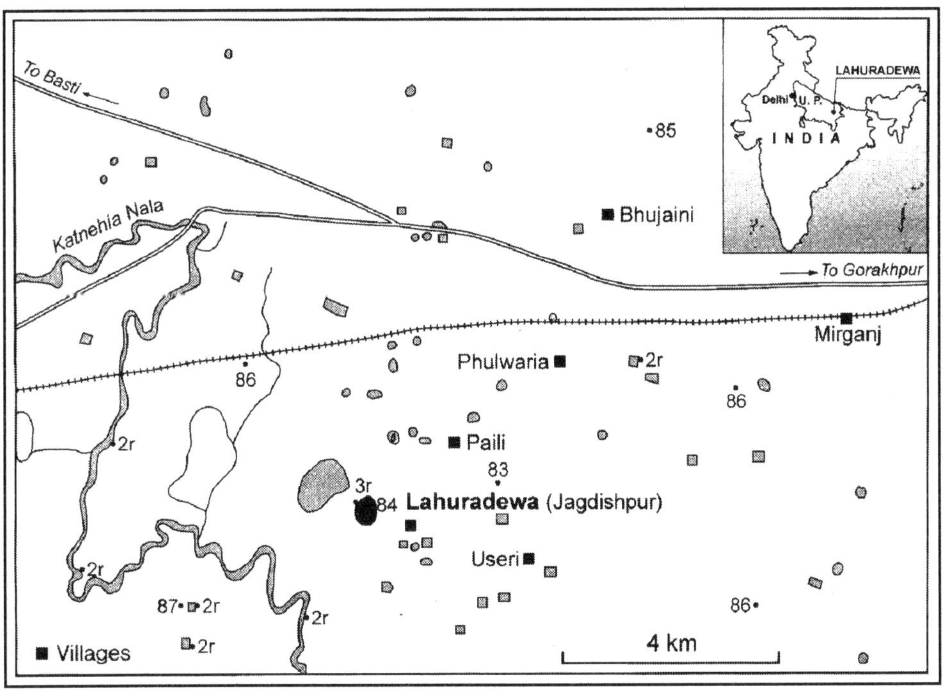

Fig. 9. Map showing location of Lahuradewa

The earliest Period I starting from the very opening of sedentary occupation at the site was sub-divided into two sub-periods, namely, IA and IB. Sub-Period IA is characterised by the presence of a coarse variety of hand-made red ware and black-and-red ware industry often displaying cord-impressions on exterior surface. A few sherds also show decoration by incised patterns and fine red slip. Inclusion of black and grey ware in a

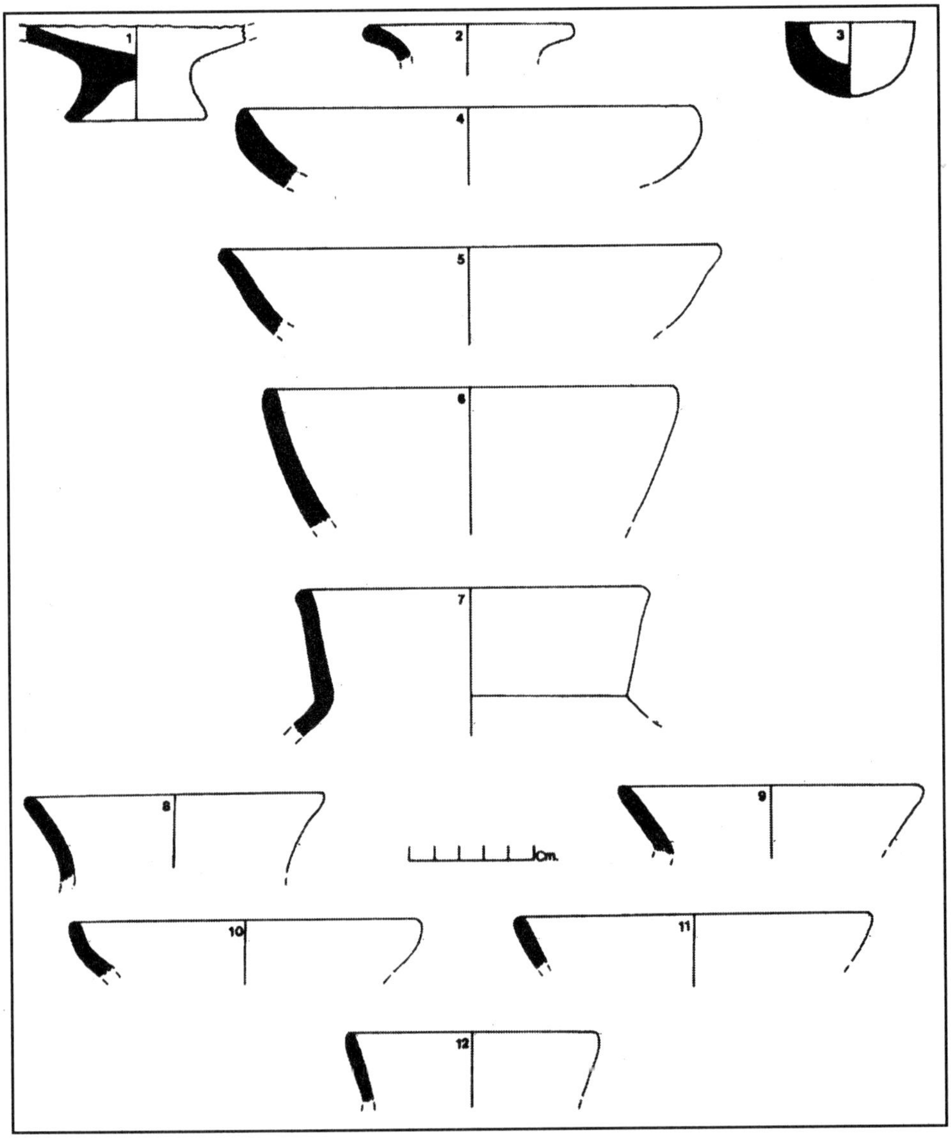

Fig. 10. Lahuradewa: Pottery of Period IA

meagre amount was noticed. Water vessels, pedestal and knobbed bowls, some of which were decorated with applied rope-pattern, were the important shapes in the ceramic assemblage. Faunal remains included some bones and a tortoise shell. Plant material consisting of incidentally carbonised material included a few grains and glume pieces of rice, conforming morphological to those of domesticated form (*Oryza sativa*), in the assortment of the grains of some widely or segetally growing rice (*Oryza* cf. *rufipogon*) and foxtail grass (*Setaria glauca*). On the basis of two conventional radiocarbon date determinations of wood charcoal from the lowermost deposits, carried out by the Radiocarbon Dating Laboratory at BSIP (BS-1951: BP 5320±90 yr: Cal. BC 4220, 4196, 4161 yr and BS-1966: BP 6290±160 yr: Cal. BC 5298 yr), the human activity and the agriculture practices during the early phase of occupation at the site, were ascribed to the early post-glacial times (early Holocene), during 6th-5th millennium BC (8th-9th millennium BP). However, the estimation of precise date of the cultivated rice remained unsettled, in want to direct AMS date of the material.

Sub-period IB was marked by the appearance of some new shapes in pottery such as beaker, perforated vessel, spouted vessel and dish or bowl-on-stand. Black-and-red ware continued in medium variety sometimes comprising black or red slip on one side, and quite often, burnishing on one or both sides. The quality of pottery showed improvement over Period IA. A few painted potsherds, some terracotta and stone beads, and a few micro steatite beads were the noteworthy commodities in the cultural assemblage. Charred and un-charred bones showed cut marks. Wattle-and-daub dwelling appeared in continuance, implied by the post-hole and burnt mud clots with reed-marks. Culmination on this sub-period is dated by a radiocarbon date of charcoal from the upper level of deposit in this occupational phase (BS-1950: BP 3750±90 yr; Cal. BC 2135, 2079, 2056 yr).

Period II succession beginning from about 2000 BC was characterised by an acclaimed presence of copper artefacts at Lahuradewa. In continuation of ceramic industries of Period I, this period was marked by the appearance of plain and painted black slipped and black-and-red ware. The proportion of spouted and lipped vessel, bowl/dish-on-stand, pedestal bowl, disc based bowl increased manifold. Earthen storage bins, baked terracotta tiles, legs of some terracotta objects, steatite beads in fairly large numbers, some lithic artefacts, beads of semi-precious stones, socketed and tanged bone or antler arrowheads with ravishing micro-encircled decorations, indicate considerable spurt in the material prosperity. In

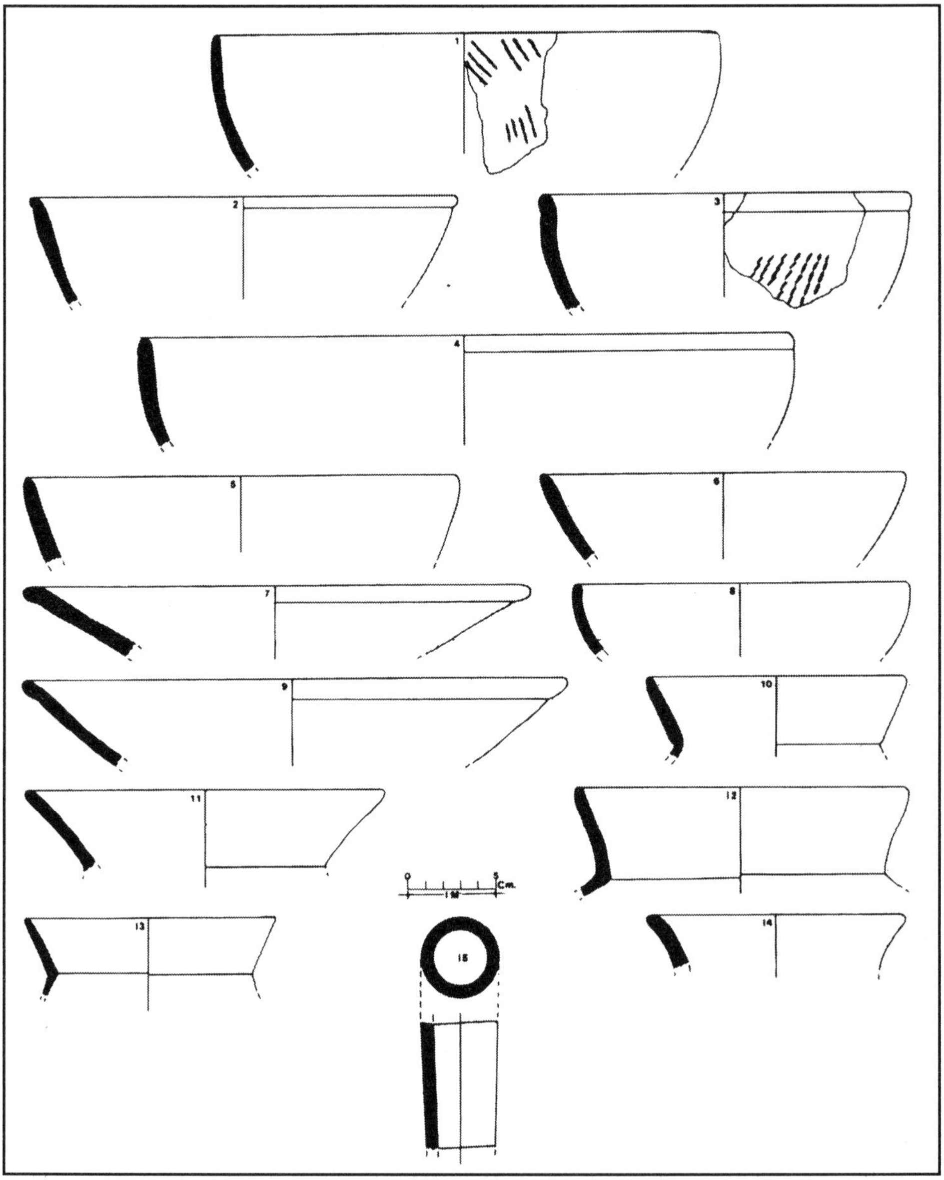

Fig. 11. Lahuradewa: Pottery of Period IB

addition to dwelling structures, rammed earthen floors, hearths and a mud-wall augment improvement in the settlement plan.

Period III was marked by the appearance of highly rusted iron artefacts. This period also comprised all types of ceramic industries of the

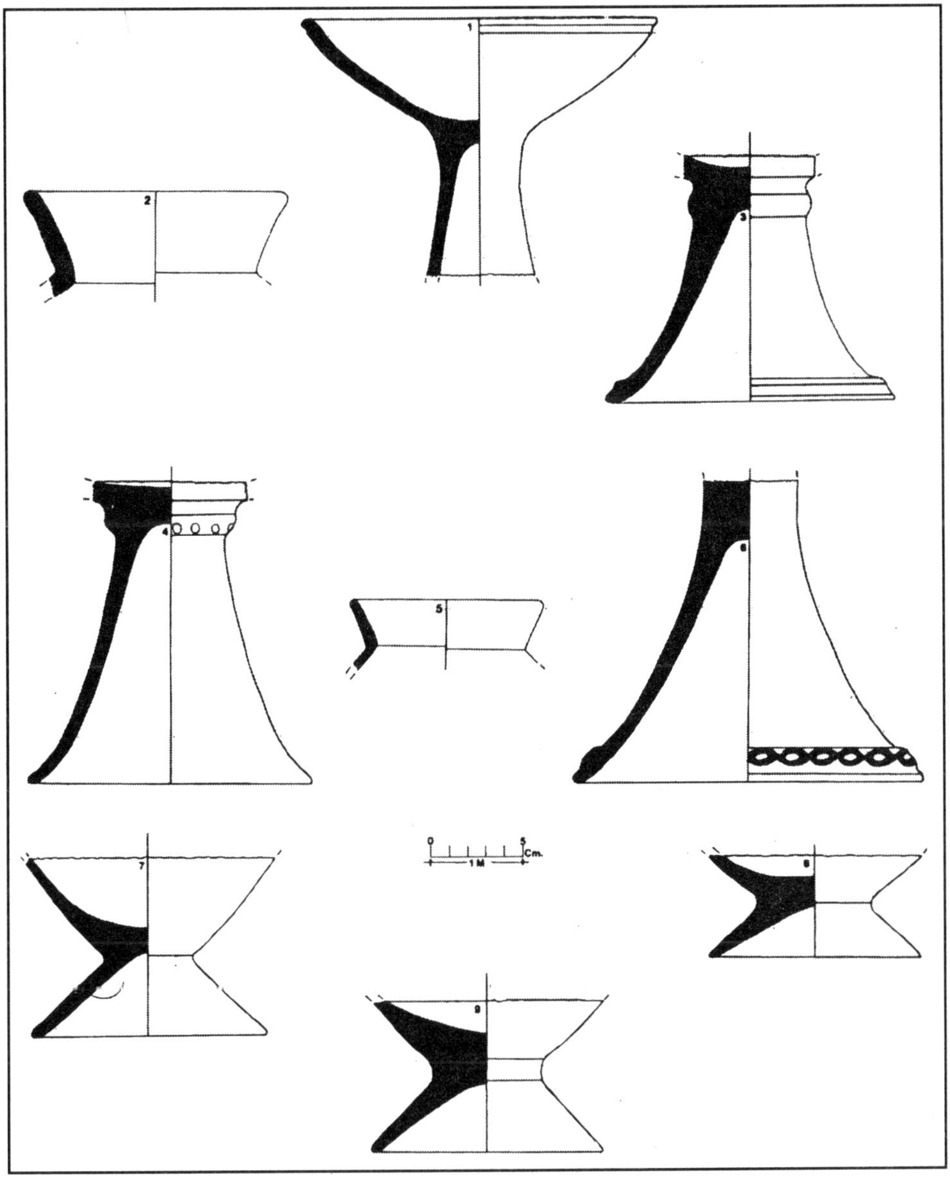

Fig. 12. Lahuradewa: Important shapes in the pottery of Peroid IB

earlier period. Important iron objects included sickles (?). Earthen floors, hearths, burnt clay lumps with reed and straw impressions indicated the continuation of earlier structural traditions. Bone and antler arrowheads and awls were present in a good proportion, which show a considerable variation in shape and decoration. A radiocarbon date for a charcoal sample collected from the lowest iron yielding deposit of this period is 2940±100 yr BP; Cal. BC 1205, 1205, 1188 yr (BS: 1939).

Period IV was characterized by well known NBPW in an occupation deposit of about 1.20 m thickness. Painting tradition on pottery continued considerably even in this period. Some NBPW sherds of deluxe variety also exhibited painted decorations. The proportion of finely made black slipped, grey and red ware increased, while black-and-red ware and coarse variety of pottery declined in their proportion. Presence of iron slag was noted.

The main achievements of Lahuradewa excavation are as follows (Tewari *et al.*, 2006a: 62):

There is good evidence to show that human activity was going on in the Ganga Plain from Early Palaeolithic Period. The presence of micron-charcoal pieces in the lake-sediments of Sanai Tal and Lahuradewa lake from lower to upper levels indicates human activity in their vicinity from circa 15000 and 10000 yr. respectively. Obvious closeness and exploitation of wild flora by the foragers would have culminated in the plantation of certain plants. On the basis of the presence of domesticated rice grains from Lahuradewa, datable to mid-9th millennium BP, it may be surmised that this process was probably initiated during latest Pleistocene/Early Holocene. Mostly coarse variety of hand-made red and black-and-red ware appear along with such rice grains from the very beginning. The settlers, related with these finds, were making wattle-and-daub dwellings having mud-plastered screens made of reed-like material. Aquatic fauna formed a considerable proportion of their subsistence economy. These people were interacting directly or indirectly with distant regions to procure steatite/ steatite beads and beads made of semi-precious stones. These interactions, particularly with the western part of the Indian subcontinent, enhanced considerably since the early half of the 5th millennium BP onwards, which are evidenced by the appearance of copper arrowhead and fishing hook, dish-on-stand, barley, increased numbers of steatite and other beads, wheat and pulses, spouted and pedestal vessels, a few painted potsherds, improvement in pottery making, etc. Earlier ceramic industries, decorations on them and architectural tradition continued. Around 4000 yr. BP some new cultural traits appeared, represented by thin-sectioned plain and painted black slipped ware, plain and painted black-and-red ware, baked tiles, terracotta legs of an indeterminate object and a good number of storage bins. Since the settlement extended in an area of about 500 x 200 m by this time, a considerable growth in demography is apparent.

The presence of earthen bins of this time period at every location, which has been subjected to excavation and a large granary, show surplus agricultural production. However, baked clay titles, earthen bins and terracotta legs did not continue for a longer time and are restricted to only in the lower phase of this period. Except for the appearance of iron artefacts around 3200 BP, no major change appears in the cultural traits of the Lahuradewa settlers for the period of about early 3rd millennium BP. The next phase is marked by the appearance of the famous NBPW, which covers the pre- and post-Buddha periods.

Imlidih Khurd

The ancient settlement of Imlidih Khurd is an inconspicuous, featureless mound located on the left bank of the Kuwana, a tributary of Ghaghara River in district Gorakhpur. It was excavated during 1992, 1993 and 1995 by the author (Singh, 1991-92; 1992-93, 1993-94). The main results of the three-fold culture sequence are as follows:

The major achievement of Imlidih excavation is the discovery of a Neolithic culture, noticed earlier at Sohgaura and represented by hand-made cord-impressed pottery as its diagnostic trait, an antecedent phase of culture having a cultural deposit of 50-60 cm and stratigraphically occurring just below the Narhan culture, hence termed as 'Pre-Narhan' by us. The diagnostic trait of this culture is its characteristic pottery hitherto unrecorded at Narhan, Khairadih, Manjhi, etc. but supposedly found at Sohgaura in the limited dig of 1963.

The inhabitants of Period I (Neolithic culture) lived in wattle-and-daub huts represented by reed marks discovered in large number. Several floors made of mud, ovens and hearths marked the other structural activities. An almost circular pit, with a diameter of 1.95 metres, was found. A circular structure with an internal diameter of 85 cm and 7 cm thick walls was supposedly used as a grain silo or bin. Remains of a mud floor with an average thickness of 25-30 cm was also found in another trench. The small finds comprise a large number of micro beads of steatite, other beads of terracotta, agate and faience, bone points and pottery discs.

The pottery of Neolithic culture is essentially crude, some of it bearing cord impressions on the exterior of the pots and hence termed 'corded ware', the others being vessels of plain red ware. In both cases, the clay contained good amount of degraissant, which got burnt during firing and it resulted into the porous surface. Most vessels, particularly the globular vessels, have thin, sandy, friable core, some of them having mica pieces. The vessels are generally ill-fired, leaving a black core.

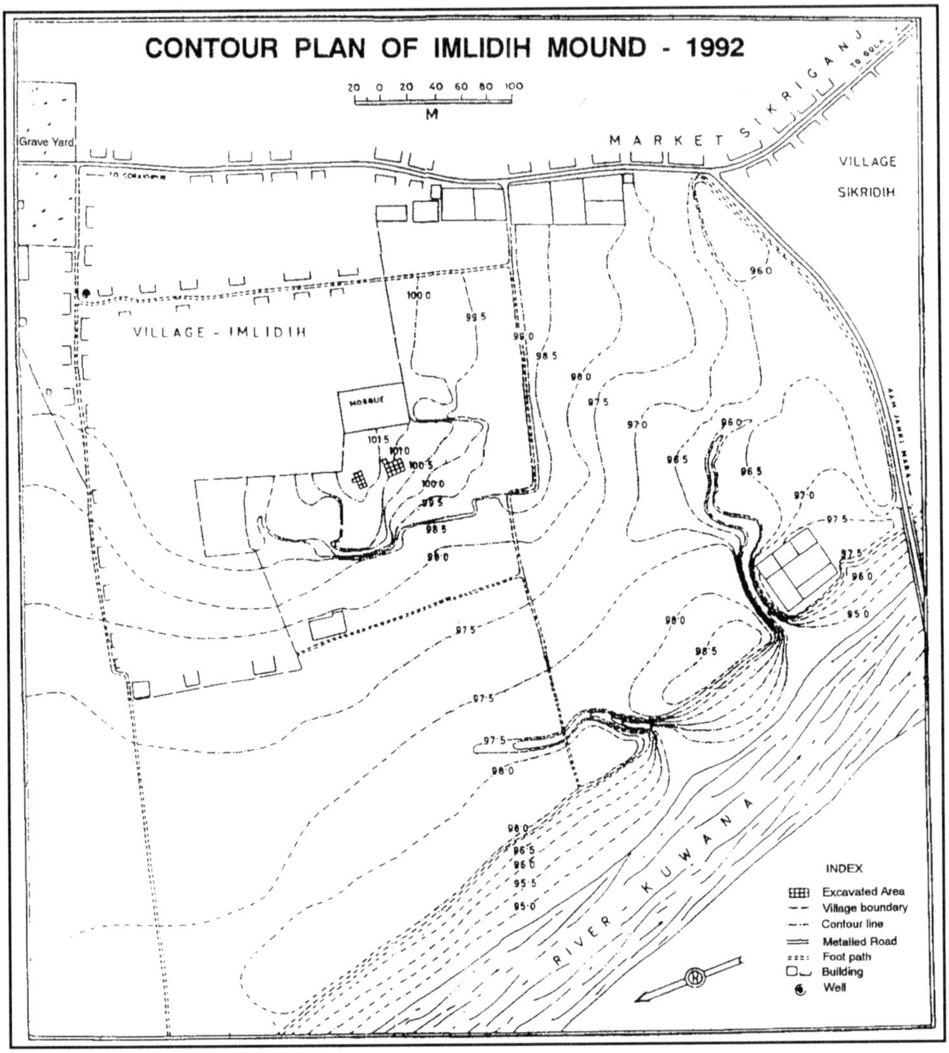

Fig. 13. Contour plan of Imlidih Khurd mound

Some pottery vessels bear post-firing scratched designs done by a sharp instrument which essentially includes geometrical pattern (opposed triangles, etc.) within concentric circles. A few floral motifs have also been noticed. The second method of decorating a vessel was by painting the pot with dots and dashes in red colour over a bright red surface. However, such paintings are very limited in our collection. Another method of decorating pottery vessel was appliqué method. This method is confined to *handis* only. A strip of clay was generally affixed on the exterior of the

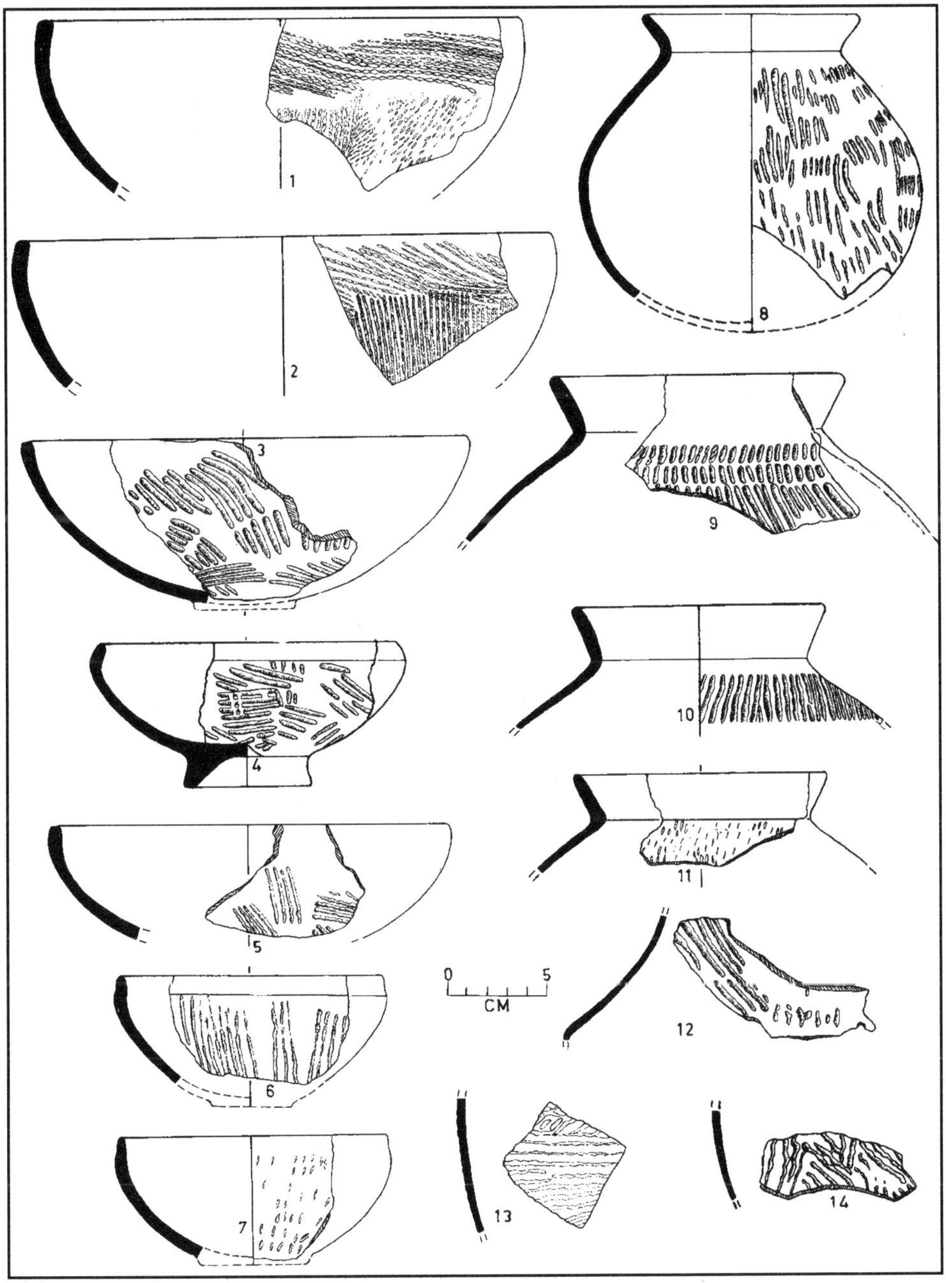

Fig. 14. Imlidih Khurd: Corded ware of Period I

vessel at the point of carination below the shoulder and by cutting, incising and other methods, various types of rope and chain patterns were executed

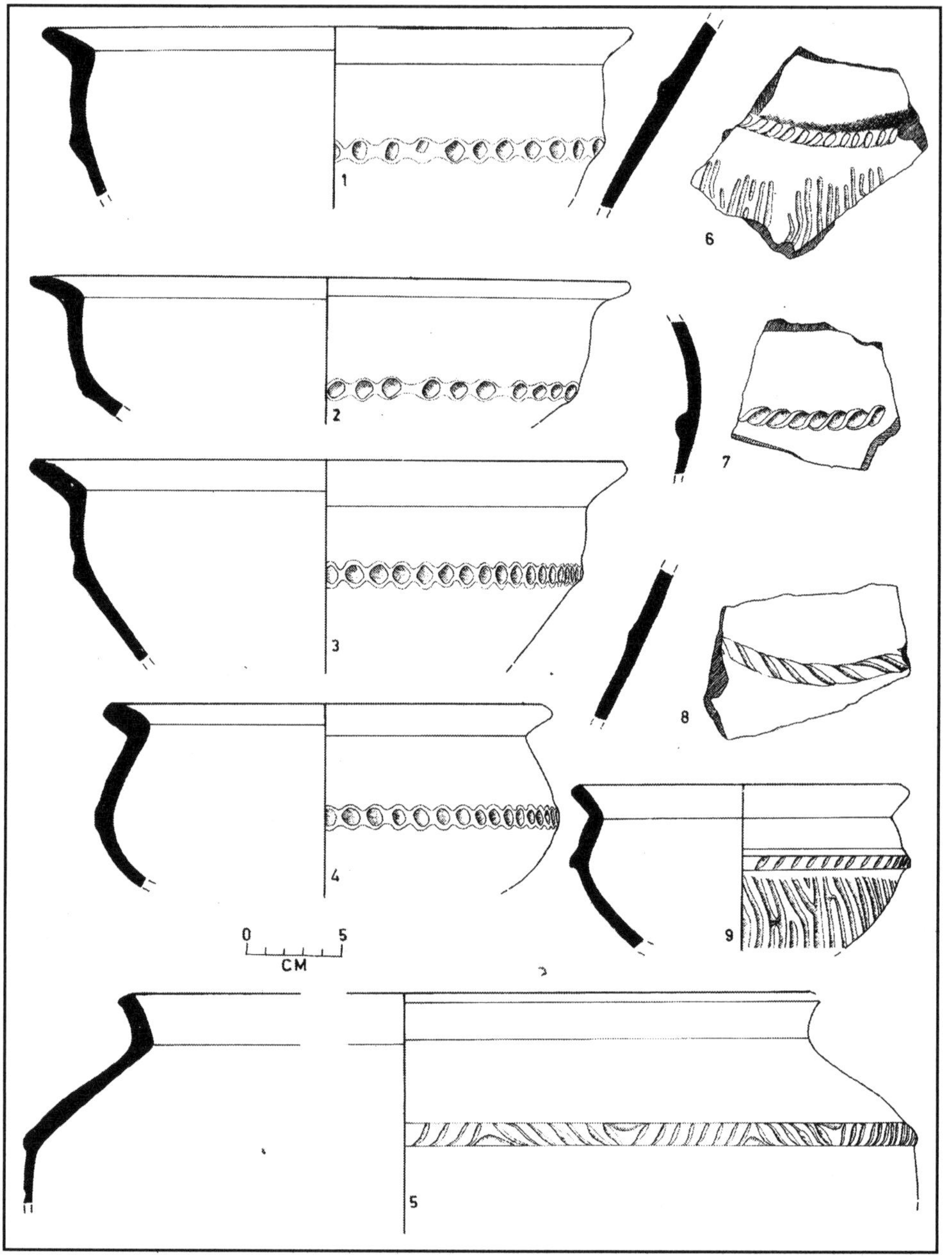

Fig. 15. Imlidih Khurd: Corded ware with appliqué designs, Period I

on the added strip of clay. Below the carination, the *handi* generally has a corded exterior.

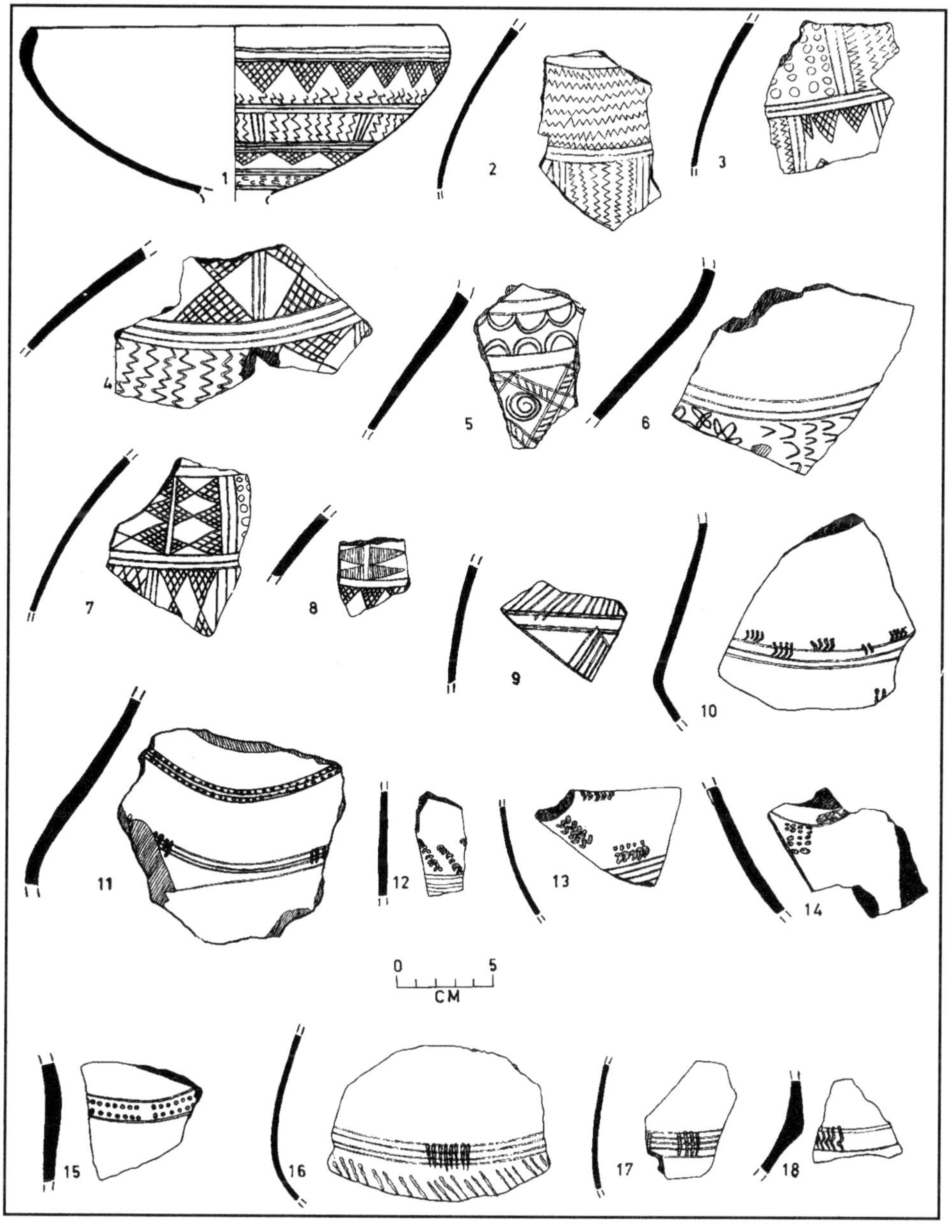

Fig. 16. Imlidih Khurd: Post-firing scratching and painted designs, Period I

A good quantity of animal bones was collected in the process of excavation, particularly from the large refuse pits cut into the natural soil. A tentative taxonomic classification of these bones shows that cattle,

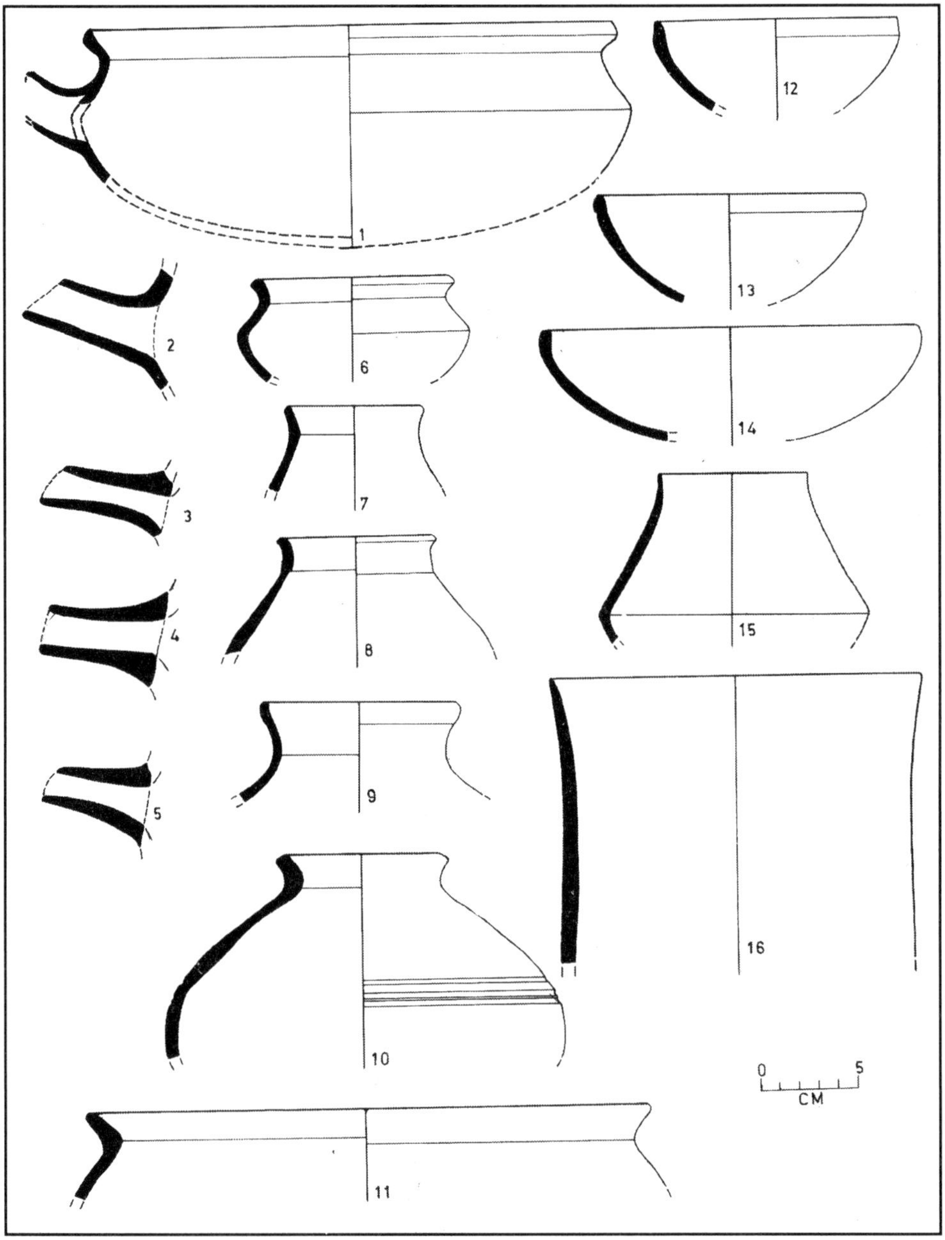

Fig. 17. Imlidih Khurd: Plain red ware Period I

sheep/goat and presumably pig had already been domesticated in Period I. Among these, cattle remains predominate and often bear characteristic butchery marks. The wild ungulates comprise horned deer and a large canid, possibly wolf. The aquatic resources comprised two species of fresh-water turtle, fish of small and medium size and freshwater mollusca. Examination of archaeobotanical remains has shown that the pre-Narhan settlers of Imlidih Khurd cultivated two crops a year. The cereals comprise rice, barley, wheat, jowar, millet and bajra (pearl millet). The pulses included lentil, field pea, grass pea (*Khesari)* and green gram or *mung*. The oilseeds comprised field *brassica* and sesame or *til*. Jujube, *anwla* and grapes were the fruits eaten by the inhabitants.

DHURIAPAR

The ancient settlement of Dhuriapar is situated on the left bank of the Kuwana River about 46 km south of Gorakhpur. The settlement presently spreads over a length of about 1.5 km along the river bank and is occupied by three small villages, viz., Jagdishpur, Basudeopur and Dhuriapar. According to the local tradition, the history of the present settlement began with the invasion of Kaushika Kshatriyas under their Raja Dhurchand who established a fortified settlement in the middle of the 14th century. This ancient settlement was named Dhuriapar after the name of its founder, Dhurchand.

While conducting archaeological excavation at Narhan about 25 km east of Dhuriapar in 1984-89, the present author had seen this site. This site had also come in the prominence as a medieval sculpture presumably representing the various incarnations of Lord Vishnu was stolen from this site in January 1987. Hence, at the request of local inhabitants, the present team explored this site. In excavation it was found that the earliest ceramic industry available at this site are the black-and-red ware, black slipped ware, NBP ware and red ware. Bowls and dishes of black slipped ware and vases of black-and-red ware are the principal shapes. This mound was inhabited up to the medieval period. Burnt brick structures of Kushana and Gupta periods were seen in the eroded section of the mound. Besides, our excavation at Narhan had revealed the existence of altogether distinct culture termed by us as Narhan culture, datable between 1300-800 BC. Therefore, the next logical step was to determine the extent of this culture. The occurrence of black-and-red ware encouraged us to undertake trial excavation of this site so that the full potential of this settlement could be assessed. In order to fulfil the aim, five 3 m × 3 m text pits were excavated in different parts of this mound in a five-week period in April-May, 1991 (Singh *et al.,* 1991-92). The total cultural deposit measuring between 2-5 metres has been divided into five periods, which are as follows:

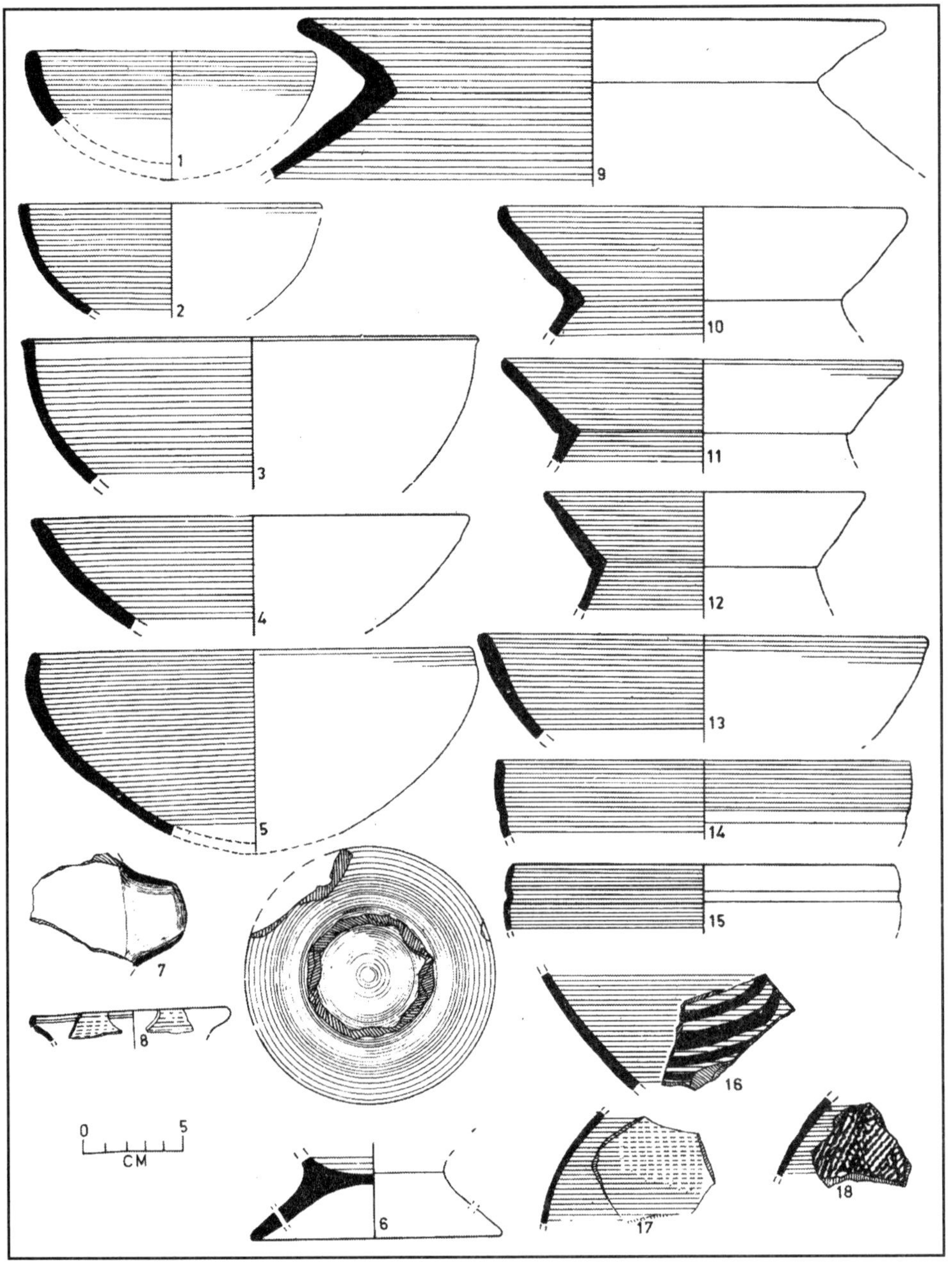

Fig. 18. Dhuriapar: Painted black-and-red ware No. 18 is a sherd of cord-impressed pottery

Period I

This period is represented by black-and-red ware with linear paintings in white (having pedestal bowls, basins and vases as the main types); black slipped ware (main types, bowls and dishes); grey ware (main types, bowls and dishes) and red ware (bowls and vases). The small antiquities comprise terracotta beads, balls, points and combs of bone and pottery discs. The cultural deposit broadly conforms to the assemblage of Narhan culture. Therefore, this period has been dated between circa 1300 BC and 600 BC.

Period II

Period II is characterised by the NBP ware and its associated ceramic industries. The NBP levels were found to be disturbed in almost all tenches. It has been dated to 600 BC-200 BC.

Period III

Period III was marked by red ware comprising basins, vases and other types of the Kushana and Gupta periods; bangles made of terracotta and glass, iron objects, stone beads and terracotta pestles. Tentatively it has been dated between 200 BC and 500 BC.

Period IV

This site seems to have been deserted for about four centuries, to be re-occupied once again in Period IV. This period was marked by red ware with such characteristic types as spouted vases, cooking vases with flared featureless rim, multi-grooved concave neck carinated to a sagger base; knife-edged bowl with featureless rim and hollow conical knob rising above the rim level. Walls made of burnt bricks have several structural phases and a width of 75 cm. These structures were traced up to a depth of 1.05 m in one of the trenches. This period has been dated between AD 900 and AD 1500.

The settlement was occupied during the British period as well and several burnt brick structures, including dying vats of indigo, are still visible to the west of the present-day Dhuriapar village. Besides, a small fortified area just on the banks of the Kuwana River and located almost in the central part of the mound is believed to represent remains of the fortified settlements of King Dhurchand.

WAINA

Waina is an important protohistoric settlement in Ballia district (Singh, P. *et al.*, 1994-95). This ancient settlement is situated on the main Ballia-

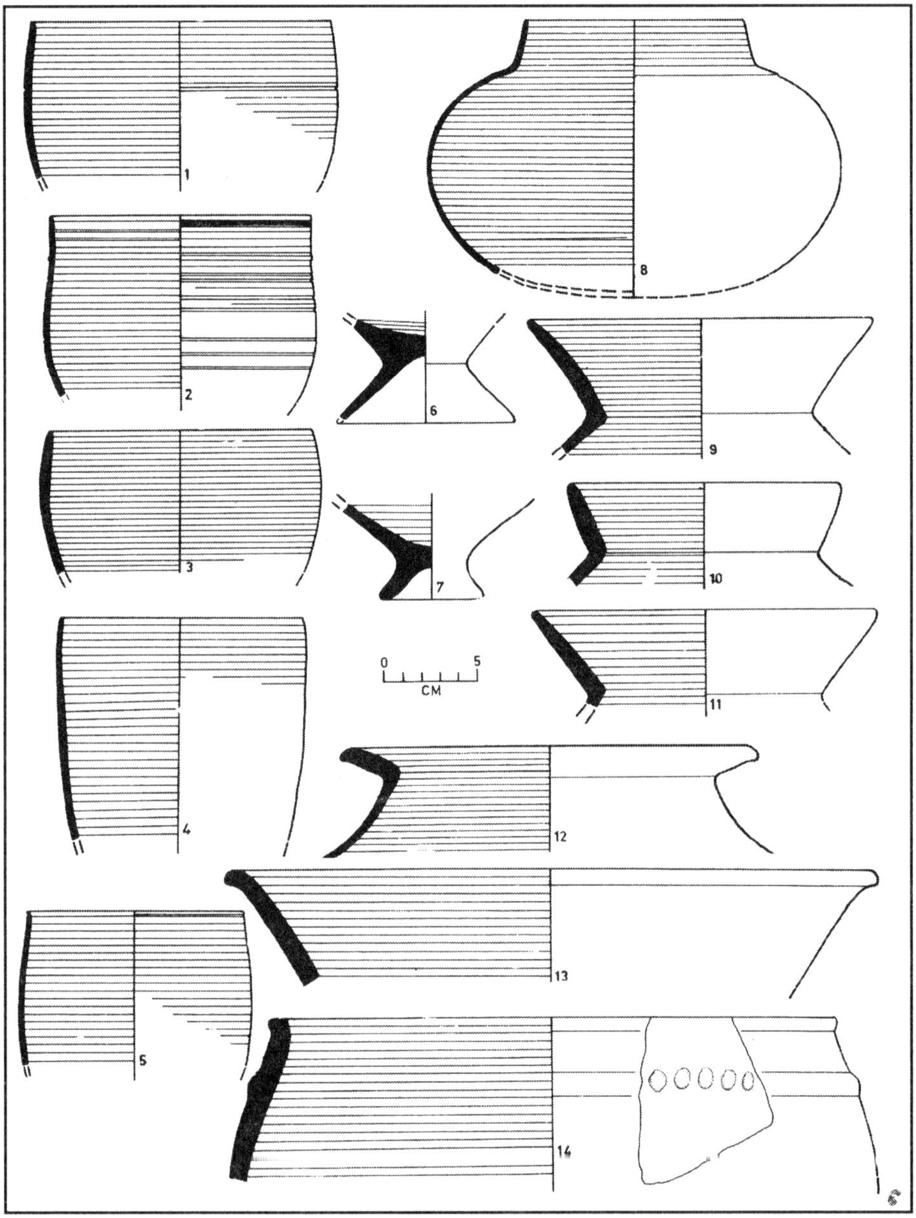

Fig. 19. Waina: Black and red ware shapes

Ghazipur road, about 8 km to the west of Ballia town. The ancient settlement lies on the left bank of the ancient bed of Chhoti Saraju (Tons), which joins the Ganga about 3 km south-east of the present site. It is situated between the Gazipur-Ballia metalled road and the railway line (NER) between Phephana and Ballia. The small railway station of Sagarpali is located about 1.5 km east of Waina.

The ancient settlement is spread over an area of about 10 acres and the extant height of the mound from the surrounding plain is about 7 m. Trial excavation conducted at this site during March-May 1995 yielded a cultural deposit of 8 m divisible into four periods. The earliest period has been further subdivided into IA and IB. The settlement of Period IA was found in the south-west corner of the mound. It is represented by cord-impressed red ware with spouted vessels, bowls and vases as principal types. The pottery assemblage is comparable with pre-Narhan pottery found at Imlidih Khurd (Singh *et al.*, 1995-96: 42).

Bhunadih

The ancient settlement at Bhunadih is located two km east of Janwan on the right bank of Bahera nala, about 28 km north of Ballia town on the Ballia-Sikanderpur road. The mound extends in an area of about 4 acres and the extant height gradually rises to well over a metre. Human activity in recent years has disturbed the stratigraphic position of archaeological relics to a large extent. However, carefully conducted excavation in May-June 1996 (Singh *et al.*, 1997-98: 11-29) resulted into a two-fold culture sequence which is as follows:

Period IA – Pre-Narhan (Neolithic)
Period IB – Overlap phase (between Neolithic and Narhan cultures)
Period II – Narhan culture (Chalcolithic)

Deposits of Period IA were found on the western portion of the mound where 2 m × 2 m test pits were excavated. This resulted into identification of this sub-phase on the basis of ceramic evidence. The pottery of sub-phase is well documented at Imlidih Khurd, represented by cord-impressed red ware, plain red ware with spouted vessels, beakers, and vases. Straight-sided beaker of red ware with short spout (*Martban*) is a new discovery at this site. Other important shapes comprised vessels of red ware with closing mouth and basins of red ware having flaring rim and grooves on the exterior.

The inhabitants of Period IA lived in wattle-and-daub houses represented by burnt clay lumps bearing reed marks. The small finds comprised a few micro beads of steatite, terracotta and pottery discs (Singh *et al.*, 1997-98: 12).

Period IB represents an overlap phase between Neolithic and Narhan culture. The structural activity is the same as in Period IA. The ceramic assemblage of this sub-period is cord-impressed and plain black-and-red ware, black slipped ware and red ware. The principal shapes and characteristic features are pedestal bowl, and dish-on-stand of black-and-red ware, *Lota*-shaped vessels of black slipped ware, post-firing scratching on the exterior (comprising geometric patterns) and a few painted sherds of red ware with dots and dashes. The small finds comprised beads of steatite, terracotta and semi-precious stones and pottery discs.

CHIRAND

Chirand, also called Cherand or Cheran, is situated on the bank of the Ghaghara in district Saran, 11 km west of Chhapra. This site has been mentioned in Hunter's *Statistical District Account* of 1887 who mentions it as on the bank of the Ganga but Carlleyle saw it on the junction of an old river channel (old bed of Ghaghara) with the Ganga. After a long gap of time, this site was visited by A.S. Altekar in July 1954 and on the basis of his exploration, he dated the mounds to the 5th century BC. In June 1960, this site was explored by B.S. Verma who collected sherds of black-and-red ware belonging to the Chalcolithic culture (Verma, 1997: 75). Subsequently, excavations were conducted by the Directorate of Archaeology and Museums, Bihar for seven seasons between 1962-63 and 1972-73 which revealed five cultural periods, viz., Period I (Neolithic), Period II (Chalcolithic), Period III (NBPW culture), Period IV (Sunga-Kushana) and Period V (Pala period).

Period I, covering a 3.5 m thick deposit, has revealed a full-fledged Neolithic culture represented mainly by bone tools and decorated pots, besides other associated finds. Bone (including antler) implements include different types of celts, scrapers, chisels, hammers, needles, points, borers, awls, diggers, a shaft-straightener (*baton de commandment*), pins, styli, tanged and socketed arrow-heads and many unfinished tools, such as the shoulder bone of an ox probably used as a shovel. Bone ornaments are represented by pendants, ear-rings, bangles of ivory and tortoise, bone discs and combs. The neoliths include celts, hammers, pestles, querns, balls, etc. usually made of quartzite, basalt and granite. Microliths are represented by parallel-sided blades, scrapers arrowheads, serrated points, notched blades, points, lunates, borers and a few geometric microliths generally made of chalcedony, chert, agate, jasper, etc. Beads of chalcedony, agate, jasper, marble, steatite and faience represent different types, such as long tubular, long barrel, short barrel, cylindrical, triangular and disc-shaped. Terracotta objects include humped bulls, birds, *nagas*, bangles, beads and punctured decorated objects (Roy in Ghosh, 1989: II: 104).

The Neolithic people of Chirand did not use bone for manufacturing only implements, but also made a number ornaments. Neolithic stone axes were copied in bone in small sizes for making pendants. Bangles and disc were prepared out of tortoise bone. The discovery of a broken comb is also very interesting. A reel-shaped object having perforation horizontally across it, is also remarkable. The people, therefore, seem to have mastered the technique of making all types of tools and ornaments of bone even by drilling the big hour-glass holes. Besides these, they also manufactured ground stone tools. About half a dozen Neolithic celts besides other ground implements, such as hammers were recorded from the excavation. A fairly good number of other rectangular tools, pestles, querns, balls, etc. are worth mentioning. The stones used were quartzite, basalt and granite.

The microlithic industry was an integral part of the Neolithic culture complex of Chirand. The tool types included micro-parallel blades, scrapers, arrow-heads, points, borers, etc. In addition, a few geometrical microliths were also discovered. The materials used for these tools are chalcedony, chert, agate, jasper, etc. Carnelian is totally absent. A fairly good number of nodules and cores were discovered in the course of excavations. It is significant to note that not a single blade has the crested ridge. The frequency of cores and nodules indicates that the microliths were locally manufactured. The source of the raw materials has not yet been determined. However, it is presumed that the nodules were collected from the bed of the river Son which is not far from Chirand.

Among the terracotta objects, humped bull, bird, figurines, *naga* figurines (one is of coiled variety), a female and a male figurine, bangles, beads and balls were reported from the excavations. Two partially broken but giving complete picture of rectangular piece of pendants with incised and punctured decorations are very interesting. One of them had a hole in an appliqué knob on the reverse side. This gives an idea of a modern brooch used by ladies. A small pipe of terracotta, probably a smoking pipe, (soot is found inside) was another significant object. Terracotta wheels were also discovered. One wheel-shaped object (without hole) with convex sides and flat edge with thick section was discovered from this phase. The exact purpose of this object is difficult to determine. A few terracotta discs having hole in the centre have also been discovered. Perhaps they were used as spindle whorls. Many burnt clay pieces in different sizes were also collected from the excavations. Their exact purpose is not yet clear. Several of them had paddy-husk impressions. In one of the burnt clay pieces is an impression of a *pipal* leaf.

There is some indication that in the early phase people lived on floors partially dug underground. It may have been roofed. Later we find them living on level floors with reed walls plastered with mud. A circular paved floor was discovered from the late phase of this period. It measures about 4 m in diameter. This circular hut was provided with oblong ovens. Outside the circular platform, post-holes were located at regular intervals. A fairly large number of burnt chunks of clay with reed or bamboo impressions were discovered close to the hutments suggesting that the houses perished due to fire. They practised community cooking which is proved by the discovery of a series of continuous elongated hearths dug in the floors.

Rice was known to them as paddy-husk impressions have been noticed on some of the burnt clay pieces. It has further been confirmed by the discovery of a few specimens of charred rice along with other charred cereals like wheat, *mung, masoor,* etc. The cereals have been examined by the Birbal Sahni Institute of Palaeobotany, Lucknow. They were not pure vegetarians as is evident from the discovery of a large number of animal and bird bone pieces and sedimented dumps of fish scales. The frequency of bone and lithic tools and weapons indirectly suggests that their main source of livelihood was fishing and hunting. River shells and snails were also eaten since they have been attested by the discovery of their dumps.

The pottery of this period is by and large hand-made. A few examples might have been made by turn-table method. Beating or dabbing was done for shaping the pots. The bulk of the pottery is red ware. However, grey, black and black-and-red ware were also manufactured. The types included vase with broad mouth and narrow neck, spouted vases, several varieties of bowls, footed cup, channel spout, miniature pot, spoon or ladle. Knobbed pottery was also made. A new type representing a miniature hand-made dish in red ware was also discovered. It has double perforations on its four points at equidistance. Post-firing scratched decoration was also done on some pots. In one sherd (burnished portion of shoulder of a pot of red ware) is the representation of a wheel with hub and sixteen spokes in post-firing scratching decoration. In another sherd, there is mat pottery which indicates that they knitted mat out of some kind of reed. Such types of impressed pottery are also mentioned as corded ware by many archaeologists.

An interesting feature of the pottery was the post-firing paintings in red ochre on grey and black-and-red ware. Only the linear design was common. Criss-cross designs in groups of five lines, concentric circle or semi-circle wavy lines, etc. were found on some of the sherds. In one sherd, there is a painting in dots representing *trisula* (trident). Rim band painting was very popular. Similar paintings have been reported from Utnur and Piklihal and probably at Brahmagiri (Verma, 1997: 78).

The skeletal remains from Chirand have been studied by Nath and Biswas (1980: 115-24). In all, twelve species have been identified. They are: cattle, buffalo, sheep (*Ovis areies dolichura Durest*), chital, barasinga, pig, elephant, rhino, dog, a carp and two varieties of turtle.

The Neolithic complex discovered at Chirand with its developed technique in manufacturing of bone articles and in bead making together with post-firing painting in elaborate and variety of designs and highly burnished pottery taken together tend to indicate that it is an advanced Neolithic culture without any knowledge and experience of metal working.

The Neolithic strata representing Period I without any hiatus was succeeded by Period II which has been characterised as the Chalcolithic culture having painted black-and-red ware. This period has been subdivided into two sub-periods – IIA and IIB – due to emergence of iron in the later sub-period; otherwise the assemblages of these two sub-periods remained the same.

Senuwar

Senuwar is located 7 km south of Sasaram in district Rohtas, Bihar. The two seasons' work (1986-87 and 89-90) conducted by the Department of AIHC & Archaeology, Banaras Hindu University, brought to light deposits of four cultural periods: I-IV. I – Neolithic, II – Chalcolithic, III – NBPW phase and IV – Kushana. The earliest Period I is divisible into two sub-periods – IA and IB. Period IA is marked by the presence of copper and thus has been termed Neolithic-Chalcolithic. Both sub-periods IA and IB, however, showed cultural continuity. Period II is chalcolithic in character for a total thickness of 3.30 m occupational deposit. It is represented by (i) unslipped and slipped red ware (the latter being plain as well as painted), (ii) black-on-red ware, (iii) black-and-red ware (plain as well as painted), (iv) black slipped ware (plain as well as painted), (v) burnished black ware (plain as well as painted), (vi) cord-impressed pottery and (vii) rusticated pottery. The excavations at Senuwar had a significant bearing on our knowledge of the Neolithic culture.

The noteworthy copper objects included bangle, tool of indeterminate use, (pin?), ear-ring (?), pendant (?), copper pieces and a potsherd in which a layer of copper is found still adhering throughout on its inner surface. The lithic assemblage consisted of marginally retouched bladelets, partly backed bladelets, flakes, blades and cores. The material employed for manufacturing these tools are chalcedony and chert.

Besides, polished stone axes, hammers, rubber stones, pestles, sling balls, sharpeners, discs, *ukhali*, beads of agate, chalcedony, faience and steatite are also found. The bone tools comprised of borer, point, needle (?), chisel and arrow-head, both socketed and tanged. Among objects of terracotta, mention may be made of beads decorated with incised designs, animal and bird figurine, hop-scotch, stopper, etc. Recovery of grains by flotation method was obtained. The associated strata yielded evidence of the following crops: Rice (*Oryza sativa)*), Barley (*Hordeum vulgare*), Dwarf wheat (*Triticum sphaero coccum),* Bread wheat (*T. aestivum*), Sorghum millet or *jowar* (*Sorghum bicolor*), Chickpea (*Cicer arietinum),* Green gram or mung (*Vigna radiata*), Field pea (*Pisum arvense),* Lentil (*Lens culinaris*), Horse gram (*Dollhos biflorus*), Grass pea (*Lathyrus sativus*), Oil seeds belonging to Sesame or *til* (*Sesamum indicum*) and Linseed (*Linum usitatissimum).*

THE EMERGING PICTURE

The Neolithic people of the Ganga valley as those of the Vindhyas were farming and pastoral communities which is attested by the cultivated variety of rice, barley, wheat, field pea, lentil, green gram, etc. recovered from the excavated sites. However, the botanical evidence obtained from Senuwar and Jhusi in mid Ganga valley read with its counterpart of Tokwa in the Vindhyas suggests that in the early phase only rice and some primitive millets were being cultivated (Misra, 2007). With the passage of time other cereals were also added. The Neolithic deposit at Senuwar is divided into two sub-periods – IA and IB. In the later phase of IA new cereals like barley, wheat, *jowar,* millet, lentil, field pea, finger millet (*ragi*) and *kheshari* were introduced (Saraswat, 2004). The available evidence shows that by the late phase of Neolithic culture in the mid Ganga valley, double crop pattern had become a regular feature. Cereals of the winter and rainy crops including rice (*Oryza sativa*), six rowed hulled barley (*Hordeum vulgare*), bread wheat (*Triticum aestivum*), dwarf wheat (*Triticum sphaerococcum*), lentil (*Lens culinaris*), field pea (*Pisum arvense*), grass pea (*Lathyrus sativus*), horse gram (*Macrotyloma uniflorum*), green gram (*Vigna radiate*), (*Sesamum Indicum*), linseed (*Linum usitatssimum*), etc. have been reported from the early levels of Jhusi (Pokharia *et al*., 2009).

Domesticated animals include cattle (*Bos indicus*), buffalo (*Bubalus bubalis*), sheep, goat and pigs. Domesticated pig has been found from Senuwar. Domesticated mammals that were not included in food are dog and cat. Besides these, the bones of elephants, rhinoceros, stag, deer, etc. have also been found from some of the sites. Of aquatic fauna whose bones have been found, mention may be made of fish and turtle. Bones of birds have also been found. That meat was part of their diet is attested by charred bone fragments and bones with sharp cut marks (Joglekar *et al.*, 2008). The available evidence, thus, indicates that besides agriculture and domestication the Neolithic people of the mid Ganga plain also practised hunting, catching and fishing (Pal, 2009: 10).

The Neolithic culture of the Ganga plain is marked by a rich and varied ceramic industry. The available evidence indicates that in the early stage of the culture, as indicated at Chirand, Lahuradewa, Jhusi and Hetapatti, people were using hand-made pottery but subsequently the slow wheel appears to have been used for the purpose. The ceramic assemblage includes cord-impressed ware, ordinary red ware, lustrous red ware, burnished ware (red, black and grey), rusticated ware and crude black-and-red ware. The clay used for manufacturing the pots is not well levigated. It contains grits, husks and chaff as degraissant. Pots are generally ill-fired and have blackish grey core. Pottery types including bowls with varying profile, vases, vessels, basins, miniature *jars, handis,* etc. suggest that these were used for storing, cooking and also kitchen wares. A large number of vases with rustication and soot mark on outer surface indicate that these were also used for cooking, possibly for boiling rice. Bowls, basins and vases also have sometimes spouts, suggesting consumption of liquid or semi-liquid food. The cord-impressed pottery is a distinguishing feature. Some times rustication or burnishing is done on the cord-impressed surface. A variety of patterns in cording have been found at Jhusi and Hetapatti. Some of the pots, generally vases, were made in two parts separately – the body and the rim portion and subsequently these were luted together. This feature was noticed in the ceramics of Imlidih Khurd. Spouts were also luted to the bowls or basins after making then separately. Painted sherds have also been reported from Imlidih Khurd, Lahuradewa, Chirand and Senuwar. The post-firing paintings in red ochre confined to the rim of pots were found at Chirand and Senuwar. The painted motifs consist of linear designs of criss-cross lines and concentric circles. At Imlidih Khurd painting executed in white red pigment over a bright slip has been found. Post-firing scratch designs consisting of generally geometric patterns like opposed triangles with concentric circles and floral motifs is another feature of decorating the pots. Scratching is done by sharp instruments. Appliqué decorations, especially on the shoulder of basins and *handis,* also have been found at many sites. On these appliqué are executed chain and rope patterns or incised decorations. Wheel-thrown pots are also reported from the late Neolithic phase of some of the sites like Senuwar (Pal, 2009: 12).

As revealed from the excavated sites, the culture is associated with microlithic industry. Microlithic element is comparatively more prolific at the sites which are nearer to the Vindhyas. Bladelets, flakes, blades, scrapers, arrowheads, serrated points, lunates, borers, etc. fashioned on chert, chalcedony, agate, jasper and quartz has been found form some of the sites like Chirand, Maner, Jhusi, etc. However, celts of basalt and granite has been obtained from Lahuradewa, Chirand and Senuwar. Heavy-duty stone objects included fragments of querns, mullers, balls, hammer stones, etc. fashioned on sandstone or quartzite. Spindle whorls also have been found from many sites. Beads finished and unfinished and fashioned on chalcedony, agate, etc. have been found at Jhusi, Chirand and Senuwar. Chirand, Imlidih Khurd, Lahuradewa, Jhusi and Hetapatti have also yielded micro-beads of steatite and/or faience.

Bone tools have been found at Jhusi, Senuwar and Chirand. The last site has yielded a corpus of bone tools and weapons including celts, scrapers, chisels, hammers, needles, points, borers, awls, arrowheads, etc. Other bone objects comprise ornaments like pendants, earrings, bangles discs, comb, etc.

CHRONOLOGY

The problem of the antiquity of the Neolithic culture of the region is still not finally settled but now we have some relevant C^{14} dates from the excavated Neolithic sites of the Vindhyas and Ganga plain. Considering three of C^{14} dates reading 4530±185 BC (PRL 101), 5440±240 BC (PRL 100) and 6570±210 BC (PRL 224) obtained from Koldihwa as dependable, the culture was dated to the 7th-6th millennium BC (Sharma *et al.*, 1980). But being the only site of such antiquity, doubts were raised by several scholars. The C^{14} date belonging to the transitional phase of the Neolithic to Chalcolithic at Koldihwa is 1440±120 BC (PRL 223). The absolute dates obtained from Mahagara also indicated a late date to the culture, though these dates have the possibility of contamination of samples. Two TL dates reading 2265 BC and 1616 BC and four C^{14} dates reading 1440±150 BC (PRL 409), 1330±120 BC (PRL 408), 1440±100 BC (PRL 407) and 1480±110 BC (BSIP) have been obtained from the samples from Mahagara. These dates are not consistent with the stratigraphy possibly due to contamination of samples. In the light of calibrated C^{14} date obtained from Kunjhun, reading 3530-3335, the beginning of the Vindhyan Neolithic culture was proposed to 4th millennium BC. Three C^{14} dates have come to light from recent excavations at Lahuradewa in the middle Gangetic plain, which read as

5320±90 BP (BS 1951) (Cal. BC 4220, 4196, 4161) and 6290±160 BP (BS 1966) (Cal BC 5298) (Tewari *et al.*, 2001-2002, 2002-2003). Recently three relevant C^{14} dates have been obtained from Tokwa. When calibrated these read 6591 BC (BS 2417), 5976 BC (BS 2369), 4797 BC (BS 2464). An AMS C^{14} date for a carbonised domesticated rice would push the antiquity of the Neolithic culture at Lahuradewa in 7th millennium BC (Tewari *et al.*, 2004-2005: 40). From the Neolithic horizon of Jhusi, three C^{14} dates have been obtained. These dates when calibrated read 7477 BC (BS 2526), 5837 BC (BS 2524) and 6196 BC (BS 2525). The earliest date obtained from the site would put the beginning of the Neolithic culture of the site in 8th millennium BC (Pal, 2008: 277).

Regarding the span of the Neolithic culture, the observation of P. Singh is very significant, "domestication was a process which took considerable time and domestication of each type of domesticable animal and plant species would have been taken place in different ecological niches at different times" (Singh, 1991: 5; Singh, 2002: 128). In the Ganga plain, Neolithic culture and Neolithic way of life lasted for a long time starting from 8th-7th millennium BC to 3rd-2nd millennium BC (Pal, 2009: 15-16).

Table 1. Early C^{14} dates from Neolithic sites

Site	Calibrated C^{14} dates	Remark
Koldihwa	4530 ± 185 BC=5432-5051 BC, 5440 ± 240 BC=6190-5764 BC, 6570 ± 210 BC=7505-7033 BC (Chakrabarti 2006: 216)	On the Belan in the Vindhyas
Tokwa	4797 BC, 5976 BC, 6407 BC	On the confluence of the Belan and Adwa in the Vindhyas
Kunjhum	1565 BC, 2675 BC, 3530 BC	On the right bank of the Son in the Vindhyas
Lahuradewa	4220 BC, 5298 BC, An AMS date 6442-6376 (mid-7th millennium BC); three more new and early radiocarbon dates from Lahuradewa are: 8317-8555 (8436), 8340-8696 (8518). 8813-9171 (8992)	On the bank of a horseshoe lake in the mid Ganga plain
Jhusi	7110 BC, 5649 BC, 5938 BC, later half of 8th millennium BC	On the confluence of the Ganga and Yamuna

REFERENCES

Alur, K.R. 1980. Faunal remains from the Vindhyas and the Ganga Valley, in G.R. Sharma, V.D. Misra, D. Mandal, B.B. Misra and J.N. Pal (eds.), *Beginning of Agriculture*, Allahabad, Abinash Prakashan: 201-227.

Charurvedi, S.N. 1985. Advance of Vindhyan Neolithic and Chalcolithic cultures to the Himalayan Tarai, *Man and Environment*, IX: 101-108.

Joglekar, P.P, V.D. Misra, J.N. Pal and M.C. Gupta. 2008. Faunal Remains from Neolithic-Chalcolithic phases at Tokwa, Mirzapur District, Uttar Pradesh, *Man and Environment*, XXXIII (2): 51-59.

Misra, V.D. 1977. *Some Aspects of Indian Archaeology*, Allahabad, Prabhat Prakashan.

———. 2007. Stone Age Cultures, their Chronology and Beginnings of Agriculture in the North-Central India, *Man and Environment*, XXXII (1): 1-4.

Misra, V.D., B.B. Misra, J.N. Pandey and J.N. Pal. 1995-96. A Preliminary Report of Excavation at Jhusi-1995, *Pragdhara*, No. 6: 63-66.

Misra, V.D., J.N. Pal and M.C. Gupta. 1999-2000. Further Excavation at Jhusi, District Allahabad (Uttar Pradesh), *Pragdhara*, No. 10: 22-30.

———. 1998-99. Further Excavation at Jhusi, District Allahabad (Uttar Pradesh), *Pragdhara*, No. 9: 45-50.

Misra, V.D., B.B. Misra, J.N. Pal and M.C. Gupta. 2000. Exploration at Tokwa: A Neolithic Chalcolithic Settlement on the Confluence of the Belan and Adwa Rivers, in S.C. Bhattacharya, V.D. Misra, J.N. Pandey and J.N. Pal (eds.), *Peeping through the Past: Prof. G.R. Sharma Memorial Volume*, Department of Ancient History, Culture & Archaeology, University of Allahabad: 45-57.

Nath, B. and M.K. Biswas. 1980. Animals Remains from Chirand, Saran District, Bihar, *Rec. Zool. Survey India*, Vol. 76: 115-124.

Narain, A.K. and T.N. Roy. 1977. *Excavations at Rajghat*, Part I, Varanasi, Banaras Hindu University.

———. *Excavations at Prahladpur*, Varanasi, Banaras Hindu University.

Pal, J.N. 1983. Base of the Neolithic Culture of the Middle Ganga Valley, *(Baldev Upadhyaya Felicitation Volume of the G. N. Jha Kendriya Sanskrit Vidyapeeth)*: 205-16.

———. 1986. *Archaeology of Southern Uttar Pradesh, Ceramic Industries of Northern Vindhyas*, Allahabad, Swabha Prakashan.

———. 1987. Neolithic Cord-impressed ware of the Vindhyas, *Man and Environment*, XI: 61-65.

———. 2000. Mesolithic and Neolithic Societies of the Vindhyas in the Middle Ganga Plan, in V.D. Misra and J.N. Pal (eds.), *Social History and Social Theory*, Allahabad, University of Allahabad: 7-13.

———. 2008a. Recent Excavations at Tokwa: Fresh Light on the Early farming Culture of the Vindhyas, in Lallanji Gopal and V.C. Srivastava (eds.), *History of Agriculture in Ancient India (upto. C. 1200 AD)*, New Delhi, Concept Publishing Company: 48-69.

———. 2008b. The Early Farming Culture of the Middle Ganga Plain with Special Reference to the Excavation of Jhusi and Hetapatti, *Pragdhara*, No. 18: 263-282.

_____. The Early Farming Culture of the Northern Vindhyas, *Bulletin of the Deccan College Post-Graduate Research Institute*, Vol. 49: 297-310.

_____. 2009. Beginnings of Agriculture in the Middle Ganga Plain, Sectional Presidential Address (Ancient Section). U.P. History Congress, XXth Session, VBS Purvanchal University, Jaunpur. October 3-4, 2009.

Pokharia, A.K., J.N. Pal and Alka Srivastava. 2009. Plant macro remains from Neolithic Jhusi in Ganga Plain: Evidence for grain-based agriculture, *Current Science*, Vol. 97, No. 4, 25August: 564-572.

Possehl, G.L. and Paul C. Rissman. 1992. The Chronology of prehistoric India: From Earliest Times to the Iron Age, in Robert W. Ehrich (ed.), *Chronologies in Old World Archaeology*, Vol. I, India. The University of Chicago Press, Chicago and London: 461.

Rao, S.N. 1977. Excavation at Sarutaru, *Man and Environment*, I: 39-43.

Rivett-Carnac, H. 1882. Stone implements found in Bundelkhand, *Proceedings of the Asiatic Society of Bengal.*

Roy, S.R. 1989. Chirand, in A. Ghosh (ed.).

Shahu, B.P. 1988. *From Hunters to Breeders*, Delhi, Anamika Prakashan.

Sharma, G.R. and D. Mandal. 1980. *Excavations at Mahagara*, Allahabad.

Sharma, T.C. 1966. *Prehistoric Archaeology of Assam*. Unpublished Ph. D. Thesis, London University, London.

_____. 1997. The Neolithic Pattern of Eastern India, in V.D. Misra and J.N. Pal (eds.), *Peeping through the Past: Prof. G.R. Sharma Memorial Volume*, Allahabad.

Singh, B.P. 1989-90. The Chalcolithic Culture of Southern Bihar as revealed by the Exploration and Excavations in District Rohtas, *Puratattva*, No. 20: 83-92.

_____. 1995-96. Transformation of Cultures in the Middle Ganga Plain: A case study of Senuwar, *Pragdhara*, No. 6: 75-94.

Singh, P. and A.K. Singh. 1995-96. Trial excavations at Waina, District Ballia, U.P., *Pragdhara*, No. 6: 41-61.

_____. 1997-98. Trial excavations at Bhunadih, District Ballia, U.P., *Pragdhara*, No. 8: 11-29.

Singh, P. 1991-92. Excavation at Imlidih Khurd, *Puratattva*, No. 22: 120-22.

_____. 1991-92. Trial Digging at Dhuriapar, *Pragdhara*, No. 2: 55-60.

_____. 1992. Neolithic-Chalcolithic Cultures of Eastern U.P., in Rakesh Tewari (ed.), *Archaeological Perspectives of Uttar Pradesh and Future Prospects*, Part I, Lucknow: 67-76.

_____. 1992-93. Archaeological Excavations at Imlidih Khurd-1992, *Pragdhara*, No. 3: 21-36.

_____. 1993-94. Further Excavations at Imlidih Khurd-1993, *Pragdhara*, No. 4: 41-48.

_____. 1999. Rise of Cultures in Eastern India, in G.C. Pande (ed.), *History of Indian Science, Philosophy and Culture*, Vol. No. I, The Indian Council of Philosophical Research, New Delhi.

Singh, S.K. 2000-2001. Lithic industries of Waina, District Ballia, U.P., *Pragdhara*, No. 11: 105-107.

Tewari, R., R.K. Srivastava and K.K. Singh. 2002. Excavations at Lahuradewa, District Sant Kabir Nagar, Uttar Pradesh, *Puratattva*, No. 32: 54-62.

Tewari, R., R.K. Srivastava, K.K. Singh, K.S. Saraswat and I.B. Singh. 2002-2003. Preliminary Report on the Excavations at Lahuradewa, District Sant Kabir Nagar, U.P. 2001-2002: Wider Archaeological Implications, *Pragdhara,* No. 13: 37-68.

Tewari, R., R.K. Srivastava, K.K. Singh, K.S. Saraswat, I.B. Singh, M.S. Chauhan, A.K. Pokharia, A. Saxena, V. Prasad and M. Sharma. 2006a. Second Preliminary Report of the Excavation of Lahuradewa, District Sant Kabir Nagar, U.P. 2002-2003-2004 & 2005-06, *Pragdhara,* No. 16: 35-63.

Tewari, Rakesh, R.K. Srivastava, K.K. Singh and K.S. Saraswat. 2006b. Further Excavations at Lahuradewa, District Sant Kabir Nagar, U. P. 205-06: Preliminary Observations, *Puratattva,* No. 36: 68-75.

Verma, B.S. 1997. A Short Note on Chirand Excavations, in J.P. Joshi (ed.), *Facets of Indian Civilization: Recent Perspectives,* (Essays in Honour of Professor B.B. Lal), New Delhi, Aryan Books International, Vol. I: 75-80.

5

The Chalcolithic Cultures

The Neolithic phase in the Middle Ganga Plain and the Vindhyas was succeeded by the Chalcolithic cultures. There is no time gap between the two cultures and a gradual evolution from the former to the latter has been witnessed at a number of sites. Excavations at sites like Koldihwa, Sohgaura, Imlidih Khurd, Waina, Bhunadih, Chirand, Chechar and Senuwar have furnished evidence pertaining to the transitional stage from the preceding Neolithic culture of the region to the Chalcolithic. The only perceptible change during the Chalcolithic is the introduction of copper in this region sometime in the later half of third millennium BC, which resulted into a tremendous economic activity further leading to agricultural surplus in a big way and the consequent increase in human population. Whereas the Neolithic settlements were few and far between, in the Chalcolithic phase the number as well as size of the settlements increased several-fold. Exploration carried out in 14600 sq. km area has revealed more than 200 sites. Of these, about two dozen sites have so far been excavated (Misra, B.B., 2000: 66). Important among them are Kakoria, Magha, Koldihwa, Khajuri, Banimilia-Bahera, Takiaper, Malhar, Raja Nal Ka Tila in the Vindhyas and Jhusi, Kausambi, Sringaverapura, Rajghat, Prahladpur, Masondih, Sohgaura, Narhan, Imlidih Khurd, Khairadih, Chirand, Chechar, Maner, Oriup, Champa, Sonpur, Taradih, Manjhi and Senuwar in the Ganga valley. The general features of the Chalcolithic culture in the Vindhyan hills can be listed as follows:

The Chalcolithic inhabitants lived in wattle-and-daub structures, circular or oval on plan and in houses having mud walls. The ceramic assemblage comprises the red ware, the black slipped ware and black-

and-red ware. The pots are usually wheel-thrown though hand-made specimens are also met with. The red ware, the most prolific ceramic industry, is characterised by the bowl, including the lipped and pedestalled varieties, with convex sides and everted rim; convex or straight-sided dishes with sagger or flat base; shallow disc, basin including the lipped variety and storage jar. The types in black-and-red ware include the deep carinated lipped or pedestalled bowl; dish with convex or straight sides and sagger base; small vase, basin, and straight sided troughs. Though in general the pottery is plain, decoration in the form of paintings, incisions and applied patterns are also met with.

Microliths consisting of cores, flakes and finished tools – parallel-sided, blunted back, and serrated blades, points, lunates, scrapers and triangles, fashioned on chalcedony, chert, agate, carnelian, etc. have also been found. The assemblage is characterised by the crested ridge technique. From Koldihwa have also been obtained tanged and socketed bone arrowheads. The use of copper appears to have been very limited. Only a few fragments have been found. Mention may be made of a thin knife from Koldihwa. Beads of semi-precious stones and terracotta, sling balls of stone and clay, querns and mullers are the other objects. At Kakoria the Chalcolithic culture is characterised by Megalithic monuments. The tombs – cairn circles, cists and cists within cairn circles – were located at the foot of the Hathinia and Bhadahawan hillocks. Out of hundreds, 12 monuments, which have been excavated, have yielded sherds of the red, black slipped and black-and-red ware, identical in shape and fabric with their counterparts of the habitation area, located at Kakoria. Among the other antiquities obtained from the burials, mention may be made of a gold bangle, microliths and jaw and teeth of the bovid. A C14 date of 3390+120 BP has been obtained from the chalcolithic horizons of Koldihwa. Misra proposes a time-bracket ranging from the later half of the second millennium to the early centuries of the first millennium BC for this culture.

The Chalcolithic cultures of the middle Ganga region have been documented in the excavations at Chirand, Sonpur, Oriup and other sites. At the first two sites the Chalcolithic people lived in houses made of mud plaster, reeds or bamboos. The 5.50 m thick Chalcolithic deposit at Chirand revealed in its earliest level a circular hearth and post-holes and floors of burnt earth. The exposed lime floors at Sonpur had circular pits representing circular huts, with varying diameters of 1.84 to 2.44 m and with bones of animals and birds inside (Roy in Ghosh, 1989: I: 98-99).

The ceramic industry is represented by kiln-burnt plain and painted black-and-red, black, steel grey and red ware. The pottery, of sandy clay and porous section, is both wheel-turned and hand-made and has a thick

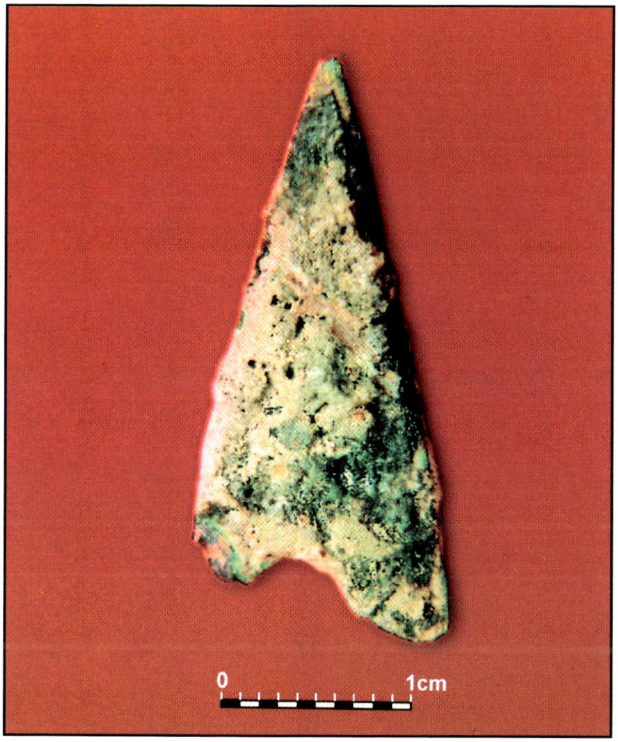

Pl. IXA. Lahuradewa: Copper arrowhead, Period IB

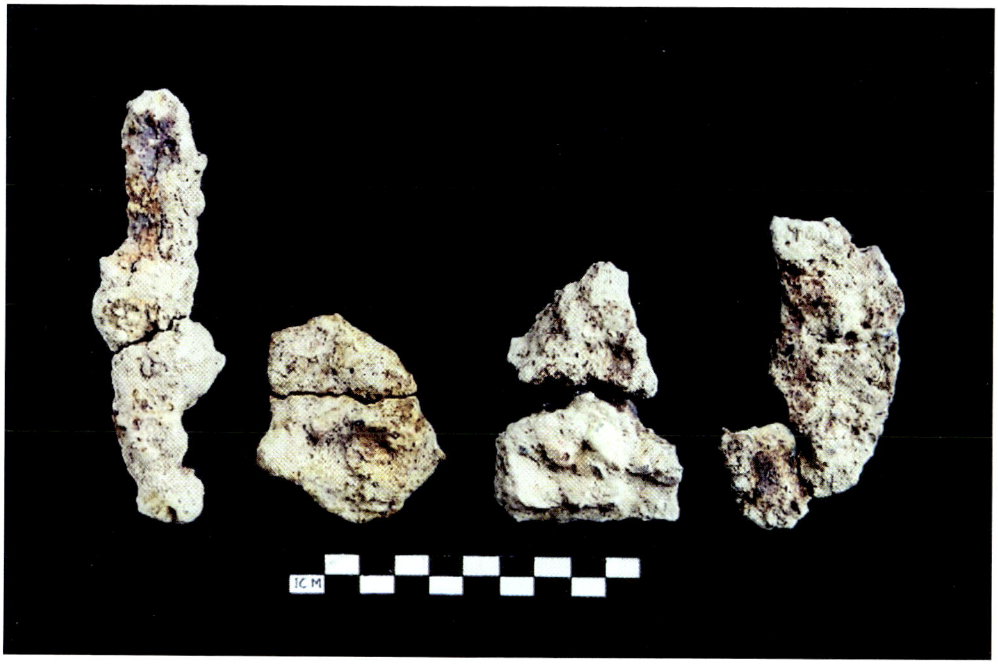

Pl. IXB. Lahuradewa: Broken iron implements, Period III

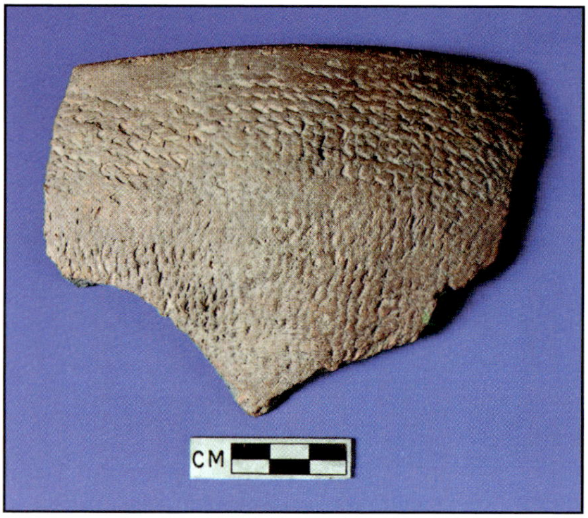

Pl. XA. Imlidih Khurd: Cord Impressed Ware, Period I

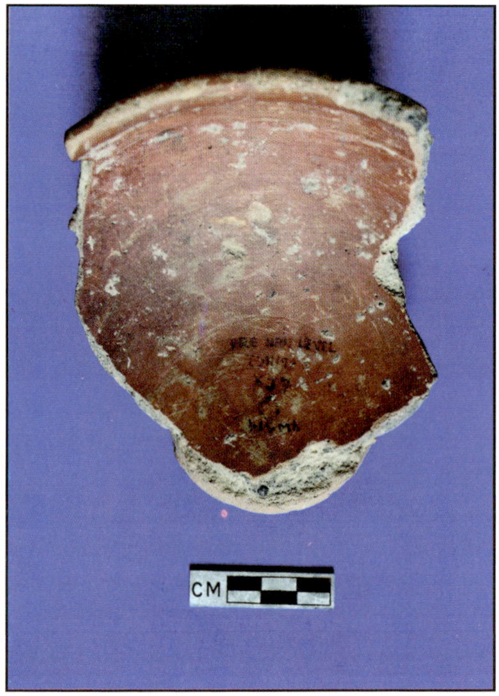

Pl. XI. Imlidih Khurd: Bowl of Cord Impressed Ware, Period I

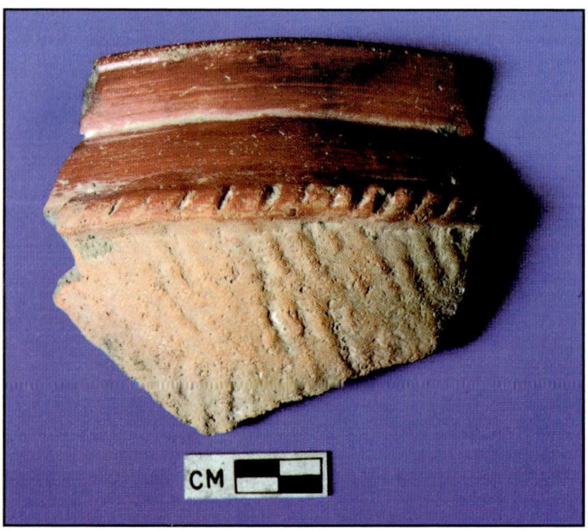

Pl. XB. Imlidih Khurd: Cord Impressed Ware Period I

Pl. XIIA. Imlidih Khurd: Painted Red Ware, Period I

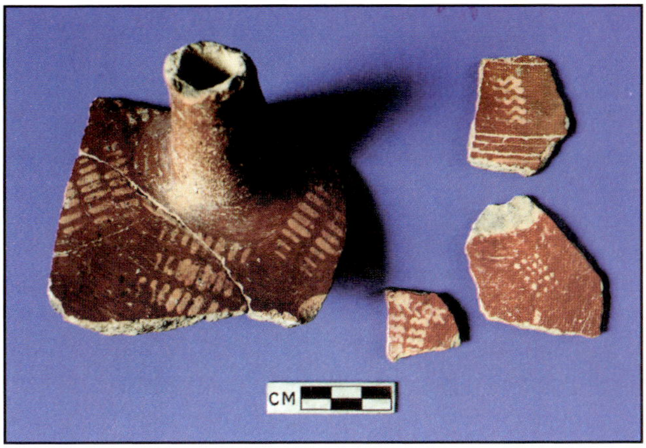

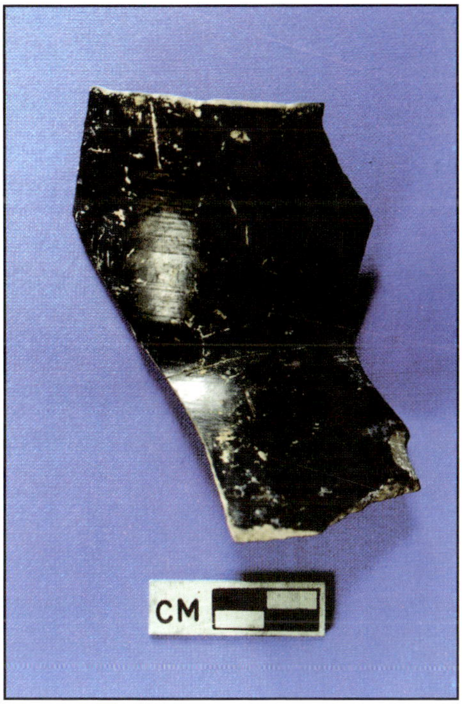

Pl. XIIB. Imlidih Khurd: Painted Black Slipped Ware, Period II

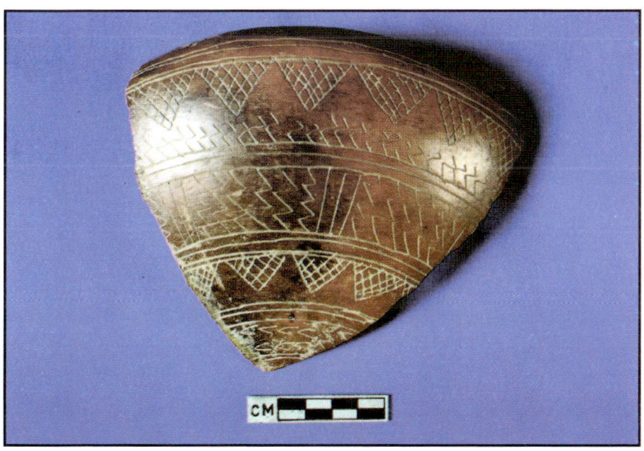

Pl. XIII. Imlidih Khurd: Post-firing scratched designs, Period I

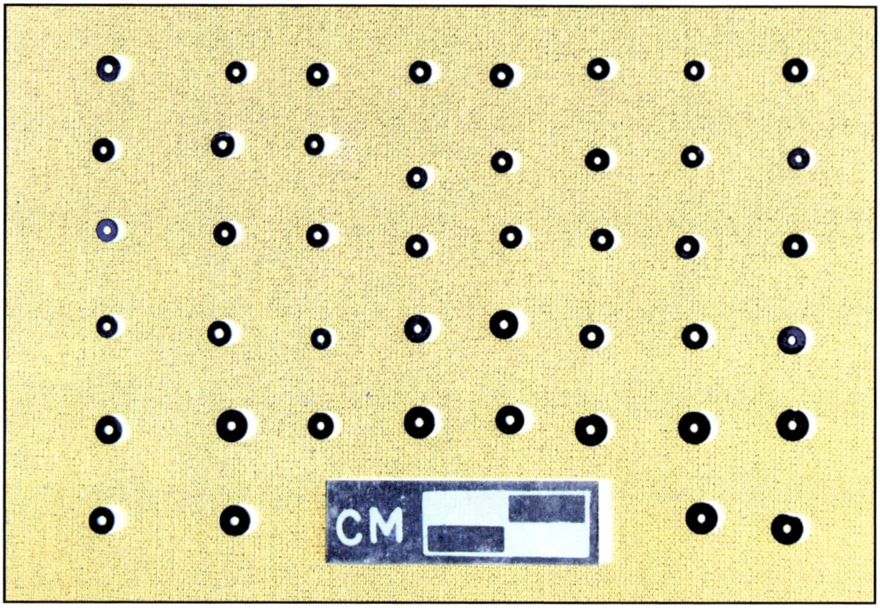

Pl. XIVA. Imlidih Khurd: Steatite beads

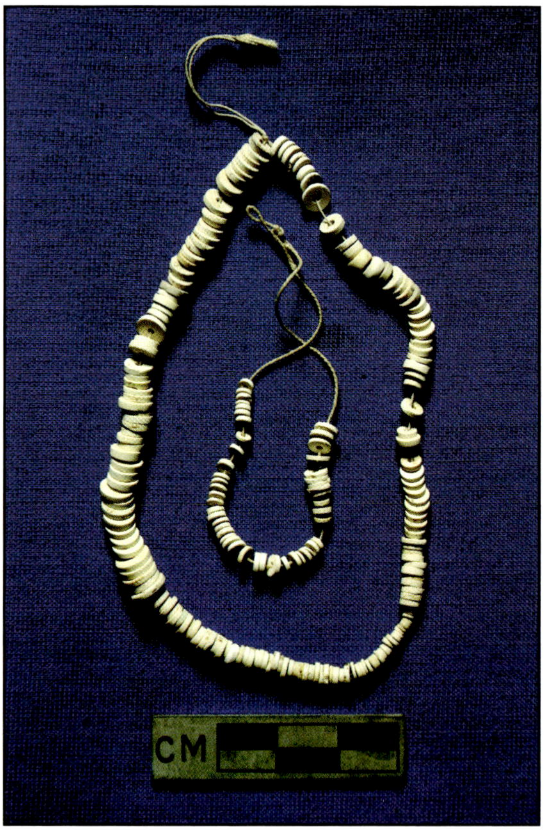

Pl. XIVB. Imlidih Khurd: Steatite beads

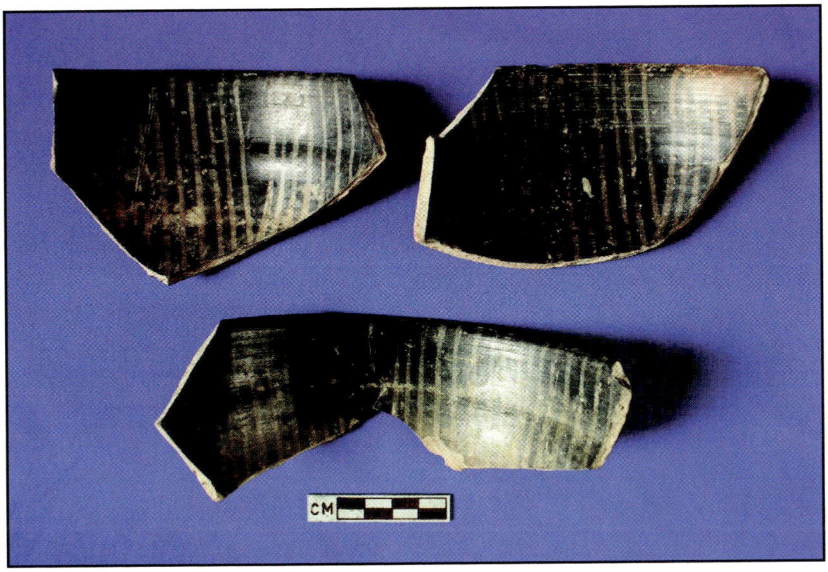

Pl. XVA. Narhan: Painted Black-and-Red Ware, Period I

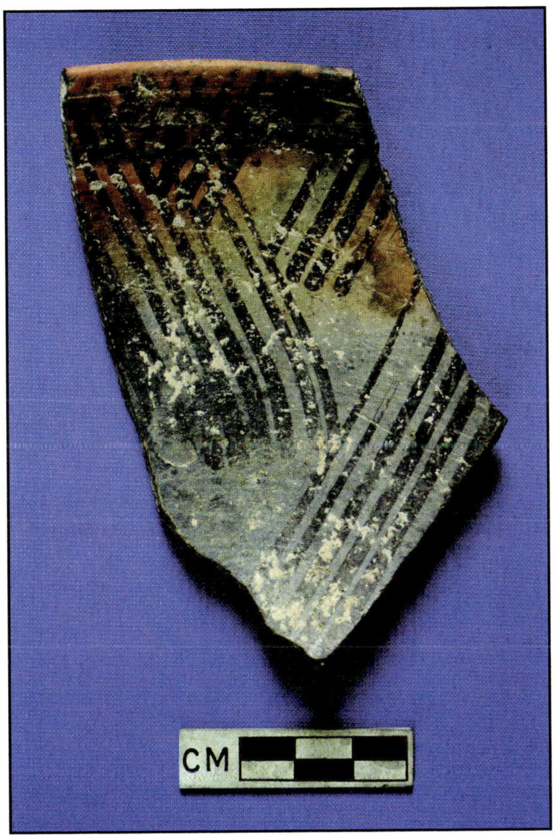

Pl. XVB. Narhan: Painted Black-and-Red Ware, Period I

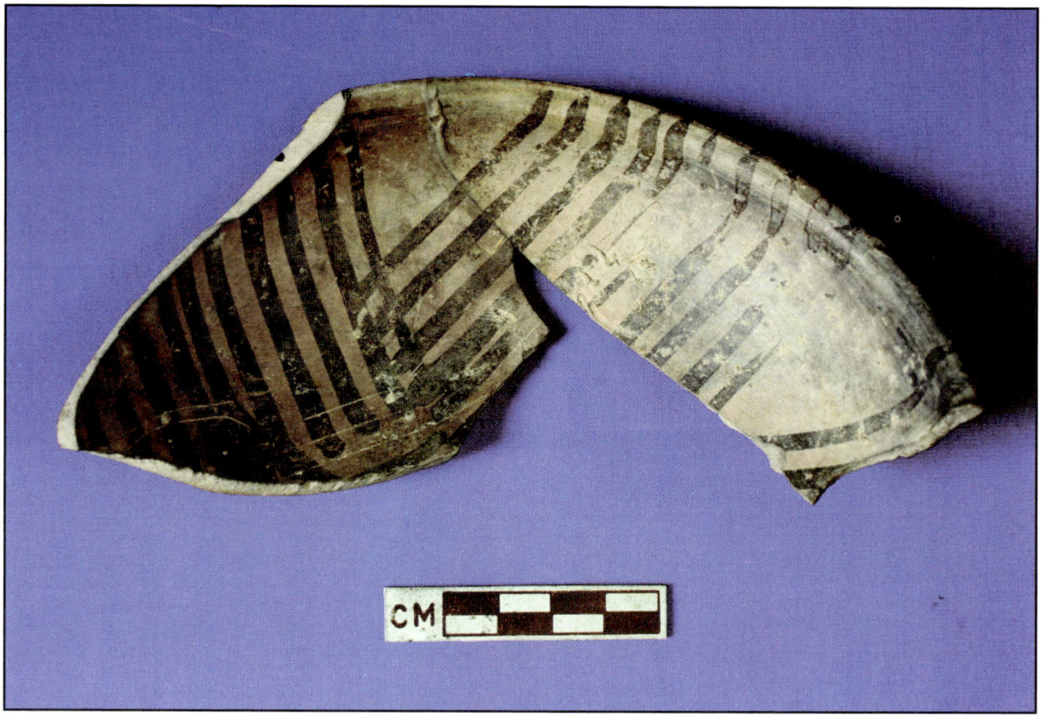

Pl. XVIA. Narhan: Painted Black-and-Red Ware, Period I

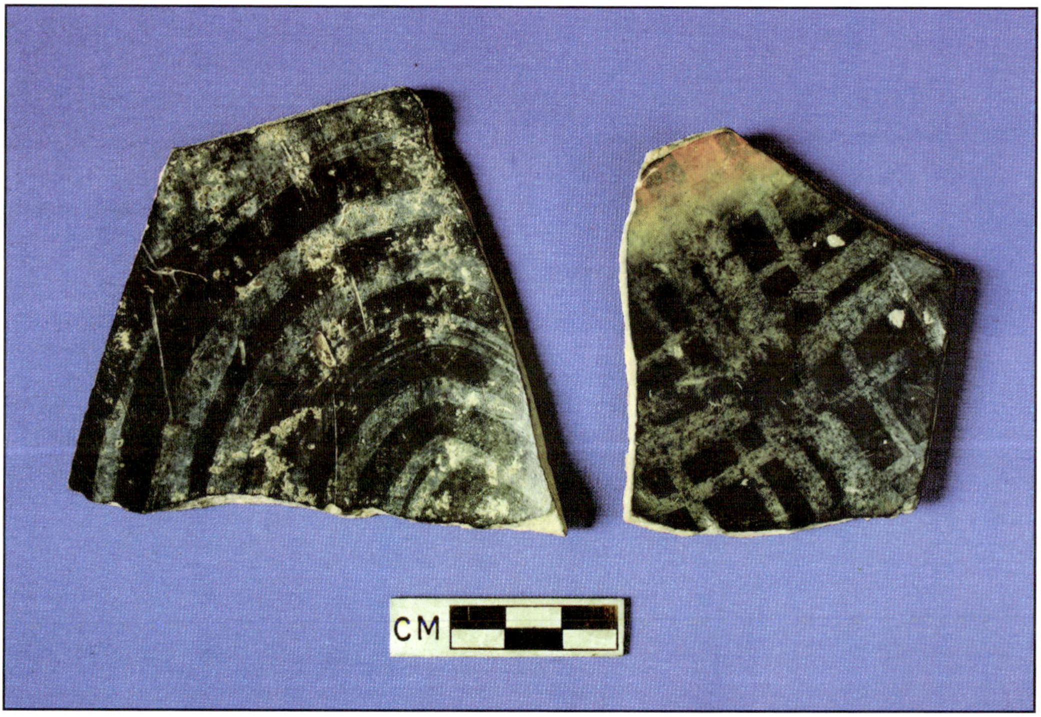

Pl. XVIB. Narhan: Painted Black-and-Red Ware, Period I

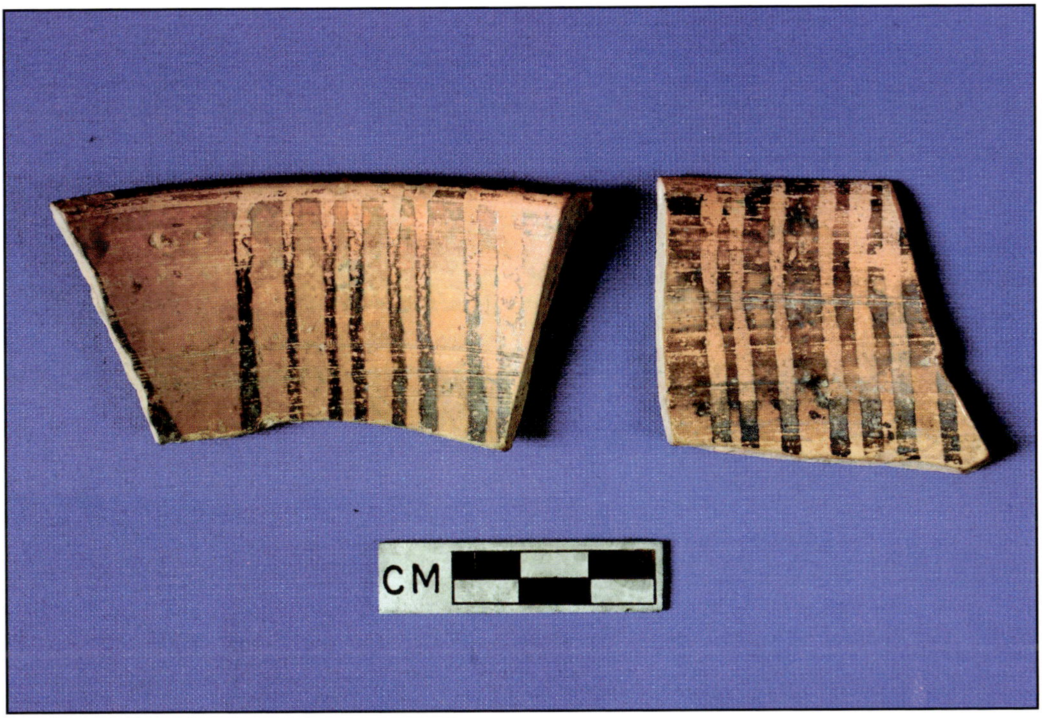

Pl. XVIIA. Narhan: Painted Red Ware, Period I

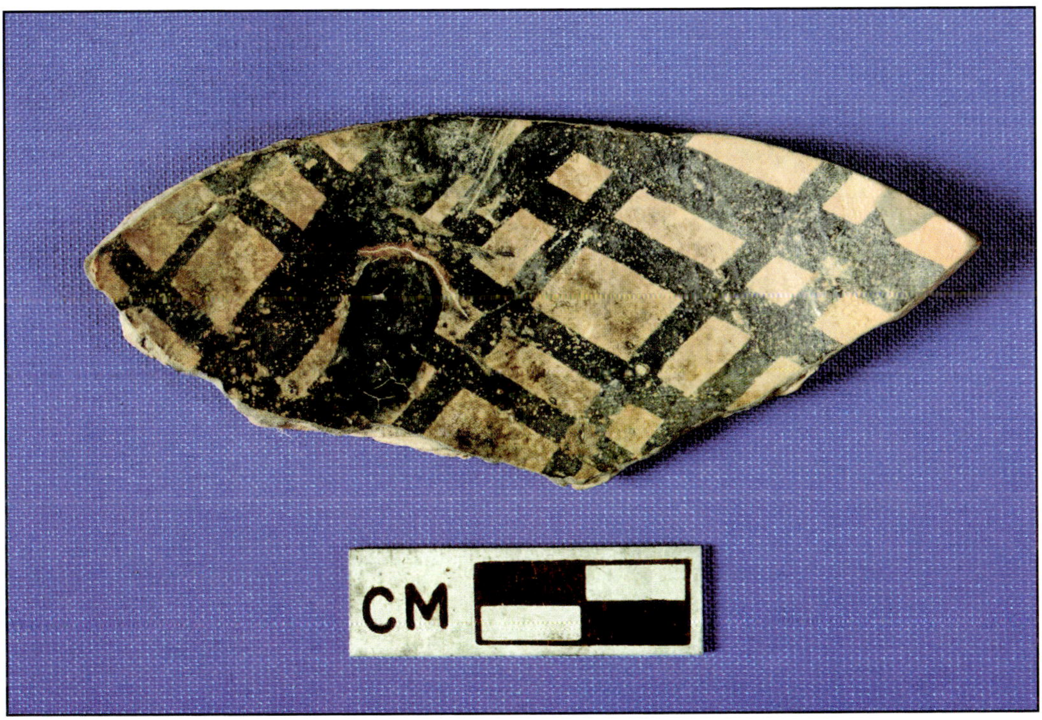

Pl. XVIIB. Narhan: Painted Red Ware, Period I

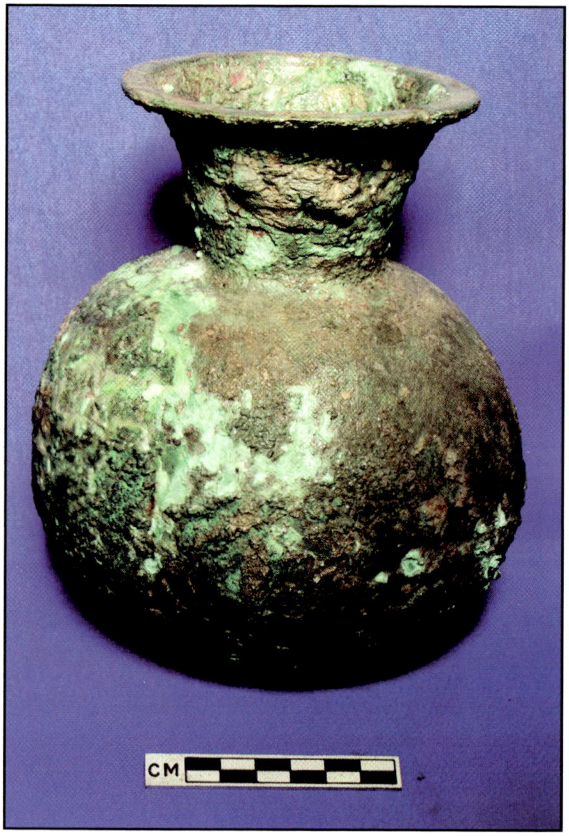

Pl. XVIIIA. Agiabir: Copper vessel (*Lota*), Period III

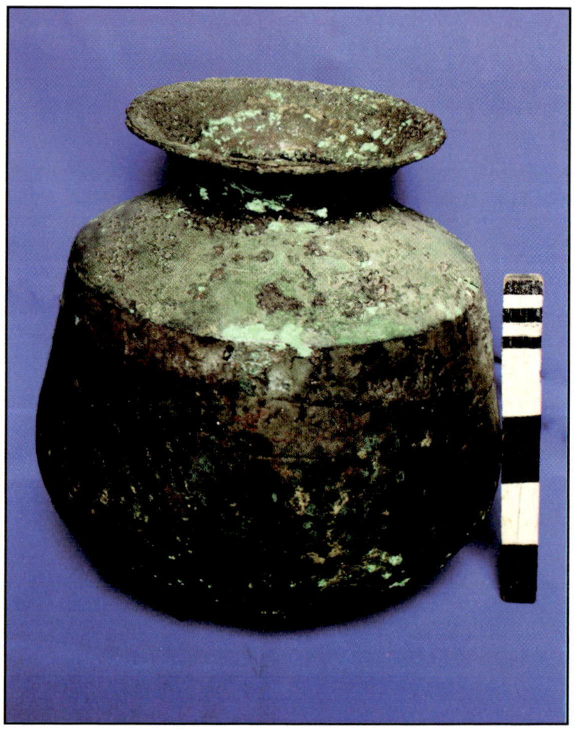

Pl. XVIIIB. Agiabir: Copper vessel (*Handa*), Period III

slip over it. The early specimens of Sonpur are brittle and too small to indicate any shape, but the types at Chirand include dish-on-stand, long-necked jar, lipped bowl, basin, bowl with ring base, spouted vessel, four-legged and ring-based perforated pot in black-and-red ware, and high-necked jar, lipped bowl, basin; bowl with ring base, spouted vessel, *lota* with corrugated shoulders in black slipped ware. Generally bowls and dishes bear painted designs comprising groups of wavy and straight lines or dashes executed in white on black surface.

The negligible occurrence of copper objects, which include a few small corroded pieces from Sonpur and Chirand, a bead from Chirand and a bangle piece from Oriup reflects the scarcity of the metal. Microliths from the sites are represented by cores, waste flakes, blades and numerous small nodules of carnelian, chalcedony, quartz and chert. The appearance of iron in the uppermost Chalcolithic levels of Sonpur and Chirand is significant. A similar situation obtains at Narhan also.

The other associated finds from Sonpur and Chirand include tanged and socketed arrowheads having circular or square section and pins of bone, arrowheads of ivory and styli of both materials. Besides, there are terracotta beads, some pear-shaped and some others with incised decorations, beads of steatite, chalcedony, etc., balls, pestles and querns of stone, bones of birds and fish and a few Neolithic celts from Chirand.

The post-cremation circular pit-burials at Sonpur and suspected such burials at Chirand are noteworthy (Roy in Ghosh, 1989, I: 99). The Sonpur burials having diameters of 1.82 to 2.12 m and a depth of 91 cm and containing ash, charred bone pieces and sherds of black, red and black-and-red wares and a hand-made jar with 5 kg of charred rice, suggests that the people burnt their dead and buried their charred bones, and also cultivated rice.

In the Sarayupar plain, the Chalcolithic cultures have been identified at Sohgaura, Narhan, Khairadih, Waina, Bhunadih and other sites. At all these sites, this phase is characterised by the occurrence of black-and-red ware (plain and painted), black slipped ware (plain and painted), red ware (both slipped and unslipped), burnished black ware, cord-impressed pottery and rusticated ware. The last three ware are found in limited number. At Narhan the painted black slipped ware is meagre, the prominent ware being the painted black-and-red ware. About twenty per cent sherds in this ware are reported. On the contrary, the painted black slipped ware is the prominent industry at Khairadih (Singh, 1992: 78).

Other common noteworthy finds found at Khairadih, Narhan and Sohgaura constituted beads of agate, chalcedony, carnelian, jasper, steatite, socketed and tanged arrowheads of bone, points, pottery discs, etc. Terracotta beads decocrated with incised designs are common to both Khairadih and Sohgaura. At Khairadih, the use of glass is attested by the presence of a micro bead of blue glass (Singh, 1992: 79), while at Narhan a polished celt is reported (Singh, 1994: Pl. XXIX A). The presence of a socketed copper arrowhead, an indeterminate object, a coin, a rod and a copper piece respectively found at Khairadih, Narhan and Sohgaura suggests the scarce use of the metal. A noteworthy point which needs our attention is the complete absence of lithic tools at these sites which is considered an essential chalcolithic appellation (Singh, 1992: 79).

The results of principal excavated sites of this culture are presented below:

Sohgaura

As stated earlier, the earliest settlement at this site is Neolithic which is followed by this Chalcolithic which has been divided into two periods at this site (Period II = Chalcolithic I and Period III, Chalcolithic II) (Chaturvedi, 1985: 103). Chalcolithic I has a deposit of 55 cm. It shows the beginning of new ceramic industries although the earlier tradition of the corded and the rusticated ware continues. The new ceramic industries comprise black slipped, black-and-red, burnished grey and red wares, beside the earlier ceramics. Jars with splayed-out rim or constricted-necked bowls and dish-on-stand are the principal types in the black-and-red ware. The black slipped ware has jars and bowls which have paintings with vertical lines in white pigment. In the red ware, jars, bowls, basins and perforated pots with legs are the principal types. The only structural activity comprises a working floor having an underground oven (*Chulha*). Chalcolithic II has some new elements, mainly in the pottery ornament, the most noteworthy being the painted varieties. The finer variety of black-and-red ware is now painted with the linear patterns including the lipped one. The coarse variety of black-and-red ware is represented by globular vessels.

Among the antiquities of this period, a bone arrow-head with circular section is a noteworthy find. Copper is represented by a round rod with a slightly bulbous end. Beads of terracotta, jasper, agate, carnelian and rimmed hearths were found in the lower levels of this period.

The chronology of Chalcolithic Sohgaura is based on two radiocarbon dates. A sample (PRL-178) from near the junction of Periods II and III has given a date of 1330+110 BC and another sample (PRL-179) from the lowermost level of Period III has been dated to 1230+130 BC (Chaturvedi, 1985: 107).

Commenting upon the chronology of Sohgaura, Chaturvedi observes:

> Since some defect in the packing of the samples might have given a younger date, it would be reasonable to suggest the beginning of Period III in circa 1500 BC i.e., around the middle of the second millennium BC, which shall also be the terminal date of Period II. A rough calculation of the rate of the deposit during the Chalcolithic period on the basis of the two samples separated by an accumulation of 13 cm in a span of 100 years would suggest that the deposit of 55 cm of Period II might have taken about 400 years. Thus the beginning of Period II may be fixed around 1900 BC. The deposit of Periods II and III totalling 140 cm belonging to the Chalcolithic period might have accumulated in about 1000 or 1100 years and, therefore, the end of this phase may be fixed around 900-800 BC (Chaturvedi, 1985: 107).

NARHAN

Narhan is located on the left bank of river Ghaghara in Gola Tehsil of district Gorakhpur. There are two mounds at the site. Our limited sampling of both mounds has brought to light a five-fold culture-sequence ranging in date from middle of the second millennium BC to the seventh century AD (Singh, 1994). Details regarding each period are as follows:

Period I: Represented by an average deposit of 1 m on Mound-1 is marked by the occurrence of white painted black-and-red ware, black slipped ware with occasional paintings in white, red slipped ware and plain red ware. The principal pottery types in black-and-red ware are bowls, basins and vases. Dishes are conspicuous by their absence in this ware. More than 20% sherds in the fine and medium fabrics of this ware are painted.

The first settlers lived in wattle-and-daub houses. Remains of post-holes and reed marks in burnt clay lumps have been found. Although the first settlers practised agriculture, meat was an important component of their diet as is evidenced from the presence of charred animal bones; some of them having cut marks. Bones of humped Indian cattle (*Bos indicus* L.), sheep/goat (*ovis/Capra)*, remains of a wild ruminant like deer or antelope (? *Axis* sp.) and horse (*Equus* sp.) have been identified in the limited collection of bones studied so far. The small finds include pottery discs in large numbers. Of these, four pieces are perforated and might have been used as toy-cart wheels. Bone points account for 15 pieces and nine terracotta dabbers and two balls, one each of terracotta and stone. No evidence of any metal was reported from the limited dig.

A good quantity of archaeo-botanical remains obtained by flotation give a fair idea of the agricultural practices of the people. Grains of hulled

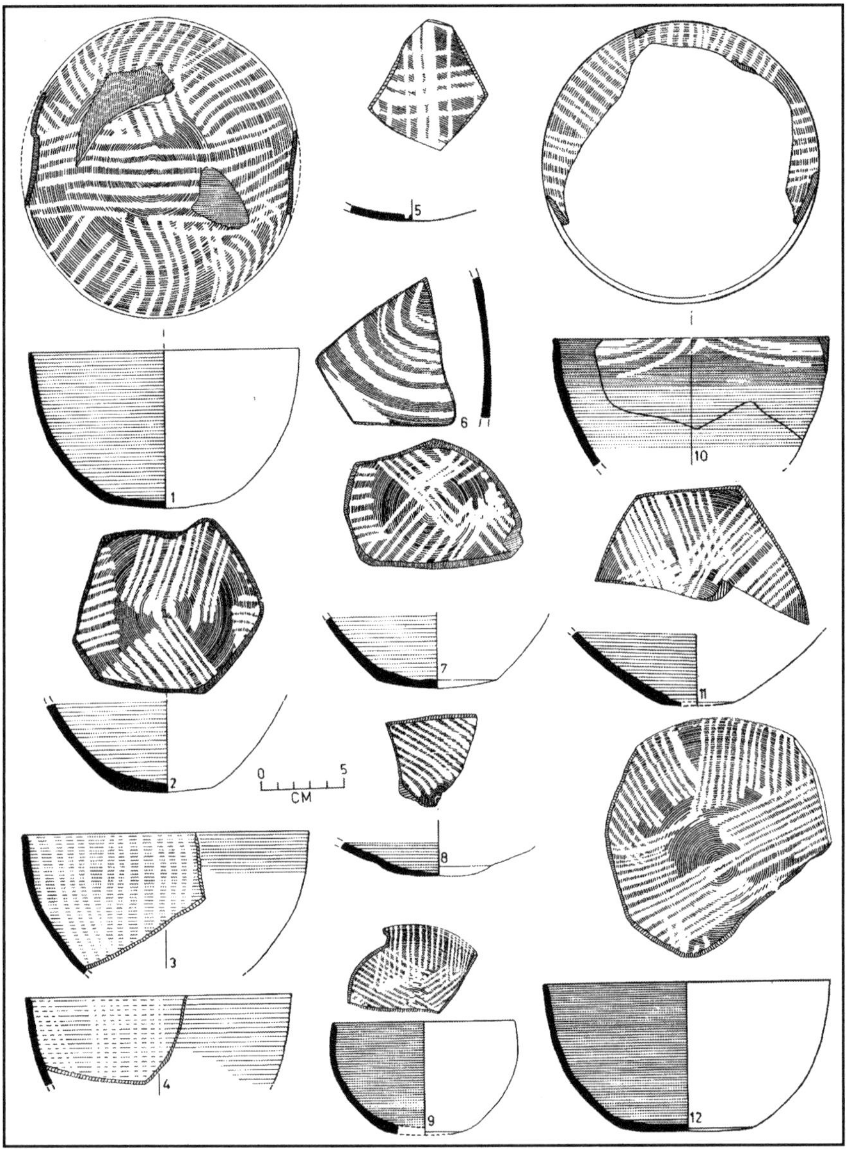

Fig. 20. Narhan: Painted black-and-red ware, Period I

and six-row barley (*Hordeum vulgare*), club wheat (*T. compactum*), bread wheat (*T. aestivum*), dwarf wheat (*T. sphaerococcum*) and cultivated rice (*Oryza sativa*) have been identified. The pulses include pea (*Pisum sativum*), green gram (moong: *Vigna radiata*), gram/chickpea (*Cicer arietinum*), khesari (*Lathyrus sativus*), besides mustard oilseeds and flax/linseed. Seeds

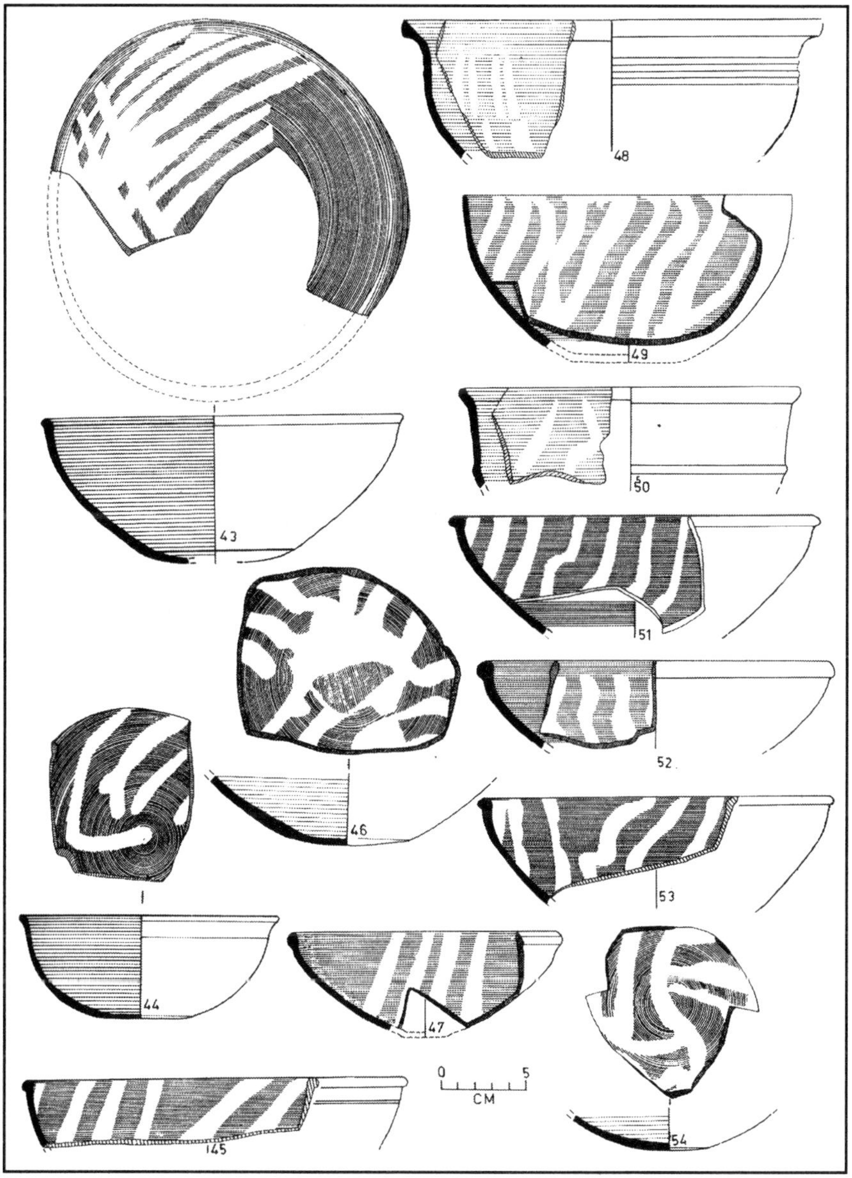

Fig. 21. Narhan: Painted black-and-red ware, Period I

of jack fruit (*Artocarpos integrifolious*) found from these levels is an important discovery. Jack fruit grows wild in the western ghats and it was taken to cultivation in North India. The present evidence suggests that the Narhan inhabitants cultivated it for its fruit.

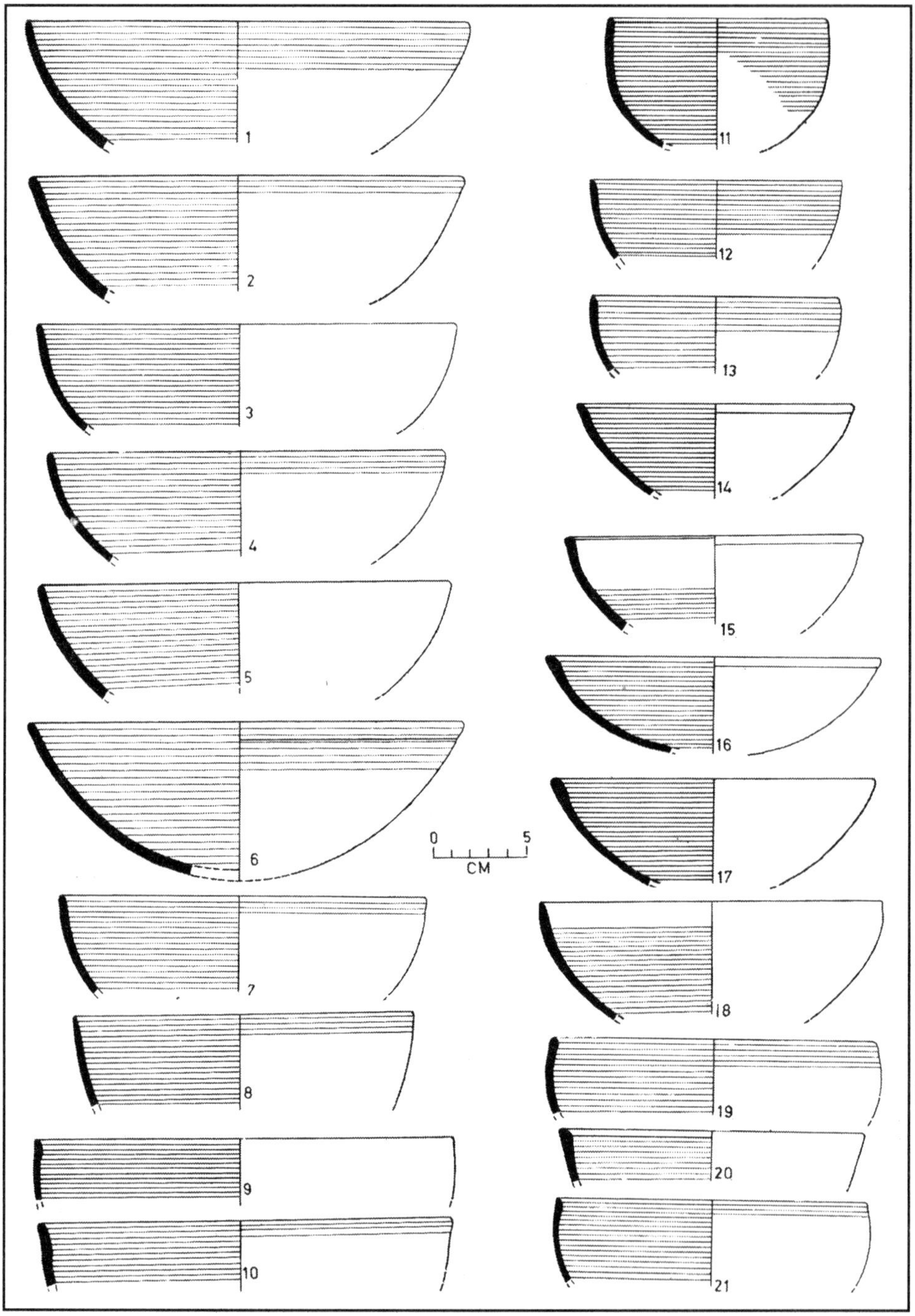

Fig. 22. Narhan: Bowls of black-and-red ware, Period I

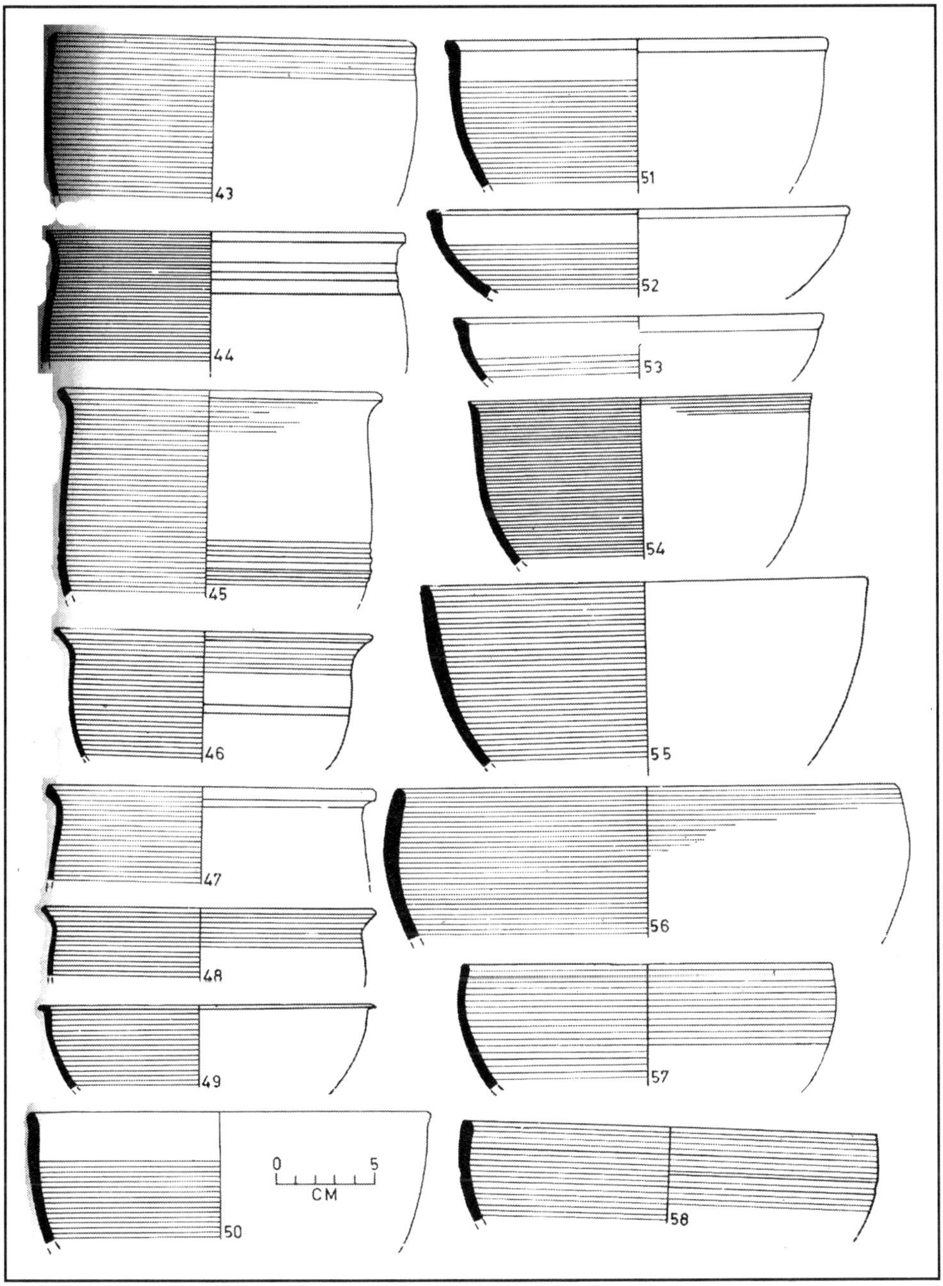

Fig. 23. Narhan: Deep bowls of black-and-red ware, Period I

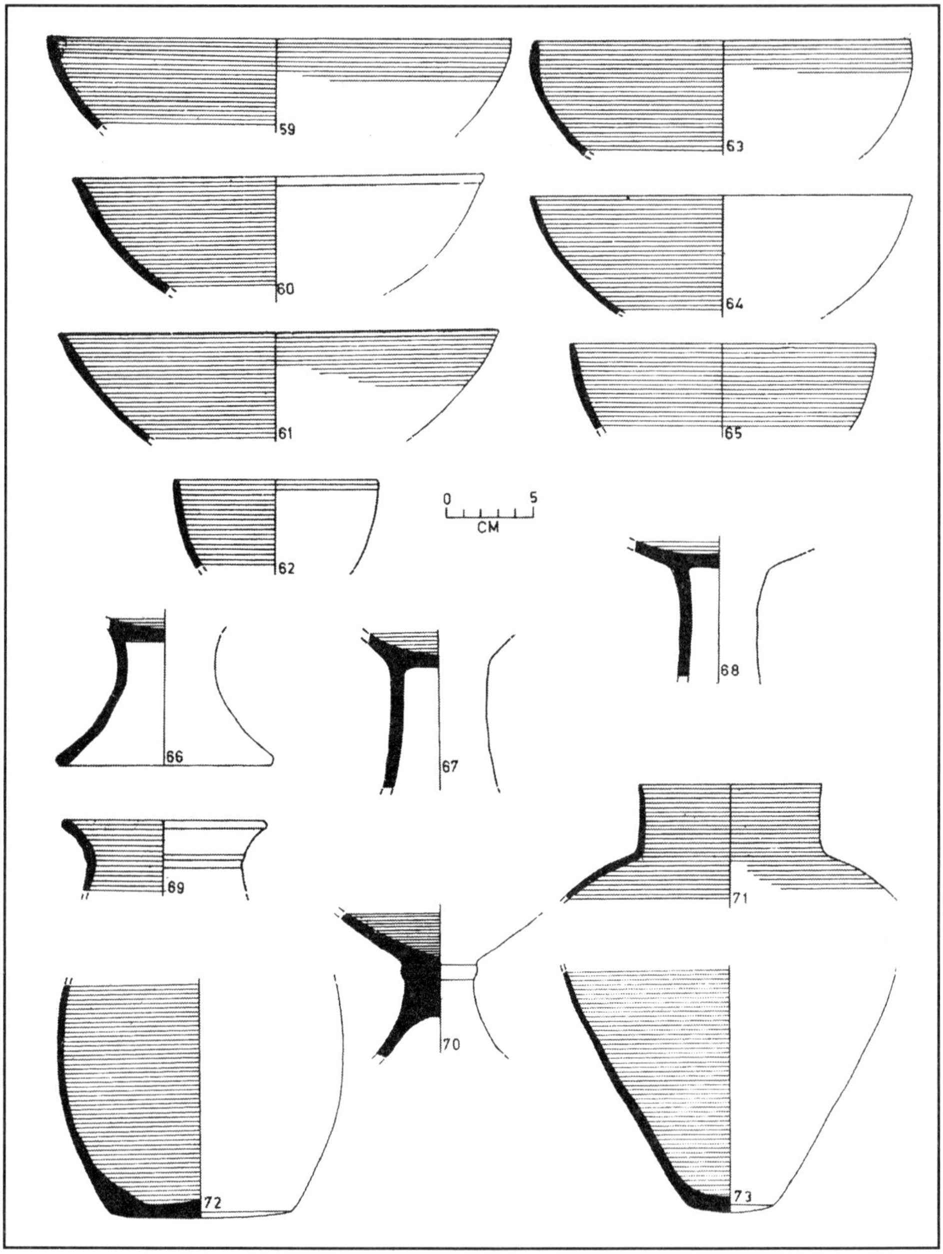

Fig. 24. Narhan: Bowl, dish-on-stand, pedestalled bowl, etc. Black-and-red ware, Period I

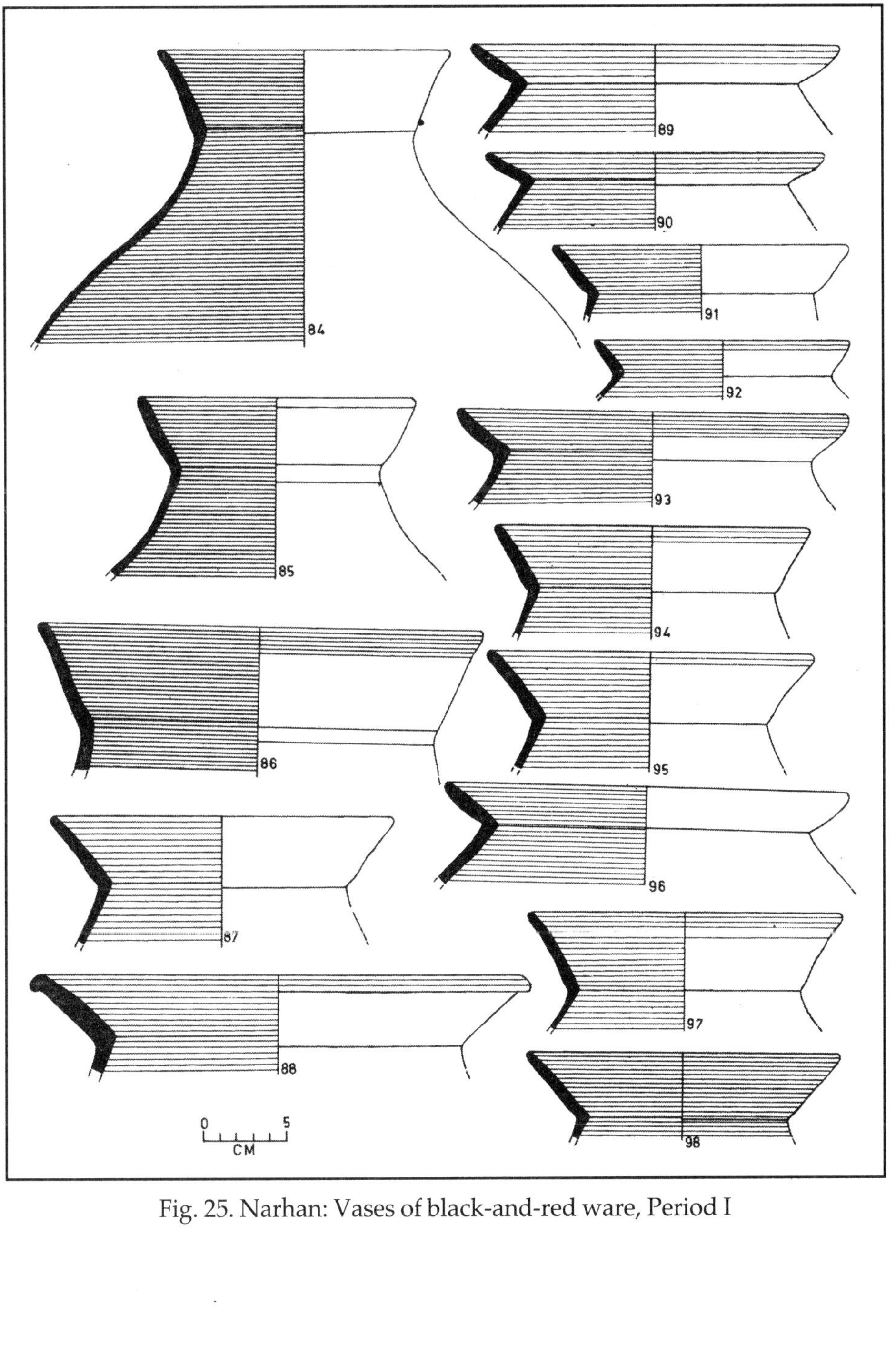

Fig. 25. Narhan: Vases of black-and-red ware, Period I

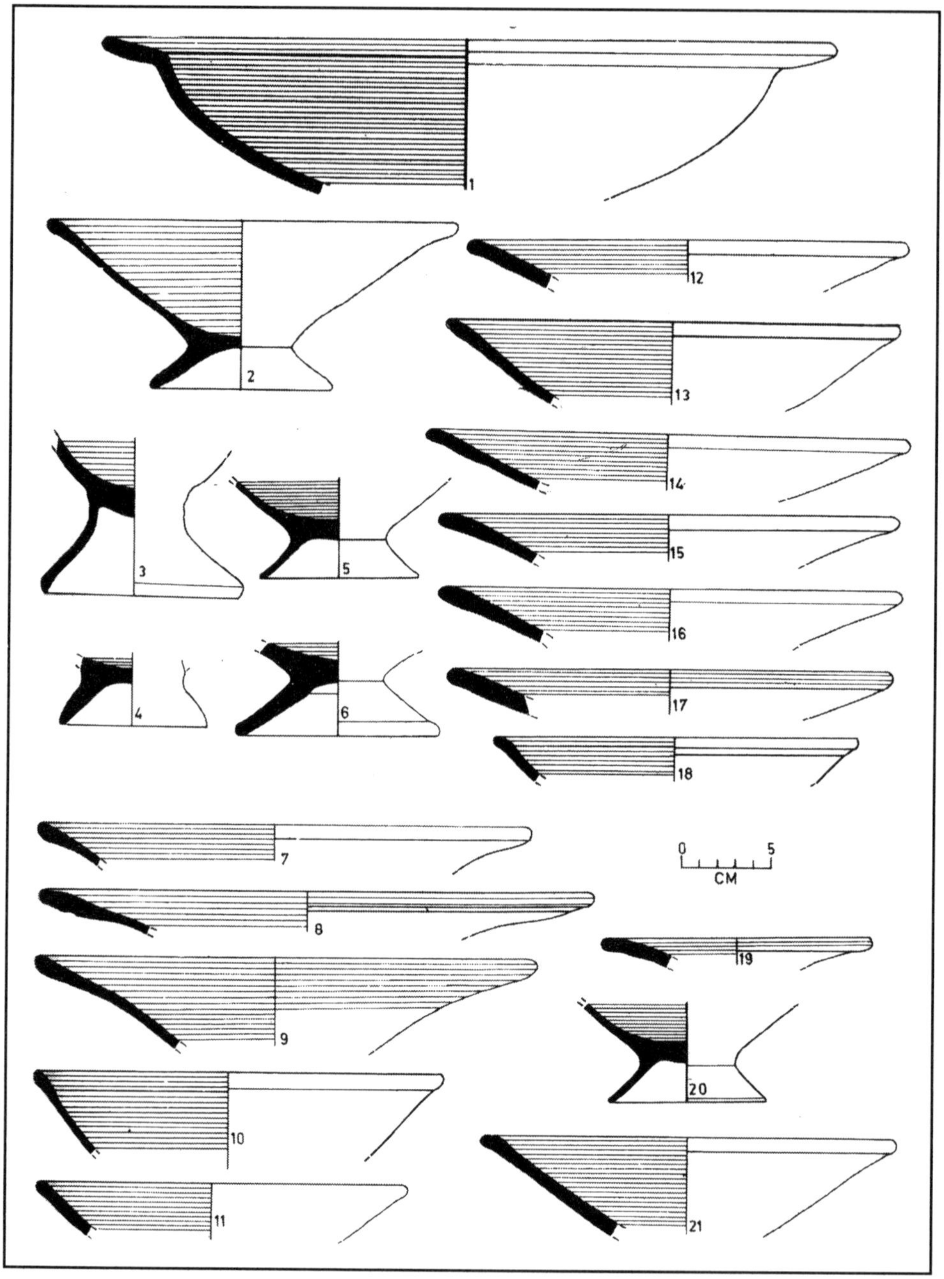

Fig. 26. Narhan: Pedestalled bowls and basin of black-and-red ware, Period I

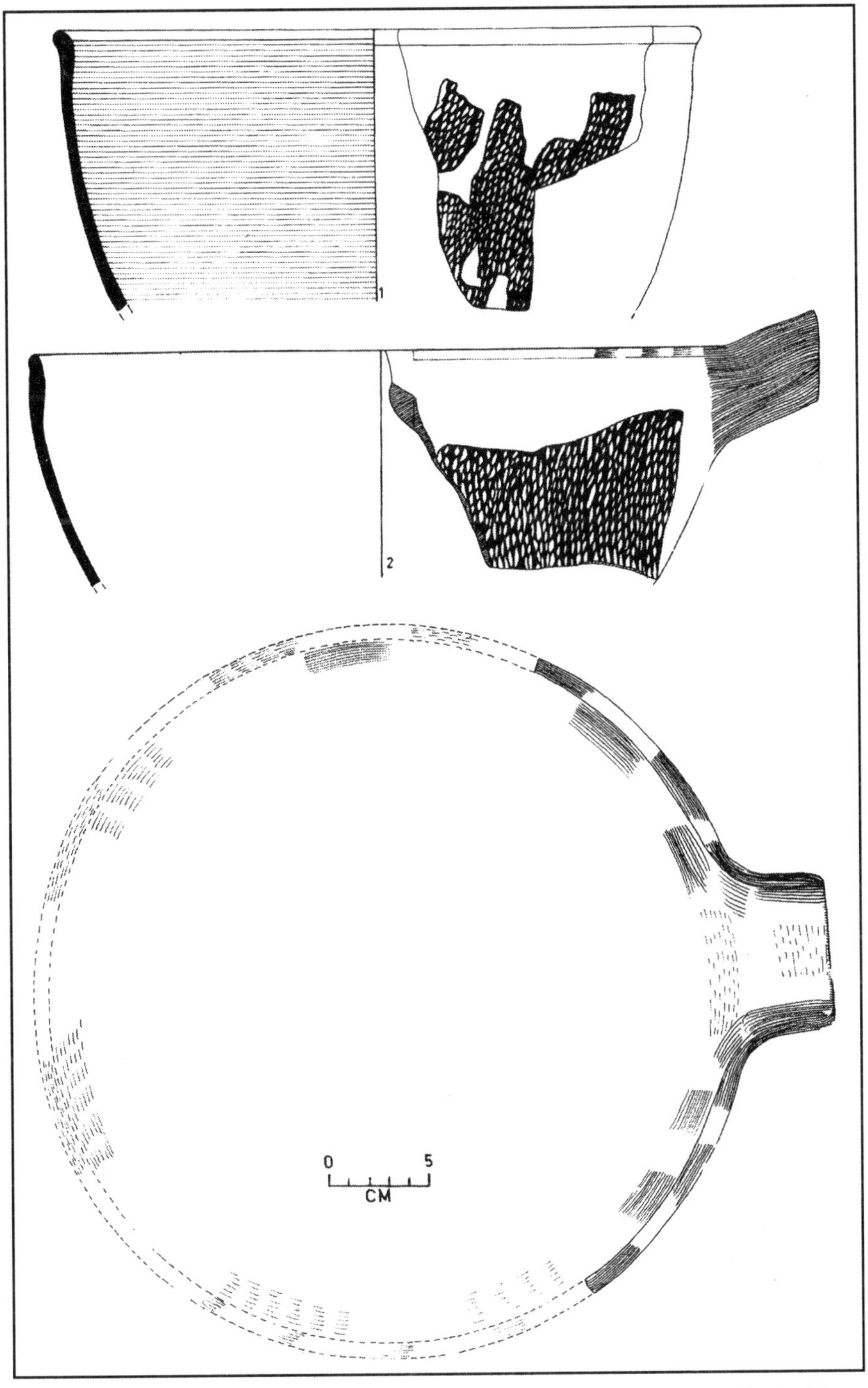

Fig. 27. Narhan: Deep bowl and lipped basins of corded ware, Period I

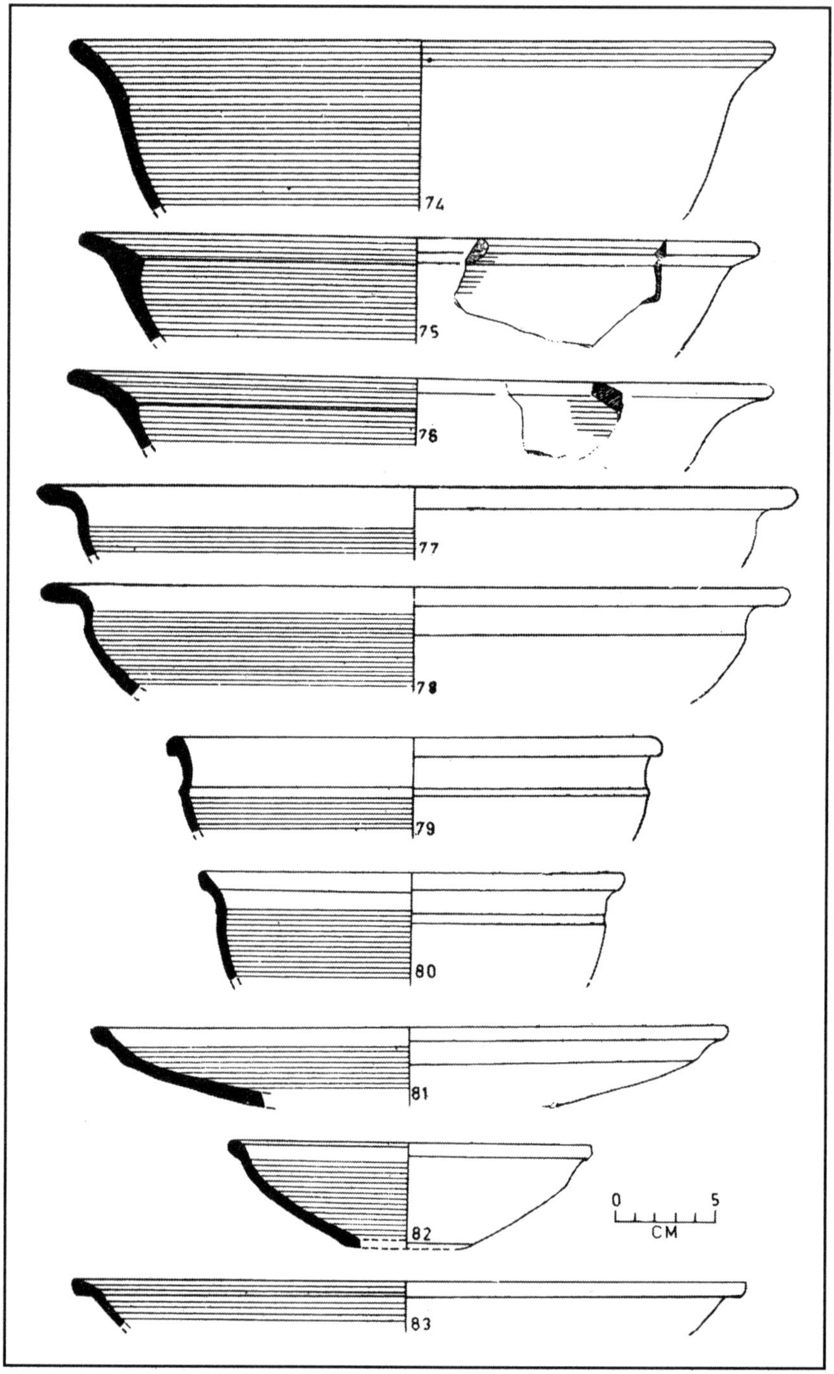

Fig. 28. Narhan: Bowls, basins and platter of black-and-red ware, Period I

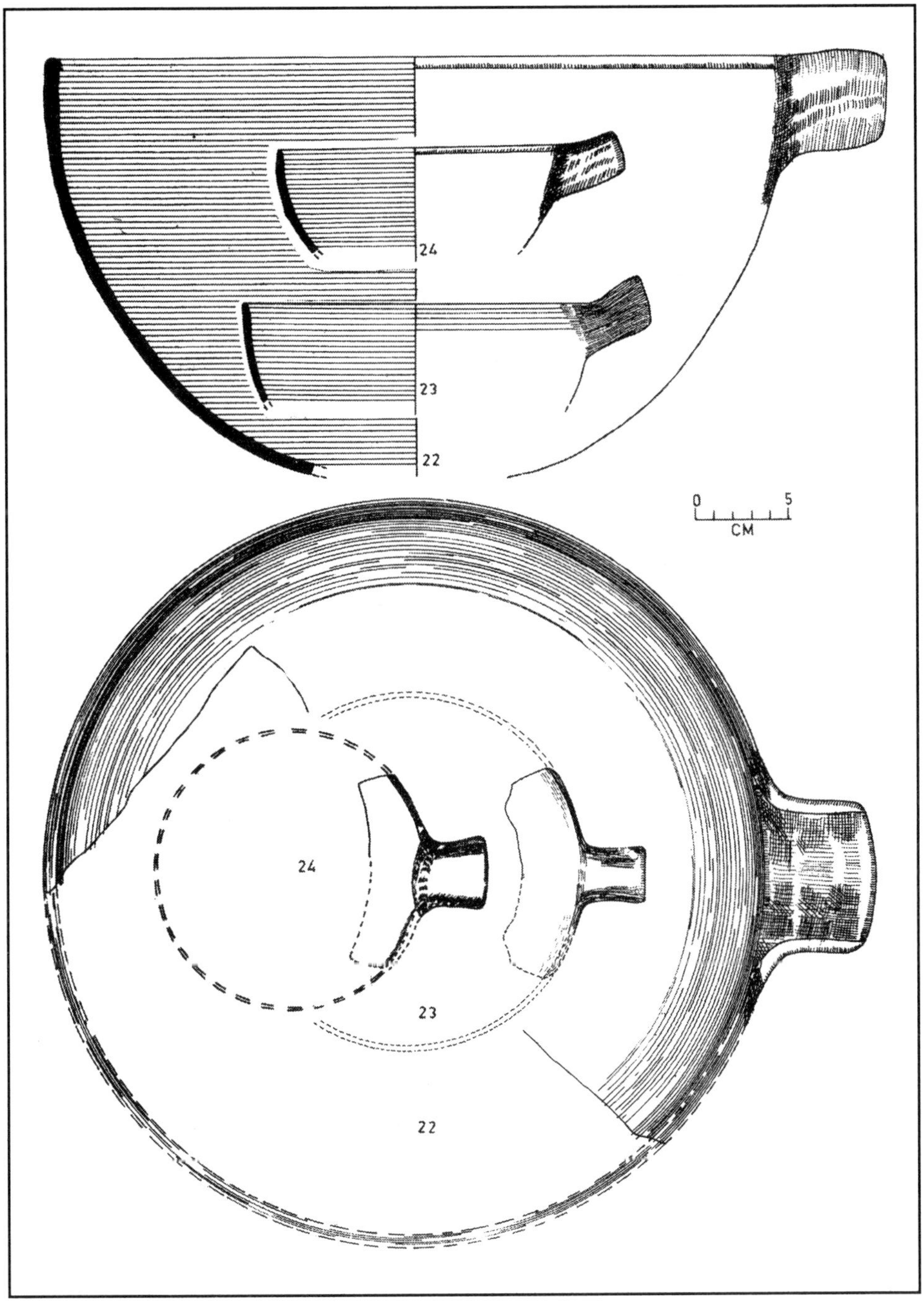

Fig. 29. Narhan: Lipped basins of burnished black-and-red ware, Period I

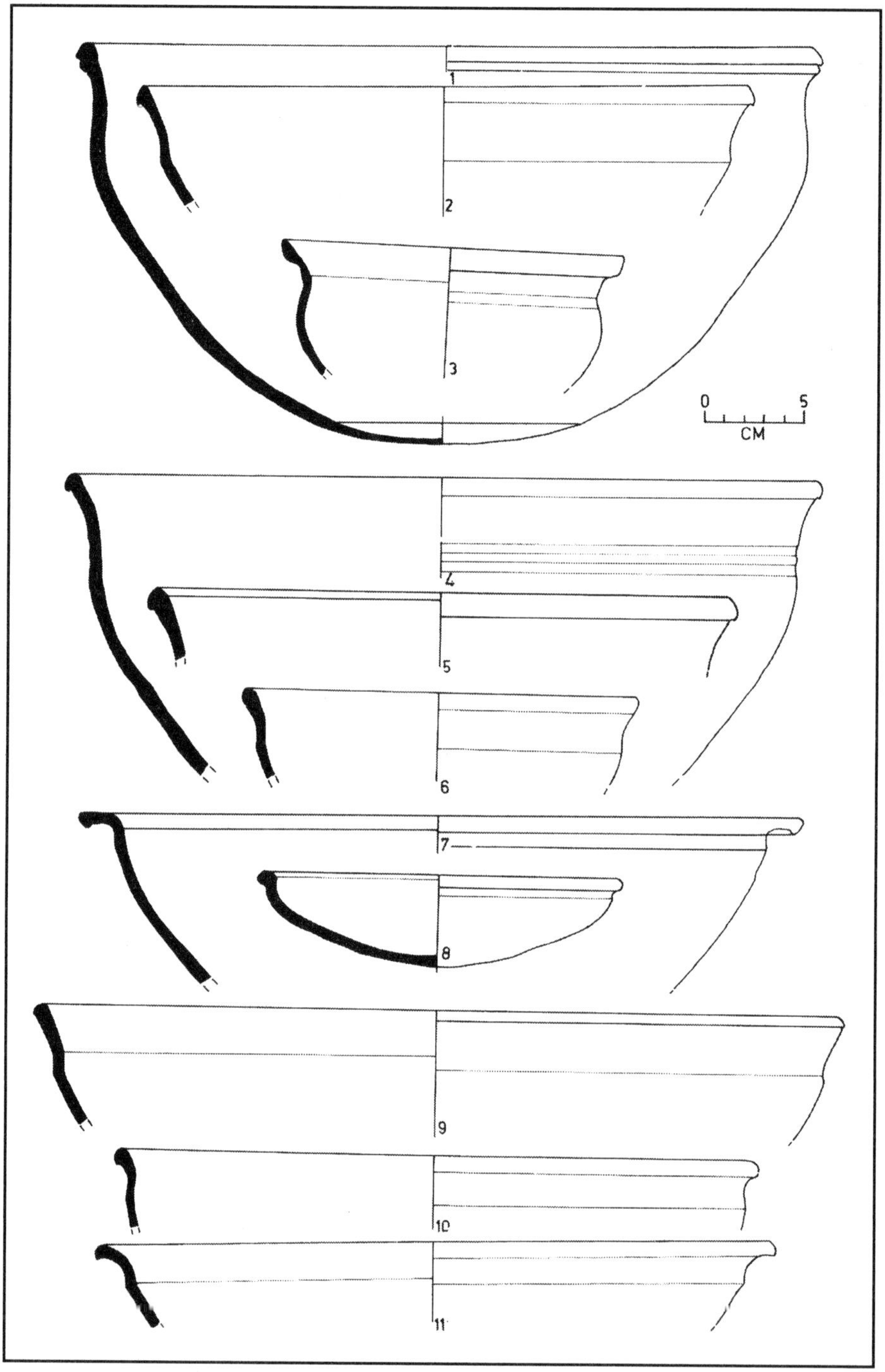

Fig. 30. Narhan: Red slipped ware, Period I

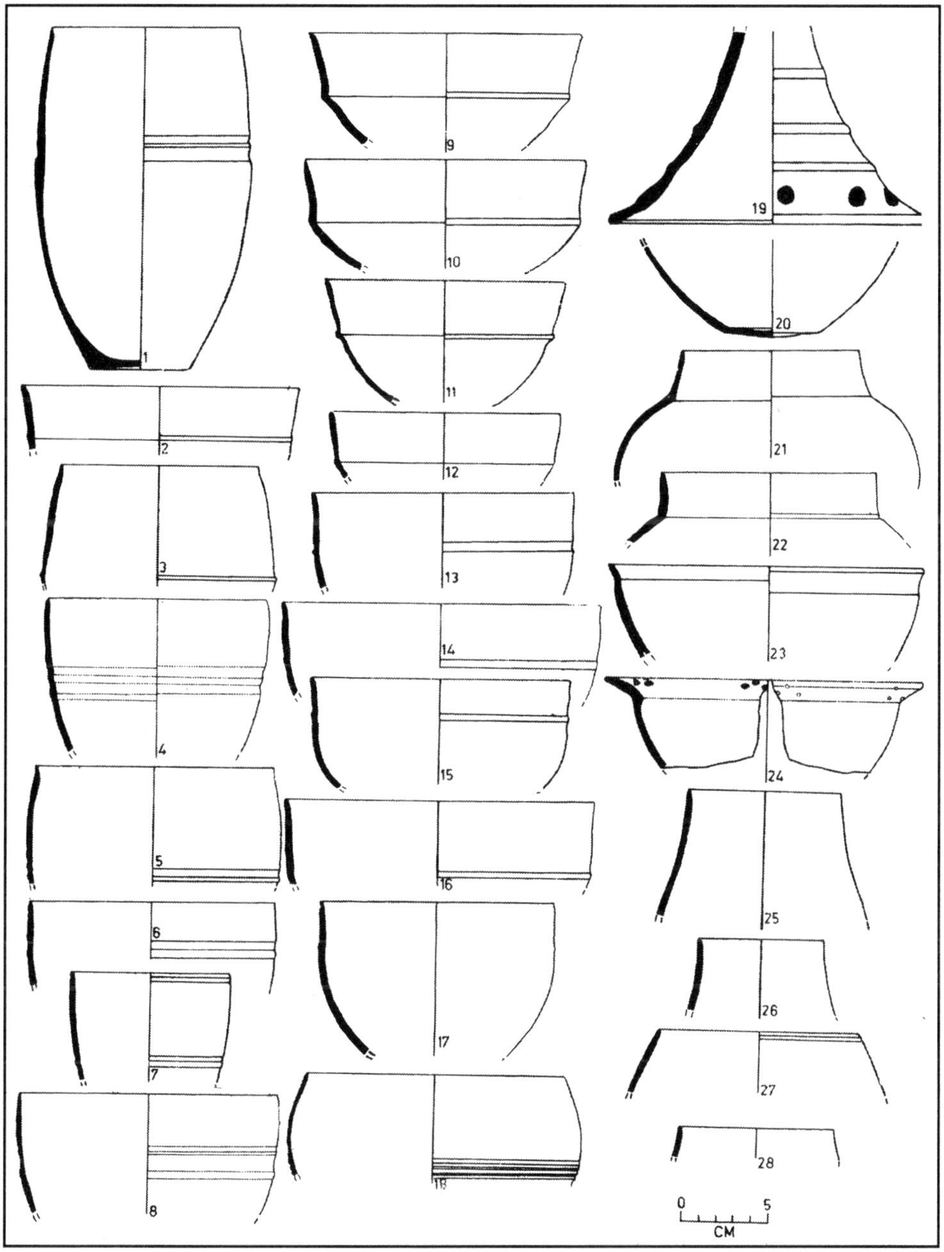

Fig. 31. Narhan: Beakers and bowls of black slipped ware, Period I

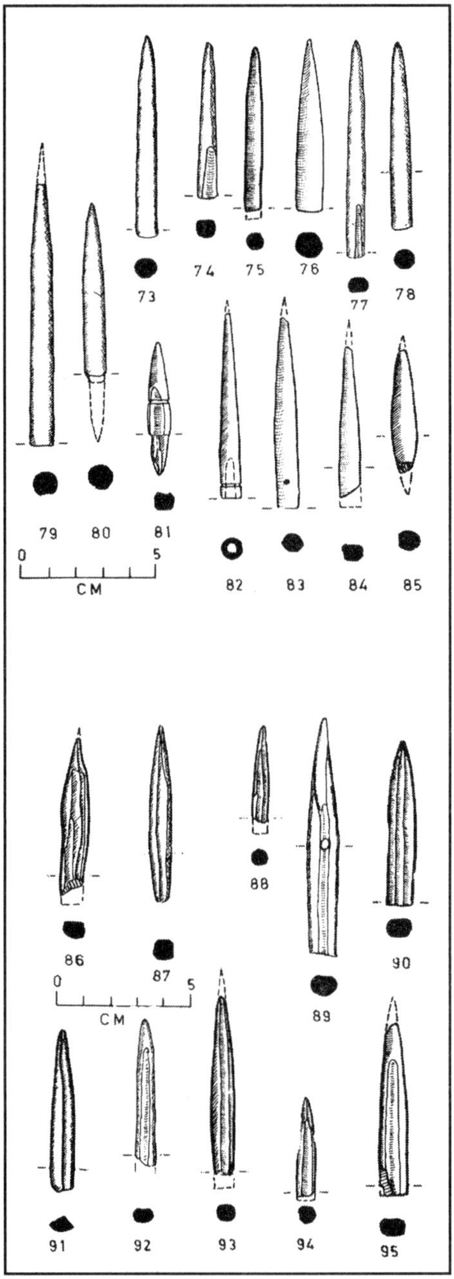

Fig. 32. Narhan: Bone points, Period II

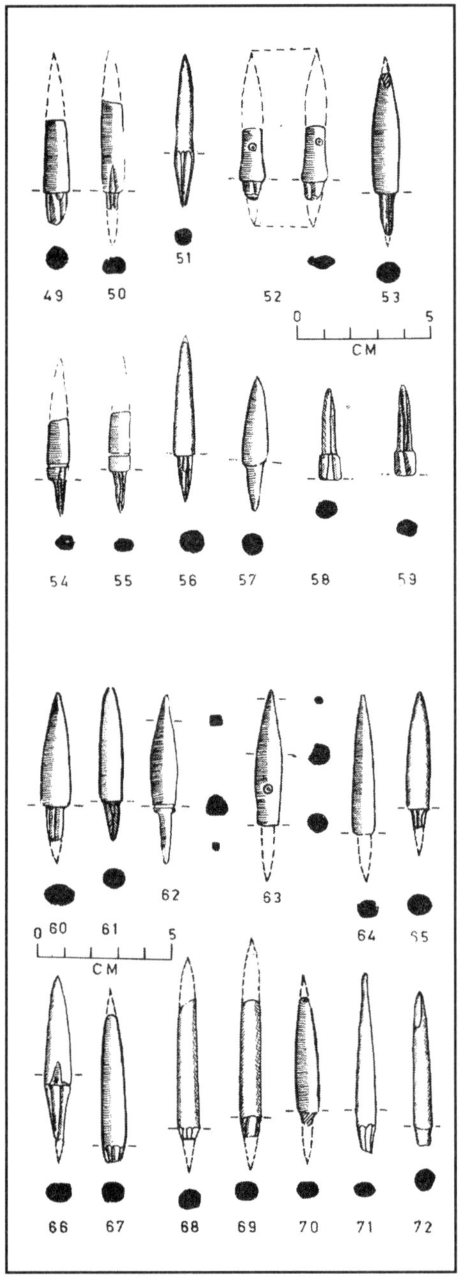

Fig. 33. Narhan: Tanged arrowheads, Period II

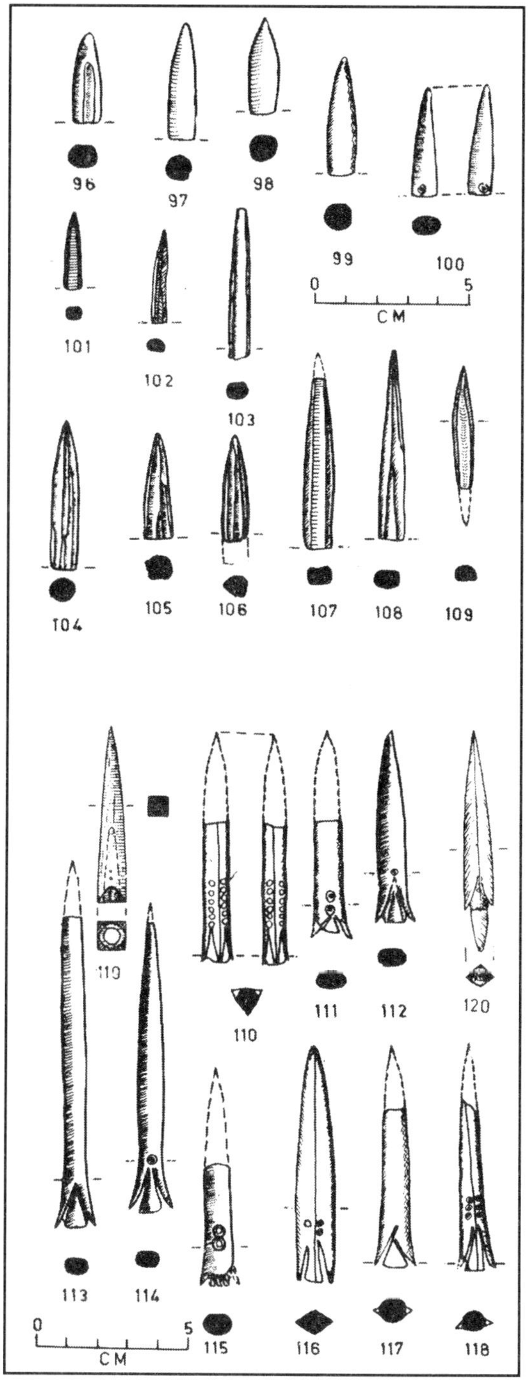

Fig. 34. Narhan: Bone arrowheads, Period II

Bhunadih

As stated earlier, Bhunadih is located on the bank of a Nala in Ballia district and was excavated by the present author in 1996. The earliest settlement (Period IA) at this site belongs to the Neolithic period while Period IB represents an overlap phase between Neolithic and Narhan culture. The structural activity is the same as in Period IA. The ceramic assemblage of this sub-period is cord-impressed and plain black-and-red ware, black slipped ware and red ware. The principal shapes and characteristic features are pedestal bowl, and dish-on-stand of black-and-red ware, *Lota*-shaped vessels of black slipped ware, post-firing scratching on the exterior (representing geometric pattern) and a few painted sherds of red ware with dots and dashes. The small finds comprised beads of steatite, terracotta and semi-precious stones and pottery discs.

Period II: This site is marked by the assemblage of Narhan culture (Chalcolithic) documented at the type-site. The inhabitants of this period lived in the wattle-and-daub houses, evidenced by a large number of reed marks. The small objects comprised beads of steatite, semi-precious stones, terracotta and pottery discs (Singh *et al.*, 1997-98: 11-29).

Archaeobotanical samples and animal bones of these two periods are presently under examination.

Waina

Waina is an important protohistoric settlement in the middle Ganga valley. It was excavated by the present author in 1995 which resulted in the discovery of a Neolithic settlement in the earliest layers (Period IA), represented by cord-impressed pottery, comparable with pre-Narhan pottery found at Imlidih Khurd. Period IB is marked by the pottery assemblage of Narhan culture. The principal ware comprise black-and-red ware, black slipped ware and plain red ware. The settlers of this period lived in wattle-and-daub houses. Remains of post-holes, ovens and storage pits were found. The small antiquities comprise bone points, beads of terracotta and semi-precious stones and pottery discs. Period II is represented by dishes, straight-sided beakers and bowls of black-slipped ware, vases and lipped basins of red slipped ware and plain red ware. Among the NBP associated ware, dishes with incurved rim are the principal type.

A preliminary observation of K.S. Saraswat on the archaeobotanical samples from this period shows that an advanced agriculture was practised by the settlers of Waina. They were well acquainted with the rotation of crops and grew cereals, pulses and oilseeds in the summer and winter seasons. Samples from the strata datable between 1300 BC to 600 BC show that the following crops were grown:

Rice (*Oryza sativa*)
Barley (*Hordeum vulgare*)
Wheat (*Triticum aestivum*)
Green-gram (*Vigna radiata*)
Lentil (*Lens culinaris*)
Field-pea (*Pisum arvense*)
Grass-pea or Khesari (*Lathyrus sativus*)
Gram/Chick-pea (*Cicer arietinum*)
Field-brassica (*Brassica juncea*)
Til/sesame (*Sesamum indicum*)

A large number of animal bones were collected from various strata of Period I. Period III is marked by the Sunga-Kushana pottery, terracotta human and animal figures, terracotta balls, beads, pestles, bone points, antlers, and iron and copper objects. Period IV is dated to Gupta period. The settlement was occupied for a brief period in the post Gupta times also.

Khairadih

Khairadih is a small village situated on the right bank of the Ghaghara River in the Ballia district of U.P. The ancient mound covers an area of 710 m east-west and 510 m north-south and rises to a maximum height of 11 m above the river bed. This mound was excavated for five seasons (1980-81 to 83-84 and again in 1985-86) by the Banaras Hindu University. This excavation brought forth a culture-sequence divisible into three periods Period I (Chalcolithic), Period II (c. 600-200 BC) and Period III (c. 200 BC-AD 300) (Singh, B.P. 1987-88: 33).

The inhabitants of the Chalcolithic period settled directly over the virgin soil and were confined to a small area along the river bank. The people lived in mud huts as evidenced by remains of post-holes, reed marks in burnt clay lumps and fragmentary remains of a mud wall in the earliest level of this period (Singh, 1987-88: 8). However, no exact plan either of huts or mud houses could be made due to limited area undertaken for digging. The ceramic industry consisted of the following ware:

1. Black-and-red ware, both plain and painted.
2. Black slipped ware, both plain as well as painted.
3. Red ware consisting of both slipped and unslipped variety.
4. Black ware, distinct from the black slipped ware.

Except for the pottery of category 4, all other categories of pots are available at the neighbouring site of Narhan.

The use of copper is attested by the occurrence of a socketed arrow-head having two perforations on the socket and an indeterminate object. But iron was not encountered in this period. Among other notable finds, mention may be made of tanged and socketed arrow-heads akin to the type mentioned above. Bones of birds and animals were frequently met with from the strata of this period. The bones showed cut-marks caused by sharp instruments. All these suggest that they might have formed part of diet of the people. Agriculture was known to the inhabitants of Period I at Khairadih. Rice-husk was found mixed with clay on some of the potteries. Cattle breeding formed another important occupation of the people.

Among other finds of this period, mention may be made of disc-shaped beads of steatite of varying sizes, beads of carnelian, agate, chert, and chalcedony, mostly cylindrical in shape, hop-scotch, dabber, whirl-wind of terracotta and a large-sized hand-made terracotta figurine most probably of an animal (Singh, B.P., 1987-88: 32). Like at Narhan, there is complete absence of lithic tools at Khairadih. Even then, the apallation 'Chalcolithic' has been used for the cultural assemblage of Period I of this site (Singh, B.P., 1987-88: 33).

As regards the chronology, the earliest settlement at this site goes back to c. 1100 BC. Radiocarbon dates for Period I at Khairadih are as follows:

BSIP 3070 + 9-0 BP
PRL 1049 1030 + 160 BC
940 + 150 BC

These dates have been calculated on 5730 years as the half-life value of the carbon. These C-14 dates from Khairadih are in agreement with the chronology suggested for the Chalcolithic cultures of eastern India, particularly of Pandu Rajar Dhibi, Mahishdal and Chirand (Singh, B.P., 1987-88: 33).

CHIRAND

The Neolithic settlement of Chirand has been discussed in the preceding chapter. Suffice it to mention that Period II, having at places about 5.50 m thick cultural deposit, belongs to the Chalcolithic period. It has three occupational levels divided into two sub-periods. Like their predecessors, the Chalcolithic folk lived in houses made of reed and bamboos with mud plaster, their dwellings, comparatively huge in dimension, having floors of burnt earth. The earliest level of this period has revealed 9 circular hearths and a few post-holes. A post-cremation burial has been suspected on the top level of this period (Roy in Ghosh, 1989, I: 104). A miniature sarcophagus with ridge to support the cover and having paintings on its outer surface in creamish white pigment representing spotted deer and a bull in dots and lines is very rare in this area (Verma, 1997: 79).

The ceramic industries comprised black-and-red ware (both painted and plain), red, grey and black slipped ware. The noteworthy forms included dish-on-stand, some with corrugated stem, long-necked vases, bowls, lipped bowls, basins, perforated vessels, four-legged pots, spouted pots, lipped jugs, trough and dishes. Some of the pots have paintings comprising dashes and wavy lines in creamish white pigment executed on the shoulder and neck.

The associated finds include microlithic core, waste flake and small nodules, a few neolithic celts, pins and tanged and socketed arrowheads of bone, styli of bone and ivory, a bead and a few corroded pieces of copper, stone beads of steatite and chalcedony, balls, pestles and querns of stone, and bones of birds and fish.

The earliest level of this period was dated by C-14 to 1650+100 BC. The upper levels of Period IIB have yielded numerous iron objects and exposed animal burials.

Taradih

The ancient settlement of Taradih is located just to the south-west of Mahabodhi Temple at Bodh Gaya (Bihar). Archaeological investigations carried out at the site by the Directorate of Archaeology and Museums, Government of Bihar, brought to light a sequence of cultures ranging in date from the Chalcolithic to the Pala period (Prasad, 1980-81: 180-81). The earliest settlement belongs to the Chalcolithic culture which had a developed rural economy in which agriculture, hunting and fishing played an important role. The remains of huts and earth-rammed floors indicate the structural activities. Ovens of different sizes, met with during this period, were most probably meant for melting copper besides cooking purpose.

The ceramic industry comprises black-and-red ware, black ware and red ware. The main types include dish-on-stand, bowl with a pedestal, perforated bowl, lipped bowl, spouted vessels and deep dish. A fairly good number of painted black-and-red ware along with painted black ware and red ware were also found. The painting is done in white on creamish white colour and includes wavy lines, straight and oblique strokes and dots.

The small finds include celt, carnelian beads, querns, pestles, balls and fish-hooks. Among the bone objects, mention may be made of socketed, tanged and barbed arrowheads, points and chisels. The terracotta beads and conical objects and a few disc-shaped beads of white colour (steatite?) with perforation at the centre were also noteworthy.

SENUWAR

As stated earlier, this site is situated on the right bank of the river Kudra in the Rohtas district, Bihar. Excavations conducted by the Banaras Hindu University during 1986-87 and again in 1989-90 brought to light deposits of four cultural periods: Neolithic, Chalcolithic, NBPW phase and Kushana (Singh, B.P., 2004). Period II at Senuwar is Chalcolithic. The ceramic industry of this period is represented by black-and-red ware (plain as well as painted), black slipped ware and other associated ceramic industries. Other objects include microliths, copper, beads of semi-precious stones, bone tools, etc. The black-and-red ware recovered from the Chalcolithic phase is similar in fabric and shape to that recovered from Khairadih (Singh, B.P., 1987-88: 33 f.n. 4). The occurrence of black-and-red ware is not only the first of its kind to have been noticed in this region but shows a resemblance with the Chalcolithic ware of Central India suggesting some kind of contact (Singh, 1987-88: 34, f.n. 10).

As regards the structural activity in Chalcolithic levels at Senuwar, it may be stated that the people lived in huts made of wattle-and-daub, plastered over with husk-mixed earth. No house plans could be made out but remains of a circular mud structure, 4.26 m and 3.80 m in diameter, was exposed (Singh, B.P., 1989-90: 83). Several clay-lined pits, circular, oval or rectangular in shape, associated with floors, constitute other structural activity.

Among the small finds, the use of copper is witnessed by the presence of bangle; a tool of an indeterminate use, pin (?) ear-ring (?), pendants (?), copper pieces and a pot-sherd in which a layer of copper is found still adhered all along its inner surface which indicates that it was a pot used in smelting copper ore. The lithic assemblage consisted of retouched bladelets, flakes, blades and cores made of chalcedony and chert. Significantly polished stone axes, together with hammers, rubber stones, pestles, sling balls, etc. were a survival from the preceding Neolithic culture. Bangles of bone, beads of agate, chalcedony and faience formed objects of personal adornment. Besides, faience slags were reported strewn in an area measuring 2.45 m × 1.60 m suggesting an evidence of an industry of faience. The beads of faience were introduced in Period IB which continued in Period II also.

The bone tools include point, needle (?), chisel and arrow-heads, both socketed and tanged. Among objects of terracotta, mention may be made of beads, animal and bird figurines, hop-scotch, stopper, etc.

Recovery of grains by floatation from the Chalcolithic levels indicate that agriculture was practised on large scale. The study revealed the following crops (Singh, B.P., 1989-90: 90):

1. Rice (*Oryza sativa*)
2. Barley (*Hordeum vulgare*)
3. Dwarf-wheat ((*Triticum sphaerococcum*)
4. Bread wheat (*T. aestivum*)
5. Sorghum-millet or Jowar (*Sorghum bicolor*)
6. Chickpea (*Cicer arietinum*)
7. Green gram or *mung* (*Vigna radiata*)
8. Field-pea (*Pisum arvense*)
9. Lentil (*Lens culinaris*)
10. Horse-gram (*Dolichos biflorus*)
11. Grass-pea (*Lathyrus sativus*)
12. Oilseeds belonging to sesame or *til* (*Sesamum indicum*)
13. Linseed (*Linum usitatissimum*)

Table 1. Remains of crop plants from Senuwar

Senuwar, Sasaram: Crop Remains	***Neolithic Period*** **(2200-1950 BC)**	***Neolithic-Chalcolithic Period*** **(1950-1300 BC)**	***Chalcolithic Period*** **(1300-700 /600 BC)**
Rice (*Oryza sativa*)	*	*	*
Barley (*Hordeum vulgare*)	*	*	*
Dwarf-wheat (*Triticum sphaerococcum*)	*	*	*
Bread-wheat (*Triticum aestivum*)		*	*
Ragi-millet (*Eleusine coracana*)	*		
Jowar-millet (*Sorghum bicolor*)	*	*	*
Kodon-millet (*Paspalum scrobiculatum*)		*	
Lentil (*Lens culinaris*)	*	*	*
Field-pea (*Pisum arvense*)	*	*	*
Grass-pea (*Lathyrus sativus*)	*	*	*
Green-gram (*Vigna radiata*)	-	*	*
Chick-pea (*Cicer arietinum*)	-	*	*
Moth-bean (*Vigna aconitifolia*)	-	-	*
Horse-gram (*Dolichos biflorus*)	-	*	*

Til (*Sesamum indicum*)	-	-	*
Field-brassica / Lahi (*Brassica juncea*)	-	-	*
Linseed (*Linum usitatissimum*)	-	-	*
Safflower (*Carthamus tinctorius*)	-	-	*
Castor (*Ricinus communis*)			
(Evidenced by wood charcoal)	-	-	*
Water-melon (*Citrullus lanatus*)	-	-	*

*Recorded in the collection

The study of animal bones provides a detailed status of food economy, anatomical and nutritional preferences of the inhabitants, animal represented at Senuwar are mostly large to medium-sized herbivorous, both domestic as well as wild.

There are a total of 21 taxa of which 15 are mammals, one small mammal (rodent), two reptiles and three molluscan species (Sathe and Badam, 2004). The taxa are given as under:

Equus sp.: horse family
Bos indicus Linn., 1758: domestic cattle
Bubalus bubalis Linn., 1758: domestic buffalo
Boselaphus tragocamelus Pallas, 1766: nilgai
Antiloe cervicapra Linn., 1758: blackbuck
Tetraceros quadricornis Blainville, 1816: four-horned antelope
Mutiacus nuntjak Zimmermann, 1780: barking deer
Ovis aries Linn., 1758: domestic sheep
Capra hircus Erxl., 1777: goat
Sus scrofa cristatus Linn., 1758: domestic pig
Cervus spp.: barasingha / sambar
Axis azix Erxl., 1777: chital
Canis familiaris Linn, 1758: domestic dog
Canis lupus Linn, 1758: wolf
Felis catus domesticus: domestic cat
Rattus rattus Linn, 1758: house rat
Trionyx gangeticus: turtle
Varanus sp.: monitor lizard
Lamellidens sp.
Pila sp.
Bithynia sp.

The composition and ratio of wild and domesticated animals indicated over-dependence of inhabitants on domesticated stock. As regards the food value, wild fauna may have provided occasional requirements to supplement the regular supply of primary and secondary products from domestic stock (Table 1 & 2).

The number of animals represented at the site revealed a stable and family rich status of food economy. Domestic fauna out-member their wild counterparts throughout successive occupational layers at the site. The Neo-chalcolithic levels yielded maximum number of cattle bones while buffalo is under-represented. In terms of the ratio of abundance, sheep and goat come next only.

Table 1. Distribution of identifiable taxa in Neolithic period

Domestic	**NISP**	**MNI**
Bos indicus	132	24
Babalus bubalis	49	12
Ovis aries	2	3
Capra hircus	1	1
Sus cristatus domesticus	4	3
Canis familaris	1	1
Felis catus domesticus	2	2
Wild		
Cervus spp.	8	5
Antilope cervicapra	2	2
Muntiacus muntjak	1	1
Boselaphus tragocamelus	3	3
Total	**205**	**57**
	(6.57%)	(27.31%)

NSIP: No. of identical specimens
MNI: Minimum number of individuals

Table 2. Distribution of identifiable taxa in Chalcolithic period

Domestic	**NISP**	**MNI**
Bos indicus	45	13
Babalus bubalis	16	7
Capra hircus	2	2
Sus cristatus domesticus	9	2
Eguus sp.	1	1
Wild		
Cervus spp.	3	1

Antilope cervicapra	2	1
Boselaphus tragocamelus	2	2
Total	**80**	**29**
	(2.55%)	(36.25%)

NSIP: No. of identical specimens
MNI: Minimum number of individuals

Dependence on the wild fauna for subsistence appears quite less at Senuwar. They were hunted in wild and dismembered and only important body parts were brought into the habitational areas. Further, there was no major shift in dietary habit from Neolithic to Chalcolithic periods at the site. It is believed that the Neolithic people who came to settle at Senuwar brought along with them already domesticated animals which were subsequently raised for stock breeding (Sathe and Badam, 2004: 564).

Thus, it is obvious that the subsistence economy of the Chalcolithic Senuwarians depended mainly on agriculture, cattle-breeding, hunting and partly on some cottage industries which included pottery making, lapidary, bone tool making and faience industry.

Lastly, the stratigraphic position of this culture at Senuwar needs to be understood. Period II (Chalcolithic) is represented by 2.30 m thick occupational deposit suggesting that the duration of this phase is fairly long at this site as also at most of the sites of eastern U.P., Bihar and parts of the Vindhyan area. Further, the lowermost deposit of Chalcolithic culture at Senuwar overlapped with the preceding Neolithic sub-phase and its uppermost deposit with the succeeding Period III, which is characterized by the introduction of iron and the NBP ware. Thus, the Chalcolithic culture on the one hand, is a gradual development of the preceding Neolithic culture, and on the other, it paved the way for the growth of the NBP culture (Singh, B.P., 1989-90: 83).

Among the Chalcolithic cultures of the middle Ganga plain, except Narhan, Senuwar is the only other site whose detailed report is available. The importance of this site lies in the fact that it has provided evidence for uninterrupted growth of cultures from the Neolithic to the NBPW culture, ranging in date from circa third millennium BC to the fifth century BC. The following four stages of growth of cultures have been delineated:

Stage IA: Early Neolithic (circa 2200 BC to circa 2000 BC)

This stage is marked by pastoralism, supported by incipient agriculture and large scale food collection, exploitation of aquatic fauna and hunting. In archaeological record, this stage is represented by typical Neolithic traits comprising small polished celts, food processing lithic equipment such as pestles, saddle querns, rubber stones, etc. and microlithic industry (Singh, B.P., 2004: 605). Other noteworthy items were bone and small tools and a limited number of terracotta animal figurines. The personal ornaments comprised beads of semi-precious stones and terracotta and small pendants and bangles of bone. In the ceramic collection burnished red, burnished grey, combed, rusticated and red ware dominate. In addition, a small proportion of crude black-and-red ware was also found. The economy of this stage was marked by domestication of animals and incipient farming which included the cultivation of only *Oryza sativa* variety of paddy. The latter fact is rather surprising as only rice was cultivated at Senuwar in the Neolithic period while in the middle Ganga plain, multiple crop raising is evident from all the early Neolithic horizon. The domesticated animals comprise cattle, buffalo, sheep, goat and pig (Sathe and Badam in Singh, B.P., 2004) while deer, antelope, barking deer and *nilgai* were hunted but their contribution in the Neolithic food economy was marginal.

Stage IB: Late Neolithic (circa 2000 BC to circa 1950 BC)

This stage is marked by a major shift in the agricultural practices and consequently the economy. The new cereals included barley, wheat, jowar millet, lentil, field pea and finger millet (*Ragi* and *Khesari*). This shows that agriculture now played a major role in the economy. Saraswat believes that since Harappan trade with Mesopotamia had declined around 2000 BC, the Late Harappan people migrated from their homeland to different regions and some of them came to the Kaimur region. From the Kaimur region, the tradition spread in inland regions of the middle Ganga plain and a number of sites like Chirand Taradih, Maner and Chechar-Kutubpur are a testimony to this (Singh, B.P., 2004: 607). Harappan influence has also been noticed by some scholars in the pottery types of this period. The bottom-less goblet, dish-on-stand and knobbed ware from Chirand (Sinha, B.P., 1982: 135-39) are taken as further proofs of the eastward migration of the late Harappans.

Stage II: Neolithic-Chalcolithic (circa 1950 BC to circa 1300 BC)

This stage has been designated Neolithic-Chalcolithic as metal (copper) appears for the first time during this stage. It witnessed an overall advancement in the living pattern. In the field of agriculture, new cereals and pulse crops were introduced. These comprise bread wheat, Kodon millet, green gram/*mung*, horse-gram, *kulthi* and chickpea/gram. The faunal complex now included some more wild species of animals like wolf, four-horned antelope and chital along with the species found in Period IA. Besides, various crafts such as clay moulding, lapidary, chiselling of bone, shell and stone show gradual refinement and the high proficiency in bead making at Senuwar remind one of Harappan craftsmanship. But as stated above, the most important contribution of this period was the introduction of metal (copper). As many as 19 objects made of pure copper (99%) were recovered from the limited excavations.

The introduction of this metal helped in the development of various crafts and the increased prosperity led to interaction and trade with other regions. Beads and pendants of marine shells *Turbinella pyrum* (Linn.) found at Senuwar were probably imported from the Gulf of Kutch and copper was obtained from the Rakha mines and lead from Bhagalpur district of Bihar (Singh, B.P., 2004: 609).

Stage III: Chalcolithic (circa 1300 bc-7th century bc)

This stage of techno-cultural development is characterised by production of bronze objects, improvement in agriculture and introduction of plain and painted pottery comprising black-and-red ware and other associated ceramic industries. Several new shapes in pottery forms were introduced; noteworthy among them are dish-on-stand, bowls of varying shapes and capacity, vessels with long vertical sides and dish. The appearance of the last-named pottery form suggests a change in the food habits of the people.

This stage also witnessed the evidence of alloying (tin around 5%) which may be considered a technological advancement over the preceding stage. Now the economy of the Chalcolithic Senuwarians depended mainly on agriculture, cattle breeding, hunting and partly on some cottage industry which included pottery making, lapidary, bone tool making, etc. In the realm of agriculture, a new pulse crop – the moth bean – was added and the cultivation of *til*, field brassica/ brown mustard, safflower, linseed/*alsi* and castor was started. Besides, orchard husbandry began to be practised. Water melon seeds, mango and jack fruit have been reportd from this period. Thus, the agricultural base of the Ganga valley was laid down by the pre-iron farmers and no new crops were added after the introduction of iron (Chakrabarti, 1986: 73).

Stage IV: (Circa 7th century bc-5th century bc)

The Chalcolithic phase at Senuwar transforms itself into the Iron Age in this stage. This stage witnessed the use of iron which played an important role in the life of the people. The principal cultural traits of the preceding stages such as the use of the microliths, shell and bone objects now became insignificant and the NBP ware becomes the principal ceramic industry.

At the end of Stage IV (Period III), Senuwar was abandoned and the site was reoccupied around the beginning of the Christian era.

Champa

The ruins of the capital city of the state of Anga, which was one of the sixteen major political principalities during the time of Buddha, lies in the general area of Nathnagar on the outskirts of modern Bhagalpur town. The visible ruins of the site form a high, square plateau (about 14 m or more high, from the level of the ground below), rising almost straight on all sides (Chakrabarti, 2001: 166-67).

Champa was subjected to archaeological excavation by Patna University for six seasons between 1969-70 and 1976-77 and again in 1982-83 on a limited scale. The Chalcolithic remains were found in the excavations of 1974-75; 1976-77, and 1982-83 but these levels could not be examined properly as the sub-soil water prevented the excavations from reaching the virgin soil.

As stated above, the Chalcolithic deposit of Champa was found for the first time in the excavation of 1974-75 in the water-logged trench CMP-IB, where recourse had to be undertaken to pumping set for draining out the sub-soil water (*IAR*, 1979-75: 8). The cultural deposit of 2 m thickness, overlying the natural soil, yielded a fairly large number of black-and-red ware sherds of coarse fabric. The pottery types include bowls and vases with flared rim, similar to the Chalcolithic black-and-red ware from Sonpur and Chirand, and indicate the earliest occupational culture on this site prior to the NBPW phase.

In another trench – CMP-IM excavated in 1976-77 – fragments of coarse black-and-red ware were recorded in a 1.20 m thick deposit of compact greenish and red clay, overlying the natural soil (*IAR*, 1976-77: 11).

In yet another trench dug towards the northern side of the Bishop's Office at Champa during 1982-83, a one metre thick deposit represented by layers 8A and 8, yielded coarse black-and-red ware along with red ware (*IAR*, 1982-83: 15). This deposit was found overlying the natural soil.

Thus, the Chalcolithic character of this site was well-documented, although the 'lithic' component and structural remains of this period could not be recorded because of the high water table on the site.

Manjhi

The huge mound of Manjhi, nearly 14 metres in height from the ground level, extends from north-east to south-west along the left bank of river

Ghaghara (Sarayu) in district Saran (Chhapra), Bihar. The present-day village of Manjhi occupies a part of the ancient settlement which extends for about 526 metres north to south but only about 390 metres from east to west. These dimensions, however, may not represent the overall area covered by the ancient people, since as the excavation has revealed, the ancient people had once removed a substantial portion of older settlement for the construction of a huge fortification wall and a moat (Roy, 1985-86: 29). Chakrabarti (2001) observes that this fortified rectangular site measures about 17 to 18 acres. On the northern side across the modern road, which is about half a kilometre away, there is another high but much smaller mound (7 to 8 acres; 8 m high) within a moat. The major mound was excavated marginally for two seasons in 1984 and 1985 (Roy, 1985-86: 29-32) which resulted into a culture-sequence from the Chalcolithic to the Medieval period. This culture sequence has been divided into the following four periods:

Period I – Black slipped ware culture
Period II – NBPW period to circa 50 BC
Period III – circa 50 BC to AD 300
Period IV – Medieval period.

It is the earliest settlement which is relevant to the present context. This period has an average deposit of about two metres above the natural soil and has been termed black slipped ware culture by the excavator as it is the predominant ceramic industry. However, the black-and-red ware, the hallmark of almost all the Chalcolithic cultures of U.P. and Bihar, is also present side by side. The Chalcolithic shapes of this ware bowls with the everted and featureless rim, platters and dish-on-stand are present at this site. The last named shape is also represented in red ware (Roy, 1985-86: 30). No other antiquity was recovered from this phase except pottery discs and two fragments of stone of indeterminate use.

Remnants of burnt earth with reed impressions suggest that the hutments of this period were constructed of wattle-and-daub. This period overlaps with the NBPW culture of Period II, which has a cultural deposit of nearly 4 metres. According to the excavator, the earliest period at Manjhi could be dated to the beginning of the first millennium BC (Roy, 1985-86: 30).

Raja Nal Ka Tila

This site is situated at a distance of about 29 km east of Robertsganj in Sonbhadra district, near Pannuganj. Excavations conducted at this site for two seasons (1996, 1997), have exposed four-fold culture sequence as given below:

Period I: Pre-Iron (ca. 1700-1300 BC); Period II: Early Iron; Period III: NBPW ware; and Period IV: Gupta and post-Gupta.

Raja Nal Ka Tila is situated within a loop-like curve of the Karamnasa River which surrounds the ancient site from three sides, while the western side is blocked by a *nala*. The ancient settlement extends over an area of about 50 acres and is mostly under cultivation. This site was explored in the year 1994 and the first phase of excavations was conducted from March to May 1996. The second season's digging was performed in the year 1996-97 (Tewari and Srivastava, 1996-97: 77-96; Tewari and Srivastava, 1997-98, 99-106).

Period I is represented by a deposit of about one metre and is found to be devoid of any metallic remains. A few floors prepared with rammed earth, pit hearths and remains of wattle-and-daub structures were found in the first season's dig. A few post-holes forming oval or circular plan were noticed in the second season (Tewari and Srivastava, 1997-98: 101). The floors were prepared with rammed earth mixed with tiny pot-sherds. A few bone implements – mainly arrow-heads – were found on the floors. Terracotta and stone beads, chips and bladelets, stone pestles and balls are the other notable finds of this period.

Archaeobotanical remains were collected in both season's work. A preliminary examination of these samples by K.S. Saraswat showed that the earliest settlers of Period I had sufficient experience of agriculture and they cultivated rice, barley, lentil, field pea, *ragi* millet and fox-tail millet, besides *khesari* and *moong*.

The presence of *ragi* and fox-tail millet in the collection indicate that the inhabitants of Raja Nal Ka Tila gave due consideration to their ecological surroundings. These millets require little water and can thrive on the soil too poor for other cereals. Double cropping, i.e., rice in rainy seasons and lentil, pea, etc. in the winter, was practised in the inundated area of river Karamnasa.

A number of C-14 dates have been obtained from this site (see Table 1).

Period II (1300-700 BC) is represented by a cultural deposit of 1.50 to 2 metres at this site. This period marked the appearance of iron in considerable number from lower to upper levels. The artefacts include implements such as knife, arrow-heads, chisel, spear-head, etc. besides iron slags.

Ceramic industries are almost similar to those of the preceding period. Black-and-red ware bearing ochre and black coloured paintings are the typical representatives of this period. Structural remains comprise primary and secondary post-holes forming similar plans as of the earlier period. Four successive floors prepared with rammed clay were observed. Occurrence of *Kothilas* provide evidence of storage of grains. A large number of charred bones, some with cut marks, show that animal meat formed a considerable part of the diet.

Agiabir

Agiabir is located on the left bank of the Ganga about 2 km south-east of Katka railway station on the Varanasi-Allahabad section of the Northern Railway, on the border of Mirzapur and Ravidasnagar (Bhadohi) districts. Katka is situated 38 km west of Varanasi on Varanasi-Allahabad G.T. Road. The ancient settlement extends in an area of more than a kilometre along the river and it has been partly eroded by it. The main mound measures about 500 m × 500 m. The excavation was carried out in the western part of the main mound (ABR-1) and also in the eastern part of the settlement (ABR-2) by the present author (Singh *et al.*, 2004). On Mound-1 ten trenches, measuring 3 m × 3 m square, were excavated, while on Mound-2 only one trench measuring 5 m × 5 m was excavated which was subsequently restricted to only 2 m × 2 m area because of increased structural activity. This trench was excavated up to a depth of 7 metres without reaching the natural soil. These excavations revealed the following culture sequence (Singh and Singh, 2004).

Period I (Chalcolithic Culture)

Remains of Narhan culture were met within the lowermost 60 cm cultural deposit. The main ceramic industries of this period comprised black-and-red ware (mostly of medium and coarse fabrics), black slipped ware (in a limited quantity but in fine fabric) and red ware. The main types in black-and-red ware and black slipped ware are bowls, storage jars, lipped basins and dish-on-stand. Some sherds of black-and-red ware bear cord impressions on the exterior, and linear paintings in white as in the case of Narhan. The main types in black-and-red ware are bowls, storage jars, lipped basins and dish-on-stand. Some sherds of black-and-red ware bear cord impressions on the exterior. In black slipped ware, the important shapes are deep bowls, *lota*-shaped vessels and bowls with pedestal. In red ware no kitchenware vessels were reported except for legged perforated

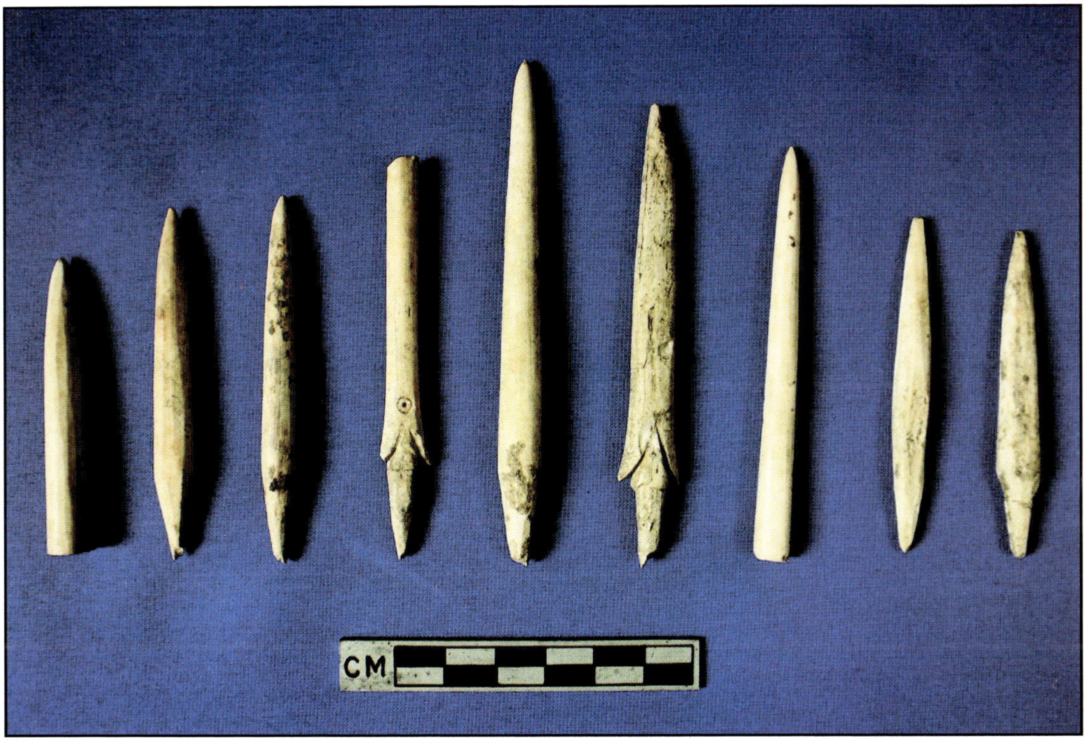

Pl. XIXA. Agiabir: Bone points, Period I

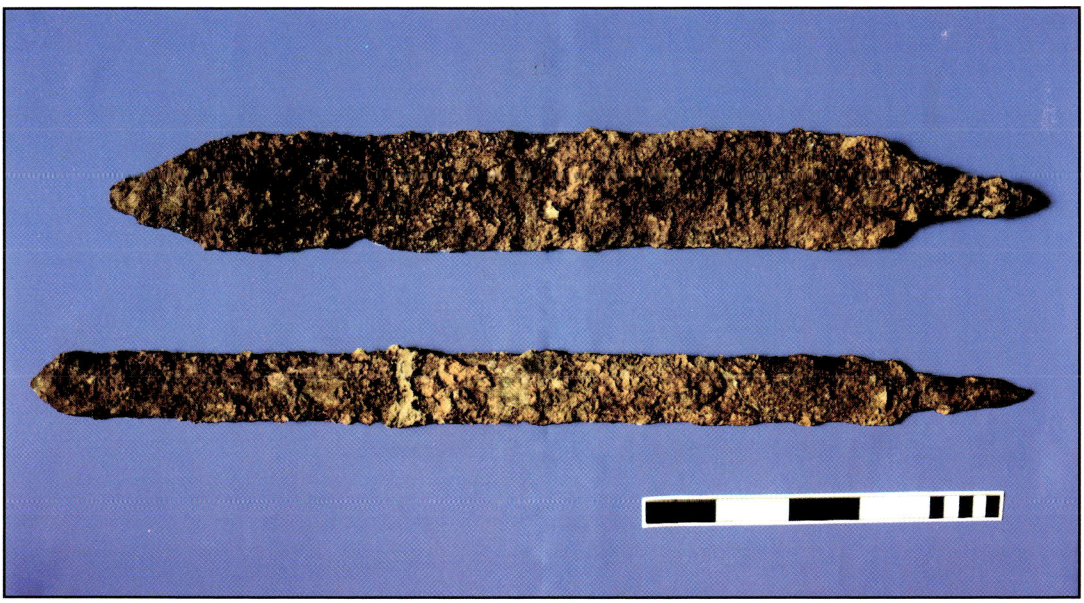

Pl. XIXB. Agiabir: Iron swords, Period III

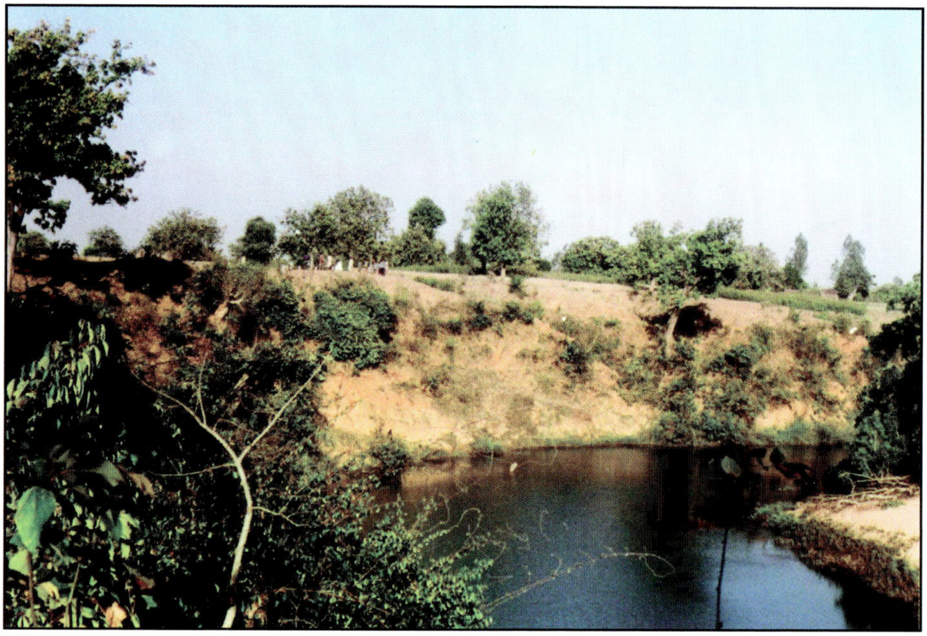

Pl. XXA. Raja Nal Ka Tila: General view of the mound

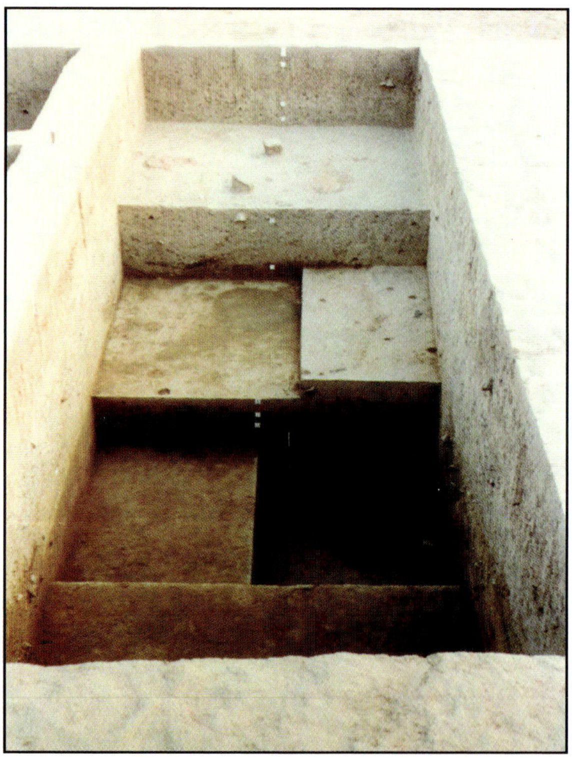

Pl. XXB. Raja Nal Ka Tila: General view of the excavated trench

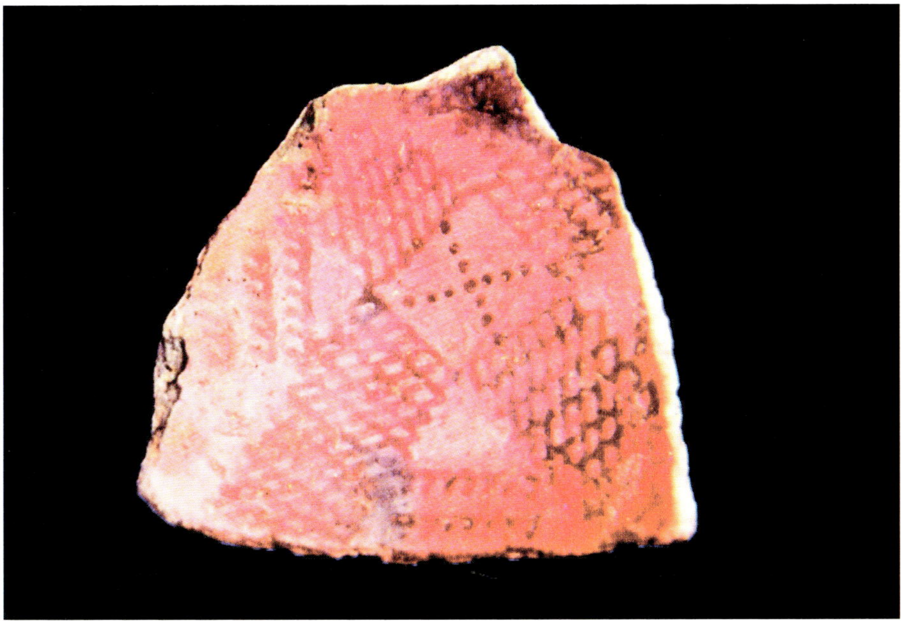

Pl. XXIA. Raja Nal Ka Tila: Decorated potsherd, Period I

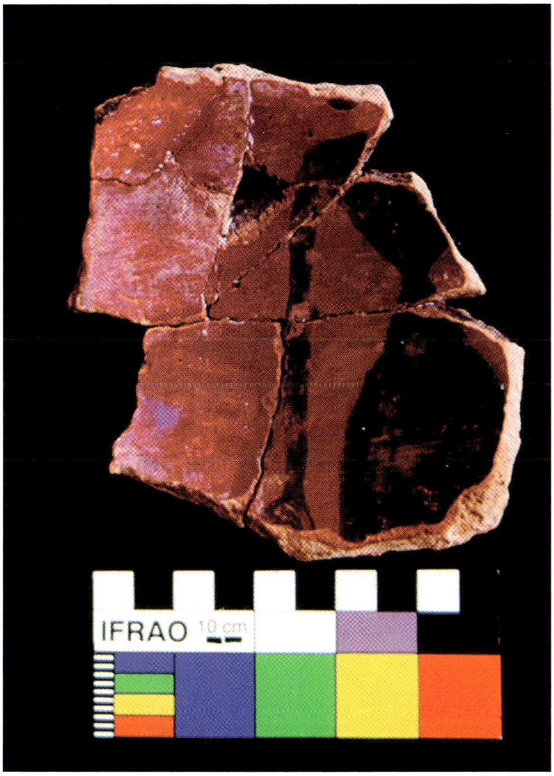

Pl. XXIB. Raja Nal Ka Tila: Painted potsherd, Period I

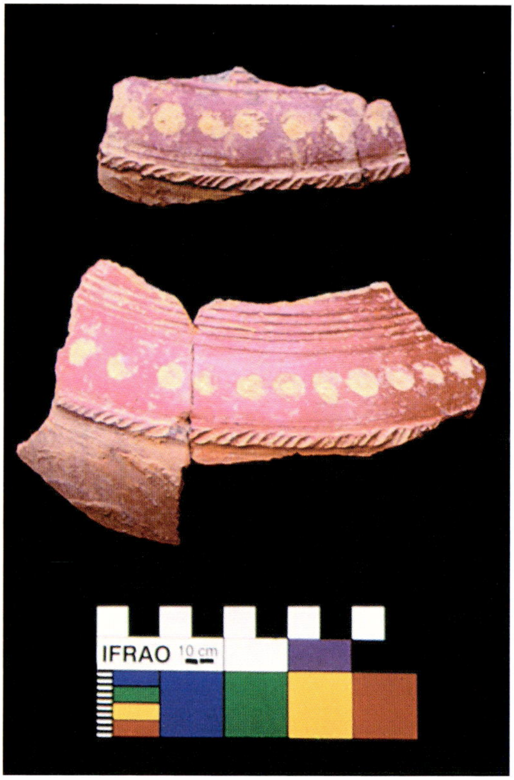

Pl. XXIIA. Raja Nal Ka Tila: Decorated potsherd (vase), Period I

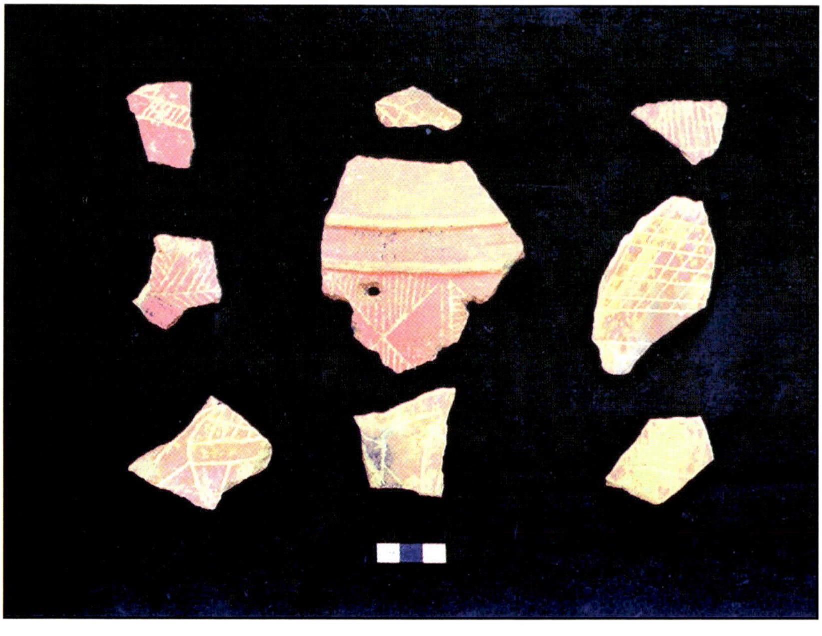

Pl. XXIIB. Raja Nal Ka Tila: Potsherds with incised designs, Period I

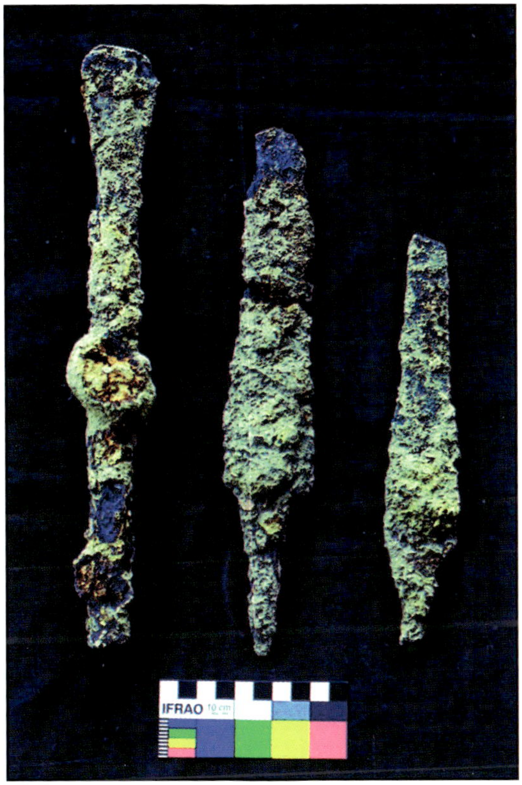

Pl. XXIIIA. Raja Nal Ka Tila: Iron artefacts, Period II

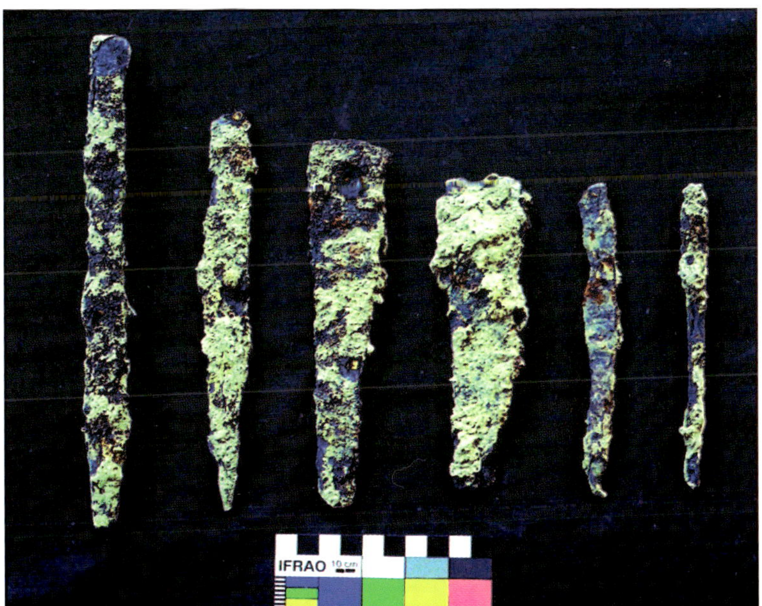

Pl. XXIIIB. Raja Nal Ka Tila: Iron artefacts, Period II

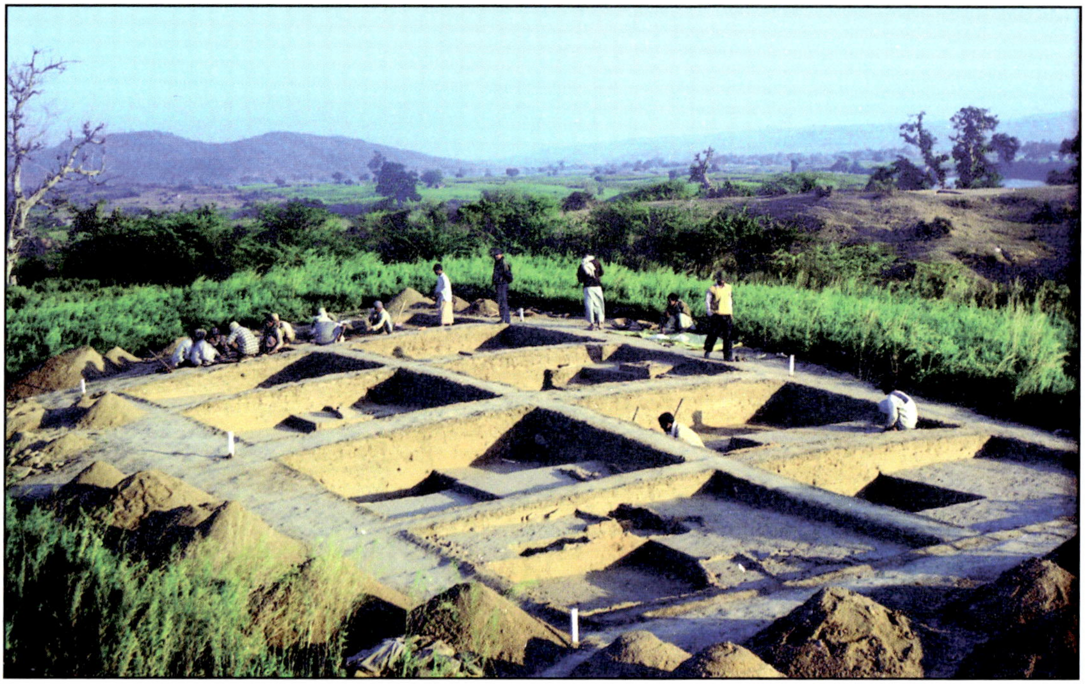

Pl. XXIVA. Malhar: General view of the excavated trenches

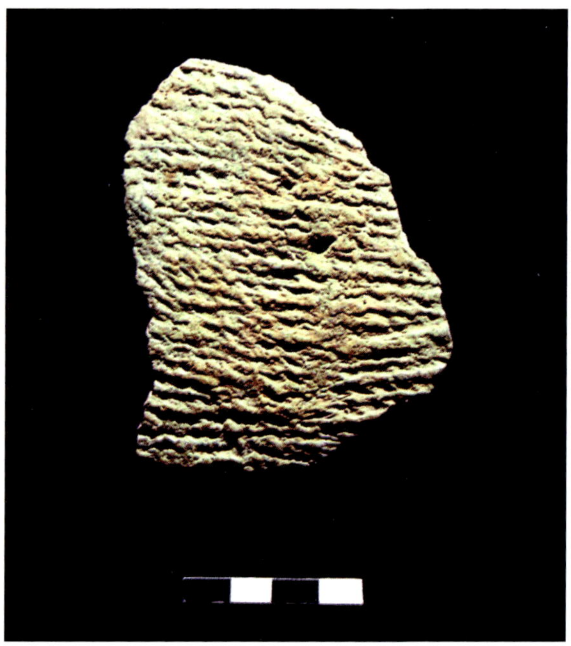

Pl. XXIVB. Malhar: Potsherd with cord impression on exterior, Period I

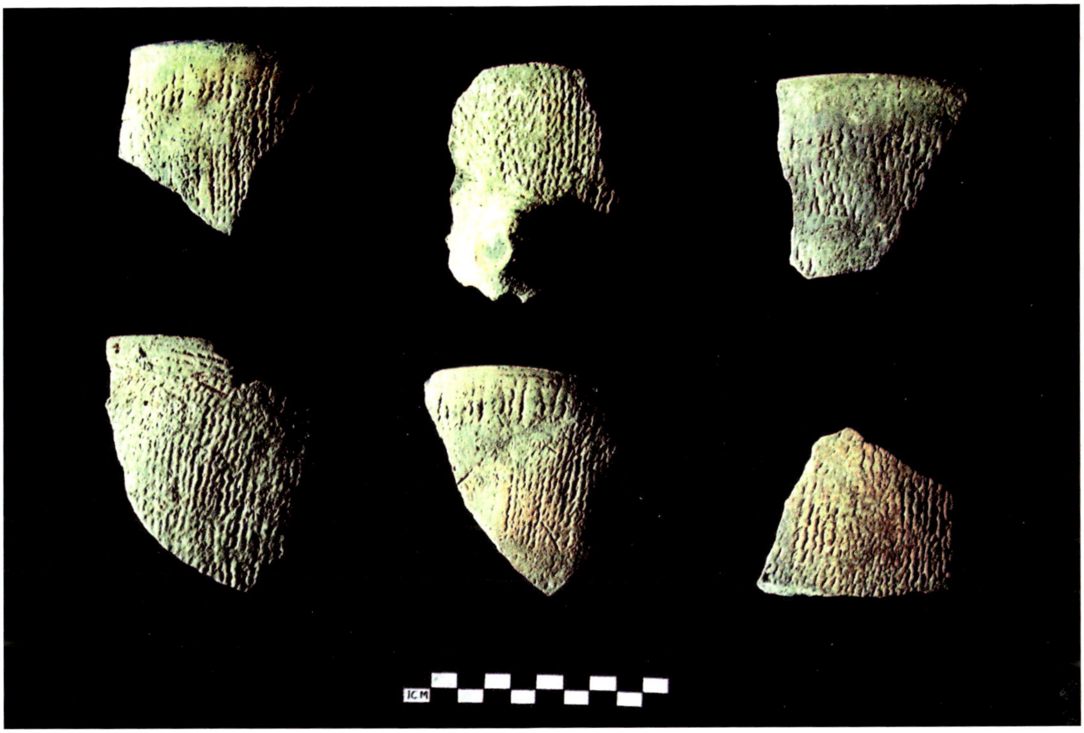

Pl. XXVA. Malhar: Potsherds of Corded Ware, Period I

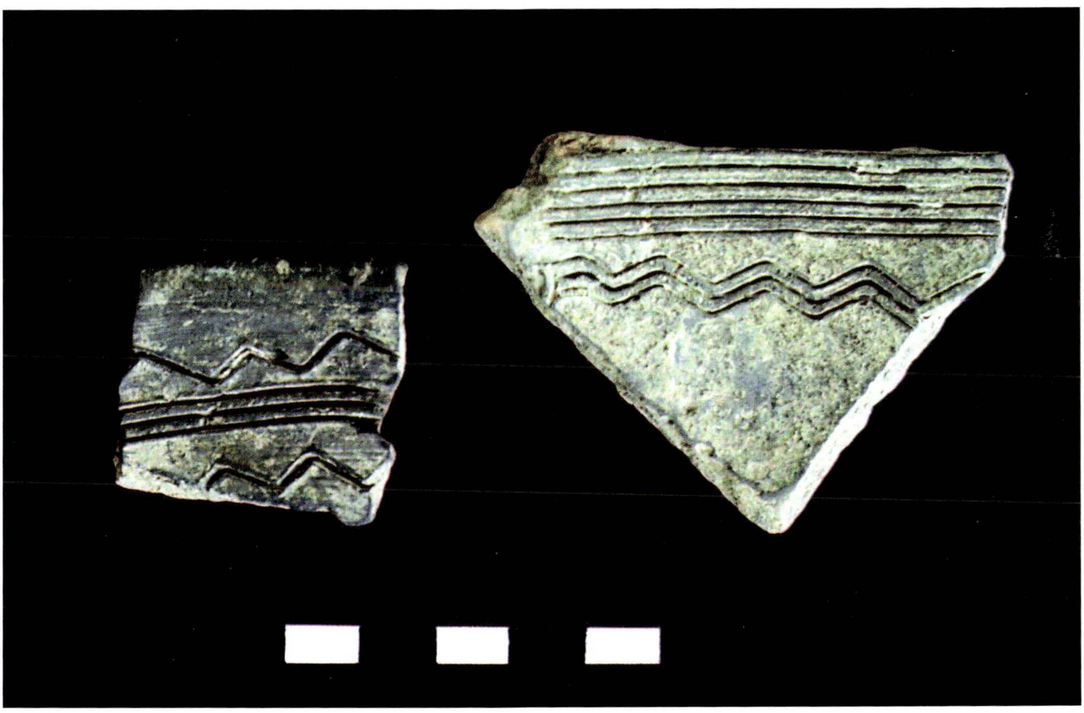

Pl. XXVB. Malhar: Incised potsherds, Period I

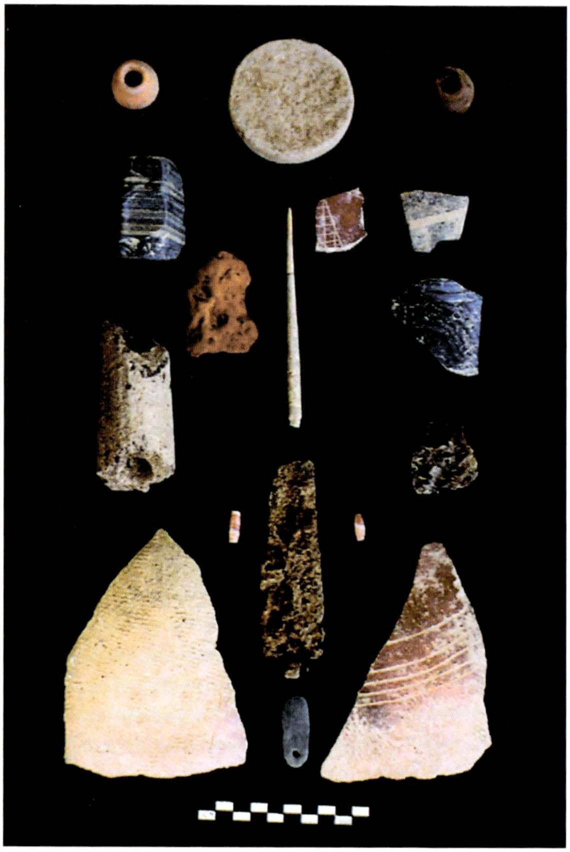

Pl. XXVIA. Malhar: Components of Early Iron Age culture, Period II

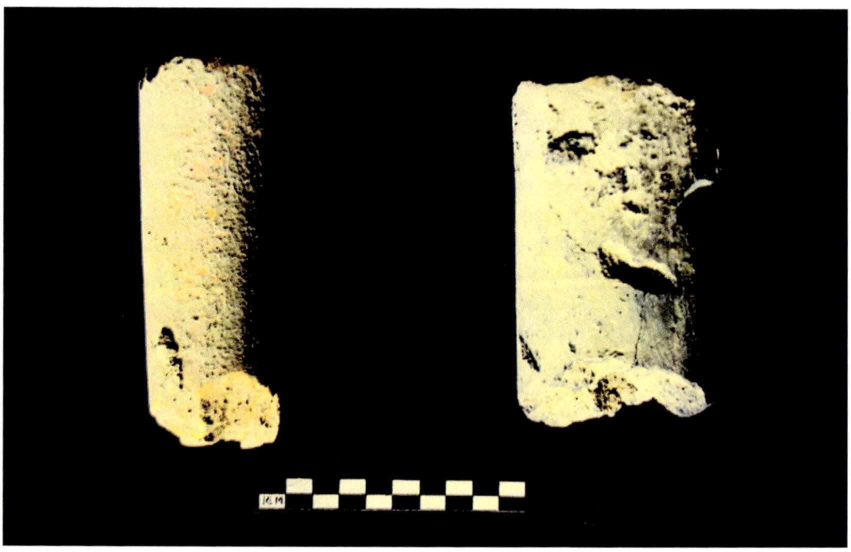

Pl. XXVIB. Malhar: Terracotta pipes (tuyeres), Period II

bowls with several perforations at the base. Vases and storage jars, some bearing appliqué designs on the exterior, are the other types in this ware.

The inhabitants of this period lived in wattle-and-daub houses. Fragment of burnt clay with reed marks and patches of floors, ovens and post-holes have been recorded. Two silos, obviously used for storage of grains, were brought to light. A bead manufacturing workshop is an important discovery of this period. Twenty-six stone beads (18 finished and 8 unfinished) together with stone chips were recovered. Other antiquities comprised net sinkers, bone points and pottery discs. A large number of bones and charcoal samples were collected from various strata of this period. Their study will furnish valuable information regarding the fauna and chronology of this period.

Excavations at Agiabir were resumed again by Vibha Tripathi of the same organization who excavated six trenches on the main mound (Mound 2) in March-May 2006 up to a maximum depth of 7 metres without reaching the natural soil. Several burnt brick structures of Kushana and Gupta periods were exposed (Tripathi and Upadhyaya, 2007). However, the five period culture-sequence established earlier by P. Singh remains unchanged.

In this context mention may be made of field investigations carried out at a number of sites by the Banaras Hindu University in recent years. The excavations at Aktha located to the north-east of the city of Varanasi revealed that it was inhabited since eleventh century BC (Jayaswal, 2003, 2009). Similar was the case of Sarai Mohana situated on the left bank of the Varuna River just before it joins the Ganga. The two excavations demonstrate that the antiquity of the city of Varanasi may be traced back to the eleventh century BC if not earlier (Singh and Singh, 2004). It was only after three centuries that Rajghat was selected as a dwelling area. Further small-scale digging made at Ramnagar, on the right bank of the Ganga, just opposite to the present city of Varanasi in 2006 has revealed a thick deposit of black slipped ware and NBP ware. This settlement continued to flourish till the Gupta period. It has been suggested that Ramnagar was a craftsman's colony catering to the needs of Varanasi city (Jayaswal and Kumar, 2006: 85).

Again small scale excavation conducted at Anai, located about 35 km north-west of Varanasi, revealed that this settlement was inhabited during the pre-NBPW period (ca. 900 BC-600 BC) and continued to flourish till the late phase of NBPW (200 BC). This site was re-occupied briefly during the early medieval period (Tripathi and Upadhyay, 2006: 95).

MALHAR

One of the most crucial sites of Chalcolithic period, excavated in recent years, is Malhar, located on the left bank of the Karamnasa, at a distance of about 10 km from Chakia in district Chandauli. Most of the ancient settlement at Malhar is under cultivation but a small portion is considerably preserved (Tewari, 1997-98: 59; Tewari *et al.*, 2004: 1-112). Sherds of red ware, black slipped ware, black-and-red ware and associated pottery were picked up during 1997-98. This site was subjected to archaeological excavations during January-March 1999 by the U.P. State Archaeology Department and the maximum cultural deposit of 1.34 m to 1.50 m in thickness was divided into the following four periods (Tewari *et al.*, 2004: 23):

Period I – Pre-Iron Phase or Early Farming Phase (ca. 2200-1800 BC)
Period II – Early Iron Phase (ca. 1800-800 BC)
Period III – NBPW Phase (ca. 700-300 BC)
Period IV – Early Historic Phase (ca. 200 BC-AD 300)

The earliest period is Chalcolithic in character and it has a maximum deposit of about 50 cm in thickness. The main ceramic industries are red ware (plain and corded), black-and-red ware (plain and corded) and black ware. Here the black-and-red ware is the principal ceramic industry accounting for as much as 42.60% (Tewari *et al.*, 1999-2000: 70; 2004: 23). An examination of archaeobotanical samples reveals while rice was the principal cereal grown at Malhar, other grains and seeds belonging to barley, *mung*, field pea, dwarf wheat, bread wheat, four varieties of millets, lentil and *khesari* were cultivated (Saraswat, 2004: 137-72). Bone remains indicate that meat also played considerable role in the protein-rich diet of ancient settlers.

Field crops documented from Malhar

	Vernacular and Botanical names	Period-I Pre-Iron Phase 1900 BC (Cal. 2150 BC)-1700-1600 BC (Cal. 1840-1740 BC)	Period-II Early-Iron Phase 1700-1600 (Cal. 1840-1740 BC) – 800 BC (?)
1.	Rice (*Oryza sativa*)	•	•
2.	Barley (*Hordeum vulgare*)	•	•
3.	Dwarf-wheat (*Triticum sphaerococcum*)	•	•
4.	Bread-wheat (*Triticum aestivum*)	•	•
5.	Italian-millet (*Setaria italica*)	•	-

6.	Jowar-millet (*Sorghum bicolor*)	-	•
7.	Ragi-millet (*Eleusine coracana*)	-	•
8.	Kodon-millet (*Paspalum scrobiculatum*)	-	•
9.	Field-pea (*Pisum arvense*)	•	•
10.	Lentil (*Lens culinaris*)	•	•
11.	Grass-pea (*Lathyrus sativus*)	•	•
12.	Green-gram (*Vigna radiata*)	•	•
13.	Horse-gram (*Macrotyloma uniflorum*)	-	•

• Indicates presence (Note: A seed of sesame (*Sesamum indicum*) from Period-II in highly brittle condition, crumbled during handling

The presence of burnt clay lumps with reed marks suggests that the earliest inhabitants lived in huts having screens made of reeds and plastered with mud. No other structural remains such as floor on post-holes could be found in excavation.

Small finds from the earliest deposits are limited in number. Simple and double-evolved arrowheads and points comprise the bone objects. A few bladelet-shaped objects are representatives of stone objects (Tewari *et al.*, 1999-2000: 76). Terracotta beads comprise mainly vase-shaped specimens. A large pit found in one of the excavated trenches has been interpreted as an earthen bin. It was excavated in the virgin soil. Similar bins have been found at Imlidih Khurd, Chechar-Kutubpur and Lahuradewa (Tewari, 2004: 24).

There is no hiatus between the deposits of Period I and the succeeding period which has a deposit of 60-80 cm. The characteristic features of Period II are the appearance of iron artefacts, iron slag, a particular type of oval structures (furnaces), besides black slipped ware and fine grey ware. The oval structures have lengths varying from 0.60 m to 2.56 m and their maximum and minimum widths are about 70 and 46 cm. The material found within the oval structures consists of pot-sherds, broken stones, burnt clay nodules and a few pieces of iron lag. Further, a considerable number of terracotta pipes (tuyeres) were found in different trenches. On circumstantial evidence, the oval structures were taken to be fine-flakes in which burning activities were carried out, and the ash content used to be discharged as a regular feature, after cleaning of the structure (Tewari *et al.*, 1999-2000: 78). Similar furnaces were also located at the nearby site of Lohsanwa (Tewari *et al.*, 1999-2000: 78). A large number (71 pieces) of iron artefacts have been found from various trenches which suggests that from the very beginning of Period II, iron technology was in an evolved form at Malhar. It has been argued that in Period II some new people, with considerable experience of iron technology, came and settled at Malhar. They were bearers of iron-metallurgical tradition in this region of India and not the authors of it. The immigrants indubitably hailed from some community of skilled iron-smiths established elsewhere (Tewari *et al.,* 1999-2000: 81).

Four radiocarbon dates are available for the samples from Periods I and II at Malhar. Their uncalibrated as well as caliberated values are given in the following table:

Radiocarbon ages from Malhar

S. No.	Laboratory Number	Radiocarbon Ages in BP/BC on the Basis of Half Life		Cal. BC Stulver *et al.* One Sigma
		5568 ± 30 years	5730 ± 40 years	
1.	BS-1623, MLR II Trench No. XA 1, Layer No. (3) Depth 0.55 cm	3450 ± 90 BP 1500 ± 90 BC	3550 ± 90 BP 1600 ± 90 BC	1882 (1743) 1639 BC
2.	BS-1614, MLR II Trench No. A 1, Pit sealed by Layer No. (3) Depth 61-63 cm	6380 ± 110 BP 4430 ± 110 BC	6570 ± 110 BP 4620 ± 110 BC	5475 (5358, 5351, 5340, 5329, 5323) 5262 BC
3.	BS-1593, MLR II Trench No. A 1, Pit sealed by Layer No. (3) Depth 90-100 cm	3540 ± 90 BP 1590 ± 90 BC	3650 ± 90 BP 1700 ± 90 BC	2012 (1882, 1836, 1834) 1742 BC
4.	BS-1590, MLR II Trench No. XA 1, Layer No. (4) Depth 80 cm	3740 ± 90 BP 1790 ± 90 BC	3850 ± 80 BP 1900 ± 80 BC	2283 (2141) 1984 BC

TOKWA

As mentioned earlier, Tokwa is one of the largest and well-preserved Neolithic-Chalcolithic settlement in the Vindhyas. Though this site was explored in the early sixties of the last century, its true potential was realized for the first time in the limited excavation conducted in February-March 2000 and again in 2003 by the University of Allahabad. The culture sequence comprises Neolithic, Chalcolithic and Early Iron Age deposits.

The Chalcolithic settlement exposed at the site has yielded identical ceramic industries as obtained from Kakoria on the Chandraprabha, Koldihwa on the Belan and Magha in the Adwa valley (Misra *et al.*, 2000-2001: 70). This phase is characterized by black-and-red ware, black slipped ware and red ware. Besides the ceramic tradition, short blade industry, beads fashioned on semi-precious stones and terracotta, bone arrowheads particularly of socketed variety, are the other salient features of this culture.

The excavators observe that there was a gap between the disappearance of the Neolithic culture and arrival of the Chalcolithic culture as these two cultures exhibit different traits in ceramic tradition. However, this point needs some closer observation in future investigation (Misra *et al.*, 2000-2001: 70).

The osteological remains from the Chalcolithic levels were studied by Joglekar *et al.* (2008). A total of 324 faunal elements were recovered from the Chalcolithic levels. It was found that the overall proportion of domestic mammals was much large than wild animals. The cattle and buffalo together formed the major part of the faunal assemblage (88.12%). The proportion of cattle as compared to buffalo was much more. Among other animals, domestic pig, sheep and domestic ass were found from Chalcolithic levels. The spectrum of wild animals is much narrower than the Neolithic phase. Only three wild mammals were found in this phase – gaur, blackbuck and spotted deer.

JHUSI

Jhusi, the ancient Pratisthanpur, is located on the left bank of the Ganga, very close to the Ganga-Yamuna confluence at a distance of about 7 km to the east of Allahabad city. The ancient site extends for about 3 km along the river. Its width from west to east measures about 1.5 km (Misra *et al.*, 1995-96: 63). Originally one compact mound, it has now been dissected into a number of smaller mounds by rain gullies and encroachment by people.

This site has been known as an early historical settlement and potteries and antiquities were picked up from time to time by the University of Allahabad. However, the first scientific excavation was conducted in March-April 1995 by V.D. Misra and his team (1995-96). This excavation revealed a gradual material development ranging from Neolithic to early Medieval period. The culture sequence has been divided into the following seven periods:

Period I : Neolithic
Period II : Chalcolithic

Period III: Early Iron Age (Pre NBPW with iron)
Period IV: NBPW
Period V: Saka-Kushana
Period VI: Gupta Period
Period VII: Early Medieval Period

The Chalcolithic deposit has a total thickness of 70 cm and is characterised by black-and-red ware, black slipped ware, black burnished ware and red were with characteristic pottery types. Burnt clay lumps with reed marks and a few microliths completed the inventory during 1995.

The excavations at Jhusi were resumed again in March-June 1998 and 4 trenches, each measuring 5 metres square, were laid out on the Samudrakup mound. The five cultural periods, delineated in 1995 was reconfirmed in this excavation. It was found that the cultural deposit of the earliest period (Chalcolithic) was 4.36 m – perhaps the thickest deposit anywhere of this culture. Besides the characteristic pottery noted above, beads fashioned on ivory were recorded. On the basis of presence or absence of iron objects, the pre-NBPW deposit has been divided into two sub-groups – IA and IB. While the sub-group IA representing layers 52 to 63 did not yield any iron object, group IB comprising layers 45 to 51 is associated with iron objects (Misra *et al.*, 1998-99: 46).

Excavations at Jhusi were resumed for the third season during March-June 1999 and some more details regarding the pre-NBPW culture were obtained. It was found that sub-phase IA (pre-iron) has a cultural deposit of 2.75 m comprising layers 53 to 68. The ceramic industries were the same as noted in this first season's excavation. This pottery compares well with its counterparts in the Vindhyas on the one hand and those of the Chalcolithic site of the Ganga valley on the other (Misra *et al.*, 1999-2000: 24). In addition, barbed and socketed arrowheads with engraved circlets were recorded from sub-phase IA. This type of arrowheads also occur at Narhan, Chirand, Senuwar and Koldihwa. Besides, beads fashioned on semi-precious stones and terracotta, were recorded. The animal bones found in the hearths comprise those of cattle, sheep, goat and pig. Charred grains of wheat, barley, rice and *moong* were obtained from the pits. Post-holes, floors and hearths constituted the structural activity. On the basis of two radio-carbon dates from the pre-Iron (Chalcolithic) phase, the sub-period IA has been dated to a period from mid-second millennium BC to circa 1000 BC (Misra *et al.*, 1999-2000: 28).

Sub-period IB has a deposit of 1.60 m comprising layers 45 to 52 and is characterised by the presence of iron.

SRINGAVERAPURA

This site is located on the left bank of the Ganga at a distance of 36 km north-west of Allahabad. It was excavated between 1977 and 1980 (Lal and Dikshit, 1978-79). The culture sequence, divisible into seven cultural phases, ranges in date from the last quarter of the second millennium BC to the early Medieval period. Among them, the earliest settlement (Period) has a thickness of 30 to 50 cm and is relevant in the present context.

The earliest inhabitants lived in huts made of reed and bamboo and plastered over with mud. The archaeological relics are represented by burnt clay lumps with reed impressions. The pottery is a kind of red ware, some of which resembles the ochre-coloured ware. The types include jars with prominently out-turned rim, bowl with featureless or everted rim, shallow basins with horizontally splayed-out rim, vases with disc base and platters (Lal and Dikshit, 1978-79: 1). The small finds are not many and comprise pottery discs, with or without a central perforation, and a flake of carnelian. The suggested date of Period I is circa 1050-1000 BC.

Period II (ca. 950-700 BC), with an average deposit of about 1.5 m, has yielded besides ceramic industries, points and arrowheads of bone, a bone pendant, and beads fashioned on terracotta, jasper and gold.

The archaeo-botanical specimens from the earliest period were examined by K.S. Saraswat (1980-81: 79-89) who has identified grains of six-rowed *Hoerdeum* species, paddy, sesame (*Seasmum* sp.) and cotton (*Gossypium* sp.).

REFERENCES

Chakrabarti, Dilip K. 1986. Iron and Urbanization: An Examination of the Indian Context, *Puratattva*, No. 15.

_____. 2001. *Archaeological Geography of the Ganga Plain: The Lower and the Middle Ganga*, Delhi, Permanent Black.

Charurvedi, S. N. 1985. Advance of Vindhyan Neolithic and Chalcolithic cultures to the Himalayan Tarai, *Man and Environment*, IX: 101-108.

Jayaswal, V. 2003. Aktha: A Satellite Settlement of Sarnath, *Bharati*, No. 26: 61-180.

_____. 2009. *Ancient Varanasi: An Archaeological Perspective*, New Delhi, Aryan Books International.

Jayaswal, V. and M. Kumar. 2006. Excavations at Ramnagar: Discovery of the Supporting Settlement of Ancient Varanasi, *Puratattva*, No. 36: 85-92.

Joglekar, P.P, V.D. Misra, J.N. Pal and M.C. Gupta. 2008. Faunal Remains from Neolithic-Chalcolithic phases at Tokwa, Mirzapur District, Uttar Pradesh, *Man and Environment*, XXXIII (2): 51-59.

Kajale, M.D. and B.C. Deotare. 1988-89. Pollen analysis and chemical examinations of a prehistoric lake site at Damdama, *Puratattva*, No. 19: 27-30.

Lal, B.B. and K.N. Dikshit. 1978-79. Sringaverpura: A Key site for the protohistory and early history of the central Ganga Valley, *Puratattva*, No. 10: 1-7.

Lal, B.B. 1993. *Sringaverapura Excavations*, New Delhi, Archaeological Survey of India.

Misra, B.B. 2000. Chalcolithic cultures of the northern Vindhyas and the mid-Ganga Valley, in S.C. Bhattacharya, V.D. Misra, J.N. Pandey and J.N. Pal (eds.), *Peeping through the Past* (Prof. G.R. Sharma Memorial Volume), Allahabad, University of Allahabad: 66-85.

Misra, V.D., B.B. Misra, J.N. Pal and M.C. Gupta. 2000. Explorations at Tokwa: A Neolithic-Chalcolithic Settlement on the confluence of the Belan and Adwa rivers, in S.C. Bhattacharya, V.D. Misra, J.N. Pandey and J.N. Pal (eds.), *Peeping through the Past* (Prof. G.R. Sharma, Memorial Volume), Allahabad, University of Allahabad: 45-57.

Misra, V.D., B.B. Misra, J.N. Pandey and J.N. Pal. 1995-96. A Preliminary Report of Excavation at Jhusi, 1995, *Pragdhara*, No. 6: 63-66.

Misra, V.D., J.N. Pal and M.C. Gupta. 1998-89. Further Excavation at Jhusi, District Allahabad (Uttar Pradesh): 1998, *Pragdhara*, No.: 45-50.

_____. 1999-2000. Further Excavation at Jhusi, District Allahabad (Uttar Pradesh): 1999, *Pragdhara*, No. 10: 22-30.

_____. 2000-2001. Excavations at Tokwa: A Neolithic-Chalcolithic Settlement, *Pragdhara*, No. 11: 59-72.

_____. 2001. Neolithic Cultures of Northern Vindhyas with Special Reference to Tokwa, *Bharati*, No. 25 (Parts I & II): 211-233.

_____. 2002-2003. Further excavations at Jhusi: Evidence of Neolithic Culture, *Pragdhara*, No. 13: 227-230.

Misra, V.D. and B.B. Misra. 2000. Chalcolithic Cultures of the Northern Vindhyas and the Middle Ganga Valley: Some Observations, in V.D. Misra and J.N. Pal (eds.), *Social History and Social Theory*, Allahabad, University of Allahabad: 14-22.

Narain, A.K. and T.N. Roy. 1963. *Excavations at Prahladpur*, Varanasi, Banaras Hindu University.

_____. 1977. *Excavations at Rajghat*, Varanasi, Banaras Hindu University.

Prasad, A.K. 1980-81. Exacavations at Taradih, *Puratattva*, No. 12: 180-81.

Pal, J.N. 1986. *Archaeology of Southern Uttar Predesh*, Allahabad, Swabha Prakashan.

_____. 2008. The Early Farming Culture of the Middle Ganga Plain with Special Reference to the Excavation of Jhusi and Hetapatti, *Pragdhara*, No. 18: 263-282.

Roy, T.N. 1985-86. Excavations at Majhi, 1983-85: A Preliminary Report, *Puratattva*, No. 16: 29-32.

Saraswat, K.S. 1980-81. Plant Economy at ancient Sringaverapura, Phase I (1050-1000 BC), *Puratattva*, No. 12: 79-89.

_____. 2004. Plant Economy in Ancient Malhar, *Pragdhara*, No. 14: 137-172.

Sathe, V. and G.L. Badam. 2004. Faunal Remains, in B.P. Singh, *Early Farming Communities of the Kaimur*, Jaipur, Publication Scheme, Vol. II: 536-584.

Singh, B.P. 1987-88. Khairadih: A Chalcolithic Settlement, *Puratattva*, No. 18: 28-33.

_____. 1989-90. The Chalcolithic Culture of Southern Bihar as revealed by the Exploration and Excavations in District Rohtas, *Puratattva,* No. 20: 83-92.

_____. 1995-96. Transformation of Cultures in the Middle Ganga Plain: A case study of Senuwar, *Pragdhara,* No. 6: 75-94.

_____. 2004. *Early Farming Communities of the Kaimur (Excavations at Senuwar),* Jaipur, Publication Scheme.

Singh, B.P. and A.K. Singh. 2004. Excavation at Sarai Mohana 1967-68, *Bharati,* No. 27: 1-20.

Singh, P. 1991-92. Excavation at Imlidih Khurd, *Puratattva,* No. 22: 120-22.

_____. 1992: Neolithic-Chalcolithic Cultures of Eastern U.P., in Rakesh Tewari (ed.), *Archaeological Perspectives of Uttar Pradesh and Future Prospects,* Part I, Lucknow: 67-76.

_____. 1992-93. Archaeological Excavations at Imlidih Khurd-1992, *Pragdhara,* No. 3: 21-36.

_____. 1993-94. Further Excavations at Imlidih Khurd-1993, *Pragdhara,* No. 4: 41-48.

_____. 1994. Excavations at Narhan (1984-89), Varanasi and Delhi, Banaras Hindu University and B.R. Publishing Corporation.

_____. 1999. Rise of Cultures in Eastern India, in G.C. Pande (ed.), *History of Indian Science, Philosophy and Culture,* Vol. No. I, The Indian Council of Philosophical Research, New Delhi.

Singh, P., A.K. Singh and Brahmanand Singh. 1994-95. Protohistoric Investigations in Ballia District, Uttar Pradesh, *Pragdhara,* No. 5: 21-36.

Singh, P. and A.K. Singh. 1995-96. Trial excavations at Waina, District Ballia, U.P., *Pragdhara,* No. 6: 41-61.

_____. 1997-98. Trial excavations at Bhunadih, District Ballia, U.P., *Pragdhara,* No. 8: 11-29.

_____. 2004. *The Archaeology of Middle Ganga Plain: New Perspectives (Excavations at Agiabir*), Shimla, Indian Institute of Advanced Study and New Delhi, Aryan Books International.

Singh, S.K. 1999-2000. Lithic industry of Agiabir, District Mirzapur (U.P), *Pragdhara,* No. 10: 57-63.

_____. 2000-2001. Lithic industries of Waina, District Ballia, U.P., *Pragdhara,* No. 11: 105-107.

Sinha, B.P. 1982. Harappan Fall out (?) in the Mid Gangetic Valley, in Gregory L. Possehl (ed.), *Harappan Civilization,* New Delhi.

Tewari, R. 1997-98. In Quest of early Iron Age Sites in the Karamnasa Valley, *Pragdhara,* No. 8: 57-68.

Tewari, R., R.K. Srivastava, K.S. Saraswat and K.K. Sinha. 1999-2000. Excavations at Malhar, District Chandauli, U.P. 1999: A Preliminary Report, *Pragdhara,* No. 10: 69-98.

Tewari, R., R.K. Srivastava and K.K. Singh. 2003-2004. Report of Excavation at Malhar, District Chandauli, U.P. 1998-99, *Pragdhara,* No. 14: 1-112.

Tripathi, V., A.K. Singh and P. Upadhyaya. 2005-06. Excavations at Agiabir (2005-06), District Mirzapur, Uttar Pradesh, *Bharti*, No. 30: 1-38.

Tripathi, V. and P. Upadhyaya. 2006. Anai: A Settlement in Varuna Region, *Puratattva*, No. 36: 93-102.

_____. 2007. Further Excavations at Agiabir (2005-06), *Puratattva*, No. 37: 121-129.

Verma, B.S. 1997. A Short Note on Chirand Excavations, in J.P. Joshi (ed.), *Facets of Indian Civilization: Recent Perspectives*, (Essays in Honour of Professor B.B. Lal), New Delhi, Aryan Books International, Vol. I: 75-80.

6

Material Culture and Social Formations

A study of archaeological data presented in the preceding pages brings forth the following points regarding the development of material culture in the middle Ganga plain through the ages and the crystallization of social formations:

SETTLEMENT PATTERN

As stated earlier, the lakes formed by meandering rivers in the south-central margin of the Ganga plain attracted the Mesolithic population. Biological remains from sites in this region show that the settlers exploited both terrestrial and aquatic fauna. Elsewhere people lived in the open, on the tops of low hills and in the valleys and along the banks of perennial or seasonal streams (Misra, V.N., 1996: 322). The colonization of virgin areas like the Ganga plains, and intensification of habitation in previously colonized areas, like Mewar, Central India and the Deccan plateau, clearly suggests that Mesolithic period saw a dramatic rise in human population (Misra, V.N., *Ibid.*).

The Mesolithic sites in the middle Ganga plain have fairly dense but discontinuous distribution. The Mesolithic settlement pattern is seen either along rivulets and their seasonal tributaries or in close association to horse-shoe lakes. Very few sites are located away from rivers and lakes. Obviously the settlements are related to the availability of water and aquatic resources. The settlements are generally small in size and measure around 5 metre square. Very few large settlements like Sarai Nahar Rai, Mahadaha and Damdama are seen. The average spacing between two sites is between 5 and 10 km.

Field investigations carried out by us in the Sarayupar plain shows that during the Neolithic and Chalcolithic periods, the prehistoric man inhabited the area which was comparatively more fertile and which was drained by smaller tributaries of large rivers like the Ghaghara. Thus, the preferred rivers were the Kuwana, the Ami, the Manwar and the like. They avoided other rivers like the Rapti, Burhi Rapti, Parasi, Banganga, Jamuar, etc. as they are flood prone and create havoc during rainy season. Further, they generally preferred *Tals* like the Bhuila, Skahara Lahuradewa Awaina, Nagar, Tahari, Bakhira and others. Of the 165 sites explored by S.C. Singh in the Basti district, 23 belonged to the Chalcolithic period; 47 settlements contained NBPW deposits and the remaining 80 sites have been assigned to the Kushana-Gupta period (Singh, S.C., 1991: 219). A close examination of the data indicates that there was a sudden rise and concentration of settlements belonging to the first-second century AD. The increase in structural activities was also noticed in the excavations at Bhuila and Piprahwa (Srivastava, 1985). Our own field investigations carried out along the Kuwana River in Basti district provided interesting results (Singh *et al.*, 1991-92: 34). It was observed that:

1. The earliest settlers belonging to the Narhan culture preferred to settle mainly on the banks of the river and not away from it. For avid agriculturist communities, water was of prime importance to sustain their crops.
2. Subsequently, with the advancement of irrigation techniques the people of later periods could afford to spread out in the adjoining areas. It is our observation that sites of later periods are generally located comparatively away from the river.
3. The density of sites is less in the flood plains as the annual floods would inundate and damage the crops. Even today the area is sparsely populated.
4. It was also noted that the density of settlements in the area explored by us was comparatively more in the richer soil as compared to the areas where the soil is less fertile.
5. It was also observed that the large settlements were located mainly on such spots where the river was comparatively more navigable. Incidentally these navigable places continued to be used as *ghats* (ferry-crossings) in later times as well.
6. As compared to the Ghaghara, which becomes terribly violent during the rainy season, the Kuwana is a slow flowing and meandering river and it provided added attraction to the earliest inhabitants as their settlements and crops would not get damaged by annual floods.

7. Our exploration revealed that the number of sites on the Kuwana upstream from Basti town is greatly reduced. The river has been reduced to be only a small nullah to the north-west of Basti proper as it originates from that area, further up in district Bahraich. Obviously, the volume of water available in the river, particularly in the lean months was not adequate enough to sustain agricultural operations. This might perhaps account for the sparseness of settlements of Narhan culture in this region.
8. Our exploration revealed that Narhan related sites occur in clusters comprising four to five sites in each cluster. The distance between such clusters varies from 3 km to 5 km.

As regards the settlement pattern of Neolithic-Chalcolithic sites in Bihar, it has been noted that all major Neolithic sites excavated so far, are situated on the river banks. Chirand has an about 1 km long mound at the confluence of the Sarayu and the Ganga. Chechar Kutubpur lies on the bank of the Ganga near Biddupur, on the opposite side of Patna while Senuwar lies on the bank of a stream in a fertile plain in the foot of the Kaimur range not far from Sasaram. Maner lies on the bank of an old course of the Ganga near Patna and Taradih is present-day Bodh Gaya. Basically, they are all river bank sites. They comfortably formed villages in such widely spaced areas as Bodh Gaya and Chirand directly on the banks of major rivers like the Ganga in the third millennium BC.

There are 70 odd reported Chalcolithic and Iron Age black-and-red ware sites in West Bengal. They are distributed mostly in the area to the west the Bhagirathi. The river valleys are, from the north to the south, Dwaraka, Mayurakshi, Bakreshwar, Kopai, Ajay, Damodar, Dwarakeshwar, Silai, and Kasai and their smaller tributaries, all flowing through a sloping plateau region from the west to the east towards the Bhagirathi. A study of their individual locations suggests that some of the sites in the western part of the state were located in agriculturally less attractive areas and were perhaps geared towards the raw material resources of the main part of the Chotanagpur plateau. Otherwise, the overall preference was for the fertile stretches along rivers and for a general nearness to low-lying lands (Chakrabarti, 1999: 242-43).

AGRICULTURE AND PASTORALISM

The transition from foraging to farming, which began some ten thousand years ago, was most fateful change as it enabled more food to be obtained, and more people supported, per unit area of exploited land. It thus facilitated long-term sedentary settlement and maintenance of larger and more complex social groups, which, in turn enabled urban society to develop (Harris, 1996: Preface). The beginning of agriculture, variously termed as 'Food Producing Revolution', the 'Neolithic Revolution' or the 'Agricultural Revolution', not only changed the subsistence pattern of man but at the same time brought in significant changes in his socio-economic pattern. However, it needs to be stressed that domestication was not an event but a long-term process. It required a scientific understanding of the natural phenomena, development of tools and skill, sense of right season for sowing various crops, correct method of storage and preservation of grains from insects, right type of grains for seed, domestication, control, training and use of draft animals, water management, fertilization, weeding out, reaping, threshing, grinding, pounding, invention of methods of cooking and processing including pottery.

In the process of domestication, the physical characteristics of plant and animal species changed. Domestication changed the whole pattern of human society, behaviour and psychological outlook. To cope with the necessity of life based on domestication of crops and animal, permanent settlements, villages, family unites and many organizational setup were formed. The surplus agricultural produce set in motion complex system of trade and commerce, formation of cities, specialization of labour and formation of social groups. (Varma, 2003).

The beginning of agriculture in Indian sub-continent is shrouded in obscurity. Effective use of querns and mullars, microlithic blades and bladelets with particular type of gloss on their cutting edge; and dental decay are some of the indicators of effective use of grains in subsistence economy which can be detected in archaeological record. Further, archaeobotanical evidences, if carefully collected, throw much more light on the complex phenomena of domestication of cereals and other plants.

In the Vindhyas cereal grains have been recovered from Chopani Mando in the Belan valley. Here remains of charred or carbonized rice of wild variety were found imbedded in lumps of burnt clay. These remains came from the Proto-Neolithic levels and have been dated to the 9th-8th millennium BC. In the same locality domesticated rice and hand-made pottery were recovered from the Neolithic levels of Koldihwa and Mahagara, situated at a distance of only three km from Chopani Mando and have been dated 7000-6000 BC. This evidence has been assigned considerable significance, indicating the presence of rice in wild form in the area, which was subsequently cultivated in the Neolithic period (Bose, 2003: 44).

As stated earlier, evidence regarding human-plant interation during the Mesolithic period in the middle Ganga valley and the Vindhyas, comes from botanical and dental remains, together with analysis of lithic artefacts. Nearly ten wild species representing broad spectrum vegetal food have been identified at Damdama in district Pratapgarh of eastern U.P. A carbonized and extremely poorly preserved grain of rice was found at this site. It was taken to be of wild species. However, recent findings by K.S. Saraswat have indicated that the Mesolithic inhabitants of Damdama exploited both cultivated and wild rice (Bose, 2003: 42; also see Pant, 2001). Investigations at the Mesolithic rock-shelter site of Lekhahia have confirmed both the wild and cultivated strains of rice (*Oryza rufipogon* and *Oryza sativam*) (*IAR*, 1983-84: 178; cf. Bose, 2003: 43).

Similar evidence comes from the rock-shelter of Lekhahia in district Mirzapur but this site is comparatively late as it has been dated to circa 3rd millennium BC only (Kajale, 1991: 164 and Bose, 2003: 44).

Microwear study of the microlithic industry reveals that in addition to hunting with bow and arrow and fishing with harpoons, people were using sickles for collecting wild fruits, tubers and grains. The gloss on the working edges on some blades suggests that they may have been used for cutting plant material (Pal, 1994: 97). The numerous quern and muller fragments from Mahadaha and Damdama represented food processing equipment. The concave surfaces of querns and the convex surfaces of mullers were lustrous and glossy indicating heavy use, possibly for crushing wild grains. The mullers must also have been used as pounders and anvils (Pal, 1994: 97). Since they are used for processing vegetal food, it seems gathering formed an important factor in their economy.

Besides, the dental pathology profile of Mesolithic sites in the Gangetic plains revealed features typically associated with hunting-gathering or foraging adaptation.

NEOLITHIC PLANT ECONOMY

The Neolithic plant economy has been worked out from evidence obtained from Koldihwa, Mahagara, Manigara, Baraunha and Tokwa – all in the Vindhyas; Lahuradewa in Uttar Pradesh and Senuwar, Chirand, Taradih and Oriup in Bihar. Potsherds obtained from the Neolithic strata of Koldihwa were found to bear imprints of rice (*IAR*, 1974-75: 80). These imprints have been identified as *Oryza sativa, Oryza rufipogon* and *Oryza nivara*. This suggests that during the Neolithic age, the inhabitants of Koldihwa had known along with the cultivated rice, a perennial wild and also an annual wild (*Oryza nivara*). Wild rice (*Oryza rufipogon*) is still of common occurrence in the region (Kumar, 1988: 111). Besides rice, charred wheat and *moong* were other cereals and legumes at Koldihwa (Sharma *et al.*, 1980: 184). At Mahagara, rice has been found in two conditions: in loose form as well as embedded in potsherds. Imprints of caryopsis, stalk, glum, etc. found on the cord-impressed and rusticated ware suggests their utilization as temper in the clay for manufacturing (Sharma *et al.*, 1980). The rice husk impressions found on potsherds confirmed the use of both wild and cultivated strains of rice. The wild strains of rice (*Oryza rufipogon*) were found to be spontanea rice, a hybrid between wild and cultivated strains (*IAR*, 1982-83: 149). Thus, the evidence of rice cultivation from both Koldihwa and Mahagara is conclusive. Besides, two carbonized grains retrieved from the Neolithic Mahagara have been referred to as barley (*Hordeum vulgare*) (*IAR*, 1980-81: 110). Radiocarbon dates suggest the antiquity of Koldihwa Neolithic to as early as 7th-5th millennia BC. However, reservations have been expressed against such an early date (Pal, 1986). But recent evidence for the presence of cultivated rice in an early context at Lahuradewa indicates an antiquity as early as late sixth the fifth millennium BC (Tewari *et al.*, 2001-2002: 55-56).

In this context, it may be mentioned that rice husk remains have also been found in potsherds from Manigara in the Adwa Valley in district Mirzapur (*IAR*, 1981-82: 106). However, this site has dated to circa second millennium BC only (Kajale, 1991: 164). Similar evidence comes from Baraunha, situated in same river valley. Scan microscopy of these imprints from the Neolithic site confirm the identification of wild perennial rice *Oryza rufipogon* besides rice husks of the cultivated strain *Oryza sativa* (*IAR*, 1982-83: 149). Cultivated rice has also been reported from Oriyup in district Bhagalpur, Bihar (Kajale, 1991: 160) as also from Chirand, district Saran, Bihar. Besides rice, Chirand has also yielded remains of wheat, barley, lentil, field-pea, grass-pea and some leguminous weeds (Bose, 2003: 51). Although the radiocarbon dates from Chirand put the Neolithic culture to the middle of the third millennium BC (2590±105; 2665±105; *IAR*, 1975-76: 86), the beginning of occupation at this site may be even earlier (Chakrabarti, 1999: 244). Uninterrupted evidence for plant husbandry from Neolithic, Chalcolithic and early Historical culture has also been reported from Taradih in district Gaya, Bihar (Kajale, 1991: 172) but the richest evidence of a complete sequence of crop cultivation practices comes from Senuwar.

The lower half of the Neolithic deposit at Sanuwar suggests that initially these people were cultivating only rice (*Oryza sativa*) which along with fox-tail grass was encountered in the bottom layers, just above the natural soil. Subsequently, the inclusion of job's tear (*Coix lachryma jobi*), a cereal native to South-East Asia and still cultivated in the Philippines and New Guinea and by the hill tribes of Vietnam, Cambodia, Laos and eastern India has also been noted (Saraswat, 2004: 498). The grains of wild and cultivated types are used as food. Presumed to be an older domesticate than rice, its cultivation spread to areas where rice culture had not yet penetrated (Saraswat, 2004: 498). It is also suspected that fox-tail grass (*Setaria glauca*) also encountered in the bottom layers of Sanuwar was also taken to cultivation (Saraswat, 2004: 498). From the middle levels of deposits of Period IA, the Senuwarians also started cultivating barley, and after some time, wheat and finally, millet and pulses as well (Bose, 2003: 53).

As regards our knowledge of the food grains encountered in the earliest and metal-free Neolithic period (ca. 2200-1950 BC) at Senuwar, the cereals include cultivated rice (*Oryza sativa*), barley (*Hordeum vulgare*), dwarf-wheat (*Triticum sphaerococcum*), jowar-millet (*Sorghum bicolor*) and finger/ragi-millet (*Eleusine coracana*). Pulses, which occupied an important place in the dietary of Neolithic people, have been represented by the remains of lentil (*Lens culinaris*), field-pea (*Pisum arvense*) and grass-pea/khesari (*Lathyrus sativus*). These cereals and pulses are primarily those which form staple food resources of advanced agricultural societies today. The finds of cultivated rice, barley, dwarf-wheat, lentil, field-pea, similar to these from Senuwar, were earlier reported by Vishnu-Mittre from Neolithic Chirand in the alluvial tracts of Ghaghara in northern Bihar, dated between 1900-1400 BC. In the associated remains of weeds and wild taxa, the grains of wild rice (*Oryza rufipogon*), fox-tail grass (*Setaria cf. glauca*) and job's tear (*Coix lachrymal-jobi*), belong to the category of true cereals of grass family. Vetch (*Vicia sativa*) is a common edible weed in the pulse-crop fields. It seems reasonable to regard that these grains and seeds might have also played role in the food economy of Neolithic people (Saraswat in B.P. Singh, 2004: 488).

Recently R.P. Singh (2010) has made a detailed study of the rise of agriculture in the Ganga plain. From his study the following picture emerges:

Wheat and Barley

It is now common knowledge that the staple food of the pre-Harappans and Harappans was basically the two winter crops – wheat and barley. These cereals were growing in their natural habitat zone on the hilly flanks of the Zagros range extending from the present-day Turkey to the borders of Iran. These cereals were cultivated by the Neolithic man some time during the eighth millennium BC (Singh, 1974, 1991). These cereals were also cultivated by the Neolithic man at Mehrgarh in around seventh millennium BC and was subsequently adopted by the Harappans. Of the former, three varieties, viz., the Indian dwarf wheat, the club wheat and *Triticum aestivum* were grown by the Harappans. In case of barley, though the six-rowed variety *Horduem vulgare* was dominant, two other varieties, viz., *Hordium vulgare nudum* and *Hordium sphaerococcum* were also grown (Costantini, 1984).

Rice

Rice seems to have been unknown to the Mature Harappans at least in the Indus valley although it occurs at Lothal and Rangpur in Gujarat and Hulas in western Uttar Pradesh. In the Ganga valley evidence for the first cultivation of rice comes from Koldihwa, Jhusi and Lahuradewa datable seventh millennium BC and since then it has been a staple food of Indians till today. It has been reported from all the sites of mid Ganga valley since Neolithic onwards.

Pulses

Chickpea or Chana

Among the various pulse crops, gram (*Chana*) is the most important pulse accounting for more than a third of the area and about 40 per cent of the production of pulses in this country. Presently it is grown in the arid areas of the Punjab, Haryana, Rajasthan, Bihar, Uttar Pradesh, Gujarat and Madhya Pradesh. Chickpea is believed to be of Western Asiatic origin. The earliest known specimen of chickpea is reported from the Neolithic site of Hacilar near Burdur in Turkey. In India the introduction of chickpea may be attributed to the Harappans who were the earliest to cultivate it (Randhawa, 1980: 166). Chickpea was grown at Kalibangan and Harappa in the third millennium BC and at several sites in the Ganga basin and Maharastra in the second millennium.

Peas (Pisum Sativum var. arvense) or Matar

Today the major part of the area under this crop is in the Indo-Gangetic plain, Uttar Pradesh, accounting for 0.5 million hectares and 0.47 million tones. *Matar* also is believed to have originated in South-West Asia. It was grown at Jericho in Palestine in the 8th millennium BC and Abu Hureyra in Syria in the 7th millennium. It occurs at numerous sites from Iran to Turkey. In India *Pisum* occurs at Burzahom (Kashmir) 2400-1700 BC; at Harappa (2500 BC) and Balathal in Rajasthan (Misra, 2007) in the date-range of 2000-1800 BC.

Pigeon pea

Pigeon pea or red-gram is extensively used as *dal*. In India pigeon pea is grown almost in every state. The earliest pigeon pea yet reported comes from Peddamudiyam in Andhra Pradesh (ca. 1700-1300 BC) and the Jorwe period (ca. 1200-900 BC) at Tuljapur Garhi, Maharashtra. Archaeological remains of pigeon pea in India are from Bhagi Mohari (ca. 750-500 BC), Nevasa (ca. 250 BC-AD 200) and Bhokardan (ca. 200 BC-AD 200). It also occurs at Sangankallu in Karnataka in the second millennium BC. In Indian historical and literary texts, pigeon pea is mentioned in the Sutra period (800-300 BC); early Buddhist and Jain works (800-300 BC), Kushana and Saka Satavahana period (AD 75-300) and Gupta period (AD 300-750). This would tend to suggest a latter start for the cultivation of pigeon pea in the eastern peninsular region around Bastar and southern Orissa, although archaeobotanical evidence from this region itself is lacking. In the mid Ganga valley its earliest record is from Charda dated to circa 800 BC.

Lentil (Lens culinaris) or Masur

Lentil ranks among the oldest and the most appreciated legumes of the Old World. Lentil is grown throughout northern India, Madhya Pradesh and some parts of Maharashtra. *Masur* is also believed to be of south-western Asiatic origin. It was cultivated at Jericho in Palestine in the 8th millennium BC and at Abu Hureyra, in Syria during the 7th millennium BC. It also occurs at numerous sites from Iran to Turkey.

In India lentil is present in the Harappa culture and at Navdatoli in Central India and at Inamgaon in the Deccan. In North-Western India, the earliest occurrence of lentil seeds together with wheat and barley has been reported from Neolithic Gufkral in Kashmir valley (Period IA) dating back approximately to circa 2600-2100 BC. At Rohira this pulse crop was cultivated throughout the pre-Harappan and Harappan times (ca. 2300-1700 BC). Lentil has been recovered from the Late Harappan site of Hulas (district Saharanpur) in western U.P. Occurrence of lentil at Neolithic Chirand in the alluvial tract of northern Bihar, dating back to circa 1900-1400 BC, suggests the widespread cultivation of this pulse crop during second millennium BC from North-Western to North-Eastern India. In the mid Ganga valley, the earliest evidence for the cultivation of this pulse crop comes from the Neolithic levels of Jhusi.

Black gram (Urd or Mash)

Black gram (*urd, mash*) is a highly prized pulse, very rich in phosphoric acid. It is used, more or less, in the same way as green gram (*mung*). *Mash* is grown all over India, mainly in the monsoon season, the main areas of production being Madhya Pradesh, Uttar Pradesh, Punjab, Maharashtra, West Bengal, Andhra Pradesh and Karnataka.

Himalayan foothills are belived to be the region of its origin. Botanical evidences suggest that the original home of *mash* is India, where it seems to have been first domesticated (Randhawa, 1980: 243). This pulse crop was consumed by the Chalcolithic (1500 BC) people of Navdatoli. It was a favourite *dal* during the Vedic period. It occurs at Balathal (Rajasthan) and at several sites of Maharashtra. It was grown by the Jorwe culture people at Inamgaon. Evidence for the earliest cultivation of black gram comes from the Neolithic levels of Jhusi.

Green gram or Mung

Green gram or *mung* is presently grown in about 2.5 million hectares. It is spread all over the country, with a production of about 0.8 million tonnes. The important states producing this pulse are Madhya Pradesh, Maharashtra, Uttar Pradesh, Punjab, Andhra Pradesh, Rajasthan, Karnataka and Tamil Nadu.

Botanical evidence shows that the original home of *mung* is India. A wild relative of *mung* – *Vigna sublobata (Phaseolus sublobata*) – is found in the tarai jungle near Pantnagar, district Nainital. Grains of *mung* were discovered at Navdatoli.

Mung is widely found on Southern Neolithic sites which await dating but could push its origin back into the early or mid-third millennium BC along with horse gram. Otherwise *mung* comes from Malwa phase at Apegaon, Jorwe levels at Inamgaon, Rojdi level C and Hulas in the Ganga-Yamuna Doab region, all dating between 2000 BC and 1700 BC. From India, *mung* spread to other countries in ancient times.

Grass pea (Lathyrus sativus L.) or Khesari

This crop is considered to have originated in South-West Asia. It is present in the pre-pottery Neolithic levels in Turkey. In India grass pea is present at Harappa (2500 BC), Babar Kot (2200 BC), Rojdi in Gujarat and Ahichchhatra in Uttar Pradesh.

Horse gram (Dolichos biflorus) or Kulthi

Carbonised seeds of *kulthi* have been recovered from the Neolithic site of Tekkalakota in Karnataka as also from the Neolithic levels of Paiyampalli in district North Arcot (Tamil Nadu). *Kulthi* occurs at Harappa and

Mitathal, Kunjhun (2500 BC) at Rojdi (ca. 2000-1700 BC) and at several sites in Chalcolithic Maharashtra and several southern Neolithic sites.

From the above account, it is clear that Chick pea (*chana*), Lentil (*masur*), Pea (*matar*) and Broad Bean (*bakla*) are not native to India. These pulses were introduced into India from Western Asia.

OILS SEEDS

Brown Mustard (Rai/rayaor laha; Brassica juncea)

Among the oil seed crops, *Sarson* oil is used in India for cooking. The seeds of *Brassica juncea* have been recovered from Chanhu-daro. Some sort of mustard was also probably cultivated for its oily seeds, with occasional finds of *Brassica* from Rojdi, Babar Kot, Oriyo Timbo and Mohenjo-daro.

After sesame, Field Brassica seems to be another popular oilseed crop in the Ganga Valley. While this oilseed is absent in the Harappan levels at Kunal and Balu, it occurs in the second millennium BC levels at several sites in the Ganga Valley. It is present in Period II (1300-600 BC) at Senuwar and in Period I (2000-1400 BC) at Imlidih Khurd. At Narhan Field Brassica has been reported from Period I (1300-800 BC) and in Period I and II at Waina (1600-800 BC and 800-600 BC). A similar story is reported at Khairadih where it occurs in Periods I and II dated to 2000-700 BC and 700-200 BC respectively. At Raja Nal Ka Tila, it has been documented from Period II dated to 1300-700 BC.

Sesamum (Sesamum indicum L.)

Sesamum (*Sesamum indicum* L.), also known as sesame, *til* and gingelly, is an important and ancient oil-yielding crop. The sesamum seed is a rich source of edible oil. The recovery of a lump of charred sesame by Vats at Harappa suggests that it was cultivated by the Indus Valley people.

Sesame or *til* has been recorded from sub-period IC (2600-2500 BC) at Kunal. It also occurs in the Mature Harappan phase at Balu in district Kaithal, Haryana. In the Ganga valley, sesame seeds have been reported from at least six sites, namely, Jhusi (Neolithic level), Senuwar, Imlidih Khurd, Narhan, Khairadih and Raja Nal Ka Tila. At Senuwar it occurs in Period II (1300-600 BC) but at Imlidih Khurd, it is present in an earlier context Period I (2000-1400 BC) as also in the subsequent period. At Narhan sesame occurs in Period I (1300-800 BC) and again in Period III (600-200 BC). At Khairadih it is present in Period II dated to 700-200 BC while at Raja Nal Ka Tila, it is has been reported from Period II (1300-700 BC).

Linseed (Linum usitatissimum L.)

Linseed (*Linum usitatissimum* L.) belongs to the family Linaceae and the genus *Linmum* which has 100 species. It has been grown from ancient times for fibre (flax) and for its seed, which is rich in oil.

Along with sesame and Field Brassica, linseed is an important oilseed crop of ancient India. Linseed has been reported from the Early Harappan Kunal (Sub-period IB, 2850-2600 BC) but has not been reported from Balu. In the Ganga valley, it occurs in Period II (1300-600 BC) at Senuwar: in Periods I and II at Imlidih Khurd (2000-1400 BC and 1300-800 BC) respectively. It is present in Period I at Narhan (1300-800 BC) and in Period II at Waina (800-600 BC). Further, it occurs in Period II at Khairadih (700-200 BC) and in Period II (1300-700 BC) at Raja Nal Ka Tila in district Sonbhadra, U.P. Carbonized seeds of linseed were also found at Navdatoli.

Castor (Ricinus communis L.)

In comparison to the above-noted three oleiferous crops (sesame, field brassica and linseed), castor has been reported from very few sites in the Ganga valley. It occurs in Period II (1300-600 BC) at Senuwar and again from Period II (1300-600 BC) at Imlidih Khurd. This would indicate that the properties of castor as an oleiferous crop were known to the people at a much later date.

Safflower or Kusum (Carthamus tinctorius L.)

This oilseed probably came from South-West Asia. It has been recovered only from the sites of inner India in post-Harappan period, including Jorwe phase at Daimabad. While safflower has not been reported from the Harappan levels at Kunal and Balu, it is present at a number of sites in the Ganga valley. Safflower occurs in Period II (1300-600 BC) at Senuwar. It also occurs in Period II (1300-800 BC) at Imlidih Khurd and in Period II (800-600 BC) at Narhan. It occurs in Period II (800-600 BC) at Waina and in Period II at Raja Nal Ka Tila datable between 1300-700 BC.

THE DOMESTICATION OF ANIMALS

The transition from nomadic to settled life was largely the result of an economic revolution based on the cultivation of certain food plants like wheat, barley and rice and the domestication of some animals like cattle, sheep, goat, pig, and buffalo. This step had a profound effect on the history of mankind. The people became sedentary and the assured supply of food gave rise to rapid increase in population. With the beginning of domestication animals were kept not for traction and dairy products but more importantly for dietary purposes. Bones bearing cut and charring marks show that pork, beef and other types of animal food were taken in large number from prehistoric times onwards. A review of the faunal records from the earliest Neolithic sites shows that the domestication of animals was a gradual process that took place in different regions at different times. In India cattle, sheep, goats, pig, buffalo and other animals were tamed as early as 6000 BC and in some cases even earlier.

As Sondor Bokonyi has observed, domestication is an extremely complicated process. Capturing animals, keeping them in corrals and killing then at the appropriate time does not amount to domestication. The essential criterion of domestication is that man intends to breed the captured animals of a certain wild species. The word domestication involves man's breeding of animals under artificial conditions. Thus, domestication can be defined as: the capture and taming by man of animals of a species with particular behavioural characteristics, their removal from their natural living area and breeding community, and their maintenance under controlled breeding conditions for profit (Bokonyi, 1969: 219).

Two decades later, Bokonyi perfected his definition of the word 'domestication' and wrote:

> the essence of domestication is the capture and taming by man of animals of a species with particular behavioural characteristics, their removal from their natural living area and breeding community and their maintenance under controlled breeding conditions *for mutual benefits* (Bokonyi, 1989: 22).

The word 'domestication' has been more succinctly defined by Juliet Clutton-Brock (1989: 7) as follows:

My definition of a domesticated animal is one that has been bred in captivity for purposes of economic profit to a human community that maintains complete mastery over its breeding, organization of territory and food supply.

Domestication is both a cultural and a biological process that it can only take place when tamed animals are incorporated into the social structure of the human group and become objects of ownership. However, it must be borne in mind that domestication was a process extending over several thousand years and that it had its own special characteristics in different areas of the ancient world. Domestication did not, of course, happen only once but has recurred time and time again in different parts of the world and at different times. Domestication as a process still continues (Ucko and Dimbleby, 1969: XX)

THE DEVELOPMENT OF ARCHAEOZOOLOGICAL STUDIES IN INDIA

The beginning of palaeontological studies in India can be traced back to the nineteenth century but a systematic study of this branch gained ground in the first half of the twentieth century when important contributions to various aspects were made by scholars like Pilgrim, Brown and others. In the post-independence period, M.R. Sahni's contribution in the early sixties is noteworthy. Among others, mention may be made of K.N. Prasad, D.K. Chakravarty, E. Khan, R.V. Joshi, A.P. Khatri and others. In the nineteen seventies, G.L. Badam made noteworthy contribution to palaeontologcal studies (Badan, 1979). M.L.K. Murthy's work in the Kurnool region reflects on palaeoecology in the Late Pleistocene. Recent researches on the Karewa Vertebrates made by A. Sahni and others (Sahni, 1982, Kotlia *et al.*, 1982) shed welcome light on the age of the Karewa sediments of Kashmir (Sahu, 1988: 11). As regards the osteological remains from archaeological excavations, animals bones were not accorded due importance till 1950. F.R. Allchin (1969: 317) writes:

> Before 1947 scarcely any excavation report thought fit to mention animal remains. The work of Sewell and Guha for Mohenjo-daro (1931) and Prasad for Harappa (1936) were happy exceptions. Since 1950 a growing number of reports has appeared in which at least some reference to animal remains is made. The principal published data relates to the excavations at Hastinapura (1950-52), Piklihal (1952), Maheshwar (1952-53), Rangpur (1953-56), Maski (1954), Mundigak (1951-58), Nevasa (1954-56), Utnur (1957) and Langhnaj (1944-63). There is further a considerable volume of hitherto unpublished material relating to other excavations.

In India the history of domestication of animals goes as far back as 7000 years BP from the Mesolithic cultural phase at Bagor, district Bhilwara in Rajasthan and Adamgarh, district Hoshangabad in Central India. While sheep/goat has been identified as the principal domestic animal at the former site, cattle (*Bos indicus*), buffalo (*Butalus bubalis*), sheep (*Ovis aries*), goat (*Capna hircus*), pig (*Sus domesticus*) and ass (*Equus asinus*) are reported as domestic animals at Adamgarh.

The humped Indian cattle (*Bos indicus*) appears to be the most predominant domestic animal in the early cultures of India. Cattle were killed for meat and were a major source of subsistence for early populations and young animals around the age of three years were preferred for food (Thomas, 1989: 108). In order of preference of food economy, the next important domestic animals were sheep, goat, pig and buffalo. A solitary evidence of dog being killed for meat is reported in the late Jorwe phase (ca. 1000-700 BC) at Inamgaon (Thomas, 1984a).

The role of domestic animals further increased in the economy of the early populations. The presence of a comparatively large number of aged bulls in sites like Ramapuram (Chalcolithic) and Veerapuram (Neolithic) – both in district Kurnool, Andhra Pradesh, suggest that these animals were probably used in agricultural operations, such as traction or even for running irrigation devices (Thomas, 1984b). The cattle by-product must have been of great importance to the people. There is no direct evidence for the consumption of milking is until early historic times. One of the earliest evidence for milking as depicted in a stone relief at Mahabalipuram is dated to about 7th-8th century AD (Zeuner, 1963). The cow dung was extensively used for plastering the flood and walls of the early houses and also as fuel, is known from the prehistoric settlements. Cattle dung is the main source of domestic cooking fuel even today in Indian villages (Harris, 1966).

Food offered to the dead is an age-old custom in Indian history. At Inamgaon, bones of cattle, sheep and goat are found along with urn and extended burials. Animal sacrifices were also common in the early cultures. The important sacrificed animals were cattle, sheep, goat, dog and horse. At Burzahon, a Neolithic site in Kashmir, dog/wolf heads were buried with a human dead body (Allchin and Allchin, 1968: 159). The Chalcolithic levels of Ramapuram in Andhra Pradesh have yielded partial and complete burials of goat in the human graves.

Sharing of cattle meat between people of two different houses belonging to the same settlement is found at Inamgoan (Thomas, 1989: 111). Two equal halves of a three-year-old bull are represented in two different houses. The degree of charring and the metrical homogeneity of bones of the left and right side of the body have been studied in detail. Probably on some occasion, people of these two different houses shared this animal.

In the middle Ganga valley, animal remains obtained from Narhan, Senuwar, Malhar, Koldihwa and Mahagara have been published while those from Khairadih, Lahuradewa, Raja Nal Ka Tila, Jhusi and Tokwa have been submitted for publication. Further, animals bones from Dhuriapar, Imlidih, Waina and Bhunadih are presently in the process of study. Their results, when available, will throw further light on the impact of domestication on contemporary life.

In the Ganga valley cattle predominate among the domesticated animals. Cattle remains are by far the most abundant in all cultural periods.

The bones of young individuals are invariably encountered at all sites. Similarly, fragments bearing cut marks and signs of charring have also been repeatedly reported from site after site.

The data from Tokwa is enough to prove this point. The study of animal remains from this site has been done by Joglekar *et al.* (2008). This study revealed presence of only two domestic species-cattle and goat in the Neolithic phase. The wild mammals identified in the Neolithic context are gaur, nilgai, blackbuck, spotted deer, sambar, porcupine, house rat, and the bandicoot rat, jungle fowl, peafowl, Saras crane, crocodile, monitor, lizard, freshwater cat fish, rohu and freshwater mussel. In the Chalcolithic phase the buffalo, domestic pig, sheep and domestic ass were found in addition to the cattle and goat. The wild or domestic status of the buffalo has not been ascertained. Conversely, the spectrum of wild animals becomes much narrower in the Chalcolithic phase. Only four wild mammals have been recorded in this phase – the gaur, blackbuck, four-horned antelope and spotted deer.

The animal taxa identified in the Ganga valley and Vindhyan sites comprised eight domestic mammals and twenty wild mammals, besides birds, fish and molluscs. Among the domestic animals, cattle (*Bos indicus)* have been found at all the sites and in all the cultural periods. The other domestic animals used as food resources are sheep and goat, buffalo and pig. Four other domestic species (donkey, horse, dog and cat) are found in less than half cases and were not used for food (Joglekar, 2008a: 314).

The range of wild animals utilized is very diverse. Large as well as small mammals were utilized as food resource. The list includes two commensal species-bandicoot rat and the common house rat. Though from ethnographic work in Ganga valley we know that rats could also be consumed, these rodents were not valued as food. Two deer species, spotted deer and sambar, have been found with highest ubiquity values. The two antelope species (blackbuck and nilgai) are found at lesser number of sites than the deer (Joglekar, 2008a: 315).

The animal remains are very often kitchen refuse and hence provide a fairly good idea of the food-habits of the people. Unmistakably, beef was a preferred item of diet since the PGW period down to historic times. Besides, cattle was intimately associated with the science and practice of agriculture. For the expansion of agriculture the usefulness of cattle was fully realized and the farmer regarded it as a helpmate. The value of *Panch-Gavya* was a natural corollary of dairying community and economy (Sahu, 1988: 263). Commenting of the food value of this animal Sahu further writes:

It is clear from ancient literature that the cow was venerated and regarded as divine. The earliest Buddhist text, the *Sutta-nipata* declares the cattle to be givers of food, beauty and happiness (*annada, vannada, sukhada*) and thus pleads for their protection (Sharma, 1977: 61). However, the evidence on hand suggest that cattle were killed on several occasions. Flesh eating flourished in the sub-continent and cattle were not spared even after Buddha and Mahavira, the two greatest exponents of *ahimsa*. Nor for that matter Ashoka's zeal for non-injury of animals lay a ban on killing. Let it be remembered that the Ashokan inscriptions relate to the king's own way of life and are an exercise in gentle persuasion. In brief, cattle were slaughtered for food and sacrifice until the mid first millennium AD, in spite of the prevailing doctrine of *ahimsa* (Sahu, 1988: 263-64).

POTTERY

The technique of making earthen utensils was unknown to the Mesolithic man but with the beginning of the Neolithic, he started making clay vessels and making them durable by firing. Initially the pots were made by hand but subsequently after the invention of potter's wheel, pots were made on mass scale with comparatively less labour. Pottery constitutes the bulk of the finds unearthed in any excavation. It is an essential tool of investigation for establishing relative chronology especially within the complex context of Indian archaeology and particularly within that of Ganga Valley (De Simone, 2009: 1).

The excavations conducted at the Neolithic sites have furnished enormous data about the ceramic industry. It appears, in the early stage hand-made pottery was used but subsequently the potter's wheel was introduced. In the mid Ganga valley the earliest ceramic assemblage includes ordinary red ware and corded ware. The corded and rusticated wares are the connecting link between the Neolithic cultures of the Vindhyas and the mid Ganga valley. The clay used for manufacturing the pots is gritty. Rice husk and chaff have been used as degraissant. The pottery types include bowls (wide-mouthed, channelled, etc.) with varying profile, vases, squatted vessels, miniature jars, etc. Occurrence of painted sherds has also been reported from Chirand, Senuwar and Imlidih Khurd. At Chirand and Senuwar the painting motifs include linear designs of criss-cross lines and concentric circles. These paintings are confined to the burnished grey ware (Senuwar) or grey ware (Chirand). Imlidih-Khurd has yielded painted pots, the motifs being dots and dashes executed in creamish red colour over a red surface **(Plate XIIA)**. Post-firing incised geometric patterns are also met with at this site **(Plate XIII)**.

The cord-impressed pottery obtained from Imlidih Khurd, Narhan, Bhunadih and other sites has been studied by Daniela De Simone (2009). She observes that the chemical composition of cord-impressed ware has a high percentage of silica and low percentage of alumina. The former is given by the use of quartz (a raw material), the latter by clayey minerals (fine materials): the differences in their percentages result in the production of fine or coarse wares. The firing temperature, in an oxidizing atmosphere, was around 850^0-900^0 C. She rightly remarks that the cord-impressed pottery provides a reliable index fossil for the relative chronology of the early and developed phase of the middle Ganga valley.

The ceramic assemblage of the Chalcolithic phase exhibits variety both in ceramic traditions and pottery types. With the exception of Masondih, Maner, Manjhi and Champa, all the excavated sites are characterized with painted pottery tradition (Misra, 2006). The assemblage comprises red, black-and-red, black slipped and occasionally grey ware. The pottery is generally wheel-thrown though hand-made specimens are also met with. The clay used for manufacturing pots is not well levigated as it contains impurities like grits, quartz and lime particles. Rice-husk, sand and mica have occasionally been used as degraissant. The pots generally range from medium to course in fabric. A few pots in fine fabric are also met with in black slipped and black-and-red ware.

Black-and-red ware with painting executed in dull-white, cream, brownish and occasionally reddish colour over black surface interior or exterior or both constitutes a salient feature of the Chalcolithic cultures of the mid Ganga valley. The painting motifs consist of linear designs – wavy lines, straight and oblique strokes, dots, semi-circle, etc. The black slipped ware, another important ceramic industry represented at all excavated sites, has also been found painted at Rajghat, Prahladpur, Khairadih, Sohgaura, Taradih, etc. The painting is executed on exterior or interior surface of the pots. The painted motifs consist of wavy lines, straight and oblique strokes, dots, lattice, group of slanting or oblique lines, concentric arcs, solid dots, vertical, horizontal or curved lines.

A 'sherd count' of the ceramic range from the Chalcolithic culture at Narhan (termed 'Narhan Culture') was done. This study showed that the main ceramic industries are the white painted black-and-red ware (57.70%), black slipped ware with occasional paintings in white (8.01%), red slipped ware (8.84%) and plain red ware (25.38%). The principal pottery types in black-and-red ware are bowls (66.90%), basins (11.0%) and vases (22.09%). A complete dish-on-stand of this ware had been reported from this site earlier. Several fragmentary pieces of this vessel were found in the excavation. Some new shapes like deep bowls with paintings inside were recorded **(Plate XVA, XVB)**. However, dishes are conspicuous by their absence in the black-and-red ware. More than 20% sherds in the fine and medium fabrics of the black-and-red ware are painted. The principal types in the black slipped ware consist of bowl (83.71%), dishes (14.95%) and vases (1.2%). The quantity of basins and vases is extremely limited. In the red slipped ware, the dominant category is that of bowls (68.70%) followed by basins (23.89%), vases (7.32%) and dishes (2.04%). The red ware had bowls (50.18%), vases (29.86%), basins (15.51%) and dishes (4.44%) (Singh, 1996: 5-6).

THE EMERGING PICTURE

Mesolithic

The first effective colonisation of the middle Ganga plain was done by a band of adventurous people who made first forays in this part of the country when living conditions no longer remained hospitable in the Vindhyan hills. They were tall, well-built and robust people. They earned their livelihood by hunting wild animals (buffalo, cattle, bison, *nilgai*, wild pig, hog and different species of deer). Reptiles and birds were also eaten. Food was supplemented by gathering edible fruits, grains and tubers from surrounding forest. Fishes and molluscs also formed a substantial part of their diet. Their tool-kit comprised various types of microliths which were used as components of arrowheads, spearheads, daggers, sickles and harpoons. Besides, other types of tools like scrapers, points and burins were also used. Bone and antler tools include arrowheads, points, blades, knives, chisels, scrapers and saw. Grinding stones, querns and mullers with heavy use marks and lustrous polished surface suggest inclusion of vegetal food in the diet. The Mesolithic people after inhabited readily available rock-shelters in the hilly region but such facility was non-existent in the Ganga valley. Hence, they constructed huts made of trees, branches and leaves. Rectangular floors have been found at Sarai Nahar Rai. Post-holes found at this floor suggest some kind of superstructure over the floor. A large number of human burials excavated at all the three excavated sites provide much needed data about their racial types, eschatological beliefs and social set-up. The dead were buried in shallow and oblong graves and the dead bodies were placed in an extended supine position, the orientation of the body being from west to east, with the skull pointing to the west. The grave-goods comprised microlithic tools, animal bones and in some cases, personal ornaments. Double burials (also termed couple burials) are common at Damdama and Mahadaha. In the case of couple burials, the graves contained remains of two individuals, one male and the other female. Both the skeletons were buried simultaneously. This practice shows that the concept of male-female relationship which later ended in the evolution of the institution of marriage or the concept of a family unit consisting of a male and female can be tracked in its most rudimentary form to the Mesolithic society of the Ganga valley (Varma 1997: 31).

The available evidence suggests that at the time of the descent of the Mesolithic man in the middle Ganga valley, the area was undergoing climatic change. The last unit of the Bhagar formation was taking its final shape. We find microliths not only embedded in this formation but also overlying it, indicating thereby that even after the process of formation was over, the Mesolithic man was operating in the area. Existence of numerous horse-shoe lakes in the area at the time under discussion is fully attested. Some of these lakes were visited time and again while on others quasi-sedentary settlements were established. In this connection it may be pointed out that all the three excavated sites – Sarai Nahar Rai, Mahadaha and Damdama – are situated on the banks of horse-shoe lakes. The easy availability of water, games and aquatic creatures in or near these might have induced the Mesolithic hunter-gatherers to settle there (Misra, in Joglekar *et al.,* 2003: 25).

Neolithic

Until recently, the Neolithic stage in the middle Ganga plain was little understood, but after the excavations at Lahuradewa, Tokwa, Jhusi, Hetapatti and other sites, it is now clear that the Neolithic in the Ganga valley had two phases, i.e., the pure (early) Neolithic which is represented by rice growing culture of Lahuradewa, Tokwa, Jhusi and Hetapatti dated around 7000 BC and the Neolithic-Chalcolithic culture at Imlidih Khurd, Senuwar Chirand and other sites. Initially the Neolithic economy was primarily based on rice cultivation and animal domestication. The evidence from Jhusi, just made available (in 2008), shows that by about 7000 BC, it comprised both rice and wheat-barley together with sorghum millet and a variety of pulses and oil-seeds like seasame or *til*. When and under what circumstances its transformation took place to the succeeding Neolithic-Chalcolithic stage, documented at Sohgaura, Imilidih Khurd, Waina, Chirand and Senuwar (both sub-periods IA and IB) is anybody's guess. Obviously, more field-work is needed to unwind this riddle. However, the impact of the Neolithic revolution made earlier during its first phase was clearly manifested in every walk of life in the succeeding phase. Commenting upon the consequences of food production and domestication, Geogory L. Possehl (1999: 395) writes:

It is widely agreed that the importance of the food production and domestication revolution lies in the profound consequences that it brought to human life. Based on the thoughts of V. Gordon Childe, Robert Redfield, Esther Boserup, Robert J. Braidwood, Philip E.L. Smith and others, a series of changes and implications can be outlined that focus on three interdependent phenomena: sedentism, changes in human social organization and alterations in human demographic patterns. Settling down into villages and the symbiosis that sedentary peoples have with pastoralists and hunter-gatherers is widely regarded as the single most important act, and it clearly has an impact on other factors. But, in the end, this is a set of historical forces that act in a systemic way, with an abundance of feedback and interlocking patterns of change.

CHALCOLITHIC METAL TECHNOLOGY

As its name implies, the Chalcolithic stage is represented by cultures where *Chalkos* (copper) was used (though in limited quantity), along with *Lithos* (stones) in the form of microliths which were used as parts of composite tools. However, in the middle Ganga plain, the artefacts of copper are very limited and the lithic component is completely missing on sites like Imlidih Khurd, Narhan, Khairadih, etc. and wherever it is present (sites like Sant Ravidas Nagar district; Waina in Ballia district and Agiabir in Mirzapur), their number is exceedingly small and it is not clear if their presence made any significant contribution to the economy of these people.

The Neolithic phase in the middle Ganga plain and the Vindhyas was succeeded by the Chalcolithic culture. There is no time gap between the two cultures and a gradual evolution from the former to the latter has been witnessed at a number of sites. The excavations at sites like Sohgaura, Imlidih Khurd, Chirand, Chechar and Senuwar have furnished evidence pertaining to the transitional stage from the preceding Neolithic cultures of the region to the Chalcolithic. The only perceptible change during the Chalcolithic is the introduction of copper in this region sometime in the later half of third millennium BC, which resulted into tremendous activity resulting into agricultural surplus in a big way and the consequent increase in human population. Whereas the Neolithic settlements were few and far between, in the Chalcolithic phase the number as well as the size of the settlements increased several fold. Exploration carried out in 14600 sq. km area of the middle Ganga plain has brought to light more than 200 sites. Surely, many more sites lie buried and are yet to be documented. Of the explored sites, about two dozen have been excavated so far (Misra, B.B., 2000: 66).

Copper

The Chalcolithic context in eastern Uttar Pradesh is typified by excavations at such sites as Sohgaura, Narhan and Khairadih. The find from Khairadih which comprises a socketed arrowhead with two perforations of the socket is a typical case in point and suggests both an easy familiarity with, and a restricted use of, this metal. In western Uttar Pradesh, the most important find occurred in the Ochre Coloured Pottery (OCP) context at Saipai in the Etawah district where a metal harpoon was found in association with OCP. Another OCP site, Lal Qila in the Bulandshahr district, yielded a pendant/bead and fragments of an arrowhead and an axe. Atranjikhera in the Aligarh district yielded in its OCP level a piece of copper and fragment of a terracotta crucible with granules of copper. The succeeding Black-and-red ware context yielded three beads and a ring (Chakrabarti and Lahiri, 1996: 77).

The Neolithic-Chalcolithic is a well established level in Bihar comprising such excavated sites as Chirand, Taradih, Oriup, Senuwar, Sonpur, etc. The finds from Taradih, Sonpur and Senuwar are fairly representative. The Chalcolithic level at Taradih yielded a copper finger ring and possibly a fish-hook and a lump as well. Sonpur showed wire and miscellaneous fragments. On analysis, a Sonpur sample showed 2.35% tin. Bangle is a type which has been reported from Oriup. A major occurrence has been reported from Senuwar. The Chalcolithic context at the site yielded a bangle, a tool of interdeterminate use, a pin, an ear-ring and copper pieces. More importantly, a potsherd has been found with copper sticking to its inner surface. This was no doubt part of a terracotta crucible (Chakrabarti and Lahiri, 1996: 77).

In West Bengal, the Neolithic-Chalcolithic evidence has been discovered at Mahisdal, Pandu Rajar Dhibi, Bahiri and Mangalkot. At the same time, the levels which have yielded copper at the above-mentioned sites have also yielded iron, their dates pointing towards the close of the second millennium BC. Mahisdal dated around the middle of the second millennium, if not earlier has certainly a pre-iron level (Chakrabarti and Lahiri, 1996: 76).

The major find from Mahisdal is a flat axe measuring 18.8 by 11.3 cm. Pandu Rajar Dhibi yielded bangles (4, diam 7.4-10.7cm), knife (spearhead?) with a tang (15.8 by 2.8 by 0.3 cm) and two pieces of wire.

Mangalkot yielded ring, bangle and fish-hook. The bangle showed the following composition: cu-Fe (0.01)-pb (0.05)-Ni (0.10)-Sn (10.5)-As (0.10). Bahiri yielded bits of copper including a finger-ring which on analysis was found to contain more than 10 per cent tin like the analysed Mangalkot bangle (Chakrabarti and Lahiri, 1996: 76-77).

A large number of metal objects (copper and iron) from the middle Ganga plain were scientifically examined from time to time by scholars like D.P. Agrawal, H.C. Bharadwaj, Hari Narain, P.K. Chattopadhyay, Rajam Shesadri, R.N. Singh and C.D.P. Singh. The sites involved are Chirand, Sonpur, Taradih, Senuwar, Champa, Maner, Manjhi, Rajghat, Agiabir, Narhan, Imlidih Khurd, Waina, Ayodhya, Bhitari and Masondih. The results have been reviewed by Chakrabarti (1992), Chakrabarti and Lahiri (1996), D.P. Agrawal (1971, 2000), Tripathi (1998, 2008) and Chattopadhyay (2004). While it is not possible to summarise the results of each analysis here, suffice it to observe that alloying was found to be popular, cooling was noted and uses of annealing, casting and forging were found to be prevalent in copper objects (Singh, R.N., 2004b). Bharadwaj's (1979) analysis of copper objects from Rajghat and ores from Bihar has established that the ores from Singhbhum area were used during early Historic period.

The non-Harappan Chalcolithic cultures of India are characterised by the use of copper and stone. The Chalcolithic cultures of the middle Ganga plain make their appearance towards the end of third millennium BC and after flourishing for about a thousand years, they were eventually replaced by the iron using cultures around 1300 BC. These cultures show regional identity probably determined by smaller ecological niches (Agarwal, 2000: 112). The basic difference among them is the characteristic pottery, though economically they have a similar status. Copper is invariably present but in very limited amount.

At Chirand copper has been reported from the top deposits of Period I (Neolithic). Period II at this site is Chalcolithic. Here copper objects are few and include tanged arrowheads, a ring, bangles and antimony rod (Agarwal, 2000: 118). A similar situation obtains at Narhan.

Senuwar has yielded 61 antiquities of copper comprising an ear-ring (?), needle (?), pointed tool, miniature arrow-head and a potsherd in which a layer of copper was found still adhering throughout its inner surface. Of these, four samples from the Neolithic-Chalcolithic levels; six samples from Chalcolithic levels and fourteen samples from Kushana levels were subjected to scientific examination (Singh, R.N., 2004a: 597). This study has shown that the coppersmiths of Senuwar had definitely started smelting copper ores since 1950 BC-1300 BC for procuring metallic copper. The use of native copper is not attested for the manufacture of artefacts. Mostly they were using unalloyed copper in the beginning (i.e., Period IB) but it seems that they were acquainted with the technique of casting, cold working, annealing and later hot-working and quenching (Singh, R.N., 2004a: 597). Alloying is attested in the succeeding Period II which may be considered as an advancement. The trace elements analysis of Senuwar specimens suggests that the source of copper at Senuwar was the Singhbhum copper belt of Bihar, particularly Rakha mines (Singh, R.N., 2004a: 597). In Bihar the Singhbhum belt extends over a region 130 km long and up to 8 km wide. In 1959 the reserves of copper ore were estimated to be 3.8 million tones with an average of 2.47% copper content. New exploration have brought to light copper ore resources at Patharghora, Surdha, Kendadih Roam-Sidheshar area (Agarwal, 2000: 14).

Metallographic and chemical study of copper artefacts from Senuwar was carried out by P.K. Chattopadhyay (1998: 25). His study shows that metallurgy at Senuwar started in Period IB as early as around 1800 BC as the smiths learnt to smelt copper ore for procuring metallic copper. The use of native copper is not attested in manufacturing artefacts. There is no evidence of alloying in IB. The study confirmed the use of pure copper in manufacturing the artefacts. The purity comes to around 99%. Even with the presence of 0.20% Sn in one object, it clearly indicates that there is no evidence of alloying. The small amount of tin in that object may be due to the association of copper ores with tin. After reduction of metal, artefacts were made by hammering method. Lack of twins also clearly suggests that simple forging process, i.e., hammering in cold condition was practised. Microstructures also indicate this process without annealing.

A copper axe obtained from Narhan culture levels (Chalcolithic) from Imlidih Khurd was subjected to scientific study by (Singh, R.N., 2004b). The description of this copper axe/celt is as follows:

Description of Copper Axe/Celt from Imlidih Khurd

Site	Imlidih Khurd
Trench No.	XM8
Locus	NE 3.50 m X NW 1.20 m
Depth	40 cm
Stratum	2
Period	Narhan Culture

R.N. Singh writes:

> This axe is thinner and with more flaring edge and is very good in condition. It has a sharp rectangular edge and typologically it is comparable to similar axes from Ahar. A small sample has been taken from butt end and was hot mounted in phenolic transparent powder using Bainmount Specimen Mounting Press with 150 kg/ cm^2 pressure. Primary grinding was done using Bainline Belt Grinder and final grinding polishing was under on Bain Pol Grinder and Polisher from 150 microns to 3-4 microns Bain Met Diamond polishing Compound. Mounted specimen was then etched chemically is alcoholic ferric chloride and ammonium hydroxide. The whole operation was repeated several times to obtain a stable structure. The prepared sample was then examined using bright field microscopy under the Leica DMLM/P metallurgical microscope having Leica (canon) DC 150 digital camera.

Although the study of the object is in progress and we have yet to get its chemical composition, but our primary examination shows a very fine grain structure. Several black particles are seen at the grain boundaries, few of which turned red under polarized light. Some several clear annealing twins are also visible in photomicrograph.

From the smooth external surface of the axe, it can be inferred that the axe was cast in a smooth well-ventilated mould. The black patches that turned red under polarized light are particles of cuprous oxide. The cuprous oxide inclusions concentrated around the gas holes, are generally observed to be due to flaws in the casting technique. However, in this tool the porosity holes are very few indicating smooth well-ventilated mould. The dark globules that do not turn red might be particles of lead. In copper, lead does not form a solid solution, instead finds itself distributed in the form of globules. However, only chemical analysis may provide details regarding percentage of lead and of course, tin, if at all it is present in the metal.

The fine grained structure indicate that the axe was cooled rapidly after casting. It is likely that the axe was not covered under hot ash, instead exposed to the atmosphere which resulted in its fine grain structure. Cold work is carried out to increase the hardness of the object. Well-formed grains with twins indicate cold-working and annealing. Inclusions are elongated due to hammering.

Iron

The introduction of iron as the principal metal for tools and weapons heralded a new age in the Gangetic Doab. It gave fresh impetus to, and accelerated the pace of development in, practically every walk of life, leading ultimately to the rise of the cities in this area. The advantages of this metal were manifold: the iron ores were far more readily available than copper ores and because of its ubiquity, iron seldom needed to be deep mined in antiquity. The most early mining for the ore was of the open cast type or grubbing. Again, this new metal had definite advantages over copper and bronze in as much as it was cheaper to produce than bronze and it had more tensile properties. Besides, the cutting tools like chisels and saws are better made of iron, to which an edge is more easily put than bronze (Singh, 1979: 313).

The chronology of iron in the heartland of India has been pushed back by several centuries with the recent discovery of early iron using sites in the Ganga plains.

Two sites in the eastern parts of the Vindhyas – Raja Nal Ka Tila and Malhar near Varanasi – have yielded second millennium BC dates (Tewari, 2003, Table III.2 and III.3). Dadupur and Lahuradewa near Lucknow and the trans-Sarayu plain respectively have yielded similar dates from iron bearing layers. Iron occurs in the pre NBPW period with black-and-red ware, grey ware, red ware and cord-impressed pottery. Iron objects coming from Raja Nal Ka Tila are a nail, an arrowhead, a knife and a chisel. Radiocarbon dates from this iron-bearing period range between 1400-800 BC. Nearby, there is the site of Malhar on river Karamnasa, a tributary of the Ganga that joins the latter near Varanasi. The iron bearing Period II follows without any break in culture. The iron artefacts types are nail, spearhead, arrowhead, awl, knife, bangle, sickle and ploughshare (Tewari, 2003). Slag and tuyeres were also found in abundance at the site and in the nearby ore-rich area. One may easily conclude, seeing the massiveness of the slag heaps and other remains, that it was an iron production centre. The activity seems to have continued unabated for centuries, followed by pre-industrial working. The C^{14} dates from Period II are 1993 Cal. BC (3390±160 BP), (3430±90 BP), 1679-1442 Cal. BC. At Dandupur iron has been reported from Period I, dated between 1900-1700 BC. The objects like arrowhead are highly corroded. Lahuradewa has yielded iron nails from Period III dated between 1300-1200 BC.

Early C^{14} dates of 1170-844 BC have recently been reported from the sites of Jhusi at the confluence of the Ganga and the Yamuna in Allahabad (See C^{14} tables III. 1). Lahuradewa in district Sant Kabir Nagar (Basti) has yielded iron in Period III dated to 1300-1200 BC. Further field-work may throw light on interactions between our zones (Tripathi, 2008: 56-57).

Analytical study of ancient iron objects has been done by B.B. Lal, H.C. Bhardwaj, O.P. Agrawal, P.K. Chattopadhyay, Balasubramaniam,

Hari Narain and C.D.P. Singh. Analytical work done by O.P. Agrawal, Hari Narain and others on iron objects from Manjhi, Khairadih, Jajmau, Hulaskhera, Sringaverapura, Kausambi and other sites has revealed different stages of development of iron technology from wrought iron to case carburized iron and finally to lamination, quenching and tempering. Iron samples from Narhan, Senuwar, Taradih and Chirand were done by R.N. Singh (2006).

Iron objects have also been recorded from different stratified Chalcolithic sites in West Bengal. Pandu Rajar Dhibi, Mangalkot, Dihar, Bahiri and Tulsipur have yielded iron objects from pure Chalcolithic context. Commenting on these discoveries, Asok Dutta (1998: 42) observes:

1. The beginning of iron technology in West Bengal may safely be placed to eleventh/twelfth century BC.
2. Two-fold developmental stages of iron technology can be ascertained on the basis of chemical and metallographic study.
3. The study shows that initial development of iron technology was made by the Chalcolithic people. But due to inability of successful reduction, much of the iron was lost in slag during Stage I. The specimens from Mangalkot belong to this stage which contain high percentage of impurities as compared to the specimens from Pandu Rajar Dhibi and Hatikra.
4. But soon after, the technology was modified and perfected during Stage II and as such the iron implements of this stage are completely free from slag particles due to successful reduction under sufficiently high temperature. The iron objects from Pandu Rajar Dhibi and Hatikra belong to this stage.
5. Stage II also witnessed the introduction of mild steel as evidenced from the presence of carbon contents. The deliberate addition of carbon with iron is definitely a step forward in iron technology. This high technical knowledge was acquired by the blacksmiths of West Bengal by about 6th/7th century BC.
6. Finally, we can conclude that technology which was developed independently by the Chalcolithic people of West Bengal, in course of time (Stage II) became very sophisticated and must have played the most crucial role in the formative stage of second urbanization.

Commenting on the archaeo-technological assessment of iron in the Ganga Valley, R.N. Singh writes:

On the basis of impurities pattern obtained from the SEM-X Ray and EPMA analysis of the iron objects from Taradih, Chirand, Senuwar and Narhan, it can be observed that Sulphur, Silicon, Titanium and Manganese are invariably present along with Aluminum and Calcium. It can be inferred that titaniferous ores might have been used for smelting. The nearby sources for such ores are Singhbum and Mayurbhanj area (Singh, 2006: 128).

To conclude, the present archaeological picture clearly suggests India to be an independent and early centre of iron technology. That this cannot be explained by any diffusinary postulate. As discussed above, the case for independent beginning of iron in India has been considerably strengthened by the new radiocarbon dates. On the basis of the above discussions, it may be concluded that the iron in Central, Eastern and South India is, on present showing, earlier that the iron in North-Western periphery of India. Iron seems to have entered the Indian productive system by circa 1800 BC, particularly in the ore abundance area. A look at the list of iron areas of India will show that all these centres are either in or near the ore areas. The evidence of pre-industrial smelting and ethnographic data also comes from almost all these areas (Tewari, 2003: 544).

CONCLUDING REMARKS

A study of the data obtained through excavations of Chalcolithic sites in the middle Ganga plain reveals that:

1. The introduction of metal (copper) witnessed a spurt in activity in every walk of life and a significant increase in the number and size of the settlements. These sites are found below the 90 m contour line and are located on higher *bhangar* land which is above the flood level. These sites are almost always found along the river banks. Of the nearly 200 sites, 13 have been excavated. The radiocarbon dates from Sohgaura, Khairadih, Narhan, Chirand, Sonpur and Senuwar indicate that Chalcolithic cultures were firmly established in around 2500 BC in the Sarayupar plain and by 2000 BC in Bihar.
2. As compared to the preceding Neolithic culture, there is a dramatic increase in the number and size of the Chalcolithic sites. Obviously, this was due to a sharp increase in population. The social structure of the Chalcolithic folk has not been worked out in detail because the excavation at most of these sites were conducted on a very modest scale. Some sort of stratification in the society during the Mesolithic period has been suspected on the basis of grave-goods from Mahadaha. A similar situation must have taken place in the Chalcolithic society as well. The presence of various type of ceramic ware and small objects of stone, bone, ivory, etc. indicates the specialization of crafts by certain individuals/families in the Chalcolithic society.

3. We do not have any indication about the religious beliefs of the Chalcolithic inhabitants of the middle Ganga plain. It may be recalled that 'a place of worship' has been identified at Baghor in district Sidhi in Madhya Pradesh. This place of worship has been dated to the Upper Palaeolithic period. Further, the discovery of a figurine of a Mother Goddess made on bone and found from the eroded Gravel III in Lohanda Nala, a tributary of the Belan River, has been dated to the Upper Palaeolithic period. It provides the earliest evidence of a belief in the supernatural. The burials of the Mesolithic sites of Pratapgarh provide ample evidence of belief in the after-life, but no such evidence is forthcoming from the Chalcolithic sites. The only evidence is that of the post-cremation pit-burials from Sonpur and Chirand which indicates that this custom was prevalent in some parts of Bihar but this evidence is missing on the other sites. The absence of burials in the Chalcolithic levels indicates that the method of cremation for the disposal of the dead body, which became the principal mode in the later-day Hindu society, had its roots in the Chalcolithic culture.
4. The faunal remains from these excavations have received adequate attention in recent years and a broad picture of animal exploitation has begun to emerge. It is now clear that while hunting was the main occupation during the Mesolithic age, selective domestication of some animals began during the Neolithic times. For example, while only two domestic species – cattle and goat – are present in the Neolithic phase at Tokwa, in the succeeding Chalcolithic phase four more animals – buffalo, domestic pig, sheep and domestic ass – were added to this list (Joglekar, 2008: 51). At the same time the spectrum of wild animals became much more narrower in the Chalcolithic phase as compared to the preceding Neolithic phase. Only four wild animals – gaur, blackbuck, four-horned antelope and spotted deer – are present in the Chalcolithic levels of Tokwa. The wild fauna at Senuwar comprises only four-horned antelope, spotted deer, nilgai, barking deer and wolf (Sathe and Badam, 2004). More or less, a similar picture obtains at other sites also.
5. An insight into the economic activity of the Chalcolithic inhabitants has been provided by the 'site catchment analysis' in the case of Senuwar. A catchment area is that area from which resources are taken to support human population and occur within reasonable walking distance from a site. The technique was first used by Vita-Finzi and Eric Higgs in 1970 for reconstructing the prehistoric economy of Mount Carmel in Palestine. From this study it has been shown that several resources were available within and in the close

vicinity of the ancient site of Senuwar such as clay for pottery and terracotta objects, house-building materials, domestic animals, fishes and other domesticated animals. The arable land around this site was quite sufficient for agriculture. However, the raw material for preparing the lithic blades (agate, chalcedony, jasper, milky-quartz, etc.) was obtained from a distance of 8 to 9 km, from the foothills of the Kaimur hill ranges (Pappu, 2004: 410). A similar situation must have obtained on other Chalcolithic sites also.

6. The archaeo-botanical remains from Jhusi, Malhar, Imlidih, Narhan and Senuwar have been studied in quite a great detail. This study indicates that by about 7000 BC almost all cereals, pulses and oil seeds which form the staple food of the present-day inhabitants of the middle Ganga plain were grown in this region. The only serious omission is the pigeon-pea (*Arhar*), which is presently missing from the archaeological record. Presently its first cultivation in the Ganga valley has been recorded at Charda and is datable to circa 800 BC.
7. The economic base of the Chalcolithic culture of the lower Ganga plain (including Sarayupar region) comprised rice as well as wheat and barley. Here we find that the cultivation of two crops a year was firmly established during the Chalcolithic period and almost all the cereals which were the staple food of the urban settlement of the Harappa culture in the north-west, were being cultivated by the Chalcolithic people in this part of the country as well.
8. The radiocarbon dates from the Neolithic-Chalcolithic sites of the middle Ganga plain have conclusively proved that these cultures were a younger contemporary of the Harappa culture. Here the natural question arises as to whether the Chalcolithic people were in contact with this mighty city-civilization. The discovery of more than one hundred tiny beads of steatite from the Neolithic deposits at Imlidih Khurd and Lahuradewa and several steatite beads from Chirand provide an indication of such a contact, but this remains to be firmly established by further research. This link between two cultures is further buttressed by certain pottery types like the dish-on-stand which occurs on several sites like Lahuradewa, Narhan and Chirand (Sinha, 1996).
9. On the basis of the archaeo-botanical evidence, Saraswat (2004) believes that since Harappan trade with Mesopotamia had declined around 2000 BC, the late Harappan people migrated from their homeland to different regions and some of them came to the Kaimur region. From the Kaimur region the tradition spread in inland regions of the middle Ganga plain and a number of sites like Chirand, Taradih,

Maner and Chechar-Kutubpur are a testimony to this. Harappan influence has also been noticed by some scholars in the pottery types of this period. The button-based goblet, dish-on-stand, and a knobbed ware from Chirand are taken as further proofs of this eastward migration of the late Harappans.

10. Analysis of copper objects from Senuwar (Singh, R.N., 2004a: 597) shows that the coppersmiths of this site had definitely started smelting copper ores since 1950 BC-1300 BC (Neolithic-Chalcolithic) for procuring metallic copper. The trace element analysis of this metal from Senuwar suggests that the source of copper was Singhbhum copper belt of Bihar, particularly the Rakha mines. The metallurgical analysis of a copper axe from Imlidih Khurd has been given above.
11. Excavations at Raja Nal Ka Tila, Malhar and Dadupur provided early dates for the introduction of iron in the middle Ganga valley (Tewari, 2003: 536). A number of radiocarbon dates from these sites put the introduction of this metal to about 1600 BC, if not earlier (See Appendix F). This is a new development which has wider ramifications and the stratigraphic position of this metal in future excavations needs to be watched carefully.
12. The discovery of well-established village cultures based on the cultivation of two crops a year by rotation method in eastern U.P. and Bihar demonstrates an uninterrupted cultural continuity uninfluenced by any external stimuli from about from circa 2500 BC in the Sarayupar plain and circa 2000 BC in Bihar. This discovery has exploded the popular theory that this part of the country was 'aryanised' by clearing dense forests only around the eighth to seventh century BC, as proposed by some scholars while giving a historical explanation of the Videgha Mathava legend of the *Satapatha Brahmana.* We know that there is only casual reference to this region in the early Vedic literature, but by the late Vedic period it had become an important administrative unit due to the formation of the Kosala and Videha kingdoms. The region is first mentioned in the *Satapatha Brahmana,* a text that relates to the spread of Aryan culture. In this text we read about Videgha Mathava, the king of Videhas. Accompanied by the priest Gotama Rahugana, he carried the sacrificial fire from the banks of the Saraswati River eastward across Kosala and the Sadanira and established a settlement known as Videha after the tribal name of Mathava.
13. That the Neolithic-Chalcolithic of the middle Ganga plain are non-Harappans and non-Aryans is generally accepted on all hands. The contributions of these pioneers in the making of Indian culture are

too many to be enumerated. However, the question remains as to whether we can give a name to these people. It is suggested that they could be Vratyas and Kikatas who are forefathers of the present-day tribal population of the Vindhyas and the Chotanagpur plateau. The term 'Vratya' was possibly a collective name given to a group of people whose way of life was different from those who claimed to be Aryans. As the primitive people of India, they seem to have contributed much to the growth and development of Indian culture. They differed from the Vedic Aryans and developed their own system of thought and culture.

The Vratya has been glorified in the *Atharvaveda* (XV). According to Monier-Williams (*Sanskrit-English Dictionary*, p. 1043), the word Vratya means a man of mendicant or vagrant class, a tramp, outcaste, low or vile person, either a man who had lost caste through the non-observance of ten principal *Sanskaras*, or a man of particular low caste descended from a Shudra and a Kshatriya and according to some the illegitimate son of a Kshatriya who knows the habits and intentions of soldiers.

Weber (*Indische Studien*, I, 35, 51, 121-40) believes that the Vratya is derived from the word Vrata (troop), the chief of a band of wanderers of Aryan extraction, but absolutely independent, free from the fetters of Brahmanical hierarchy and not following the Aryan way of life.

Radhakrishna Choudhary (1964: 148) thinks that the Vratyas were a class of people different from the Aryans and did not abide by the Vedic law or custom. They were original inhabitants of eastern India (Magadha). The *Atharvaveda* and the *Kausitaki Upanishad* are the living examples of their contributions in the intellectual field (Choudhary, 1964: 150). They were worshippers of the pre-historic form of Shiva. It is only in the Vratya tradition (*Prasna* and *Svetasvatara Upanishads* of the *Atharvaveda*) that we have a succinct account of their cult.

14. It has been suggested that these first farmers may be tribals like the Kikatas of the *Rigveda* who have been said to be relying more on pastoralism. They seem to have abandoned their habitations by the fourth millennium for reasons not known to us. In this context, it may be pointed out that the earliest settlement at Mehrgarh (Pakistan) belonging to the 6th millennium (Stage I consisting of Periods I-II, Neolithic) has been found to have some biological affinity with those in the Ganga valley (Possehl, 2002: 35). This observation of biological anthropologists is significant and needs further probe (Dhavalikar, 2006: 28).

REFERENCES

Agrawal, D.P. 1971. *Copper Bronze Age in India*, Delhi, Munshiram Manoharlal.

_____. 2000. *Ancient Metal Technology and Archaeology of South Asia: A Pan-Asian Perspective*, New Delhi, Aryan Books International.

Agrawal, O.P., H. Narain, J. Prakash and S.K. Bhatia. 1992. Development of Iron Metallurgy in Ancient India, *Archeometallurgia Richerche e Prospettive*, Bologna.

Allchin, F.R. 1969. Early Domestic Animals in India and Pakistan, in P.J. Ucko and G.W. Dimbleby (eds.), *The Domestication and Exploitation of Plants and Animals*, London, Duckworth: 317-322.

Allchin, F.R. and Allchin, B. 1968. *The Birth of Indian Civilization*, London, Penguin.

Badam, G.L. 1979. *Pleistocene Fauna of India*, Pune, Deccan College.

Bharadwaj, H.C. 1979. *Aspects of Ancient Indian Technology*, New Delhi, Motilal Banarsidass.

Bhatt, S.K. 1966. *A Study of Ceramic Industries in Basti District of Uttar Pradesh (up to 600 AD)*, A Dissertation for P.G. Diploma in Archaeology (unpublished), Dept. of AIHC & Archaeology, Banaras Hindu University.

_____. 1969-70. Archaeological Explorations in Basti District (U.P.), *Puratattva*, No. 3: 77-88.

Bokonyi, S. 1969. Archaeological Problems and Methods of Recognising Animal Domestication, in P.J. Ucko and G.W. Dimbleby (eds.), *The Domestication and Exploitation of Plants and Animals*, London, Duckworth: 219-229.

_____. 1989. Definition of Animal Domestication, in Juliet Clutton-Brock (ed.), *The Walking Larder*, London, Unwin Hyman: 22-27.

Bose, Shibani. 2003. *Forests and Fields in the Middle Gangetic Plains (From the Mesolithic up to C. 3rd Century BC)*, M.Phil Dissertation, Delhi University (Unpublished).

Chakrabarti, Dilip K. 1992. *The Early Use of Iron in India*, Delhi, Oxford University Press.

_____. 1999. *India: An Archaeological History*, New Delhi, Oxford University Press.

Chakrabarti, Dilip K. and Nayanjot Lahiri. 1996. *Copper and its Alloys in India*, Delhi, Munshiram Manoharlal.

Chattopadhyay, P.K and B.P. Singh. 1998. Metallographic and Chemical Study of Copper Artefacts from Senuwar, in Vibha Tripathi (ed.), *Archaeometallurgy in India*, Delhi, Sharada Publishing House: 20-26.

Chattopadhyay, P.K. 2004. *Archaeometallugy in India*, Patna, Kashi Prasad Jayaswal Research Institute.

Chaturvedi, S.N. 1985. Advance of Vindhyan Neolithic and Chalcolithic Cultures to the Himalayan Tarai: Excavations and Explorations in the Sarayupar Region of Uttar Pradesh, *Man and Environment*, IX: 101-108.

Choudhary, R.K. 1964. *The Vratyas in Ancient India*, Varanasi, The Chowkhamba Sanskrit Series Office.

Clutton-Brock, Juliet. 1989. Introduction to Domestication, in Juliet Clutton-Brock (ed.), *The Walking Larder: Patterns of Domestication, Pastoralism and Predation*, London, Unwin Hyman: 7-9.

Costantini, L. 1984. The Beginnings of Agriculture in the Kachi Plain: The Evidence of Merghgarh, in B. Allchin (ed.), *South Asian Archaeology, 1981*, Cambridge: 29-33.

Datta, Asok. 1998. Iron Technology at the Chalcolithic Phase of West Bengal, in Vibha Tripathi (ed.), *Archaeometallurgy in India*, Delhi, Sharada Publishing House: 36-47.

Dhavalikar, M.K. 2006. Aryan Agro-Pastoralists in the Ganga Valley, *Purattatva*, No. 36: 24-29.

Harris, David R. (ed.). 1996. *The Origins and Spread of Agriculture and Pastoralism in Eurasia*, London, UCL Press.

Harris, M. 1966. The Cultural Ecology of India's Sacred Cattle, *Current Anthropology*, 7(1): 51-66.

Joglekar, P.P., V.D. Misra, J.N. Pal and M.C. Gupta. 2003. *Mesolithic Mahadaha: The Faunal Remains*, Allahabad, Department of A.H.C. & Archaeology, University of Allahabad.

——. 2008. Faunal Remains to Neoltithic-Chalcolithic phases at Tokwa, Mirzapur District, Uttar Pradesh, *Man and Environment*, XXXIII (2): 51-59.

Joglekar, P.P. 2008. A Fresh Appraisal of the Animal based Subsistence and Domestic Animals in the Ganga Valley, *Pragdhara*, No.18: 309-322.

Kajale, M.D. 1991. Current Status of Indian Palaeoethnobotany: Introduced and Indigenous Food Plants with a Discussion of the Historical and Evolutionary Development of Indian Agriculture and Agricultural System in General, in Jane Renfrew (ed.), *New Light on Early Farming – Recent Developments in Palaeoethnobotany*, Edinburgh, University Press: 155-189.

Kotlia, B.S., A.K. Sahni, D.P. Agrawal and R.K. Pant. 1982. New Vertebrate Evidence for the Age of the Karewa Sediments, Kashmir, *Man and Environment*, VI: 13-15.

Kumar, R. 1989. *Archaeology of Middle Gomati Basin: With Special Reference to Sultanpur District*. Unpublished Ph.D. Thesis, Dept. of AIHC & Archaeology, Banaras Hindu University.

Kumar, Tuk-Tuk. 1988. *History of Rice in India – Mythology, Culture and Agriculture*, Delhi, Gian Publishing House.

Misra, V.D. 2006. Chalcolithic Cultures of North-Central Vindhyas, *Pragdhara*, No. 16: 171-186.

——. 2007. Stone Age Cultures, their Chronology and Beginnings of Agriculture in the North-Central India, *Man and Environment*, XXXII (1): 1-4.

Misra, V.D. and M.C. Gupta. 2006. Pre N.B.P. Cultures of the Middle-Ganga Valley, *Pragdhara*, No. 16: 21-34.

Misra, V.N. 1996. Mesolithic India: History and Current Status of Research, in G.D. Afanas'ev, S. Cleuziou, J.R. Lukacs and M. Tosi (eds.), *Bioarchaeology of Mesolithic India: An Integrated Approach*, Colloquium XXXIII of the International Union of Prehistoric and Protohistoric Sciences, Forli, ABACO Edizioni: 321-328.

——. 2007. *Rajasthan: Prehistoric and Early Historic Foundations*, New Delhi, Aryan Books International.

Murthy, M.L.K. 1979. Late Pleistocene Fauna of Kurnool Caves, South India, in F.R. Allchin and D.K. Chakrabarti (eds.), *A Source Book of Indian Archaeology*, Delhi, 335-341.

Mushrif-Tripathy, Veena, A.R. Sankhyan and V.R. Rao. 2009. Palaeopathological Observations on Human Skeletal Remains from Sarai Nahar Rai at Anthropological Survey of India, Kolkata, *Man and Environment* XXXIV (1): 77-82.

Pal, J.N. 1986. *Archaeology of Southern Uttar Pradesh, Ceramic Industries of Northern Vindhyas*, Allahabad, Swabha Prakashan.

_____. 1994. Mesolithic Settlement in the Ganga Plain, *Man and Environment*, XIX (1-2): 91-101.

_____. 2008a. Recent Excavations at Tokwa: Fresh Light on the Early farming Culture of the Vindhyas, in Lallanji Gopal and V.C. Srivastava (eds.), *History of Agriculture in Ancient India (upto. C. 1200AD)*, New Delhi, Concept Publishing Company: 48-69.

_____. 2008b. The Early Farming Culture of the Middle Ganga Plain with Special Reference to the Excavation of Jhusi and Hetapatti, *Pragdhara*, No. 18: 263-282.

_____. 2009. Beginnings of Agriculture in the Middle Ganga Plain, Sectional Presidential Address (Ancient Section), U.P. History Congress, XXth Session, VBS Purvanchal University, Jaunpur: October 3-4, 2009.

Pant, P.C. 2000. Indus Civilization Versus Mahagara Neolithic Culture: A Note on Acculturation, in S.M. Mishtra (ed.), *Puravritta* (Journal of Department of Ancient Indian History and Archaeology, Lucknow University), Vol. I: 65-70.

Pappu, R.S. 2004. Site Catchment Analysis, in B.P. Singh, *Early Farming Culture of the Kaimur*, Jaipur, Publication Scheme, Vol. II: 405-415.

Pokharia, A.K., J.N. Pal and Alka Srivastava. 2009. Plant macro remains from Neolithic Jhusi in Ganga Plain: Evidence for grain-based agriculture, *Current Science*, Vol. 97, No. 4, 25August: 564-572.

Possehl, Gregory L. 1999. *Indus Age: The Beginnings*, Philadelphia, University of Pennsylvania Press.

_____. 2002. *The Indus Civilization: A Contemporary Perspective*, New York, Alta Mira Press.

Randhawa, M.S. 1980. *A History of Agriculture in India*, Vol. I, New Delhi, Indian Council of Agricultural Research.

Sahni, A. 1982. Karewa Vertebrates: Biostratigraphy, Palaeohistology and Palaeoecology, *Man and Environment*, VI: 16-20.

Sahu, B.P. 1988. *From Hunters to Breeders*, Delhi, Anamika Prakashan.

Saraswat, K.S. 2004. Plant Economy of Early Farming Communities, in B.P. Singh, *Early Farming Culture of the Kaimur*, Jaipur, Publication Scheme, Vol. II: 416-535.

Sharma, G.R., V.D. Misra, D. Mandal, B.B. Misra and J.N. Pal. 1980. *Beginnings of Agriculture*, Allahabad, Abinash Prakashan.

Sharma, R.S. 1977 (Reprint). Material Background of the Origin of the Buddhism, in M. Sen and M.B. Rao (eds.), *Das Kapital Centenary Volume: A Symposium*, New Delhi: 59-66.

Simone, Daniela De. 2009. Neolithic and Chalcolithic Cord-Impressed Ware of the Middle Ganga Valley, in Shahnaj Husne Jahan (ed.), *Abhijnan: Studies in South Asian Archaeology and Art History of Artifacts, Felicitating A. K. M. Zakariah,* (British Archaeology Reports, International Series S 1974), Oxford: 1-6.

Singh, C.D.P. 2004. On Metallic Iron Tools, Slags and Ore Artefacts of Malhar Site, District Chandauli, (U.P.), *Pragdhara,* No. 14: 173-179.

Singh, P. 1974. *Neolithic Cultures of Western Asia,* London, Seminar Press.

_____. 1979. Early Iron Age in Gangetic Doab, in D.P. Agrawal and Dilip K. Chakrabarti (eds.), *Essays in Indian Protohistory,* Delhi, B.R. Publishing Corporation.

_____. 1991. *The Neolithic Origins,* Delhi, Agam Kala Prakashan.

_____. 1994. *Excavations at Narhan (1984-89),* Varanạsi and Delhi, Banaras Hindu University and B.R. Publishing Corporation.

_____. 1996. Prelude to Urbanization in the Sarayupar Plain, Presidential Address Section V, *Indian History Congress,* 56 Session, Chennai.

_____. 2003. Archaeology of the Middle Ganga Plain, *Man and Environment,* XXVIII (1): 1-6.

Singh, R.N. and John F. Merkel. 2001. A Study of Iron Objects from Chirand and Taradih, *Pragdhara,* No. 11: 135-142.

Singh, R.N. 2003. Iron in Middle Ganga Plain: A Study of Iron Objects from Narhan, *Pragdhara,* No. 13: 141-150.

_____. 2004a. Analysis of Metal Objects, in B.P. Singh, *Early Farming Culture of the Kaimur,* Jaipur, Publication Scheme, Vol. II: 591-603.

_____. 2004b. A Note on Copper Axe from Imlidih Khurd: An Archaeo-Technological Assessment, Paper read in the *Workshop on the Archaeology of the Middle Ganga Plain,* held at Lucknow, on 13-14 March 2004.

_____. 2006. Scientific Study of Ancient Metal Objects of the Middle Ganga Plain: Some Observations, *Pragdhara,* No. 16: 125-131.

Singh, S.C. 1991. *Archaeology of North Eastern Uttar Pradesh: With Special Reference to Basti District,* Unpublished Ph.D. Thesis, Banaras Hindu University.

Sinha, B.P. 1996. Harappan Fallout (?) in the Mid Gangetic Valley, in Gregory L. Possehl, *Harappan Civilization,* New Delhi, Oxford & IBH Publishing Co.: 135-139.

Srivastava, K.M. 1985. *Discovery of Kapilvastu,* New Delhi.

_____. 1978. *Identification of Kapilvastu in Basti District of U.P.,* Nagpur.

Tewari, R. 2003. The Origin of Iron Working in India: New evidence from the Central Ganga Plain in the Eastern Vindhyas, *Antiquity,* 77: 536-544.

_____. 1998. In Quest of early Iron Age sites in Karamnasa Valley, *Pragdhara,* No. 8: 57-61

Thomas, P.K. 1984a. The Faunal Background of the Chalcolithic Cultures of Western India, in J. Clutton-Brock and C. Grigson (eds.), *Animals and Archaeology,* Vol. 3, Oxford, BAR-202: 355-361.

_____. 1984b. Faunal Assemblage of Veerapuram, in T.V.G. Sastri, M. Kasturi Bai and J. Varaprasad Rao (eds.), *Veerapuram: A Type Site for Cultural Studies in The Krishna Valley,* Hyderabad, Bhavani Printers.

_____. 1989. Utilization of Domestic Animals in Pre-and Protohistoric India, in Juliet Clutton-Brock (ed.), *The Walking Larder: Patterns of Domestication, Pastoralism and Predation*, London, Unwin Hyman: 108-112.

Tripathi, Vibha (ed.). 1998. *Archaeometallurgy in India*, Delhi, Sharada Publishing House.

Tripathi, Vibha. 2001. *The Age of Iron in South Asia: Legacy and Tradition*, New Delhi, Aryan Books International.

_____. 2008. *History of Iron Technology in Ancient India (From Beginnings to Pre-modern times)*, New Delhi, Rupa & Co.

Ucko, Peter J. and G.W. Dimbleby. 1969. Introduction: Context and Development of Studies of Domestication, in P.J. Ucko and G.W. Dimbleby (eds.), *The Domestication and Exploitation of Plants and Animals*, London, Duckworth.

Varma, R.K. 1997. Couple and Multiple Couple Burials of the Mesolithic in the Ganga Valley, in J.P. Joshi (ed.), *Facets of Indian Civilization: Recent Perspectives*, (Essays in Honour of Prof. B.B. Lal), New Delhi, Aryan Books International: 29-34.

_____. 2003. *Early Farming Cultures of India: Keynote Address*, National Seminar held in the Department of AHC & Archaeology, University of Allahabad on 19-20 April, 2003.

Varma, R.K., V.D. Misra, J.N. Pandey and J.N. Pal. 1985. A Preliminary Report on the Excavations at Damdama (1982-84), *Man and Environment*, IX: 45-65.

Zeuner, F.E. 1963. *A History of Domesticated Animals*, London, Hutchinson.

Appendix

APPENDIX-A

Table showing C^{14} dates from excavated sites

Site	Period	Lab. N.	C^{14} Dates	Calibrated Dates in BC
Koldihwa	Chalcolithic	PRL-223 PRL-99	1450 ± 120 BC 1035 ± 155 BC	1745 1520
Malhar	Pre-Iron	BS-1590 BS-1593 BS-1623	3850 ± 80 BP 3650 ± 90 BP 3550 ± 90 BP	2283 (2141) 1984; 2012 (1882, 1836, 1834) 1742 1882 (1743) 1639 Period I may be placed between 1900 to 1700-1600 (Cal 2283-1639)
Lahuradewa	Pd. II	BS-1950	3750 ± 90 BP	2135, 2079, 2056
Lahuradewa	Pd. III	BS-1939	2940 ± 100 BP	1205
Raja-Nal-Ka-Tila	Pd. I	PRL-2046 PRL-2045	3200 ± 90 BP 3360 ± 90 BP	1500-1490, 1448-1256 1240-1212; 1622-1613 1742-1378, 1348-1613
Senuwar		BS-757 BS-755	1400 ± 110 BC 1500 ± 110 BC 1660 ± 120 BC 1770 ± 120 BC	1760 (1617) 1497 2125 (1958) 1798
Jhusi	Chalcolithic	PRL-2083	1340 ± 90 BC	1597 (1490, 1480, 1450) 1400

Khairadih		PRL-1049 PRL-722 PRL-513	1030 ± 160 BC 850 ± 50 BC 1120 ± 90 BC	1190 ± 160 900 ± 90 1290 ± 90
Narhan		BS-850 BS-852	1123 ± 110 BC 1133 ± 110 BC	1380 ± 110 1390 ± 110
Sohgaura		PRL-179 PRL-178	1230 ± 130 BC 1330 ± 110 BC	1410 ± 130 1490 ± 110
Chirand		TF-444 TF-334 TF-1029 TF-1028 TF-445	715 ± 105 BC 845 ± 125 BC 1050 ± 90 BC 1540 ± 90 BC 1650 ± 100 BC	

APPENDIX-B

Radiocarbon dates for Mesolithic sites of the Gangetic plain

Damdama	8865 ± 65[1] 5550 ± 60[2] (st 1)
Mahadaha	6160 ± 60[2] (st 4) 4680 ± 80[2] (st 1) 4110 ± 60[2] (st 2) 4010 ± 120 3840 ± 130 2880 ± 250
Sarai Nahar Rai	10395 ± 110 (burned bone) 10050 ± 110 (burned bone) 5040 ± 50[2] (surface) 2860 ± 120

Taken from Misra, V.D. (1977: 67); Kennedy *et al.* (1992); Allchin and Allchin (1982: 79); Kennedy *et al.* (1986: 52); Lucas *et al.* (1996); Lucas (n.d.)

1 Dates obtained from Accelerated Mass Spectroscopy (AMS) techniques on bio-apatite from bone.

2 Dates obtained from AMS dating technique on bio-apatite from bovid teeth.

APPENDIX-C

Table I: Lahuradewa: Radiocarbon ages

Cultural Period	Representative Finds	Cal C^{14} dates BC
Period V	RW, brick structures	
Period IV	Painted NBPW, etc.	
Period III	Continuity of earlier cultural assemblage	BS-1939: 1205, 1205, 1188

Period II	Painted and plain BSW, BRW, steatite beads, greater presence of dish-on-stand, bowl-on-stand, pedestal bowl	BS-1938: 1519 (1435) 1399; BS-2150: 2012 (1884) 1750
Period IB	RW and BRW often bearing corded patterns, a few paintings, incised designs, slipped pottery. Introduction of pedestal bowl, dish or bowl-on-stand, charcoal pieces, steatite bead. Cultivated rice and barley	BS-1950: 2135, 2078, 2056: BS-2274: 2919 (2700) 2570; ERL-6903(AMS): 2345-2200
Period IA	RW and BRW often bearing corded patterns, charcoal pieces Cultivated rice	BS-2145: 3090 (2916), 2879: BS-2148: 3363 (3328, 3223, 3174, 3159, 3119, 3106, 3105) 3020; BS-2151: 3654 (3635, 3553, 3542) 3382; BS-1951: 4220, 4196, 4161: BS-1967: 5298; ERL-6442(AMS): 6442-6376
Natural Soil	Natural Soil	Natural soil

APPENDIX-D

Table 4: Radiocarbon dates from Tokwa and Jhusi

S. No.	Name of Site	Sample No.	Trench/Layer No.	C-14 Date	Cal BC
1.	Tokwa, district Mirzapur	BS-2417	H-9 (Pit sealed by (4)	7530 ± 230 BP	6591 (6407) 6106
2.	-do-	BS-2464	I-8 (6)	5620 ± 310 BP	4797 (4456) 4051
3.	-do-	BS-2369	H-8 (14)	6850 ± 200 BP	5976 (5725) 5561
4.	Jhusi, district Allahabad	BS-2526	SF-7 (47)	8140 ± 220 BP	7106, 7105, 7080
5.	-do-	BS-2524	SF-7 (50)	6760 ± 190 BP	5660, 5649, 5612
6.	do	BS 2525	SF-7 (51)	7110 ± 170 BP	5990, 5938, 5932

APPENDIX-E

Radiocarbon ages from Malhar

S. No.	Laboratory Number	Radiocarbon ages in BP/BC on the basis of half life		Cal. BC Stulver *et al.* One Sigma
		5568 ± 30 years	5730 ± 40 years	
1.	BS-1623, MLR II Trench No. XA 1, Layer No. (3) Depth 0.55 cm	3450 ± 90 BP 1500 ± 90 BC	3550 ± 90 BP 1600 ± 90 BC	1882 (1743) 1639 BC
2.	BS-1614, MLR II Trench No. A 1, Pit sealed by Layer No. (3) Depth 61-63 cm	6380 ± 110 BP 4430 ± 110 BC	6570 ± 110 BP 4620 ± 110 BC	5475 (5358, 5351, 5340, 5329, 5323) 5262 BC
3.	BS-1593, MLR II Trench No. A 1, Pit sealed by Layer No. (3) Depth 90-100 cm	3540 ± 90 BP 1590 ± 90 BC	3650 ± 90 BP 1700 ± 90 BC	2012 (1882, 1836, 1834) 1742 BC
4.	BS-1590, MLR II Trench No. XA 1, Layer No. (4) Depth 80 cm	3740 ± 90 BP 1790 ± 90 BC	3850 ± 80 BP 1900 ± 80 BC	2283 (2141) 1984 BC

APPENDIX-F

New C^{14} dates for early iron-use from the Ganga Plain and the Eastern Vindhyas

Site	Lab-ref	Date BP	Date Cal BC	Pub-ref
			Stuiver and Reimer 1993*	Tewari *et al* 2000: 93
Raja Nal-ka Tila district Sonbhadra (U.P.)	BS-1988	2690+70	902 (828) 800	
	BS-1988	2550+110	822 (773) 486	
	BS-1378	2830+100	1118 (963) 859	
	BS-1299	3060+110	1423 (1307) 1144	
	PRL-2047	2890+80	1196-1188 1164-143 1132-976 970-930	
	PRL-2049	3050+90	1406-1198 1186-1164 1143-1132	

Malhar district Chandauli (U.P)	BS-1623 BS-1593 (Pit sealed by Layer No. 3)	3450+90 3550+90	Stuiver and Reimer 1993* 1822 (1743) 1639 2012(1822 1836 1834) 1742	Tewari *et al* 2000: 88
Dadupur district Lucknow (U. P.)	BS-1822 BS-1759 BS-1825 Pit-sealed by 12)	3270+80 3380+160 3430+90	Stuiver and Reimer 1993* 1679 (1522) 1442 1882 (1685) 1465 1739 (1706) 1695	Tewari *et al* 2002: 111
Lahuradewa district Sant Kabir Nagar (U.P)	BS-1939	2940+100	Stuiver and Reimer 1993* 1205, 1205, 1188	Tewari *et al* 2002a: 57
Jhusi district Allahabad (U.P.)	PRL-2077	2820+80	Stuiver and Reimer 1993* 1107 (973, 956, 941) 844	Misra, *et al* 2000: 28

* These dates are calibrated by Dr. B. Sekar, BSIP, Lucknow. References for datasets used: Stuiver. et.al 1998 a

APPENDIX-G

After the manuscript of this book was sent to the press, radiocarbon dates from the first three periods of Agiabir[1] and Period I of Aktha[2] have been obtained. These are reproduced below:

Table 1: C^{14} dates from Agiabir (2005-06 and 2006-07)

Sample No.	Trench Details	Radiocarbon Age in Years BP/BC	Calibrated Age in Years BP/BC	One Sigma
BS-2640 S-3458	BAR-1/Tr.A'1 Pit SB (4) 230-250cm Pd-II, Pre-NBPW	2810 ± 100 BP	2920, 2908, 2885 Cal BP 971, 959, 936 Cal BC	1125 (971, 959 936) 832 Cal BC 3075 (2920, 2908, 2885) 2782 Cal BP

BS-2641 S-3459	ABR-2/Tr. YE-5 Lr. (13) 670 cm Pd-III Middle phase of NBPW	2700 ± 100 BP	2779 Cal BP 830 Cal BC	969 (830) 797 Cal BC 2919 (2779) 2747 Cal BP
BS-2846 S-3676	ABR-2/Tr. AM-3 Lr. (10) 420-425 cm Pd-III Middle phase of NBPW	2710 ± 70 BP	2839 ± 63 BP (2776-2902) Cal BP 889 ± 63 Cal BC	
BS-2847 S-3677	ABR-1/Tr. YA-3 Lr (4) 225-230 cm Pd-I Early phase of Chalcolithic	4090 ± 110 BP	4618 ± 156 BP (4462-4774) Cal BP 2668 ± 156 Cal BC	
PRL-3127	ABR-2/Tr. AL-3 & AM-3 Pit SB (16) 680-690 cm Transitional phase of pre-NBPW and NBPW periods.	2840 ± 80 BP	2855 Cal BP to 3072 Cal BP	

Table 2 : C^{14} Dates from Aktha

Sample No.	BS (Lab) No.	C^{14} Age (Year BP)	Year BC
2	S-3580	3350 ± 160	1660 ± 218
3	S-3849	3460 ± 180	1771 ± 248

[1] Tripathi, Vibha and P. Upadhyay, 2009. Excavations at Agiabir (2006-07), *Puratattva*, No. 39: 50-57.

[2] Jayaswal,Vidula, 2009. Antiquity of Varanasi As Revealed by Excavation at Aktha (2008-09), *Puratattva*, No. 39: 141-146.

Bibliography

Agrawal, D.P. and S. Kusumgar. 1974. *Prehistoric Chronology and Radiocarbon Dating in India*, Delhi, Munshiram Manoharlal.

——. 1971. *Copper Bronze Age in India*, Delhi, Munshiram Manoharlal.

——. 2000. *Ancient Metal Technology and Archaeology of South Asia: A Pan-Asian Perspective*, New Delhi, Aryan Books International.

Agrawal, D.P. and J.S. Kharakwal. 2002. *South Asian Prehistory*, New Delhi, Aryan Books International.

——. 2003. *Bronze and Iron Ages in South Asia*, New Delhi, Aryan Books International.

Agrawal, O.P., H. Narain, J. Prakash and S.K. Bhatia. 1992. Development of Iron Metallurgy in Ancient India, *Archeometallurgia Richerche e Prospettive*, Bologna.

Allchin, F.R. 1969. Early Domestic Animals in India and Pakistan, in P.J. Ucko and G.W. Dimbleby (eds.), *The Domestication and Exploitation of Plants and Animals*, London, Duckworth: 317-322.

Allchin, F.R. and A. Goudie. 1971. Dunes, Aridity and Early Man in Gujarat, *Western Asia Man*, Vol. 6 (June 1971), No. 2: 251.

Allchin, F.R. and B. Allchin. 1968. *The Birth of Indian Civilization*, London, Penguin.

Allchin, B., A. Goudie and K.T.M. Hegde. 1978. *Prehistory and Palaeogeography of the Great Indian Desert*, London, Academic Press.

Altekar, A.S. and V.K. Misra. 1959. *Report on Kumrahar Excavations 1951-55*, Patna, K.P. Jayaswal Institute.

Alur, K.R. 1980. Faunal remains from the Vindhyas and the Ganga Valley, in G.R. Sharma, V.D. Misra, D. Mandal, B.B. Misra and J.N. Pal (eds.), *Beginning of Agriculture*, Allahabad, Abinash Prakashan: 201-227.

Badam, G.L. 1979. *Pleistocene Fauna of India*, Pune, Deccan College.

Banerjee, S. 1979-80. The archaeological material from West Bengal in the Zoological Survey of India, *Puratattva*, No. 11: 162-64.

——. 1981. Animal Remains from Bharatpur, District Burdwan, West Bengal, India, *Records of the Zoological Survey of India*, 79: 193-220.

Bharadwaj, H.C. 1979. *Aspects of Ancient Indian Technology*, New Delhi, Motilal Banarsidass.

Bhatt, S.K. 1966. *A Study of Ceramic Industries in Basti District of Uttar Pradesh (up to 600 AD)*, A Dissertation for P.G. Diploma in Archaeology (unpublished), Dept. of AIHC & Archaeology, Banaras Hindu University.

_____. 1969-70. Archaeological Explorations in Basti District (U.P.), *Puratattva*, No. 3: 77-88.

Bokonyi, S. 1969. Archaeological Problems and Methods of Recognising Animal Domestication, in P.J. Ucko and G.W. Dimbleby (eds.), *The Domestication and Exploitation of Plants and Animals*, London, Duckworth: 219-229.

_____. 1989. Definition of Animal Domestication, in Juliet Clutton-Brock (ed.), *The Walking Larder*, London, Unwin Hyman: 22-27.

Bose, Shibani. 2003. *Forests and Fields in the Middle Gangetic Plains (From the Mesolithic up to C. 3rd Century BC)*. M.Phil Dissertation, Delhi University (Unpublished).

Chakrabarti, Dilip K. *et al.* 1982. Lithic Industries of Bankura, *Puratattva*, No. 11: 39-48.

Chakrabarti, Dilip K. and S. Jamal Hasan. 1982. The Sequence of Bahiri (Chandra Hazrar Danga), District Birbhum, West Bengal, *Man and Environment*, 6: 111-149.

Chakrabarti, Dilip K. and Nayanjot Lahiri. 1996. *Copper and its Alloys in India*, Delhi, Munshiram Manoharlal.

Chakrabarti, Dilip K. 1986. Iron and Urbanization: An Examination of the Indian Context, *Puratattva*, No. 15.

_____. 1992. *The Early Use of Iron in India*, Delhi, Oxford University Press.

_____. 1999. *India: An Archaeological History*, New Delhi, Oxford University Press.

_____. 2001. *Archaeological Geography of the Ganga Plain: The Lower and the Middle Ganga*, Delhi, Permanent Black.

Charurvedi, S.N. 1985. Advance of Vindhyan Neolithic and Chalcolithic cultures to the Himalayan Tarai, *Man and Environment*, IX: 101-108.

Chattopadhyay, I. and U.C. Chattopadhyay. 1990. The Spatial Organization of Mortuary Practices in the Mesolithic Ganga Valley, in N.C. Ghosh and S. Chakrabarti (eds.), *Adaptation and other essays*, Santiniketan, Vishwa Bharati: 103-21.

Chattopadhyay, P.K and B.P. Singh. 1998. Metallographic and Chemical Study of Copper Artifacts from Senuwar, in Vibha Tripathi (ed.), *Archaeometallurgy in India*, Delhi, Sharada Publishing House: 20-26.

Chattopadhyay, P.K. 2004. *Archaeometallurgy in India*, Patna, K.P. Jayaswal Research Institute.

Chattopadhyay, R.K., Rajat Sanyal and Kumkum Bandhopadhyay. 2007. Early Village Farming Settlement in Eastern India: An Appraisal, *Puratattva*, No. 37: 68-93.

Chattopadhyay, U.C. 1988. Subsistence Variability and Complex Social formations in Prehistoric Ganga Valley: Problems and Prospects, *Man and Environment*, XII: 135-52.

Chauhan, M.S., A.K. Pokharia, R. Tewari and I.B. Singh. 2004. Preliminary pollen analytical investigation on early Holocene sediments from Lahuradewa Lake,

District Sant Kabir Nagar, U.P. Paper read in the *Workshop on the Archaeology of the Middle Ganga Plain,* Lucknow, on 13-14 March 2004.

Choudhary, R.K. 1964. *The Vratyas in Ancient India,* Varanasi, The Chowkhamba Sanskrit Series Office.

Clutton-Brock, Juliet. 1989. Introduction to Domestication, in Juliet Clutton-Brock (ed.), *The Walking Larder: Patterns of Domestication, Pastoralism and Predation,* London, Unwin Hyman: 7-9.

Costantini, L. 1984. The Beginnings of Agriculture in the Kachi Plain: The Evidence of Merghgarh, in B. Allchin (ed.), *South Asian Archaeology, 1981,* Cambridge: 29-33.

Datta, Asok. 1998. Iron Technology at the Chalcolithic Phase of West Bengal, in Vibha Tripathi (ed.), *Archaeometallurgy in India,* Delhi, Sharada Publishing House: 36-47.

De, S. and P.K. Chattopadhyay. 1989. Iron Objects from Pandu Rajar Dhibi, Archaeo-Metallurgical Studies, *Steel India,* 3 (1): 33.

Dhavalikar, M.K. 2006. Aryan Agro-Pastoralists in the Ganga Valley, *Purattatva,* No. 36: 24-29.

Diwakar, R.R. 1959. *Bihar Through the Ages,* Bombay, Orient Longman.

Dutta, P.C. 1984. Sarai Nahar Rai Man: The First and Oldest Human Fossil Record in South Asia, *Anthropologie,* 23 (1): 35-50.

Ehrhardt, S. and K.A.R. Kennedy. 1965. *Excavations at Langhnaj,* Part III (Human Remains), Poona, Deccan College.

Fuhrer, A. 1891. *Monumental Antiquities and Inscriptions in the North-Western Provinces and Oudh,* ASIR, Vol. II, Allahabad.

Ghosh, A. (ed.). 1989. *An Encyclopaedia of Indian Archaeology,* 2 vols, Delhi, Munshiram Manoharlal.

Ghosh, N.C. and A.K. Nag. 1986. Excavations at Hatikra: A Chalcolithic Site in West Bengal, *Puratattva,* No. 15: 116.

Government of India. 1965. *The Gazetteer of India,* Vol. I, Country and People, New Delhi, Publication Division.

Gupta, H.P. 1976. Holocene Palynology from Meander Lake in the Ganga Valley, District Pratapgarh, Uttar Pradesh, *The Palaeobotanist,* 25: 109-119.

Harris, David R. (ed.). 1996. *The Origins and Spread of Agriculture and Pastoralism in Eurasia,* London, UCL Press.

Harris, M. 1966. The Cultural Ecology of India's Sacred Cattle, *Current Anthropology,* 7(1): 51-66.

Hoque, M. 1993. *Pre- and Protohistoric Settlement Patterns of the Middle and Lower Ganga Valley,* Ph.D. thesis (unpublished), Pune, Deccan College.

Hunter, G.R. 1945-46. Interim Report on the Excavations in the Mahadeo Hills, *Nagpur University Journal,* No. 1: 28-57.

Jayaswal, V. 2003. Aktha: A Satellite Settlement of Sarnath, *Bharati,* No. 26: 61-180.

_____. 2009. *Ancient Varanasi: An Archaeological Perspective,* New Delhi, Aryan Books International.

Jayaswal, V. and M. Kumar. 2006. Excavations at Ramnagar: Discovery of the Supporting Settlement of Ancient Varanasi, *Puratattva,* No. 36: 85-92.

Joglekar, P.P., V.D. Misra, J.N. Pal and M.C. Gupta. 2003. *Mesolithic Mahadaha: The Faunal Remains*, Allahabad, Department of A.H.C. & Archaeology, University of Allahabad.

_____. 2008. Faunal Remains from Neolithic-Chalcolithic phases at Tokwa, Mirzapur District, Uttar Pradesh, *Man and Environment*, XXXIII (2): 51-59.

Joglekar, P.P. 2008. A Fresh Appraisal of the Animal based Subsistence and Domestic Animals in the Ganga Valley, *Pragdhara*, No. 18: 309-322.

Kajale, M.D. 1991. Current Status of Indian Palaeoethnobotany: Introduced and Indigenous Food Plants with a Discussion of the Historical and Evolutionary Development of Indian Agriculture and Agricultural System in General, in Jane Renfrew (ed.), *New Light On Early Farming – Recent Developments In Palaeoethnobotany*, Edinburgh, University Press: 155-189.

Kajale, M.D. and B.C. Deotare. 1988-89. Pollen Analysis and Chemical Examination of a Prehistoric Lake Site at Damdama, *Puratattva*, No. 19: 27-30.

Kennedy, K.A.R. 1996. Skeletal Adaptations of Mesolithc Hunter-Foragers of North India: Mahadaha and Sarai Nahar Rai Compared, in G.D. Afanas'ev, S. Cleuziou, J.R. Lukacs and M. Tosi (eds.), *Bioarchaeology of Mesolithic India: An Integrated Approach*, Colloquium XXXIII of the International Union of Prehistoric and Protohistoric Sciences, Forli, ABACO Edizioni: 291-300.

_____. 2000. *God-Apes and Fossil Men: Palaeoanthropology of South Asia*, Ann Arbor, The University of Michigan Press.

Kennedy, K.A.R., Christopher B. Burrow and Nancy C. Lovell. 1984-85. Mesolithic Human Remains from the Gangetic Plain: Sarai Nahar Rai, *Puratattva*, 15: 1-55.

Kotlia, B. S., A.K. Sahni, D.P. Agrawal and R.K. Pant. 1982. New Vertebrate Evidence for the Age of the Karewa Sediments, Kashmir, *Man and Environment*, VI: 13-15.

Kumar, R. 1989. *Archaeology of Middle Gomati Basin: With Special Reference to Sultanpur District*. Unpublished Ph.D. Thesis, Dept. of AIHC & Archaeology, Banaras Hindu University.

Kumar, Sudhir, B. Prakash, M.L. Manchanda, A.K. Singhvi and Pankaj Srivastava. 1996. Holocene land form and soil evolution of the Western Gangetic plains: Implications of Neotectonics and Climate, *Geomorph. N.F. Suppl-Bd*. 103: 283-312.

Kumar, Tuk-Tuk. 1988. *History of Rice in India – Mythology, Culture and Agriculture*, Delhi, Gian Publishing House.

Lal, B.B. and K.N. Dikshit. 1978-79. Sringaverpura: A Key site for the protohistory and early history of the central Ganga Valley, *Puratattva*, No. 10: 1-7.

Lal, B.B. 1993. *Sringaverapura Excavations*, New Delhi, Archaeological Survey of India.

Lukacs, J.R. and J.N. Pal. 1992. Dental Anthropology of the Mesolithic Hunter-Gathers: A Preliminary Reports on the Mahadaha and Sarai Nahar Rai Dentition, *Man and Environment*, XVII (2): 45-55.

Lukacs, J.R., J.N. Pal and V.D. Misra. 1996. Chronology and Diet in Mesolithic North India: A Preliminary Report on New AMS C14 dates, 13C Isotope Values, and their Significance, in G.D. Afanas'ev, S. Cleuziou, J.R. Lukacs and M. Tosi (eds.), *Bioarchaeology of Mesolithic India: An Integrated Approach*, Colloquium XXXIII of the International Union of Prehistoric and Protohistoric Sciences, Forli, ABACO Edizioni: 301-311.

Mani, B.R. 2004. On Sensitizing Recent Achievements and Future Prospects for Archaeological Investigations in Middle Ganga Plain, Paper read in the *Workshop on the Archaeology of the Middle Ganga Plain*, held at Lucknow on 13-14 March 2004.

Misra, B.B. 2000. Chalcolithic cultures of the northern Vindhyas and the mid-Ganga Valley, in S.C. Bhattacharya, V.D. Misra, J.N. Pandey and J.N. Pal (eds.), *Peeping through the Past* (Prof. G. R. Sharma Memorial Volume), Allahabad, University of Allahabad: 66-85.

Misra, V.D. and M.C. Gupta. 1995. Pre-NBP cultures in the Mid-Ganga Valley, *Prof. Agam Prasad Mathur Felicitation Volume*, Vol. III, Agra, Huzuri Bhavan, Peepal Mandi: 21-34.

Misra, V.D. and B.B. Misra. 2000. Chalcolithic Cultures of the Northern Vindhyas and the Middle Ganga Valley: Some Observations, in V.D. Misra and J.N. Pal (eds.), *Social History and Social Theory*, Allahabad, University of Allahabad: 14-22.

Misra, V.D., B.B. Misra, J.N. Pal and M.C. Gupta. 2000. Exploration at Tokwa: A Neolithic Chalcolithic Settlement on the Confluence of the Belan and Adwa Rivers, in S.C. Bhattacharya, V.D. Misra, J.N. Pandey and J.N. Pal (eds.), *Peeping through the Past: Prof. G.R. Sharma Memorial Volume*, Department of Ancient History, Culture & Archaeology, University of Allahabad: 45-57.

Misra, V.D., B.B. Misra, J.N. Pandey and J.N. Pal. 1995-96. A Preliminary Report of Excavation at Jhusi-1995, *Pragdhara*, No. 6: 63-66.

Misra, V.D., J.N. Pal and M.C. Gupta. 1999-2000. Further Excavation at Jhusi, District Allahabad (Uttar Pradesh), *Pragdhara*, No. 10: 22-30.

_____. 2000-2001. Excavations at Tokwa: A Neolithic-Chalcolithic Settlement, *Pragdhara*, No. 11: 59-72.

_____. 2001. Neolithic Cultures of Northern Vindhyas with special reference to Tokwa, *Bharati*, No. 25, (Parts I & II): 211-233.

_____. 2002-2003. Further excavations at Jhusi: Evidence of Neolithic Culture, *Pragdhara*, No. 13: 227-230.

_____. 1998-99. Further Excavation at Jhusi, District Allahabad (Uttar Pradesh), *Pragdhara*, No. 9: 45-50.

Misra, V.D. 1977. *Some Aspects of Indian Archaeology*, Allahabad, Prabhat Prakashan.

_____. 1996. History and Context of Mesolithic Research at Allahabad University, Allahabad, India, in G.D. Afanas'ev, S. Cleuziou, J.R. Lukacs and M. Tosi (eds.), *Bioarchaeology of Mesolithic India: An Integrated Approach*, Colloquium XXXIII of the International Union of Prehistoric and Protohistoric Sciences, Forli, ABACO Edizioni: 245-250.

_____. 1997. The Mesolithic Cultures of the Vindhyas and the Ganga Valley with Special Reference to Environment and Archaeology, in B.M. Khanduri and Vinod Nautiyal (eds.), *Him-Kanti* (Prof. K.P. Nautiyal Felicitation Volume), Delhi, Book India Publishing Co. 32-38.

_____. 1999. A Brief Note on Indian Stone Age Archaeology, in G.C. Pande (ed.), *The Dawn of Indian Civilisation (up to c. 600 BC)*, Vol. I, Part I: 129-138.

_____. 1999. Agriculture, Domestication of Animals and Ceramic and Other Industries in Prehistoric India: Mesolithic and Neolithic, in G.C. Pande (ed.), *The Dawn of Indian Civilisation (up to c. 600 BC)*, Vol. I, Part I: 233-266.

_____. 2006. Chalcolithic Cultures of North-Central Vindhyas, *Pragdhara*, No. 16: 171-186.

_____. 2007. Stone Age Cultures, their Chronology and Beginnings of Agriculture in the North-Central India, *Man and Environment*, XXXII (1): 1-4.

Misra, V.D. and J.N. Pal (eds.). 2002. *Mesolithic India*, Allahabad, Department of A.H.C. & Archaeology, University of Allahabad.

Misra, V.D. and M.C. Gupta. 2006. Pre N.B.P. Cultures of the Middle-Ganga Valley, *Pragdhara*, No. 16: 21-34.

Misra, V.N. 1972. Burials from Prehistoric Bagor, Rajasthan, in S.B. Deo (ed.), *Archaeological Congress and Seminar Papers*, Nagpur, Nagpur University: 58-65.

_____. 1996. Mesolithic India: History and Current Status of Research, in G.D. Afanas'ev, S. Cleuziou, J.R. Lukacs and M. Tosi (eds.), *Bioarchaeology of Mesolithic India: An Integrated Approach*, Colloquium XXXIII of the International Union of Prehistoric and Protohistoric Sciences, Forli, ABACO Edizioni: 321-328.

_____. 2001. Prehistoric Human Colonisation of India, *Journal of Biosciences*, 26 (4), Supplement: 491-531.

_____. 2002. Keynote Address, in V.D. Misra and J.N. Pal (eds.), *Mesolithic India*, Allahabad, University of Allahabad: 1-66.

_____. 2007. *Rajasthan: Prehistoric and Early Historic Foundations*, New Delhi, Aryan Books International.

Murthy, M.L.K. 1979. Late Pleistocene Fauna of Kurnool Caves, South India, in F.R. Allchin and D.K. Chakrabarti (eds.), *A Source Book of Indian Archaeology*, Delhi, 335-341.

Mushrif-Tripathy, Veena, A.R. Sankhyan and V.R. Rao. 2009. Palaeopathological Observations on Human Skeletal Remains from Sarai Nahar Rai at Anthropological Survey of India, Kolkata, *Man and Environment* XXXIV (1): 77-82.

Narain, A.K. and T.N. Roy. 1963. *Excavations at Prahladpur*, Varanasi, Banaras Hindu University.

_____. 1977. *Excavations at Rajghat*, Part I, Varanasi, Banaras Hindu University.

Nath, B. and M.K. Biswas. 1980. Animals Remains from Chirand, Saran District, Bihar, *Rec. Zool. Survey India*, Vol. 76: 115-124.

Pal, J.N. 1983. Base of the Neolithic Culture of the Middle Ganga Valley, *(Baldev Upadhyaya Felicitation Volume of the G.N. Jha Kendriya Sanskrit Vidyapeeth)*: 205-16.

_____. 1986. *Archaeology of Southern Uttar Pradesh, Ceramic Industries of Northern Vindhyas*, Allahabad, Swabha Prakashan.

_____. 1987. Neolithic Cord-impressed ware of the Vindhyas, *Man and Environment*, XI: 61-65.

_____. 2000. Mesolithic and Neolithic Societies of the Vindhyas in the Middle Ganga Plan, in V.D. Misra and J.N. Pal (eds.), *Social History and Social Theory*, Allahabad, University of Allahabad: 7-13.

_____. The Early Farming Culture of the Northern Vindhyas, *Bulletin of the Deccan College Post-Graduate Research Institute*, Vol. 49: 297-310.

_____. 1985. Some New Light on the Mesolithic Burial Practices of the Ganga Valley: Evidence from Mahadaha, Pratapgarh, Uttar Pradesh, *Man and Environment*, IX: 28-37.

_____. 1988. Mesolithic Double Burials from Recent Excavations at Damdama, *Man and Environment*, XII: 115-22.

_____. 1992. Mesolithic Human Burials in the Ganga Plain, North India, *Man and Environment*, XVII (2): 35-55.

_____. 1994. Mesolithic Settlement in the Ganga Plain, *Man and Environment*, XIX (1-2): 91-101.

_____. 1994. Mesolithic Settlements in the Ganga Plain, *Man and Environment*, XIX (1-2): 91-101.

_____. 1996. Lithic Use Wear Analysis and Subsistence Activities Among the Mesolithic People of North India, in G.D. Afanas'ev, S. Cleuziou, J.R. Lukacs and M. Tosi (eds.), *Bioarchaeology of Mesolithic India: An Integrated Approach*, Colloquium XXXIII of the International Union of Prehistoric and Protohistoric Sciences, Forli, ABACO Edizioni: 267-277.

_____. 2002. The Mesolithic Phase in the Ganga Valley, in K. Paddayya (ed.), *Recent Studies in Indian Archaeology*, ICHR Monograph Series No. 6, New Delhi, Munshiram Manoharlal: 61-80.

_____. 2008a. Recent Excavations at Tokwa: Fresh Light on the Early farming Culture of the Vindhyas, in Lallanji Gopal and V.C. Srivastava (eds.), *History of Agriculture in Ancient India (up to. C. 1200AD)*, New Delhi, Concept Publishing Company: 48-69.

_____. 2008b. The Early Farming Culture of the Middle Ganga Plain with Special Reference to the Excavation of Jhusi and Hetapatti, *Pragdhara*, No. 18: 263-282.

_____. 2009. Beginnings of Agriculture in the Middle Ganga Plain, Sectional Presidential Address (Ancient Section), U.P. History Congress, XXth Session, VBS Purvanchal University, Jaunpur. October 3-4, 2009.

Pandey, J.N. 1985. *Settlement Patterns and Life in the Mesolithic Period in Uttar Pradesh*, D. Phil. Thesis, University of Allahabad (Unpublished).

_____. 1990. Mesolithic in the Middle Ganga Valley, *Bulletin of the Deccan College Post-Graduate & Research Institute*, Pune, 49: 311-316.

Pandey, M.S. 1963. *The Historical Geography and Topography of Bihar*, Varanasi, Motilal Banarsidass.

Pandey, Neelima. 2006. Subsistence Pattern in Mesolithic Communities of India, *Puratattva*, No. 36: 217-221.

Pant, P.C. 1982. *Prehistoric Uttar Pradesh*, Delhi, Agam Kala Prakashan.

_____. 2000. Indus Civilization Versus Mahagara Neolithic Culture: A Note on Acculturation, in S.M. Mishtra (ed.), *Puravritta* (Journal of Department of Ancient Indian History and Archaeology, Lucknow University), Vol. I: 65-70.

Pappu, R.S. 2004. Site catchment Analysis, in B.P. Singh, *Early Farming Culture of the Kaimur*, Jaipur, Publication Scheme, Vol. II: 405-415.

Pokharia, A.K., J.N. Pal and Alka Srivastava. 2009. Plant macro remains from Neolithic Jhusi in Ganga Plain: Evidence for grain-based agriculture, *Current Science*, Vol. 97, No. 4, 25August: 564-572.

Possehl, Gregory L. 1988. Radiocarbon dates from South Asia, *Man and Environment*, XII: 159-196.

_____. 1999. *Indus Age: The Beginnings*, Philadelphia, University of Pennsylvania Press.

_____. 2002. *The Indus Civilization: A Contemporary Perspective*, New York, Alta Mira Press.

Possehl, G.L. and Paul C. Rissman. 1992. The Chronology of prehistoric India: From Earliest Times to the Iron Age, in Robert W. Ehrich (ed.), *Chronologies in Old World Archaeology*, Vol. I, India. The University of Chicago Press, Chicago and London: 461.

Prasad, A.K. 1980-81. Exacavations at Taradih, *Puratattva*, No. 12: 180-81.

Randhawa, M.S. 1980. *A History of Agriculture in India*, Vol. I. New Delhi, Indian Council of Agricultural Research.

Rao, S.N. 1977. Excavation at Sarutaru, *Man and Environment*, I: 39-43.

Ray, Amita. 1990. Archaeology of Mangalkot, in A. Ray and S. Mukherjee (eds.), *Historical Archaeology of India: A Dialogue between Archaeologists and Historians*, New Delhi, Books and Books: 131-140.

Rivett-Carnac, H. 1882. Stone implements found in Bundelkhand, *Proceedings of the Asiatic Society of Bengal*.

Robbins, Gwen, V.D. Misra, J.N. Pal and M.C. Gupta. 2003. *Mesolithic Damdama: Dental Histology and Age Estimation*, Allahabad, University of Allahabad.

Robinson, H. 1966. *Monsoon Asia*, London, Macdonald and Evans Ltd.

Roy, T.N. 1985-86. Excavations at Majhi, 1983-85: A Preliminary Report, *Puratattva*, No. 16: 29-32.

Sahni, A. 1982. Karewa Vertebrates: Biostratigraphy, Palaeohistology and Palaeoecology, *Man and Environment*, VI: 16-20.

Sahu, B.P. 1988. *From Hunters to Breeders*, Delhi, Anamika Prakashan.

Sankalia, H.D. 1977. *Prehistory of India*, New Delhi, Munshiram Manoharlal.

_____. 1974. *The Pre and Protohistory of India and Pakistan*, Poona, Deccan College.

Saraswat, K.S. 1980-81. Plant Economy at ancient Sringaverapura, Phase I (1050-1000 BC), *Puratattva*, No. 12: 79-89.

_____. 2004. Plant Economy of Early Farming Communities, in B.P. Singh, *Early Farming Culture of the Kaimur*, Jaipur, Publication Scheme, Vol. II: 416-535.

_____. 2004. Plant Economy in Ancient Malhar, *Pragdhara*, No.14: 137-172.

Sathe, V and G.L. Badam. 2004. Faunal Remains, in B.P. Singh, *Early Farming Communities of the Kaimur*, Jaipur, Publication Scheme, Vol. II: 536-584.

Sharma, C., M.S. Chauhan, *et al.* 2001. Proxy records of Holocene Vegetation and climate changes from Sanai Tal, Central Ganga plain, *Geol-Surv India spl. Publication* 65 (iii): 199-202.

Sharma, S., M. Joachimski, M. Sharma, H.J. Tobschall, I.B. Singh, C. Sharma, M.S. Chauhan and G. Morgenroth. 2004. Lateglacial and Holocene Environmental

Changes in Ganga Plain, Northern India, *Quaternary Science Reviews*, 23: 145-159.

Sharma, G.R. and D. Mandal. 1980. *Excavations at Mahagara*, Allahabad.

Sharma, G.R. 1960. *Excavations at Kausambi (1957-59)*, Allahabad, University of Allahabad.

———. 1969. *Excavations at Kausambi*, Memoirs of the Archaeological Survey of India, No. 74, New Delhi, Archaeological Survey of India.

———. 1973. Mesolithic Lake Cultures in the Ganga Valley, India, *Proceedings of the Prehistoric Society* 39: 129-146.

———. 1975. Seasonal Migrations and Mesolithic Lake cultures of the Ganga Valley, *(K.C. Chattopadhyay Memorial Volume)*, Allahabad, Allahabad University, 1-21.

Sharma, G.R. and J.D. Clarke (eds.). 1983. *Palaeoenvironment and Prehistory in the Middle Son Valley (Madhya Pradesh)* Allahabad, Abinash Prakashan.

Sharma, G.R., V.D. Misra, D. Mandal, B.B. Misra and J.N. Pal. 1980. From Hunting and Food-Gathering to Domestication of Plants and Animals – Epi-Palaeolithic to Neolithic-Excavation at Chopani Mando, Mahadaha and Mahagara, *History and Archaeology*, I, Allahabad University.

———. 1980. *Beginnings of Agriculture*, Allahabad, Abinash Prakashan.

Sharma, R.S. 1977 (Reprint). Material Background of the Origin of the Buddhism, in M. Sen and M.B. Rao (eds.), *Das Kapital Centenary Volume: A Symposium*, New Delhi: 59-66.

Sharma, T.C. 1966. *Prehistoric Archaeology of Assam*. Unpublished Ph. D. Thesis, London University, London.

———. 1997. The Neolithic Pattern of Eastern India, in V.D. Misra and J.N. Pal (eds.), *Peeping through the Past: Prof. G.R. Sharma Memorial Volume*, Allahabad.

Sharma, Y.D. 1953. Exploration of Historical Sites, *Ancient India*, No. 9: 116-169.

Simone, Daniela De. 2009. Neolithic and Chalcolithic Cord-Impressed Ware of the Middle Ganga Valley, in Shahnaj Husne Jahan (ed.), *Abhijnan: Studies in South Asian Archaeology and Art History of Artefacts, Felicitating A.K.M. Zakariah* (British Archaeology Reports, International Series S 1974), Oxford: 1-6.

Singh, B.P. 1987-88. Khairadih: A Chalcolithic Settlement, *Puratattva*, No. 18: 28-33.

———. 1989-90. The Chalcolithic Culture of Southern Bihar as revealed by the Exploration and Excavations in District Rohtas, *Puratattva*, No. 20: 83-92.

———. 1990-91. Gulrihwaghat and Lohra Dewa: Chalcolithic Settlements in District Basti, Uttar Pradesh, *Pragdhara*, No. 1: 89-91.

———. 1995-96. Transformation of Cultures in the Middle Ganga Plain: A case study of Senuwar, *Pragdhara*, No. 6: 75-94.

———. 1996. Harappan Fallout (?) in the Mid Gangetic Valley, in Gregory L. Possehl, *Harappan Civilization*, New Delhi, Oxford & IBH Publishing Co.: 135-139.

———. 2004. *Early Farming Communities of the Kaimur (Excavations at Senuwar)*, Jaipur, Publication Scheme.

Singh, B.P. and R. Kumar. 1993-94. Explorations in Districts Basti and Siddhartha Nagar in the Saryupar Plain of Eastern Uttar Pradeh, *Pragdhara*, No. 4: 1-12.

Singh, B.P. and A.K. Singh. 2004. Excavation at Sarai Mohana 1967-68, *Bharati*, No. 27: 1-20.

Singh, Brahmanand. 1995-96. Ballia Janapada Ka Puratattvika Utkhanana (Hindi), *Pragdhara,* No. 6: 135-148.

Singh, C.D.P. 2004. On Metallic Iron Tools, Slags and Ore Artefacts of Malhar Site, District Chandauli (U.P.), *Pragdhara,* No. 14: 173-179.

Singh, Gurdip. 1974. Late Quaternary history of vegetation and climate of Rajasthan desert, India, *Philosophical Themes of Royal Society,* London Ser. 267, 467-501.

Singh, I.B. 1996. Geological Evolution of Ganga Plain: An Overview, *Journal of the Palaeontological Society of India,* No. 41: 99-137.

_____. 2001-2002. Late Quaternary evolution of Ganga Plain and proxy records of climate change, neotectonics and anthropogenic activity, *Pragdhara,* No. 12: 1-25.

_____. 2004a. Palaeoenvironments and Anthropogenic activity in the Quaternary of Ganga Plain, Paper read in the *Workshop on the Archaeology of the Middle Ganga Plain,* Lucknow, on 13-14 March 2004.

_____. 2004b. Quaternary Palaeoenvironments of the Ganga Plain and Anthropogenic Activity, *Presidential address: Indian Society for Prehistoric and Quaternary Studies, XXXIIth Session,* Lucknow, 28-31 December 2004.

Singh, I.B., Shikha Sharma, Maneesh Sharma, Pradeep Srivastava and Govindaraja Rajagopalan. 1999. Evidence of human occupation and humid climate of 30 ka in the alluvium of southern climate plain, *Current Science,* 76 (No. 7), 10 April 1999: 1022-1026.

Singh, P. 1974. *Neolithic Cultures of Western Asia,* London: Seminar Press.

_____. 1979. Early Iron Age in Gangetic Doab, in D.P. Agrawal and Dilip K. Chakrabarti (eds.), *Essays in Indian Protohistory,* Delhi, B.R. Publishing Corporation.

_____. 1991. *The Neolithic Origins,* Delhi, Agam Kala Prakashan.

_____. 1991-92. Excavation at Imlidih Khurd, *Puratattva,* No. 22: 120-22.

_____. 1991-92. Trial Digging at Dhuriapar, *Pragdhara,* No. 2: 55-60.

_____. 1992. Neolithic-Chalcolithic Cultures of Eastern U.P., in Rakesh Tewari (ed.), *Archaeological Perspectives of Uttar Pradesh and Future Prospects,* Part I, Lucknow: 67-76.

_____. 1992-93. Archaeological Excavations at Imlidih Khurd-1992, *Pragdhara,* No. 3: 21-36.

_____. 1993-94. Further Excavations at Imlidih Khurd-1993, *Pragdhara,* No. 4: 41-48.

_____. 1994. *Excavations at Narhan (1984-89),* Varanasi & New Delhi, Banaras Hindu University & B.R. Publishing Corporation.

_____. 1996. Prelude to Urbanization in the Sarayupar Plain, Presidential Address, Section V, *Indian History Congress,* 56 Session, Chennai.

_____. 1999. Rise of Cultures in Eastern India, in G.C. Pande (ed.), *History of Indian Science, Philosophy and Culture,* Vol. No. I, The Indian Council of Philosophical Research, New Delhi.

_____. 2003. Archaeology of the Middle Ganga Plain, *Man and Environment,* XXVIII (1): 1-6.

Singh, P., A.K. Singh and Brahmanand Singh. 1994-95. Protohistoric Investigations in Ballia District, Uttar Pradesh, *Pragdhara,* No. 5: 21-36.

Singh, P., A.K. Singh and I.J. Singh. 1991-92. On the Trails of Narhan Culture, *Pragdhara,* No. 2: 33-44.

Singh, P. and A.K. Singh. 1995-96. Trial excavations at Waina, District Ballia, U.P., *Pragdhara,* No. 6: 41-61.

_____. 1997-98. Trial excavations at Bhunadih, District Ballia, U.P., *Pragdhara,* No. 8: 11-29.

_____. 2004. *The Archaeology of Middle Ganga Plain: New Perspectives (Excavations at Agiabir)*, Shimla, Indian Institute of Advanced Study and New Delhi, Aryan Books International.

Singh, P., A.K. Singh and I.J. Singh. 1990-91. Explorations along the Kuwana River in Districts Gorakhpur and Basti, *Pragdhara,* No. 1: 69-82.

Singh, P., A.K. Singh and R.N. Singh. 1996-97. Explorations Along the Chhoti Sarju (Tons) River, *Pragdhara,* No. 7: 33-50.

Singh, P., R. Tewari and R.N. Singh. 1999-2000. Explorations in Chandauli District, (U.P.), *Pragdhara,* No. 10: 135-148.

Singh, R.L. (ed.). 1971. *India: A Regional Geography,* Varanasi, National Geographical Society of India.

Singh, R.N. 2003. Iron in Middle Ganga Plain: A Study of Iron Objects from Narhan, *Pragdhara,* No. 13: 141-150.

_____. 2004a. Analysis of Metal Objects, in B.P. Singh, *Early Farming Culture of the Kaimur,* Jaipur, Publication Scheme, Vol. II: 591-603.

_____. 2004b. A Note on Copper Axe from Imlidih Khurd: An Archaeo-Technological Assessment, Paper read in the *Workshop on the Archaeology of the Middle Ganga Plain,* held at Lucknow, on 13-14 March 2004.

_____. 2006. Scientific Study of Ancient Metal Objects of the Middle Ganga Plain: Some Observations, *Pragdhara,* No. 16: 125-131.

Singh, R.N. and John F. Merkel. 2001. A Study of Iron Objects from Chirand and Taradih, *Pragdhara,* No. 11: 135-142.

Singh, S.C. 1973. *Changes in the courses of rivers and their effects on the urban settlements in the Middle Ganga Plain,* Varanasi, National Geographical Society of India.

_____. 1991. *Archaeology of North Eastern Uttar Pradesh: With Special Reference to Basti District,* unpublished Ph.D. Thesis, Banaras Hindu University.

Singh, S.K. 1999-2000. Lithic industry of Agiabir, District Mirzapur (U.P), *Pragdhara,* No. 10: 57-63.

_____. 2000-2001. Lithic industries of Waina, District Ballia, U.P., *Pragdhara,* No. 11: 105-107.

Sinha, K.K. 1967. *Excavations at Sravasti-1959,* Varanasi, Banaras Hindu University.

Spate, O.H.K. and A.T.A. Learmonth. 1967. *India and Pakistan: A General Regional Geography*, London, Methuen.

Srivastava, K.M. 1985. *Discovery of Kapilvastu,* New Delhi.

_____. 1978. *Identification of Kapilvastu in Basti District of U.P.,* Nagpur.

Stamp, Sir Dudley. 1967. *Asia : A Regional and Economic Geography,* London, Methuen & Co.

Takahashi,T., T. Yamaoka, F. Yoneda and A. Uesugi. 1999-2000. The Ancient City of Sravasti: Its Significance on the Urbanisation of North India, *Puratattva,* No. 30: 74-90.

Tewari, R. 1997-98. In Quest of early Iron Age Sites in the Karamnasa Valley, *Pragdhara,* No. 8: 57-68.

_____. 2003. The Origin of Iron Working in India: New Evidence from the Central Ganga Plain in the Eastern Vindhyas, *Antiquity*, 77: 536-544.

Tewari, R., R.K. Srivastava, K.S. Saraswat and K.K. Sinha. 1999-2000. Excavations at Malhar, District Chandauli, U.P. 1999: A Preliminary Report, *Pragdhara*, No. 10: 69-98.

Tewari, R., R.K. Srivastava and K.K. Singh. 2002. Excavations at Lahuradewa, District Sant Kabir Nagar, Uttar Pradesh, *Puratattva*, No. 32: 54-62.

_____. 2003-2004. Report of Excavation at Malhar, District Chandauli, U.P. 1998-99, *Pragdhara*, No. 14: 1-112.

Tewari, R., R.K. Srivastava, K.K. Singh, K.S. Saraswat and I.B. Singh. 2002-2003. Preliminary Report on the Excavations at Lahuradewa, District Sant Kabir Nagar, U.P. 2001-2002: Wider Archaeological Implications, *Pragdhara*, No. 13: 37-68.

Tewari, R., R.K. Srivastava, K.K. Singh, K.S. Saraswat, I.B. Singh, M.S. Chauhan, A.K. Pokharia, A. Saxena, V. Prasad and M. Sharma. 2006a. Second Preliminary Report of the Excavation of Lahuradewa, District Sant Kabir Nagar, U.P. 2002-2003-2004 & 2005-06, *Pragdhara*, No. 16: 35-63.

Tewari, Rakesh and R.K. Srivastava. 1993-94. Explorations Along the Ami River and Its Nearby Areas in Districts Siddhartha Nagar, Basti and Gorakhpur, *Pragdhara*, No. 4: 13-39.

Tewari, Rakesh, P.C. Pant, I.B. Singh, S. Sharma, M. Sharma, P. Srivastava, A.K. Singhvi, P.K. Mishra and H.J. Tobschall. 2002. Middle Palaeolithic Human Activity and Palaeoclimate at Kalpi in Yamuna Valley, Ganga Plain, *Man and Environment*, XXVII (2): 1-14.

Tewari, Rakesh, R.K. Srivastava, K.K. Singh and K.S. Saraswat. 2006b. Further Excavations at Lahuradewa, District Sant Kabir Nagar (U.P.) 205-06: Preliminary Observations, *Puratattva*, No. 36: 68-75.

Tewari, Rakesh, R.K. Srivastava, K.K. Singh, Ram Vinay, G.C. Singh and Rajiv Trivedi. 2004a. Recent archaeological excavations in the Middle Ganga Plain and North Vindhyas, Paper read in the *Workshop on the Archaeology of the Middle Ganga Plain*, Lucknow, on 13-14 March 2004.

Tewari, Rakesh, R.K. Srivastava, K.K. Singh, K.S. Saraswat, I.B. Singh, M.S. Chauhan, B. Shekar, A.K. Pokharia, A. Saxena, V. Prasad, M. Sharma and P.P. Joglekar. 2004b. Archaeological Studies in the Lahuradewa Area, Ganga Plain: Epilogue: Implications for the Archaeological Studies in Ganga Plain, Paper read in *The Annual Conference of the IAS, ISPQS, and IHC and the National Seminar on the Archaeology of the Ganga Plain*, Lucknow, 28-31 December 2004.

Thomas, P.K. 1984a. The Faunal Background of the Chalcolithic Cultures of Western India, in J. Clutton-Brock and C. Grigson (eds.), *Animals and Archaeology*, Vol. 3, Oxford: BAR-202: 355-361.

_____. 1984b. Faunal Assemblage of Veerapuram, in T.V.G. Sastri, M. Kasturi Bai and J. Varaprasad Rao (eds.), *Veerapuram: A Type Site for Cultural Studies in The Krishna Valley*, Hyderabad Bhavani Printers.

_____. 1989. Utilization of Domestic Animals in Pre-and Protohistoric India, in Juliet Clutton-Brock (ed.), *The Walking Larder: Patterns of Domestication, Pastoralism and Predation*, London, Unwin Hyman: 108-112.

Thomas, P.K., P.P. Joglekar, V.D. Misra, J.N. Pande and J.N. Pal. 1996. Faunal Evidence for the Mesolithic Food Economy of the Gangetic Plain with Special Reference to Damdama, in G.D. Afanas'ev, S. Cleuziou, J.R. Lukacs and M. Tosi (eds.), *Bioarchaeology of Mesolithic India: An Integrated Approach*, Colloquium XXXIII of the International Union of Prehistoric and Protohistoric Sciences, Forli, ABACO Edizioni: 255-66.

Tiwari, R.C. 2003. *Geography of India*, Allahabad, Prayag Pustak Bhandar.

Tripathi, V. and P. Upadhyaya. 2006. Anai: A Settlement in Varuna Region, *Puratattva*, No. 36: 93-102.

———. 2007. Further Excavations at Agiabir (2005-06), *Puratattva*, No. 37: 121-129.

Tripathi, V., A.K. Singh and P. Upadhyaya. 2005-06. Excavations at Agiabir (2005-06), District Mirzapur, Uttar Pradesh, *Bharti*, No. 30: 1-38.

Tripathi, Vibha (ed.). 1998. *Archaeometallurgy in India*, Delhi, Sharda Publishing House.

Tripathi, Vibha. 2001. *The Age of Iron in South Asia: Legacy and Tradition*, New Delhi, Aryan Books International.

———. 2008. *History of Iron Technology in Ancient India (From Beginnings to Pre-modern times)*, New Delhi, Rupa & Co.

Tripathi, Vibha, A.K. Singh and Santosh Kumar. 2000-2001. Explorations Along the Palaeo-channel of River Varuna, *Pragdhara*, No. 11: 125-130.

Ucko, Peter J. and G.W. Dimbleby. 1969. Introduction: Context and Development of Studies of Domestication, in P.J. Ucko and G.W.Dimbleby (eds.), *The Domestication and Exploitation of Plants and Animals*, London, Duckworth.

Varma, R.K. 1986. *The Mesolithic Age in Mirzapur*, Allahabad, Paramjyoti Prakashan.

———. 1992. Some aspects of the Mesolithic of the Ganga Valley, in Rakesh Tewari (ed.), *Archaeological Perspectives of Uttar Pradesh and Future Prospects*, Part I, Lucknow, U.P. State Archaeological Organisation: 47-57.

———. 1997. Couple and Multiple Couple Burials of the Mesolithic in the Ganga Valley, in J.P. Joshi (ed.), *Facets of Indian Civilization: Recent Perspectives*, (Essays in Honour of Prof. B.B. Lal), New Delhi, Aryan Books International: 29-34.

———. 1999. The Emergence of Culture in the Vindhya-Ganga Region with Special Reference to Old Stone Age, in G.C. Pande (ed.), *The Dawn of Indian Civilisation (up to c. 600 BC)*, Vol. I, Part I: 175-204.

———. 2000. A Note on Some Aspects of Society during the Mesolithic Period, in V.D. Misra and J.N. Pal (eds.), *Social History and Social Theory*, Allahabad, University of Allahabad: 1-6.

———. 2003. *Early Farming Cultures of India: Keynote Address*, National Seminar held in the Department of AHC & Archaeology, University of Allahabad on 19-20 April 2003.

Varma, R.K., V.D. Misra, J.N. Pandey and J.N. Pal. 1985. A Preliminary Report on the Excavations at Damdama (1982-84), *Man and Environment*, IX: 45-65.

Verma, B.S. 1997. A Short Note on Chirand Excavations, in J.P. Joshi (ed.), *Facets of Indian Civilization: Recent Perspectives* (Essays in Honour of Professor B.B. Lal), New Delhi, Aryan Books International, Vol. I: 75-80.

Zeuner, F.E. 1963. *A History of Domesticated Animals*, London, Hutchinson.

Author Index

Site Index